A New Handbook of Literary Terms
is an indispensable literary reference
tool that comes at a time of formidable
complexity in literary studies. David
Mikics offers a lively, informative guide
to words and concepts that every
student of literature needs to know.
His definitions are essayistic, witty,
learned, and always a pleasure to read.
They sketch the derivation and history
of each term, including especially
lucid explanations of verse forms and
providing a firm sense of literary periods
and movements from classicism to
postmodernism. The *Handbook* also
supplies a helpful map to the intricate
and at times confusing terrain of literary
theory at the beginning of the twenty-
first century: the author has designated
a series of terms—from New Criticism to
queer theory—that serves as a concise
but thorough introduction to recent
developments in literary study.

CONTINUED ON BACK FLAP

A NEW
HANDBOOK
OF LITERARY
TERMS

A NEW HANDBOOK OF LITERARY TERMS

DAVID MIKICS

YALE UNIVERSITY PRESS
NEW HAVEN & LONDON

Published with assistance from
the Louis Stern Memorial Fund.

Designed by Nancy Ovedovitz and set in Adobe
Garamond by The Composing Room of Michigan, Inc.
Printed in the United States of America by Thomson-
Shore, Inc.

Library of Congress Cataloging-in-Publication Data
Mikics, David, 1961–
A new handbook of literary terms / David Mikics
p.   cm.
Includes bibliographical references and index.
ISBN 978-0-300-10636-7 (alk. paper)
1. Literature—Terminology—Handbooks, manuals,
etc.   2. Criticism—Terminology—Handbooks,
manuals, etc.   I. Title.
PN41.M48 2007
803—dc22   2006037905

A catalogue record for this book is available from
the British Library.

The paper in this book meets the guidelines for
permanence and durability of the Committee on
Production Guidelines for Book Longevity of the
Council on Library Resources.

10 9 8 7 6 5 4 3 2 1

CONTENTS

Preface, vii

Acknowledgments, xi

A New Handbook of Literary Terms, 1

Index, 313

PREFACE

Why another guide to literary terms, in an already crowded field? This is a moment of uncertain direction for literary study. Cultural studies competes with the new aestheticism for students' attention, as deconstruction and new historicism recede into memory. What of the much-maligned New Criticism, and the great tradition of philology? I aim to supply a chart for this troubled territory, so that readers may have a sense of current trends that is informed by a greater knowledge of what lies behind them. Historical perspective is an essential part of this handbook, as I explain below.

My goal was to write a portable, persuasive account that would be helpful to students from freshman to Ph.D. level, as well as those teachers looking to reacquaint themselves with terms and ideas. The great model for this kind of book is, to my mind, *A Glossary of Literary Terms* by M. H. Abrams (recently revised by Abrams and Geoffrey Harpham), a volume that every literature student should possess. *A New Handbook of Literary Terms* is a competitor as well as a companion to Abrams's *Glossary,* and I hope a worthy one. I am more essayistic than Abrams; the *Handbook* supplies a greater number of illustrative quotations, and I devote more space to what strikes me as crucial for students to know. I am expansive and opinionated on topics like allegory, comedy, humanism, tragedy. These words govern our sense of what literature is like, and they are best defined from an individual critic's point of view. I have pursued a personal voice, not devoid of humor—and the occasional wisecrack.

I have tried to offer enjoyable lore, in addition to the strictly necessary definition: whether successfully or not, the reader must judge. As a devoted browser of reference works, I am aware of the difference between those that lure readers and those that fend them off. I hope this book will be diverting as well as instructive, though it cannot compete with that monarch of brows-ability in the reference genre, *Brewer's Dictionary of Phrase and Fable* (another necessary addition to every bookshelf).

A New Handbook of Literary Terms is, as its title announces, a handbook, not an encyclopedia. I have been ruthlessly selective in my decisions about which definitions deserve space here. J. A. Cuddon's *Penguin Dictionary of Literary Terms and Literary Theory* and Ross Murfin's and Supryia Ray's *Bedford Glossary of Critical and Literary Terms* are valuable, and in Cuddon's case comprehensive, tomes whose size makes them less than ideal for classroom use. (Cuddon is over a thousand pages long in the paperback edition.) The entries in Cuddon, useful as they are, are frequently quite abbreviated compared with mine: I offer extended commentary in cases where it is warranted. Many rhetorical terms that are excluded from the *Handbook,* from anadiplosis to hypallage and beyond, can be found in Richard Lanham's invaluable *Handlist of Rhetorical Terms.* Nor have I admitted many of the more obscure words for kinds of verse forms, feet, and syllables: anceps, catalectic, fourteener. I refer the curious reader to the sources listed under my entry on meter. I have emphasized the most important terms, while also allowing the reader to encounter those that may be unfamiliar but that promise to rouse the interest—especially when clarified by an apt, flavorsome example (amoebean song, multum in parvo).

I have given room to a few entries dealing with non-Western literature, but the majority of the terms in this book stem from the European tradition. *The Princeton Encyclopedia of Poetry and Poetics,* edited by Alex Preminger and Frank Warnke, offers a far more global portrait of literature, with substantial discussions of African, Asian, and Near Eastern genres. Again, reasons of compactness and coherence dictated a stricter focus for this volume.

A word should be said about my bibliographical suggestions, which appear in many of the entries. I have tried to be as representative as possible, allowing space to older as well as newer criticism. The critics cited most often here are the ones who have contributed most to our consciousness, and who have most actively redefined their fields of study. These include Erich Auerbach and Ernst Robert Curtius on literary history; Northrop Frye, William Empson, and Frank Kermode on genre; T. S. Eliot on literary tradition; Harold Bloom, Geoffrey Hartman, and Helen Vendler on poetry; John Hollander on verse form; Stanley Cavell on philosophy's relation to literature; Fredric Jameson on Marxism; Robert Alter on the Bible as literature; Alice Jardine and Toril Moi on feminism; and Tzvetan Todorov on recent literary theory.

An ideal bibliography should include older, respected works that continue to shape our sense of what criticism can do. Auerbach's *Mimesis,* first published in Switzerland in 1946, is still the indispensable book on realism. *Mimesis* is referred to repeatedly here, as is Northrop Frye's definitive *Anatomy of Criticism* (1957), the best treatment of genre. Frye, like Auerbach, opened up a whole new world for criticism in his book, which continues to be central to literary study fifty years after it was written. A student who wants a sure grounding in literary history, and at the same time an exhilarating experience of criticism at the height of its powers, would do well to read *Mimesis* and *An Anatomy of Criticism*—along with other synoptic and original works like James Nohrnberg's *The Analogy of the Faerie Queene,* Harold Bloom's *The Visionary Company,* Ian Watt's *The Rise of the Novel,* Geoffrey Hartman's *Beyond Formalism,* Martin Price's *To the Palace of Wisdom,* Martha Nussbaum's *The Fragility of Goodness,* Hugh Kenner's *The Pound Era,* Irving Howe's *Politics and the Novel,* Ronald Paulson's *Satire and the Novel,* Frank Kermode's *Romantic Image,* and William Empson's *Some Versions of Pastoral.* Curtius's *European Literature and the Latin Middle Ages* remains the essential guide to the topoi that engage medieval and Renaissance literature. These fourteen books, some of them published as long ago as the 1930s (Empson), provide the background and assumptions for much later work. Some more recent volumes, like Margaret Doody's *The True Story of the Novel,* share the ambition and innovative character of those I have just listed. The *Handbook* takes care not to slight younger critics—there are quite a few references from the new, twenty-first century—but I have emphasized those books that have already stood the test of time. Some of the older writers who appear here have been neglected by their heirs (like the poet-critics Josephine Miles and Howard Nemerov), or have unjustly fallen out of favor (like the great mythopoeic Shakespearean G. Wilson Knight). I hope I have redressed the balance where possible.

I also, in these pages, recommend to the reader a number of anthologies of literary criticism and theory, foremost among them Hazard Adams's *Literary Theory Since Plato.* In addition, the recent collection edited by Daphne Patai and Will Corral, *Theory's Empire,* presents a series of invigorating and worthwhile debates about the status of theory in today's academy.

A brief bibliographical note: I have listed dates of books from their first appearance in their native language, not their first translation into English. Classical dates are for the most part taken from *The Oxford Classical Dictio-*

nary (3rd ed.), edited by Simon Hornblower and Anthony Spawforth—an invaluable resource.

The reader who wants a quick overview of contemporary literary theory and its background may wish to read the following series of entries in sequence (about twenty-five pages altogether): Aristotelian criticism, formalism, New Criticism, close reading, hermeneutics, phenomenology, Marxist criticism, psychoanalytic criticism, structuralism, reception theory, reader-response criticism, deconstruction, différance, logocentrism, poststructuralism, feminist criticism, new historicism, cultural studies, gender studies, gay studies, queer theory, visual studies.

ACKNOWLEDGMENTS

I would like to thank John Hollander and Harold Bloom for their irreplaceable enthusiasm and guidance, which I have relied on so many times. John Kulka, every author's ideal editor, was essential in directing *A New Handbook of Literary Terms* to its final shape. I am grateful as well to Phillip King for expert copyediting, and also to Lindsay Toland, at Yale University Press.

Rachel Wetzsteon, Jennifer Grotz, and Stephen Burt read the book in manuscript and improved it greatly with their suggestions, as did the five anonymous readers for Yale. It is an unusual privilege to have such learned and imaginative friends—and to benefit from the greatly discerning, and kindly offered, scholarship of strangers as well.

A Martha Gano Houstoun Foundation grant made the writing of this book possible. I am grateful to the Houstoun family and to the members of the Houstoun Committee of the University of Houston's English Department for awarding me the grant.

For suggestions concerning individual entries, and for other forms of help, I thank Richard Armstrong, Terry Catapano, William Flesch, Dien Ho, Jennifer Lewin, Lewis J. Mikics, Steven Monte, Ricki Moskowitz, and Edward Schiffer. And, most of all, Katy Heinlein.

A NEW
HANDBOOK
OF LITERARY
TERMS

abject, abjection In the early 1980s, the French literary theorist Julia Kristeva introduced the concept of abjection. According to Kristeva, the abject is neither subject nor object, but something that precedes the making of the human self. Abjection is often associated with repulsive or disgusting substances that occupy the border between the self and the world outside it: vomit, excrement. These elements grow into monstrous, anti-human presences that seem to threaten life and must therefore be destroyed, or at least repressed. Paradoxically, the effort to exclude the abject represents, for Kristeva, a revolt against what gives us being: the body of the mother.

In horror and science fiction stories and films, from H. P. Lovecraft to the *Alien* movies, the monster that must be abjected (that is, somehow escaped or defeated) is frequently an amorphous, vaguely maternal, looming and terrible presence: "one of those violent, dark revolts of being" (Kristeva). See Kristeva, *Powers of Horror* (1980).

absurd An absurd situation is one that is discordant, incongruous, and illogical. The sense that human existence remains inherently absurd, supremely challenging in its apparent meaninglessness, is significant to certain twentieth-century writers and philosophers: Franz Kafka, Albert Camus, Jean-Paul Sartre (see, for example, Camus's *Myth of Sisyphus* [1942]).

The actor and writer Antonin Artaud gave the absurd a central role in the theater. In *The Theatre and Its Double* (1938), Artaud championed a dreamlike, or nightmarish, form of theater that would assault the audience like a plague or a fever. (See THEATER OF CRUELTY.) The playwrights Samuel Beckett and Eugene Ionesco were two later authors of what was sometimes called the theater of the absurd. Ionesco, describing Kafka's universe, defined the absurd as "that which is devoid of purpose," and added, "Cut off from his metaphysical, religious, and transcendental roots, man is lost: all his actions become senseless, absurd, useless."

Ionesco's definition suggests that the conviction of life's absurdity follows from what Nietzsche called the "death of God," with the result that humans inhabit a desacralized universe, one without divine plan or purpose. Yet a religious yearning often characterizes the absurdist mood. In Beckett's *Waiting for Godot* (1953), two tramps wait for a mysterious Godlike figure, Godot, who may or may not arrive; they beguile the time with inventive, desperate, and grotesquely melancholy comic routines.

Jerome Rothenberg remarks that the absurd resembles the dream in Surrealism: it "serves as the great simplifying image, which allows for *direct presentation* of conflicting impulses." Such directness is allied with the modern inclination toward immanence and disturbing intimacy in art. See Jerome Rothenberg, "A Dialogue on Oral Poetry with William Spanos," *Boundary* 2:3 (Spring 1975), 509–48. Martin Esslin's *The Theatre of the Absurd* (1961) is a very useful overview.

accommodation In theology, the practice of describing the ineffable attributes of God in earthly, graspable terms. This effort must fail, since God remains by definition beyond our intellectual capacities; but accommodated description is necessary for our appreciation of the divine. So God is accommodated to human understanding by being conceived in terms we can know: in the Gospel of John, we are told that "God is light" (John 1:5).

In Milton's *Paradise Lost* (1667), the poet relies on accommodation, translating the unimaginable immensities of heavenly time and space into the earthly features that we humans are familiar with. (Milton's angel Raphael describes the war in heaven to Adam by "likening spiritual to corporal forms" [5.573].)

act A basic unit of drama. Most stage plays are divided into acts, which are in turn divided into scenes. The beginning of a new act is frequently marked by a change of setting, the commencing of a new narrative thread, or a shift to a different group of characters (as well as, often, an intermission). The plays of Shakespeare and other Renaissance dramatists are usually divided into five acts.

Gorboduc (1565) is an early example of five-act structure in the English theater. The five-act division was adopted in Elizabethan drama in imitation of the Roman philosopher and playwright Seneca the Younger (ca. 4 BCE–65

CE), whose works were published in English as *Tenne Tragedies* (1581), securing their importance for Elizabethan playwrights. Horace, in *Ars Poetica* (Art of Poetry, ca. 20 BCE), another influential work in the Renaissance, remarks that tragedies "should not be produced beyond the fifth act."

Many modern plays (those of Chekhov and Ibsen, for example) tend to have four acts. Still more recently, dramatists have structured their plays as a sequence of scenes, rather than relying on act division; some dramatists, like Samuel Beckett, have written plays consisting of a single scene. See Wilfred Jewkes, *Act Division in Elizabethan and Jacobean Drama, 1583–1616* (1958), and T. W. Baldwin, *Shakespeare's Five-Act Structure* (1963).

aestheticism (From the Greek *aisthein*, to perceive; *aisthetes*, one who perceives.) Aestheticism means relying on seeing, the refined use of the eye. Seeing thus becomes realized thinking: present and palpable because it issues in sight. The practice of aestheticism was defined most memorably by the essayist Walter Pater, in the conclusion to his book *The Renaissance* (1873). Pater champions the idea of life as a work of art, trying to see in our experiences "all that is to be seen in them by the finest senses." He urges us "to pass most swiftly from point to point, and be present always at the focus . . ." "To burn always with this hard, gemlike flame," Pater concludes, "to maintain this ecstasy, is success in life."

To embrace life as well as art for the intensity and beauty they have to offer is the desire that unites the writers who are called aesthetes. Pater and his immediate ancestor John Ruskin share the aim of creating in the observer of art, and of life, an appropriately heightened and refined consciousness of beauty. Pater also argues that we ought to resist society's moralizing demands, which get in the way of aesthetic appreciation. This rejection of moralizing becomes positively extravagant in Pater's disciple Oscar Wilde, who claimed that "all art is perfectly useless": that the perfecting of art, and of life-as-art, requires an indifference to the sober ideals of moral responsibility. Among the nineteenth-century continental European writers allied to aestheticism in one way or another are Théophile Gautier, J. K. Huysmans, Charles Baudelaire, and Gustave Flaubert.

The slogan of aestheticism is "art for art's sake"—oft-maligned by critics who prefer literature to subordinate itself to moral, political, or philosophical agendas. (The anxious wish for literature to be guided by philosophy, with its supposedly superior thoughtfulness, begins with Plato.)

The *aesthetic poets,* who were given this name by Pater, include William Morris, Dante Gabriel Rossetti, and others associated with the Pre-Raphaelite Brotherhood from the 1840s on; they were major influences on the early work of W. B. Yeats (1865–1939). See also ANTITHETICAL and DECA-DENCE.

aesthetics Aesthetics, as a modern discipline, was inaugurated by the German philosopher Alexander Gottlieb Baumgarten in 1735. Its most influential proponent was Immanuel Kant in his *Critique of Judgment* (1790; the "third critique," following his critique of pure reason and his critique of practical reason). For Kant, aesthetic judgment is based on an experience of pleasure that claims universal validity, rather than being an idiosyncratic preference. When I say, "Cezanne's paintings are supremely beautiful," I imply that I am expecting, or at least can argue for, your agreement with my sentiment. Furthermore, aesthetics justifies itself not by reference to rules but by evoking in us what Kant calls the harmony of faculties. There is no particular property in a beautiful object that makes it aesthetically pleasing (i.e., it is not beautiful because it is symmetrical, just large enough, or because of any other rule-based criterion). Instead, Kant argues, the object's beauty resides in its stimulating of our imaginative feeling. This feeling then interacts with the impulse on the part of understanding to claim universal status for the object as beautiful. We experience the harmony or "free play" of two faculties, imagination and understanding. (See Ted Cohen and Paul Guyer, eds., *Essays in Kant's Aesthetics* [1982].) Among the significant twentieth-century writers on aesthetics are Roger Fry, Clement Greenberg, Susanne Langer, and Theodor Adorno.

affective fallacy In their book *The Verbal Icon* (1954), W. K. Wimsatt and Monroe Beardsley criticized what they called the affective fallacy: evaluating a literary work by describing the emotions aroused in its readers. Whereas the intentional fallacy confuses a literary work with its origin or cause, the author's intention (and is therefore a variety of the broader "genetic fallacy"), the affective fallacy, Wimsatt and Beardsley write, confuses a work with its result. (See INTENTIONAL FALLACY.)

Before Wimsatt and Beardsley, I. A. Richards's *Practical Criticism* (1929) had outlined some of the untutored subjective responses that a naive reader might have to a literary work. Richards wanted to distinguish what can be explained and argued concerning a text (that is, a properly interpretive response) from what can only be felt or proclaimed (a merely affective response). Describing the feeling that a text gives us, Richards suggested, is different from, and inherently far less interesting than, explaining what it means. A reader's feeling does not offer itself up for critical debate as an interpretive explanation does. For all that, Richards devoted himself to investigating the emotions of an untaught reader when confronted by a poem, as if these were somehow telling for the more educated reader.

Wimsatt and Beardsley are less interested than Richards in the feelings provoked in naive readers by a text. They write that "the report of some readers . . . that a poem or story induces in them vivid images, intense feelings, or heightened consciousness, is neither anything which can be refuted nor anything which it is possible for the objective critic to take into account." Instead, criticism ought to explore how literary narratives suggest emotions that are "presented in their objects and contemplated as a pattern of knowledge." Here Wimsatt and Beardsley return to an Aristotelian emphasis on how emotions are produced in an audience by means of literary structure and, as well, by means of the socially recognizable connotations of the matters that a work describes (a murder, a noble family).

agitprop An amalgam of the words *agitation* and *propaganda,* agitprop is didactic and propagandistic literature such as was produced by the Bolsheviks after the October Revolution of 1917. Leon Trotsky's *Literature and Revolution* (1924) advocates the use of literature as agitprop. Trotsky wrote that "each class has its own policy in art": "The proletarian has to have in art the expression of the new spiritual point of view which is just beginning to be formulated within him, and to which art must help him give form. This is not a state order, but a historic demand."

agon In Greek, a struggle or contest, whether physical or verbal. Examples are the bitter argument between Jason and Medea in Euripides' *Medea* (431 BCE), or between Achilles and Agamemnon in Homer's *Iliad.* Harold Bloom has applied the term *agon* to the struggle between authors, with a later author striving to define himself or herself against an earlier one. Keats's agon with Milton, for instance, is exemplified in his rebellious statement about the author of *Paradise Lost:* "Life to him would be death to me." An ancient example of authorial agon occurs in Aristophanes' comic drama *The Frogs* (405 BCE) when Aeschylus debates Euripides, each trying to prove that he is the better dramatist.

aleatory From Latin *alea,* a dice game; by extension, chance or hazard. An aleatory work is dependent on chance or randomness. Some significant modern artists who have used aleatory techniques in their work are the musician John Cage and the writer William Burroughs. Characteristically, aleatory art involves the kind of random events produced through a set of rules, rather than mere raw spontaneity: Burroughs used the technique of cut-ups (scraps of text collated with arbitrary rigor); Cage threw the I Ching to determine the position of musical notes. In France, the Oulipo movement designed a series of games and exercises devoted to the production of aleatory literature. (See OULIPO.)

The aleatory may be attractive to writers because it promises a liberation, even if a momentary one, from the bondage to tradition and from the thoughtful, conscious working out and working through that writing usually requires. By using aleatory techniques authors hope to abstract their words from the burden of their usual meanings, and also from associations with earlier tradition. As with some other kinds of avant-garde art, aleatory experiments run the risk of being more interesting to the writer than to the reader.

Alexandrian Alexandrian literature (also called Hellenistic literature) was written in Greek from the fourth to the first centuries BCE. This literary culture had its center in the Egyptian city of Alexandria during the reign of the Ptolemies. Alexandrian works frequently feature elaborate mythological allusions, a polished surface, and a slender, elegant style. Among the major Alexandrian poets are Apollonius Rhodius, author of the *Argonautica,* an epic on Jason's quest for the Golden Fleece, and Theocritus, a writer of pastorals from Syracuse, one of the Greek colonies in Sicily (both third century BCE).

The terse, splendid Alexandrian poet Callimachus contributed a major slogan, useful for laconic writers of the future: *Mega biblion, mega kakon* (big book, big evil).

It could be argued that a new Alexandrianism, refusing the large work and prizing the fractured and miniature, characterizes certain present-day literary forms: poetry after modernism, for example. In the early twentieth century, the discoveries achieved by Sigmund Freud and by writers like Guillaume Apollinaire suggested that the fullest revelation of the self might come in elliptical, oblique fragments, snatches of dreams. So current American poetry often sees the most pregnant meanings residing in the tiniest flicks of thought, the most broken impressions—and the shortest poems. (See Alan Williamson, *Introspection and Contemporary Poetry* [1983].)

Alexandrine The Alexandrine goes iambic pentameter one better by adding a foot, so that each line contains six feet instead of the more usual five. To great effect, Spenser uses a snaky, languorous Alexandrine as the final line of each stanza of his mammoth epic romance, *The Faerie Queene* (1590–96); and Milton echoes Spenser by doing the same in his Nativity Ode (1629). The Alexandrine is also the predominant form of French verse, culminating in the heroic oeuvre of Victor Hugo (1802–85); see Jacques Barzun, *An Essay on French Verse* (1991). See also METER; SPENSERIAN STANZA.

alienation The basic category of Karl Marx's *Economic and Philosophical Manuscripts* of 1844. According to Marx, capitalism requires (and produces) alienated labor. That is, bosses and owners purchase labor from workers, who see the work that they "sell" to the owners as fundamentally separate from themselves. The worker who performs alienated labor is aware that his bodily and mental capacities have been rented by the bosses. As a result, he finds himself unable to identify with the product of his work. The worker under capitalism therefore remains at the opposite pole from the creative artist or craftsman, who proudly identifies with the end result of his labor.

Victorian social thinkers like John Ruskin and William Morris also voiced a protest against alienation, in terms that are in some ways comparable to Marxist ones. For an appreciation of social relations supposedly untouched by the alienation characteristic of modern industrial society, see Ruskin's beautiful description of medieval craftsmanship, "The Nature of Gothic" (in *The Stones of Venice* [1853]). The Marxist idea of alienation was a basic concept for many social theorists in the 1960s, notably Herbert Marcuse (in *One Dimensional Man* [1964]). William Monroe draws on alienation as a term for literary study in *Power to Hurt* (1998). See also REIFICATION.

alienation effect (In German, *Verfremdungseffekt.*) The dramatist Bertolt Brecht described his own theatrical methods as producing an alienation effect. Instead of identifying with the characters onstage and providing an empathetic mirror for their emotions, audiences, according to Brecht, should attend in a cool, analytic manner to the statements that the actors make. The Brechtian audience is meant to remain conscious of the distance between the actors and the characters they present: this is Brecht's proposed way of securing the audience's evaluative wariness.

Brecht contrasted his own brand of theater, which he named "epic theater" or the "learning play," to Aristotelian ideas. "The Aristotelian play," he wrote, "is essentially static; its task is to show the world as it is. The learning-play is essentially dynamic; its task is to show the world as it changes (and also how it may be changed)." Rejecting the "passive empathy of the spectator," Brecht remarked of his epic theater, "Just as it refrains from handing its hero over to the world as if it were his inescapable fate, so it would not dream of handing the spectator over to an inspiring theatrical experience."

Brecht's overt opposition to Aristotle is based on his impression that the Aristotelian audience is a "mob, which must be and can be reached only through its emotions." Brecht neglects Aristotle's idea that the audience, rather than simply and instinctively pouring out its feelings, is called upon to judge the tragic hero from a certain distance, in order to determine whether he is worthy of pity.

Brecht's epic theater aims to show its onstage characters as "conscious actors on the field of history" (Edward Mendelson). His ideas are connected to the traditional worry, especially common in the eighteenth century, that an audience might identify too much with theatrical (or novelistic) protagonists, and so engage in the same dubious behavior practiced by the characters they see depicted onstage. The Brechtian dream is for the people onstage to perform rather than act (that is, to flag everything they do as sheer gesture), and for the people in the audience to observe without the vulnerability allied to the usual position of an audience—without becoming "involved." See AN-TITHEATRICAL; and see John Willett, ed., *Brecht on Theatre* (1964). There is a useful discussion of the Brechtian ideal in Stanley Cavell, *The World Viewed* (1971); and in Edward Mendelson, "*The Cherry Orchard* and *The Caucasian Chalk Circle*," in Michael Seidel, ed., *Homer to Brecht* (1977).

allegory From the two Greek words *allos* and *agoreuein,* literally "to say [something] differently." Allegories turn abstract concepts or features into characters. The formula could be reversed: allegories just as easily transform people and places into conceptual entities, so that the family farm of one's childhood might be a lost Eden, or an urban ghetto a hell, or a Red Sox—Yankees game a battle between good and evil. As James Wood remarks, "Allegory wants us to know that it is being allegorical. It is always saying: watch me, I *mean* something."

Probably the most familiar example of allegory is the movie *The Wizard of Oz*, in which cowardice is embodied in the lion, thoughtless panic in the scarecrow, and so on. (Some have claimed that L. Frank Baum's Oz books are also political allegories: that the scarecrow represents an agricultural past, for example, and the tin woodsman the industrial future.) Two of the oldest allegorical ideas are the ship of state and the body politic, both going back to Greek and Roman traditions. In Shakespeare's *Coriolanus* a character makes use of the body-politic image in order to tell a "fable of the belly" in which the members (the working classes) rebel against the stomach (the Roman senate, which consumes the food that the members produce).

Forms related to allegory are the fable (the ant and the grasshopper), the parable (the seed that falls upon stony ground [Matthew 13:3–9]), and the exemplum (the boy who cried wolf). Parables often make us speculate about the choice of metaphoric vehicle (why does Jesus use a seed as an image for the word of the gospel? what does it mean for a word to "grow"?). The fable and the exemplum, by contrast, tend to be more straightforward.

Prudentius's *Psychomachia* ("soul-battle") (ca. 405 CE) is a striking example of allegory, featuring characters like "swelling Wrath, showing her teeth with rage and foaming at the mouth" and "the maiden Chastity, shining in beauteous armor." Some well-known allegories in English are John Bunyan's *Pilgrim's Progress* (1678), which features characters with names like Hopeful, Little-Faith, and Great-Heart, and Edmund Spenser's *The Faerie Queene* (1590–96). Spenser's Britomart is an adolescent girl dressed in the armor of a male knight, a disguise that allegorizes the militant, almost magical power of her chastity. At one point she comes upon a statue of a hermaphrodite, an allegorical image (or emblem) of the union of man and woman in marriage. Medieval morality plays like *Everyman* (ca. 1509) feature characters who are personifications of human traits: Vanity, Charity, Lust.

Allegory has an affinity to ceremonial forms like the masque, and to the potentially endless battles and adventures of romance. Allegorical forms frequently evoke a combat between antitheses: often, the good city faces off against an evil empire.

Allegory is of great significance in the traditions of biblical exegesis (see TYPOLOGY). It is often used to relate the events narrated in the Hebrew Bible to the Christian gospel, so that the Old Testament becomes an allegory of the New Testament. For example, the rock split by Moses in the wilderness, providing water for the famished Israelites (Exodus 17:6), was thought to prefigure the "pure river of water of life" in the Book of Revelation (22:1), which issues from "the throne of God and of the Lamb." Of course, the images in Revelation themselves have allegorical meaning (the Lamb is Jesus).

Such readings are not necessarily fully allegorical, though. Diodore of Tarsus (fourth century CE), interpreting Paul's comments on Hagar and Sarah in Galatians 4:22–31, remarked that while these two characters could stand allegorically for unbelieving Jews and believing Christians, they must still be recognized as historical characters in the biblical narrative.

German Romanticism characteristically opposed the allegorical to the symbolic, and preferred the symbol. For a writer like Goethe, the critic Tzvetan Todorov writes, "Allegory is transitive, symbols are intransitive . . . the symbol speaks to perception (along with intellection); the allegory in effect speaks to intellection alone." Walter Benjamin combated the romantic bias when he defended allegory in *The Origin of German Tragic Drama* (1928); much later, Paul de Man and other deconstructionists continued Benjamin's polemic.

Angus Fletcher in his comprehensive and original *Allegory* (1964) gave new life to the critical discussion of allegory. On allegory and symbol, see Tzvetan Todorov, *Theories of the Symbol* (1977). Annabel Patterson explores political allegory in her *Fables of Power* (1991); also worthwhile are Rosemond Tuve, *Allegorical Imagery* (1966), Edwin Honig, *Dark Conceit* (1959), and Gordon Teskey, *Allegory and Violence* (1996). See also James Wood, "Thomas Pynchon and the Problem of Allegory," in *The Broken Estate* (1999).

In *Allegories of Reading* (1979), Paul de Man proposed that even realist narratives are hermeneutic allegories: that is, that they present stories about reading and interpreting, even when they seem to be mimetic descriptions of real-life characters and actions. See also FABLE; FIGURA; HERMENEUTICS; MIMESIS; PARABLE; SYMBOL.

alliteration Neighboring words that begin with the same consonant. This is the usual definition of alliteration, though the term is sometimes expanded to include repeated vowel sounds; see ASSONANCE.

In Shakespeare's *Midsummer Night's Dream,* Bottom chants a bit of heroic alliterative verse:

> The raging rocks
> And shivering shocks
> Shall break the locks

Of prison gates;
And Phibbus' car
Shall shine from far,
And make and mar
The foolish Fates.

"This was lofty!" Bottom then exclaims, appreciating his own performance. "Raging rocks," "shivering shocks," "make and mar," and "foolish Fates" are examples of alliteration.

In the twentieth century, W. H. Auden frequently relied on an alliterative thread in his poetry, as he evoked the hammering, repeated consonants of Old English verse: "Doom is dark and deeper than any sea-dingle." A later poet, John Ashbery (b. 1927), quoted another Auden line when he named one of his lyrics "Round the Ragged Rocks the Rude Rascals Ran," a title that embodies the vigorous, consistent nature of alliteration.

allusion When a literary work engages in allusion, it refers to—plays with, makes use of—earlier pieces of literature (or, sometimes, history). (In a broader sense, to allude to something is simply to mention it, usually obliquely or off-handedly.) Christopher Ricks defines allusion as "the calling into play . . . of the words and phrases of previous writers." A source, Ricks continues, "may not be an allusion, for it may not be called into play." Joyce's *Ulysses* (1922) and Milton's *Paradise Lost* (1667) are among the most thickly allusive works of English literature, invoking whole universes of earlier texts.

In *A Midsummer Night's Dream,* Bottom alludes conspicuously to the Bible. Upon awakening from his bestial metamorphosis and his dalliance with the fairy queen Titania, he stumblingly remarks, "Methought I was— and methought I had—but man is but a patched fool if he will offer to say what methought I had. The eye of man hath not heard, the ear of man hath not seen, man's hand is not able to taste, his tongue to conceive, nor his heart to report, what my dream was" (Shakespeare, *A Midsummer Night's Dream,* 4.1). Saint Paul in Corinthians 2:9 had written, "Eye hath not seen, nor ear heard, neither have entered into the heart of man the things which God hath prepared for them that love Him." Shakespeare adapts, and jumbles, Paul's description of religious revelation in order to convey the radical unexpectedness of imagination, the way it upsets and disorients; and he shifts from a promise of future salvation to a bizarre, haunting reminiscence.

See Christopher Ricks, *Allusion to the Poets* (2002), and his essay on the philosopher J. L. Austin, "Austin's Swink," in *Essays in Appreciation* (1996); John Hollander, *The Figure of Echo* (1981); and Eleanor Cook, *Against Coercion* (1998). See also ECHO.

ambiguity In *The Arte of English Poesie* (1589), George Puttenham identifies a simple kind of ambiguity. Puttenham cites these lines: "I sat by my Lady soundly sleeping, / My mistresse lay by me bitterly weeping." Puttenham comments, quite reasonably, "No man can tell by this, whether the mistresse or the man, slept or wept." But this seems mere confusion, rather than the usual fascinating tangle: the more representative examples of ambiguity are the complex ones.

The critic and poet William Empson defines such complex ambiguity in his *Seven Types of Ambiguity* (1930; rev. ed. 1947) as "any verbal nuance, however slight, which gives room for alternative reactions to the same piece of language." One of Empson's instances is Shakespeare's description of Isabella in *Measure for Measure:* "In her youth / There is a prone and speechless dialect / Such as move men . . ." Empson remarks, "*Prone* means either 'inactive and lying flat' . . . or 'active,' 'tending to,'" and adds that the lines make it impossible for us to decide between the two meanings. Empson adds that "'speechless' will not give away whether [Isabella] is shy or sly." Shakespeare has made it deliberately unclear whether she moves men "by her subtlety or by her purity."

Following Empson and others, the New Critics exalted ambiguity as one of the crucial features of poetic language (see NEW CRITICISM). Stephen Booth's *King Lear, Macbeth, Indefinition, and Tragedy* (2001) is an intriguing exploration of ambiguity in Shakespeare.

American Renaissance The name given to the outpouring of American classics in the 1840s, 1850s, and 1860s by Ralph Waldo Emerson, Henry David Thoreau, Herman Melville, Nathaniel Hawthorne, Walt Whitman, Emily Dickinson, Edgar Allan Poe, and a few others. F. O. Matthiessen's book *American Renaissance* (1941) defined this movement, or association, in decisive fashion, emphasizing these writers' common "devotion to the possibilities of democracy," their inheritance of religious ideas from New England puritanism, and their concern with the relation between individual and society. Matthiessen at times saw in the American Renaissance writers a conflict between an Emersonian "will to virtue" and a will to power that he associated with Melville's Ahab.

Other influential critics on the American Renaissance followed Matthiessen. Richard Chase emphasized the rebellious search for open forms; R. W. B. Lewis underlined the importance of Adamic innocence; Charles Feidelson focused on questions of unity, symbolism, and organic form; Quentin Anderson saw American literature looking back to the revolutionary generation. Ann Douglas, claiming Margaret Fuller as an important member of the group, illuminated the contention between American Renaissance writers and the popular sentimental literature of the time. Finally, David Reynolds in *Beneath the American Renaissance* (1988), an influential work of historicism, described the ties between the American Renaissance writers and the society of their time, occupied with arguments over slavery, the status of the union and national expansion. See Quentin Anderson, *The Imperial Self* (1971) and *Making Americans* (1992); Richard Chase, *The American Novel and Its Tradition* (1957); R. W. B. Lewis, *The American Adam* (1955); Charles Feidelson, *Symbolism in American Literature* (1956); Ann Douglas, *The Feminization of American Literature* (1977); Donald Pease, *Visionary Compacts* (1987).

amoebean song Features verses sung by two characters in alternation, conversation-wise; it occurs most often in pastoral poetry. This example features two shepherds, Perigot and Willye, from Spenser's *Shepheardes Calender* (1579):

Perigot	I saw the bouncing Bellibone,
Willye	hey ho Bonibell
Perigot	Tripping ouer the dale alone,
Willyes	he can trippe it very well:
Perigot	Well decked in a frock of gray,
Willye	hey ho gray is greete
Perigot	And in a kirtle of greene saye,
Willye	the greene is for maidens meete:
Perigot	A chapelet on her head she wore,
Willye	hey ho chapelet . . .

Notice how Willye's lines extend and at the same time comment on Perigot's. Their riffing becomes a contest dramatizing the friendly solidarity of two voices, as in the call-and-response work songs common among African-American slaves.

Describing the shepherds depicted in pastoral verse, George Puttenham writes in *The Arte of English Poesie* (1589), "Sometimes also they sang and played on their pipes for wagers, striving who should get the best game, and be counted cunningest." Virgil's seventh eclogue (37 BCE), with its cheerfully adversarial singers, provides one of the main models for pastoral competitive song. For allied forms, see FLYTING; STICHOMYTHIA; see also PASTORAL.

amor fati In Latin, "love of [one's] fate." The affectionate embrace of one's own life in all its sufferings and disappointments, as well as its successes: an ideal advocated by Friedrich Nietzsche in *The Gay Science* (1882–87). See also ETERNAL RETURN.

Anacreontic Anacreon was a Greek poet who lived in Teos, in Asia Minor, perhaps around 582–485 BCE. The proverbial wine, women, and song provided the subject matter of his poems. Anacreon pictures himself, and is depicted by his imitators (of which he had many), as a handsome, lascivious older man, devoted to the pleasures of drinking and sex. One of his followers, the seventeenth-century English poet Robert Herrick, has his Mistress promise him that, in Elysium, "Ile bring thee *Herrick* to *Anacreon,* / Quaffing his full-crown'd bowles of burning wine." For a sparkling evocation of the Anacreontic tradition, see Gordon Braden, *The Classics and English Renaissance Poetry* (1978).

anagnorisis. See RECOGNITION

anagogic In biblical exegesis, the anagogic (from Greek *anagoge,* "upward") is the level of interpretation oriented toward the heavenly afterlife. Often it describes the "Change," or "last things": the events of the apocalypse and the ensuing millennium, particularly as depicted in the Book of Revelation. The anagogic is one of four levels of interpretation: the others are literal, allegorical, and tropological. (See FIGURA for an explanation of these levels; see also TYPOLOGY.)

In his *Anatomy of Criticism* (1957), Northrop Frye points to the anagogic as the final possibility of metaphor, suggesting a complete union between two terms (as in Shakespeare's "The Phoenix and the Turtle"). As Frye puts it, anagogic metaphor is "pure and potentially total identification, without regard to plausibility or ordinary experience."

analytic philosophy The analytic school has dominated most philosophy departments in America and the United Kingdom since the careers of Ludwig Wittgenstein and J. L. Austin, who taught in England in the 1940s and (in Austin's case) the 1950s. But the roots of analytic philosophy existed long before Wittgenstein and Austin, in the late 1870s and 1880s, in the works of the logician Gottlob Frege. Frege and, after him, Bertrand Russell asserted the centrality of logic for philosophical understanding. (In this respect analytic philosophy differs from its rival, the continental tradition.) Beginning in 1929, the Vienna Circle, including Moritz Schlick, Rudolf Carnap, and others, developed logical positivism, the effort to subject our thinking and expression to the strict standards of meaning associated with logic.

Wittgenstein and Austin were profound, funny, and strikingly original in the ways they refounded philosophical discussion, suggesting that much of previous tradition had simply failed to pay attention to what we do and say. Now philosophy was to be established in the common, the ordinary; it had to be proven by way of experience, not wishful hypotheses about the nature of man. The inquiries of Wittgenstein, Austin, and their heirs are called *ordinary language philosophy,* since they often begin by looking closely at our routine ways of expressing ourselves. Ordinary language philosophy, it can be argued, diverges from analytic philosophy proper, since it does not share the analytic interest in logic, mathematics, and science. (For an extreme, and immensely influential, example of the analytic approach that chooses logic over ordinary language, see A. J. Ayer's *Language, Truth, and Logic* [1936]; Gilbert Ryle and G. E. Moore were also significant voices in this trend.)

More generally speaking, though, analytic philosophy is a wide term that includes ordinary language philosophy as well as logic and philosophy of mathematics. As such, analytic remains fundamentally distinct from continental philosophy. Analytic philosophers see philosophy as a meditation on a series of problems. They are less interested in understanding a tradition in which each thinker responds to or contends with previous thinkers than in developing arguments based on attentive and precise definitions. An analytic philosopher might focus on questions such as the following: What is an action? What is naming? How does memorizing differ from learning, or from recognizing? By contrast, a continental philosopher might focus on the history of a concept in philosophical tradition: *Geist* (spirit) or justice, for example. The continental philosopher suggests that our sense of these words cannot be detached from the texts that invoke them most memorably: the works of Plato, Aristotle, Nietzsche, Heidegger, and others. The analytic philosopher is at times willing to discard tradition and start from scratch—from human reason and everyday proof.

Some of the major analytic philosophers of recent years are W. V. O. Quine, Donald Davidson, Saul Kripke, Thomas Nagel, Bernard Williams, and Daniel Dennett. Analytic philosophy has also exerted an influence on thinkers in other disciplines: for example, the great sociologist Erving Goffman, who, much in the manner of an analytic philosopher, meditates on the concept of "the action" in his essay "Where the Action Is" (from *The Presentation of Self in Everyday Life* [1956]).

Recently, there have been significant rapprochements between analytic and continental styles of philosophizing, guided in part by writers like Stanley Cavell (in *The Claim of Reason* [1979]) and Richard Rorty (in *Philosophy and the Mirror of Nature* [1979] and *Contingency, Irony, and Solidarity* [1989]). For a focused account of the origins of analytic philosophy, see Michael Friedman, *A Parting of the Ways* (2000). See also CONTINENTAL PHILOSOPHY; ORDINARY.

anapest. See METER

anatomy A systematic and elaborate dissection of a field of knowledge; fundamentally a Renaissance genre. The most familiar example in English is Robert Burton's *Anatomy of Melancholy* (1621), which divides its subject into a voluminous and bewildering series of categories. A few years before Burton's exhaustive, fascinating compendium, Shakespeare's character Jacques, in *As You Like It,* offered a more compact anatomy of melancholy: "I have neither the scholar's melancholy, which is emulation; nor the musician's, which is fantastical; nor the courtier's, which is proud; nor the soldier's, which is ambitious; nor the lawyer's, which is politic; nor the lady's, which is nice; nor the lover's, which is all these: but it is a melancholy of mine own, compounded of many simples, extracted from many objects, and indeed the sundry contemplation of my travels, in which my often rumination wraps me in a most humorous sadness."

In the twentieth century, Northrop Frye's *Anatomy of Criticism* (1957) supplied an encyclopedic survey of the forms of literary creation, from pulp fiction to national epic.

ancients and moderns (battle of the) Machiavelli, in his letters, movingly describes his evening reading of the ancient Romans as an ideal refuge from his long, hard day of political duties in Renaissance Florence. Machiavelli is a modern: although he relies on Livy and other classics in his political theory, for him the ancient authors mostly offer a heartening escape, rather than a definitive guide to life, which has changed since the old days. (Similarly, the art critic Dave Hickey writes of taking down his grandfather's copy of Cicero for relief amid the glitz of Las Vegas, where he teaches.)

But it need not be assumed that, for us moderns, the ancients are out of date, mere sources of refreshing contrast. The distance between Greek and Roman wisdom and our latter-day experience can instead be seen as a genuine debate, an intellectual contest. Indeed, the ancients might judge us, and find us lacking. (Incidentally, the word *modern* in our sense probably arrived in the sixth century CE. By 800 Charlemagne's Holy Roman Empire was being referred to as a *saeculum modernum:* a modern era or rule.)

In the twelfth century Bernard of Chartres defended the authority of the ancients against the moderns. Bernard (quoted here by John of Salisbury) wrote that "we are like dwarfs seated on the shoulders of giants." (The image is from Tertullian [ca. 160–230], an early Christian church father.) We see more, and more distant, things than the ancients. But we owe our greater power of sight to their monumental presence, which necessarily boosts us. As Bernard remarks, "We are raised and borne aloft on their giant mass." The image became a familiar one, even in champions of modernity like the Renaissance Englishman Sir Francis Bacon.

In the late seventeenth century, the combat between the ancients and the moderns (in French, *la querelle des anciens et des modernes*) was reinaugurated. John Dryden's dialogue *An Essay of Dramatic Poesy* (1668) begins with a debate over whether the ancient or the modern poets are superior, and eventually adopts a position (voiced by Dryden's spokesman Neander) that recognizes the virtues of both. Charles Perrault in *The Century of Louis the Great* (1687) spoke for the superiority of current art, literature, and culture over the products of ancient Greece and Rome. Perrault's opponent Jean de la Fontaine responded on behalf of the ancients in his *Letter to Huet* (1687).

The battle between ancient and modern reached a culmination of sorts in

Jonathan Swift's viciously funny *Battle of the Books* (1697; publ. 1704), which depicts a contest between the (modern) spider and the (ancient) bee. Swift credits the moderns with "a large vein of wrangling and satire": the poison of the spider. But the ancients enjoy, according to Swift, a better advantage, the product of "infinite labour, and search, and ranging through every corner of nature": the honey sweetness of the bee. The issue remains undecided in Swift's era, but it is arguable that, with the coming of Romanticism, modernity is unavoidable. The German Romantic A. W. Schlegel writes that whereas "the poetry of the ancients was the poetry of possession, our poetry is that of yearning; the former stands firmly on the ground of the present, the latter sways between memory and presentiment." Instead of the ancient "unconscious unity of form and content," the modern, who is denied this unity, seeks a greater intimacy with both. (See also NAIVE AND SENTIMENTAL.)

The most remarkable recent revival of a case for the ancients is contained in the writings of the political philosopher Leo Strauss and his followers. See Strauss, *The City and Man* (1964), and Stanley Rosen, *The Ancients and the Moderns* (1989).

anti-masque. See MASQUE

antitheatrical The "antitheatrical prejudice," as Jonas Barish calls it, is the fear or disapproval of spectacular representations. It begins in ancient Greece, with Plato and Aristotle, and in Rome, with Horace. Aristotle's *Poetics* (ca. 330 BCE) asserts that acts of bloody violence in tragedy, murders and the like, ought to take place offstage. Similarly, in his *Ars Poetica* (Art of Poetry, ca. 20 BCE) Horace writes: "Don't let Medea murder the children before the people's gaze, or wicked Atreus cook human remains in public, or Procne be metamorphosed into a bird or Cadmus into a snake. Anything you show me like that earns my incredulity and disgust."

For both Aristotle and Horace, avoidance of onstage bloodbaths is a matter of literary decorum rather than concern for the psyche of the spectator. (See DECORUM.) But later writers use the Aristotelian and Horatian inclination against visible gore to emphasize a different point. These critics don't merely disdain grisly spectacles, in the manner of Aristotle and Horace; they fear them. They want to ward off the peculiar power of theatrical violence, and sex as well: the horrible, entrancing sights that might affect an audience, and even damage its sensibility.

The antitheatrical prejudice testifies, at times, to a mild cultural hysteria. For the puritans of the English Reformation, plays were wicked things, and playgoing a kind of frenzied idolatry, to be classed with other vicious diversions like dice playing, maypole dancing, and cosmetics.

The antitheatrical argument has two main emphases. One is that the object of the spectator's gaze is infectious: you might become what you see (a fear apparent in contemporary discussions about the dangers of horror movies and pornography). The other emphasis goes in a slightly different direction: theatrical representation exploits unreality and makes us dwell there, so that we no longer care to know the difference between lies and truth. The first argument worries about our being transported, through drama's thrills, into a brutally effective false reality; the second, about our drifting into ineffectuality, into disregard for the demands of actual life. Both these arguments stem, in large part, from Plato's case against poetry in his *Republic* (ca. 370 BCE). Plato, unlike Aristotle and Horace, does engage questions of audience psychology: he is undoubtedly the primary source of the psychotherapeutic case against the spectacular.

For an important eighteenth-century debate about theater, see Jean-Jacques Rousseau, *Letter to d'Alembert* (1758), translated with commentary by Allan Bloom under the title *Politics and the Arts* (1960); also Denis Diderot, *The Paradox of Acting* (Paradoxe sur le comédien; written ca. 1773, publ. 1830). Jonas Barish in *The Antitheatrical Prejudice* (1981) provides an overview of the tradition.

antithetical An antithesis is a rhetorical contrast between opposing ideas, often reinforced by parallel syntax. An example, from the King James Bible: "The grass withereth, the flower fadeth: but the word of our God shall stand for ever" (Isaiah 40:8). Aristotle in his *Rhetoric* (fourth century BCE) argues that rhetorical opposites, or antitheses, are effective because they remind us of refutations (arguments that depend on disproving an opposed proposition). In the Isaiah passage, the refutation might run as follows: the fragile undependability of nature illustrates, by contrast, the fact that God's word remains in scripture, cited generation after generation.

W. B. Yeats expounds the idea of the antithetical in a contrary manner to that of Aristotle. In Yeats, the stark contrast of a rhetorical opposition substitutes for, rather than depending on, the logic of a refutation. Sheer antithesis itself becomes an argument. For Yeats, in his prose works *The Trembling of the*

Veil (1922) and *Dramatis Personae* (1935), all artistic creation is essentially antithetical: that is, it requires the construction of a persona, an "anti-self" profoundly contrary to one's natural or socially available character. Yeats described the anti-self as "our simplifying image, our genius," which is "always
opposite to the natural self or the natural world." For example, Yeats depicts
Oscar Wilde as a natural man of action who dreamed himself an aesthete (his
superbly fashioned anti-self).

According to Yeats, in his autobiographies and in *A Vision* (1925), the primary antithesis is always the one between the created, organized work of art
and the chaotic life of the human author who wrote or painted it. The anti-
self must be kept for figurative enactment in an artistic work, rather than literal enactment in life, since the messiness of our actual, everyday existence
can only frustrate the high, poised aspiration of the anti-self. On Yeats's
idea of the antithetical see Harold Bloom, *Yeats* (1970), and Daniel O'Hara,
Tragic Knowledge (1981).

anxiety of influence A concept invented, or discovered, by Harold Bloom in
The Anxiety of Influence (1973). Bloom describes the agon or struggle between
the influential precursor and the ephebe, or young writer, remarking that
"poetic history" is "indistinguishable from poetic influence, since strong poets make that history by misreading one another, so as to clear imaginative
space for themselves."

Bloom's emphasis is in sharp contrast to the craftsmanlike notion of literary imitation championed by that sturdy maker of poems and plays, Ben Jonson, Shakespeare's contemporary. In a practical and genial way, Jonson describes the method of poetic creation through emulation of previous authors:
"To make choice of an excellent man above the rest, and so follow him till he
grow very he, so like him as the copy may be mistaken for the original." Jonson, in this passage, seems to neglect the fact that a later author wants to distinguish himself, rather than becoming another Virgil or Ovid. (See IMITA-
TION for more on Renaissance ideas of literary tradition.)

Bloom writes, contra Jonson, that "the poet confronting his great original
must find the fault that is not there." Sustaining himself or herself means, for
the later author, wounding the precursor. For Bloom, the ephebe's greatest
unhappiness is the fact that, while the new poem is within her, she has been
found by (made an author by means of) works that remain outside her, and
that therefore continue to threaten her: the achievements of the precursor. To
accept definition by something that remains outside the self, whether in the

shape of literary tradition, history, or official intellectual doctrine, would mean the demise of the individual imagination and its aspiration to originality. See Bloom, *The Anxiety of Influence* (1973), and Bloom, *Poetics of Influence,* ed. John Hollander (1988).

aphorism An aphorism is a many-faceted observation: speculative and not necessarily witty. The aphorist raises a sentence or two to artful integrity. Friedrich Schlegel writes that an aphorism should be "like a miniature work of art . . . entirely isolated from the surrounding world and complete in itself like a porcupine." (In Greek, *aphorizein* is to mark off by means of boundaries.) Aphorisms are compact and pointed: often, like the porcupine, pointed in several different directions. Oscar Wilde's aphorism "one's real life is often the life one does not lead" can be understood as either cynical or idealizing; it seems to ask to be taken as both at once.

The epigram, a related genre, is closer to a one-liner, and more restricted in its effectiveness than the aphorism. (W. H. Auden gives as an instance of epigram the definition of fox hunting as "the pursuit of the uneatable by the unspeakable.") William Blake's aphorism "eternity is in love with the productions of time" conveys a contemplative depth that epigrams tend to avoid in their wish to deliver a stinging conclusion.

Francis Bacon collected a set of aphorisms, and added his own commentary, in *De Augmentis Scientiarum* (1623). The Baconian aphorism is related to the *sententia* or learned opinion, and to the proverb. François de La Rochefoucauld (1613–80), Georg Christoph Lichtenberg (1742–99), and Friedrich Schlegel in his *Athenaeum Fragments* (1798) were influential aphorists. In the twentieth century, Wallace Stevens's *Adagia* is a remarkable collection of aphorisms by a poet; Paul Valéry's *Cahiers* (Notebooks) are full of equally intriguing instances. Schopenhauer's *Parerga and Paralipomena* (1851), the middle section of Nietzsche's *Gay Science* (1882–87), and Theodor Adorno's *Minima Moralia* (1951) use the aphorism for purposes of philosophy. On Bacon's aphorisms, see Brian Vickers, "The Aphorism," in *Francis Bacon and Renaissance Prose* (1968). For an idiosyncratic and dazzling selection of aphorisms, consult W. H. Auden and Louis Kronenberger, eds., *The Viking Book of Aphorisms* (1962). See also EPIGRAM; GNOMIC; PROVERB; WIT.

apocalypse, apocalyptic The word *apocalypse,* from Greek, means an opening up or revealing: the Revelation of Saint John, the last book of the Bible, depicts the Christian apocalypse. In the English-speaking tradition, William

Blake remains the prime example of an apocalyptic writer, with his many cataclysmic overturnings of order. Apocalypse in Blake keeps happening, presenting an ongoing discovery, or life history, of the cosmos. In the late twentieth century, when World War II was widely felt to be a violent culmination of historical time, Thomas Pynchon in *Gravity's Rainbow* (1973) communicated a most frightening aspect of apocalyptic thinking: the potential erasing of the human image, and of humanity itself, from existence. Other twentieth-century writers often seen as apocalyptic are Louis-Ferdinand Céline and Georges Bataille. See Harold Bloom, *Blake's Apocalypse* (1963).

apocrypha, apocryphal. See CANON, CANONICAL

Apollonian Along with the Dionysian, the Apollonian is one of the two basic antithetical principles described by Friedrich Nietzsche in *The Birth of Tragedy from the Spirit of Music* (1872). Nietzsche associates the Apollonian with the god Apollo, and with the coolness, refinement, and balance of ancient Greek sculpture and architecture. The Apollonian conception of classicism, expressed by writers like the great German scholar Johann Winckelmann, was of a "white marble Greekness, a calm Greekness" (Margaret Doody). Nietzsche detects in Plato's Socrates, with his trust in human reason as a healing and harmonizing force, the ultimate fulfillment of the Apollonian principle. By contrast, the dark, archaic tragedy of Aeschylus, vanquished by the light of the Socratic logos, remains for Nietzsche the epitome of the Dionysian. See also DIONYSIAN.

aporia From the Greek *poros,* way or road: preceded by the negating particle *a-* (alpha privative), it means a situation of irresolvable difficulty. Scholars have described as aporetic early Socratic dialogues like the *Protagoras* (ca. 380 BCE), which end in puzzlement rather than resolution, and which fail to supply convincing definitions of sought-after concepts like truth and virtue. At the end of the *Protagoras,* wrote the philosopher Søren Kierkegaard, Socrates and Protagoras resemble "two bald men searching for a comb." See Paul Friedländer, *Plato* (1928), and Gregory Vlastos, *Socrates, Ironist and Moral Philosopher* (1991).

The critic Paul de Man explored the aporetic as a crucial feature of literature. The literary, de Man argued, distinguishes itself by the characteristic appearance of an epistemological disappointment, so that we find ourselves blocked off from the knowledge that the text seemed to promise us. What literary texts "know," according to de Man, is that knowledge is aporetic, that is, unavailable, because it is subject to a double bind. By definition, we cannot have access to the truth that we seek in literature: and this is literature's truth. See de Man, *Blindness and Insight* (1971) and *Allegories of Reading* (1979).

apostrophe An apostrophe is a poetic exclamation, colored by lament or acclaim: *O tempora! O mores!* (Oh the times, the manners!), for example (a tag from Cicero), or *Hail the conquering hero! Apostrophe* is the Greek word for "a turning away": the poet breaks off to address someone or something. The Romantic poets sometimes engaged breathlessly in apostrophes: witness Percy Bysshe Shelley's lines in "Epipsychidion" (1821):

> Spouse! Sister! Angel! Pilot of the Fate
> Whose course has been so starless! O too late
> Belovèd! O too soon adored, by me!

See Jonathan Culler's discussion of the apostrophe as an essential aspect of lyric in *The Pursuit of Signs* (1981).

Arcadia A rather rocky region of the Greek Peloponnesus, sparse rather than lush in vegetation: according to literary rumor, populated mostly by shepherds. Thomas Rosenmeyer reports the legendary characteristics of the place: "Arcadia is called lovely and well-watered; she is said to be famous for her sheep; she is the land of hunters; the Arcadian diet is notorious for its simplicity; the inhabitants are autochthonous, and in fact their race is older than the moon."

Arcadia provides the setting for much pastoral poetry, from Theocritus and Virgil on (see PASTORAL). It has also supplied a landscape for prose romance, most notably in Philip Sidney's *Arcadia* (written in 1580, later versions published in 1590 and 1593).

The art historian Erwin Panofsky wrote an influential essay on the funerary inscription in a painting by Nicolas Poussin, "Et in Arcadia Ego" (I too am in Arcadia). Panofsky showed that the inscription was meant to be spoken by death himself, who could be heard asserting the presence of mortality even within the paradisal equanimity of the pastoral world. (The poet Donald Justice's version of the topos is "And there stood Death in the garden, /

Dressed like a Spanish waiter" [from "Incident in a Rose Garden"].) See Panofsky, "*Et in Arcadia Ego:* Poussin and the Elegiac Tradition" (1936), collected in his book *Meaning in the Visual Arts,* and reprinted in an excellent collection edited by Eleanor Lincoln, *Pastoral and Romance* (1969). Thomas Rosenmeyer's *The Green Cabinet* (1969) provides the best overview of the idea of Arcadia in pastoral.

archaism A deliberately obsolete or outdated use of language. A good example is Edmund Spenser's use of *wight* (for *man*) in his epic *The Faerie Queene,* a locution that already sounded antiquated and "poetically" strange when the poem was published in the 1590s. Spenser and, at times, Milton also use the prefix *y-* to change a verb to the past tense, an archaic feature associated with the Middle English of Geoffrey Chaucer and John Gower: *yplight, yclept.*

Archaism occurs especially in poetry, which clings to certain words that have long since dropped out of prose writing and everyday speech: *methought, ween, steed.* See Eleanor Cook's essay "Methought as Dream Formula in Shakespeare, Milton, Wordsworth, Keats, and Others," in her book *Against Coercion* (1998).

archetype An archetype is a resonant figure of mythic importance, whether a personality, place, or situation, found in diverse cultures and different historical periods. Among the most familiar archetypes are the quest, the garden or earthly paradise, the youthful hero, the underworld, and the battle with a dragon or other world-destroying monster. The female divinity who both destroys and creates is another important archetype, described by Robert Graves as "the cruel, capricious, incontinent White Goddess" (Graves, *The White Goddess* [1948]). Influenced by Graves and by the psychologist C. G. Jung, Northrop Frye authoritatively outlined archetypal criticism in his *Anatomy of Criticism* (1957).

Frye defined the archetype by distinguishing it from two contrasting phenomena, allegorical typification and philosophical definition. The archetype involves neither the use of an individual person or event as an instance of the typical (as in allegory), nor the submitting of individual instances to a more general form (as in philosophy), but rather the metaphorical identification of individual and type. Every protagonist who sets out on a quest becomes representative, expanding our sense of the archetype by embodying it anew.

Archetypal reading can lead to some wildly stimulating imaginative identifications. The wedding of the young, joyous couple that concludes so many stage comedies is like the union between Christ and the human soul (called a marriage in the Christian gospels), which in turn resembles the embrace of nature and human consciousness that Wordsworth, in his poetry, names marriage. These comparisons help us to understand that marriage is itself an archetype, an image of reconciliation and bliss that transports itself into metaphor. The bond between two people becomes, via the archetype, a place of wider, deeper union, where the happy couple are contained. Their happiness is capable of appearing as divine love for humanity, even as the very fit between the human and the natural.

Television shows like *Star Trek* and *Buffy the Vampire Slayer* rely on archetypes just as surely as the Sumerian epic of *Gilgamesh* or Homer's *Odyssey*. See especially Frye, *Fables of Identity* (1963); and, for a powerful interpretation of Shakespeare in terms of archetypes, G. Wilson Knight, *The Wheel of Fire* (1930).

Aristotelian criticism Aristotle—the most significant literary critic of all, and one of the first—produced his *Poetics* around 335 or 330 BCE. What survives of this work (in the form of lecture notes, possibly written down by one of Aristotle's students) is a discussion of tragedy and epic. An additional section of the *Poetics,* on comedy, remains lost.

Aristotle identifies six aspects of tragic poetry, as presented onstage: *dianoia* (thought—by which he may have meant commentary or moralizing delivered by the characters), *melos* (music), *opsis* (spectacle), *mythos* (story or plot), *lexis* (diction), and *ethos* (character).

Arguing against Plato, Aristotle defined and defended tragedy (and, by extension, literature itself) as a worthy form. Plato had condemned poetry in his *Republic* (ca. 370 BCE) on several grounds: poets don't know what they are doing, but merely reproduce the surface of things (as Nickolas Pappas notes, this is sometimes the charge against photography as an art form); they present examples of bad behavior, uncaring about the morally corrupting effect on the audience. Finally, according to Plato, poets dote on expressions of emotion, rather than illustrating the dangers of giving way to emotion and exalting the greater privilege of thinking, as philosophers do.

In his defense of tragedy in the *Poetics,* Aristotle gives poetry the knowledge and moral weight that Plato had denied it. Aristotle focuses on the idea that a tragedy presents a serious and complete imitation of an action. Poetry is not for him the portraying of (mostly bad) characters, as Plato had charged. In Aristotle's view of tragedy plot takes precedence over character. Moreover, the tragic plot has moral import. It presents the downfall of a man who is decent and who makes a mistake: one who misses the mark (the meaning of Aristotle's term *hamartia*).

Aristotle substitutes for the crude notion of recognition that Plato ascribes to poetry in Bk. 10 of the *Republic* his own much deeper concept. Plato had said that poetry merely elicits a recognition of the objects or persons depicted, much as a painting of a bed asks us to realize that it is a bed. But what we recognize when we view a tragedy, according to Aristotle, is something far less trivial: the just nature of the denouement. The hero must be neither too depraved nor too glorious; he is an ordinary mortal punished by bad luck, unfairly yet fittingly. We pity such a protagonist, and we are afraid along with him: our sympathy constitutes the morality of tragedy.

Recognition (in Greek, *anagnorisis*) and reversal (*peripeteia*) are the two key moments of tragic plot, Aristotle claims. An example of recognition is when (in Aristotle's favorite tragedy, Sophocles' *Oedipus Rex*) Oedipus realizes that he is himself the monstrous criminal he has been seeking. Reversal is the turning around from fortune to misfortune that guides most tragic narratives, including that of Oedipus.

Aristotle's ideas have had a long, sometimes eccentric afterlife. In the late seventeenth and eighteenth centuries, some neoclassical critics focused on, and misinterpreted, a few of Aristotle's passing remarks about the unity of place, time, and action, in order to insist that a tragedy must occur in a single location and in the course of a single day. Later, in the nineteenth century, critics seized on Aristotle's term *catharsis* (used only fleetingly in the *Poetics*). Catharsis in Aristotle seems to mean something like demonstration or clarification, but the primary reading of catharsis during the nineteenth and twentieth centuries was a medical one: tragedy purges pity and fear, flushing the audience's emotional system (so the critics asserted).

In the twentieth century, the "Chicago school" applied Aristotle's ideas about tragedy to other literary forms. Aristotle's *Rhetoric* is increasingly important in literary study as rhetorical criticism, inspired partly by the example of Kenneth Burke, becomes a flourishing field in English departments. See also CATHARSIS; CHICAGO SCHOOL; NEOCLASSICISM; RECOGNITION; REVERSAL; RHETORIC; TRAGEDY.

See Nickolas Pappas, "Aristotle," in Dominic Lopes and Berys Gaut, eds.,

The Routledge Companion to Aesthetics (2000); Gerald Else, *Aristotle's Poetics* (1957); Martha Nussbaum, *The Fragility of Goodness* (1982); Kathy Eden, *Poetic and Legal Fiction in the Aristotelian Tradition* (1986). In *The Reach of Criticism* (1983), Paul Fry opposes Aristotle's tradition to that of Longinus, the theorist of the sublime.

ars poetica Literally, "art of poetry": a summary description, written in verse by a poet, of how poems are, and ought to be, constructed—and, implicitly, what a poem *is*. The Roman poet Horace wrote the best-known ars poetica, around 20 BCE. An ars poetica can be as curt and bristling as Archibald MacLeish's "A poem must not mean / But be," or as expansive as Wallace Stevens's "Notes Toward a Supreme Fiction."

asceticism Derived from the classical Greek *askesis,* glossed by Walter Pater as "the girding of the loins in youth." (Pater was referring to the discipline and rigor demanded of Greek adolescents training for athletic contests.) Asceticism in the later moral sense of the term is associated with Pauline Christianity and its long tradition of self-punishment. This Christian ascetic morality, acutely diagnosed by Friedrich Nietzsche in his *Genealogy of Morals* (1887), was also undertaken in secularized form by artists and writers, who insisted that artistic creation required intense labors of purity and self-denial. Flaubert wrote to his companion Louise Colet in 1852, "I am leading a stern existence, stripped of all external pleasure . . . I love my work with a love that is frenzied and perverted, as an ascetic loves the hair shirt that scratches his belly." (See Gustave Flaubert, "Art as Ascetic Religion," in Richard Ellmann and Charles Feidelson, eds., *The Modern Tradition* [1965].)

In our era, asceticism has been embodied in some remarkable works of literature: the circuitous, stringent novels of the Austrian Thomas Bernhard, for example, or Samuel Beckett's final works, with their stark and attentive interest in a punishing blankness.

assonance The repetition of similar or identical vowel sounds, usually to create a melodious, lulling effect. Here are some lines from "August" by Algernon Charles Swinburne (1837–1909):

The colour of the leaves was more
Like stems of yellow corn that grow
Through all the gold June meadow's floor

The repeated *o* sounds in colour, more, yellow, corn, grow, gold, meadow, and floor provide a striking example of assonance. And the assonance becomes more insinuating and powerful as it continues because of a "bending" effect, involving the ineluctable difference between related sounds. In "meadow's floor," the *ow* of meadow and the *oo* of floor are close, but not the same; the first vowel seems to push or glide into the second, *ow* into *oo*.

Attic Associated with Athens or its surrounding region, Attica. The Athenians were noted for their elegant good taste in verbal expression: so an Attic prose style is a refined and smooth one, never extravagant or over the top. Cicero in his *Orator* (46 BCE) remarks that the orator in the Attic style must avoid heavy-handed, hammy rhetoric: "He will not represent the State as speaking or call the dead from the lower world, nor will he crowd a long series of iterations into a single period . . . he will be rather subdued in voice as in style."

Such calm Attic poise contrasts with the insistent rhetorical symmetries of the Greek orator Isocrates, who liked to end successive sentences with similar-sounding words (a figure called *homoioteleuton*). Attic style also rejects the extravagant figures of speech that the sophists relied on (one sophist, Gorgias, referred to vultures as "living graves"). In Hellenistic and Roman literature, Attic prose style is sometimes contrasted to the florid and overblown Asiatic manner. (See CLEVELANDISM; PLAIN STYLE; SOPHISTS.) The Attic writer or orator, writes Cicero, resembles the man who gives a tasteful and impressively organized banquet. "He will avoid extravagant display, and desire to appear thrifty, but also in good taste, and will choose what he is going to use." See J. V. Cunningham, ed., *The Problem of Style* (1966).

aubade A poetic salute to the dawn, whether joyous or lamenting, usually spoken by a poet-lover who has spent the night with his beloved mistress. (*Aubade* is French; its Provençal synonym is *alba*.)

So Shakespeare's Romeo (accompanied by Juliet, who responds with her own verses) calls out at once to her and to the morning:

> look love what envious streaks
> Do lace the severing clouds in yonder East:
> Night's candles are burnt out, and jocund day
> Stands tip-toe on the misty mountain tops,
> I must be gone and live, or stay and die.

Augustan Age Originally, the Augustan Age was the era of the Roman emperor Augustus, who ruled from 27 BCE to 14 CE and who presided over a great literary flowering (including the works of three immortal poets, Virgil, Horace, and Ovid). The first half of the eighteenth century is also called, in literary study, the Augustan Age, since its writers—Alexander Pope, Jonathan Swift, Joseph Addison—emulated the decorum, capacity for sharp judgment, and firmly shaped urbanity of the Roman authors. See Howard Erskine-Hill, *The Augustan Idea in English Literature* (1983); Margaret Doody, *The Daring Muse* (1985); Paul Fussell, *The Rhetorical World of Augustan Humanism* (1965).

aureate The poets who were close to the Roman emperor Augustus, especially Horace and Virgil, were described as *aureate* (from the Latin for golden); their successors in the following generations, notably Ovid, Statius, and Lucan, were the silver poets. *Aureate* was later applied to the style of medieval poets like John Lydgate (ca. 1370–1449) and John Gower (ca. 1330–1408). Their follower William Dunbar, in his poem *The Goldyn Targe* (1508?), wrote of Gower's and Lydgate's "sugarit lippis and tongis aureate."

The critic and novelist C. S. Lewis drew a distinction between the "golden" poets of the English Renaissance (Sidney, Surrey, Shakespeare) and the "drab" poets (George Gascoigne, Barnabe Googe, George Turberville). The golden poets prominently display the strength of poetic wonder. They praise and cherish the beloved persons evoked in their verse, especially their sonnets. The "drab" poets, by contrast, often exhibit a rather harsh, satirical, or epigrammatic manner. The cantankerous and influential critic Yvor Winters championed the drab poets of the era in such books as *In Defense of Reason* (1947). See G. K. Hunter, "Drab and Golden Lyrics of the Renaissance," in Reuben Brower, ed., *Forms of Lyric* (1970).

authenticity Ovid, the great Roman poet of seduction and adulterous excitement, asserted in his *Tristia* (ca. 9–12 CE), "Believe me, my character is different from my poetry; my life is decent, my muse sportive." The seventeenth-century English parson and erotic poet Robert Herrick wrote his own epitaph in very similar words: "*Jocund* his muse was, but his life was chaste." Such a knowing separation of the writer's life from his art remains traditional. (In our own day, Brian Wilson of the Beach Boys was fond of reiterating that he never surfed.) However, we also often prize writers who go in the opposite direction from Ovid and Herrick, who claim to have experienced what they record in print (see CONFESSIONAL POETRY).

The question of authenticity is wider than mere curiosity about whether writers have actually lived the subject matter that they work from. Instead, authenticity is an attitude, a distinctive posture of character, endorsed by our culture. The critic Lionel Trilling, in *Sincerity and Authenticity* (1972), traces the development of the ideal of authenticity, which he defines as a strenuous morality based on experience, and particularly valued in the modern age. Trilling writes that authenticity implies "a degree of rough concreteness or of extremity," and "deal[s] aggressively with received and habitual opinion." The authentic is iconoclastic, provocative, honestly against the grain: all characteristics often linked to modernism.

Trilling's *Beyond Culture* (1965) also explores the notion of modernist authenticity. For descriptions of some literary and philosophical movements associated with authenticity, see CONFESSIONAL POETRY; EXISTENTIALISM; MODERNISM.

authority In Latin as in English, the word *authority* is etymologically bound to *author* (the Latin equivalents are *auctoritas* and *auctor*). In political terms, authority implies a human source, a giving of character or face to social power. Just as books have authors, so political authority depends on this personal aspect.

For Hannah Arendt, authority in politics remains fundamentally personal: it works its effects through the character of the politician, rather than through mere force, custom, or rhetorical adeptness. Arendt notes that *auctoritas* is derived from *augere,* to augment, and that "what those in authority constantly augment is the foundation." This activity reaches into the future, since authority, whether in politics or religion, involves "the enormous, almost superhuman and hence always legendary effort . . . to found for eternity."

The authority of a work of literature seems related to the kind of political and religious authority that Arendt describes, since literary power derives neither from sheer reliance on convention, nor from the violence of powerful effects, nor from rational persuasion. Instead, what speaks is the personality of the author, along with his or her characters. The Bible and Homer stand at the beginnings of their respective traditions, and these books combine claims for their own authority with their assertions about the utmost power of character, located in divinities and godlike heroes. In the Bible, the *Iliad,* and the *Aeneid,* authority requires a personal presence: a Moses, Achilles, or Aeneas.

There is also the authority of the instinctive moment. The story is told of how the ancient painter Apelles, frustrated at his inability to paint the foam on the lips of Alexander the Great's horse, threw his brush at the canvas and inadvertently made this masterful detail. As with the abstract expressionists, so in ancient Greece, we are meant to see the artist's brusque and spontaneous gesture in the finished painting: an unpredictable act proves supremely telling. Authority here comes in the form of energy, and results from impulse, not calculation.

Finally, each writer faces an often difficult struggle to inherit and assert authority in the literary tradition (see ANXIETY OF INFLUENCE). See Hannah Arendt, "What Is Authority?" in *Between Past and Future* (1961); Harold Bloom, *Ruin the Sacred Truths* (1989); John Guillory, *Poetic Authority* (1983). Michel Foucault's "What Is an Author?" (1971) argues against the connection between authorial personality and text.

automatic writing A form of literary creation advocated in the early twentieth century by Surrealists like André Breton. The writer would sit down at his desk and, as in Freudian free association, produce whatever sequences of words came to mind. In automatic writing, according to the idealizing view of the Surrealists, the writer's unconscious does all the work, without intervention from the censorious ego. See SURREALISM; UNCONSCIOUS.

avant-garde "Advance guard," a military term for the shock troops who open the way for an invasion. The term was apparently first used in reference to art and literature in 1845, by Gabriel-Désiré Laverdant, a disciple of the philosopher and social theorist Henri de Saint-Simon. Ezra Pound stated in 1914 that "the artist has at last been aroused to the fact that the war between him and the world is a war without truce." On literary and artistic battlefields, the avant-garde aims to *épater le bourgeois:* to shock the middle classes, jar their conventional taste.

More broadly, avant-garde art aims at innovation, and at a revolutionary reassessment of the techniques and role of art. Often, it departs from organic unity and coherence in the direction of strategic randomness or obscurity; it may involve a confrontation with the nonsensical. The avant-garde work sometimes generates unfulfilled expectations, leaving the reader or viewer frustrated. It may destroy our usual sense of a referential world, as well as the normal processes of identification and sympathy involved in reading. The disclosure of meaning might seem imminent—hinted at, whether in a teasing or an abrasive manner—but might never occur. Avant-gardists imply, often, that the established means of representation are impoverished; they offer new modes of intelligibility (which may deliberately court unintelligibility) and new ways to look, listen, and read.

The critic Peter Bürger argues that the avant-garde sees as its goal the destruction of institutional or officially approved art, and that it operates by warring against the usual basis of artistic institutions: the bourgeois assumption that art is separate from ordinary life. The avant-garde intends for art and life to interfere with or contaminate each other. So, in Surrealism, bizarre dreams infiltrate waking existence, and in Dada, an everyday object like a teacup becomes a small furry monster, a piquant objet d'art. See Richard Chase, "The Fate of the Avant Garde" (1957), in Irving Howe, ed., *The Idea of the Modern* (1967); Renato Poggioli, *The Theory of the Avant Garde* (1962); Peter Bürger, *Theory of the Avant Garde* (1974); and Marjorie Perloff, *The Poetics of Indeterminacy* (1981). Roger Shattuck in *The Banquet Years* (1958) provides a fascinating history of the avant-garde of the early twentieth century; Greil Marcus's *Lipstick Traces* (1989) focuses on the Situationists, a later movement (1957–72). Finally, Paul Mann's *The Theory-Death of the Avant-Garde* (1991) sees the attachment to theory as the factor that destroys avant-garde movements. See DADAISM; FUTURISM; SURREALISM.

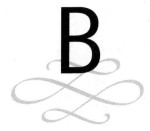

B

ballad A ballad is a popular story told, and usually sung, in verse. Ballads are products of oral tradition, handed down from one singer to another, with later singers adding variations and changes of emphasis. They are often topical, dealing (for example) with a famous local murder case or kidnapping, much in the manner of a tabloid headline. Sometimes the event narrated is of worldwide importance, as in the remarkable ballad about the sinking of the *Titanic,* "When That Great Ship Went Down" (ca. 1915).

The English-language ballad originated in the fourteenth or perhaps the early fifteenth century. Its most popular hero was Robin Hood (in nineteenth-century American ballads he is replaced by a less virtuous gangster, Jesse James). One of the richest sources of ballads was the border country between England and Scotland. Ballads from this region are often full of daring criminals, political rebels, and adventurous lovers.

The ballad stanza (which is frequently, but not always, used in ballads) is a four-line stanza that rhymes the second and the fourth lines, but not the first and third. The first and third lines have four beats, the second and fourth lines, three beats. Here is Dr. Samuel Johnson's parody of the predictable meters and restrained manner of the ballad:

> I put my hat upon my head
>> And walked into the strand,
> And there I met another man
>> Whose hat was in his hand.

Johnson shows us the lows, step by stolid step. But the heights of the ballad form are reached in "Sir Patrick Spens," one of the best traditional Scottish ballads:

> The king sat in Dumferling town
>> Drinking the blood-red wine.

"Oh where will I get good sailor
To sail this ship of mine?"

The ominous, foreshadowing tone, visible in the tint of the "blood-red wine," and the rapid opening move into narrative action are characteristic of the ballad. Ballads practice the art of "leaping and lingering": sudden transitions to climactic moments, along with a resonant dwelling on certain unforgettable scenes. They set in motion the steady and inexorable draw of tale-telling, and often cap this steadiness with the shock of a perfectly aimed narrative gesture or detail.

In the eighteenth century, a "broadside ballad" was a ballad printed on newspaper (broadside) and sold in the streets, a popular form in England until the rise of the daily newspaper in the 1860s. The eighteenth was also the century during which ballads gained new prestige. Thomas Percy's *Reliques of Ancient English Poetry* (1765) proved an important spur to the consideration of the ballad as a literary form. Among the German Romantics, the ballad enjoyed an enormous vogue, stimulated especially by the poet G. A. Bürger. Many of the most distinguished poems of Heinrich Heine and Johann Wolfgang von Goethe are ballads (Goethe's "Erlkönig," Heine's "Die Lorelei"). William Wordsworth and Samuel Taylor Coleridge in their collection *Lyrical Ballads* (1798–1800) adapted the ballad as their chosen literary form, espousing its starkness and plain language as authentic embodiments of ordinary life. Thomas Chatterton and Walter Scott, among the other Romantics, wrote distinguished ballads. Finally, John Keats's "La belle dame sans merci" is one of the most influential Romantic ballads, evoking the femme fatale who enthralls her male victim.

Among the most familiar American ballads are "John Henry," "Frankie and Johnnie," and "Staggerlee." In the twentieth century, W. H. Auden produced striking ballads, as did the African-American poet Sterling Brown. Some notable popular musicians who have drawn on or adapted the ballad are Jean Ritchie, Fairport Convention, and especially Bob Dylan (see Dylan's "Oxford Town," "Boots of Spanish Leather," and his apocalyptic revision of "Lord Randal," "A Hard Rain's A-Gonna Fall"). Johnny Cash's "Folsom Prison Blues" is actually a ballad rather than a blues, and the flourishing genre of gangsta rap depends heavily on ballad influence. See MacEdward Leach, *The Ballad Book* (1955); Gordon Gerould, *The Ballad of Tradition* (1932); David Fowler, *A Literary History of the Popular Ballad* (1968); Josephine Miles,

"In the Terms of Ballads," in *Eras and Modes in English Poetry* (1964); and, for American material, John A. and Alan Lomax, *American Ballads and Folk Songs* (1934). Francis Child's *English and Scottish Popular Ballads* (1882–98) is a standard collection.

ballade Not to be confused with the ballad (see above), the ballade is a French verse form usually consisting of three eight-line stanzas, each ending in a repeated line (or refrain), followed by a four-line stanza (the "envoi," or send-off). The rhyme scheme in this form is *ababbcbC,* with the envoi rhyming *bcbC* (*C* is the refrain). In fifteenth-century France, the ballade was perfected by Charles d'Orléans, Christine de Pisan, and (especially) François Villon. There are medieval English ballades by Geoffrey Chaucer and John Gower, and the form was revived in the nineteenth century by Algernon Charles Swinburne, among others.

bardic A bardic poet is one who, like William Blake, champions a rather archaic, quasi-religious style of poetic power, often associated with a nation or tribe. In the English-speaking countries Shakespeare is known as "the Bard."

William Collins's "Ode on the Poetical Character" (1747) speaks of the youthful poet

> High on some cliff to Heaven up-piled,
> Of rude access, of prospect wild,
> Where, tangled round the jealous steep,
> Strange shades o'erbrow the valleys deep,
> And holy genii guard the rock,
> Its glooms embrown, its springs unlock.

Charles O'Conor in 1753 described the "incendiary Bards" of Ireland as "a Race of Men who were perpetually stirring up the Natives to Rebellion," and preserving at the same time "the antient Genius of the Nation."

In the early 1760s James MacPherson contributed significantly to the image of the bardic. MacPherson produced translations of what he claimed were odes by a third-century Scottish Gaelic poet named Ossian. Ossian proved to be a figment rather than a real historical figure, but McPherson's invented bard had a huge impact. Suddenly, the rude and rustic Scottish Highlands became the site of an aboriginal sublime, a vanished, heroic ancestral past surviving in poetic song (invoked, for example, in Thomas Gray's "The Bard"). On Ossian, see Fiona Stafford, *Sublime Savage* (1988); Katie Trumpener, *Bardic Nationalism* (1997); also Geoffrey Hartman, "Blake and the Progress of Poesy," in *Beyond Formalism* (1970). For a significant reevaluation of the bardic in contemporary poetry, see Nick Halpern, *Everyday and Prophetic* (2003).

baroque As a term applied to artistic style (in visual art, music, and literature), the baroque suggests the sensuous and mystical, the florid and morbid, an extravagant and somewhat ponderous power of invention. (The name perhaps derives from the Spanish *barrueco,* a strangely shaped pearl.) The baroque characteristically spans or incorporates extremes: libertine intensity and fervent religious ecstasy, ravishing beauty and grotesque ugliness. The bizarre extended conceits of Renaissance poets, especially the Spaniard Luis de Góngora and the Italian Giambattista Marino, are considered baroque. In English, the writer most often called baroque is the seventeenth-century poet Richard Crashaw, whose poem on the ecstatic martyrdom of Saint Teresa evokes the famous sculpture by Bernini.

The art historian Heinrich Wölfflin, in *Renaissance and Baroque* (1888) and *Principles of Art History* (1915), was the key figure in the popularization of baroque as a critical term. In painting and sculpture, Wölfflin writes, the elaborate, expansive, brooding features of baroque style stand in contrast to the restrained and harmonious impact of the high Renaissance. (See also MANNERISM.) In twentieth-century criticism, Erwin Panofsky emphasized the summary, orchestrating grasp of baroque style, whereas Walter Benjamin understood (and cherished) the baroque as an outlandish, fragmentary, and extreme phenomenon. See Panofsky, "What Is Baroque?" (1934) in his *Three Essays on Style,* and Benjamin, *The Origin of German Tragic Drama* (1928).

René Wellek in *Concepts of Criticism* (1963) supplies a useful overview of the baroque as a term in literary scholarship. Readers of contemporary Spanish-language literature sometimes use the concept of the neo-baroque, associating it with the passionate and ornate practice of style in Hispanic cultures. See Lois Zamora and Monica Kaup, eds., *Baroque New Worlds* (2007).

bathos Bathos is a stylistic and intellectual low point (as distinct from pathos, an emotional height). Alexander Pope's *Peri Bathous, or the Art of Sinking in Poetry* (1727) describes "the gentle downhill way to the Bathos; the bottom, the end, the central point, the *ne plus ultra,* of true modern poesy!" Pope here parodies Longinus's *Peri Hupsous,* the famous ancient treatise on the sublime or lofty (see SUBLIME).

Martin Price writes that "Swift and Pope use bathos constantly to dramatize the collapse of mind in the very activities in which it takes pride." In their works, passions inevitably coast or plummet downward, from righteous anger to bitter raillery, from love to grasping bawdiness. See Price, *To the Palace of Wisdom* (1964).

beast fable An economically told story with a moral, in which animals dramatize human faults. The genre originated with the ancient Greek writer Aesop, who lived perhaps as early as the sixth century BCE, and some of whose pithy tales are still familiar today. The most famous example of a beast fable in English is Chaucer's Nun's Priest's Tale (ca. 1386), the story of Chanticleer, a rooster prone to grand anxieties.

The beast fable is still the central genre in Hollywood's animated films, with each animal, from Wile E. Coyote to Simba, having certain fixed emblematic qualities, as in the comedy of humors (see COMEDY). See also FABLE.

Beats The Beats, or Beat writers, were a group of Americans, bohemian in appearance and manner, who saw themselves as misfits, wanderers, outlaws, and exiles from respectable society, often on the model of French authors like François Villon and Arthur Rimbaud. The Beats championed spontaneous utterance, along with the pursuit of ecstasy through chemical and other means, including Eastern religious practices. (The word *beat* was meant to evoke beatitude, as well as the situation of one who brags of having been defeated, or "beat," by the mainstream powers that be, and who survives defiantly, separated from both money and conventional pieties.) Among the most memorable works of the movement are Jack Kerouac's picaresque novel *On the Road* (1957) and Allen Ginsberg's poem *Howl* (1955–56), the latter inspired by the prophetic voices of William Blake and Walt Whitman. William Burroughs's *Naked Lunch* (1959), a nightmarish novel of drug addiction, revealed a darkly Gothic, excrucied side of the Beats. The Beats influenced the counterculture of the 1960s substantially: there is a debt to Ginsberg's rough, aphoristic wildness in the style of that key lyricist of the American '60s, Bob Dylan.

beautiful Edmund Burke, in *A Philosophical Inquiry Into the Origin of Our Ideas of the Sublime and Beautiful* (1757), contrasts the sublime and the beautiful. The beautiful, with its smooth, convenient perfections, seduces us to indolence: "The head reclines something on one side; the eyelids are more closed than usual, and the eyes roll gently with an inclination to the object, the mouth is a little opened, and the breath drawn slowly, with now and then a low sigh: the whole body is composed, and the hands fall idly to the sides. All this is accompanied with an inward sense of melting and languor." So Burke, giving a somewhat narcoleptic impression of beauty.

The beautiful, in contrast to the sublime, exhibits harmonious, unbroken shapes, and is soothing rather than shocking in its effects. A beautiful landscape gently urges and invites, offering rolling hills and slight valleys. The sublime, by contrast, confronts and shakes us with rocky crags, lightning storms, and thundering waterfalls.

The opposition between the sublime and the beautiful is important in the work of a later philosopher (one influenced by Burke), Immanuel Kant. In his *Critique of Judgment* (1790), Kant distinguishes the beautiful from the pleasant (toward which we feel an inclination) and the good (toward which we feel esteem or respect). For the beautiful object we feel favor, according to Kant. We regard it as an example of "purposiveness without purpose," since it shows design (i.e., the marks of artistic purpose), yet it is not of instrumental use (it does not accomplish any practical goal in the world, as a tool or instrument does).

The beautiful has a "binding truth for us," as the philosopher Hans-Georg Gadamer, explicating Kant's idea, puts it. It is not the case that beautiful things are just suited to my taste, like the meals I prefer. Rather, I (quietly) demand everyone's agreement that a beautiful object is in fact beautiful, even universally appealing. Yet I know I cannot elicit this agreement merely by producing an adequate reason for my judgment, or by appealing to rules, as I might in a legal or ethical debate. I cannot "prove" beauty by showing that a beautiful object conforms to preconceived standards. What I am asking, instead, is that others cultivate their taste for, or appreciation of, such an object, in its beauty. On Kant, see Paul Guyer, *Kant and the Claims of Taste* (1979); Hans-Georg Gadamer, *The Relevance of the Beautiful* (1977). See also SUB-LIME.

belatedness A key term in Harold Bloom's theory of literary influence (which was in turn influenced by W. Jackson Bate, *The Burden of the Past and the English Poet* [1970]). For Bloom, any significant author must eventually become conscious of his or her belatedness: of coming after earlier, overshadowing presences who pervade the later author's work. These earlier writers are, in Bloom's terminology, the author's "precursors." Wallace Stevens, for example, is belated in respect to his precursors Keats and Whitman. He perceives these earlier authors as larger than and prior to him, and he can be seen reacting to their work in his own poems. The meaning of Stevens's poems is, then, in some sense a function of these earlier ones. "The meaning of a poem can only be another poem," writes Bloom in *The Anxiety of Influence* (1973).

Belatedness involves an ambivalence toward the precursor. When Stevens writes,

> What good is it that the earth is justified,
> That it is complete, that it is an end,
> That in itself it is enough?

he challenges Keats's espousal of a "poetry of earth" in the name of his own precarious doubt. Yet Stevens also knows that he himself yearns after, and cannot have, Keats's more harmonious attitude, his reliance on the common pleasures of the earth. Precisely because Stevens comes after Keats, his vision remains diminished in comparison with his precursor's: more severe and intense, less assured that "in itself it is enough." But the narrow, stringent stance of the belated writer can also be a source of strength, because the later one arrives, the more one has seen and the more one knows. See also ANXIETY OF INFLUENCE.

belletristic From the French term *belles lettres,* "fine literature." A piece of prose writing that is belletristic in style is characterized by a casual, yet polished and pointed, essayistic elegance. The belletristic is sometimes contrasted with the scholarly or academic; it is supposed to be free of the laborious, inert, jargon-ridden habits indulged by professors.

Reflection on literature has most often been belletristic: practiced by authors themselves and (later) by journalists, outside academic institutions. Literary study, beginning with research on the classics, became a systematic academic discipline only in the eighteenth and nineteenth centuries. See GEISTESWISSENSCHAFT; PHILOLOGY.

beloved, the The beloved is, often, the object of a lyric poet's effusions. In classical Roman poetry, Catullus's Lesbia and Propertius's Cynthia (both first century BCE) might be based on sheer invention, biographical reality, or something in between. Dante's beloved was Beatrice, immortalized in his

Vita Nuova (ca. 1292–93) and then in his epic *Divine Comedy* (ca. 1308–21); Petrarch's goes by the name Laura, the elusive star of his *Rime Sparse* (Scattered Rhymes, 1374). Shakespeare's sonnets are occupied, or possessed, by two enigmatic beloveds, an aristocratic "young man" and a "dark lady."

The beloved usually represents a sustained fictive source of poetic inspiration, a muse figure, rather than a day-to-day reality. Dante and Petrarch had only a glancing acquaintance, if that, with their ladies.

Bildungsroman *Bildung,* often translated as "education," means in German the development of the self through knowledge. (*Roman* is the German word for novel.) As a form of study united with personal experience, Bildung enhances, and even makes, an individual. (Emerson remarks in "The American Scholar" [1837] that "the main enterprise of the world for splendor, for extent, is the upbuilding of a man. Here are the materials strown along the ground.")

The Bildungsroman, then, is the novel of Bildung, usually devoted to the story of a young person learning his or her way. A classic example is *Wilhelm Meister's Apprenticeship* (1795–96), by Johann Wolfgang von Goethe. Other notable instances are George Eliot's *Middlemarch* (1872), D. H. Lawrence's *Sons and Lovers* (1913), James Joyce's *Portrait of the Artist as a Young Man* (1916), Saul Bellow's *The Adventures of Augie March* (1953), and, in African-American literature, James Weldon Johnson's *Autobiography of an Ex-Colored Man* (1912), Zora Neale Hurston's *Their Eyes Were Watching God* (1937), Ralph Ellison's *Invisible Man* (1952), and Toni Morrison's *Sula* (1973).

Franco Moretti's *The Way of the World* (1987) presents a study of the Bildungsroman, as does Martin Swales, *The German Bildungsroman from Wieland to Hesse* (1978). On the "female Bildungsroman," see Elizabeth Abel, Marianne Hirsch, and Elizabeth Langland, eds., *The Voyage In* (1983), and Susan Fraiman, *Unbecoming Women* (1993). For a related genre, see KUNST-LERROMAN.

biography Literary biography begins with Plato's account of Socrates (fourth century BCE), with the Greek historians Herodotus and Thucydides (both fifth century BCE), and with the *Parallel Lives of the Greeks and Romans* by Plutarch (ca. 50–120 CE), which depicts the lives of its protagonists as exemplary instances of different virtues and vices.

In English, the great early examples of literary biography are Samuel Johnson's *Lives of the English Poets* (1779–81) and James Boswell's *Life of Johnson* (1791). Johnson and Boswell were preceded by John Aubrey, with his tart, satisfying, and sometimes fanciful *Brief Lives* (published after Aubrey's death in 1697).

Spiritual autobiography, beginning with the *Confessions* of Saint Augustine (354–430 CE), centers on a crucial turning point in the author's life, a crisis and recovery into faith. Spiritual autobiography shares with secular autobiographies like Jean-Jacques Rousseau's *Confessions* [1782–89], and with the memoir, a plotline animated by crisis, profound recognition, and change of life. From Rousseau to Goethe to Henry Adams, many authors have produced remarkable autobiographies. At the beginning of the twenty-first century, autobiography (and its subcategory, the memoir) has become a major genre of American writing.

Guy Davenport writes of our fascination with authors' lives, of such anecdotal (and partly imaginary) glimpses as "Wordsworth pushing a wheelbarrow containing Coleridge with blistered heels; the grave infant Milton watching lean Will Shakespeare and fat Ben Jonson staggering home from the Mermaid; . . . Joyce and Proust in a taxi, the one lowering the windows because of his claustrophobia, the other raising them because of his asthma, up and down, down and up, all the way to Maxim's . . ."

It is arguable that biography has, in our era, become the main form of history: that for us, in Emerson's words, "there is no history, only biography." Adam Phillips in *Darwin's Worms* (2000) writes interestingly on Freud's resistance to biography. See also Guy Davenport, "Seeing Shelley Plain," in *Geography of the Imagination* (1981).

Black Arts Movement A group of African-American intellectuals, writers, and artists began the Black Arts Movement around 1965. Many of them were cultural nationalists who aimed to define a distinctive black aesthetics, ethics, and way of life. Among the major figures of the movement were Amiri Baraka (Leroi Jones), Ed Bullins, Nikki Giovanni, Adrienne Kennedy, Larry Neal, and Sonia Sanchez. See Harold Cruse, *The Crisis of the Negro Intellectual* (1967).

Black Mountain An experimental and progressive college founded in 1933 near Asheville, North Carolina, in the Blue Ridge Mountains. The early era of Black Mountain, 1933–49, was dominated by the abstract painter Josef

Albers. (Among other residents at the college were artists and thinkers like John Cage, Merce Cunningham, and Buckminster Fuller.) After Albers's departure, Charles Olson became the presiding spirit of the college. Olson was a poet and follower of Ezra Pound who trusted in "free" poetic forms that were supposed to mimic, or carry forward, the human voice. The poem was thought of as a series of spontaneous, expansive movements on an "open field," akin to a painter's canvas. "No persona and no personality—VOICE," was Olson's credo: the statement reveals his adaptation of the modernist idea of impersonality (see IMPERSONALITY). Robert Duncan, who generated expansive and highly imaginative texts echoing Pound, William Carlos Williams, and Walt Whitman, was another important poet associated with Black Mountain. As the critic Willard Spiegelman points out, the Black Mountain idea of the poem as an "open field" was influential on several later poets, including Charles Wright and Jorie Graham.

blank verse Introduced into English by the Earl of Surrey in his translation of Virgil's *Aeneid* (ca. 1540), blank verse is unrhymed iambic pentameter, the most common meter in English poetry. (See METER.) "Good day and happiness, dear Rosalind," says Orlando to his beloved in Shakespeare's *As You Like It*. The melancholy satirist Jacques, standing by, comments on Orlando's statement, "Nay then, God b' wi' you, an you talk in blank verse," because Orlando, in a prose passage, has lapsed into iambs: "Good dáy | and hápplinéss, | dear Róslalínd."

John Milton, in a prefatory note to his great epic *Paradise Lost* (1667), championed blank verse as the vehicle of "ancient liberty recovered to heroic poem from the troublesome and modern bondage of rhyming." See Anthony Hecht, "Blank Verse," in Annie Finch and Kathrine Varnes, eds., *An Exaltation of Forms* (2002). See also RHYME.

blazon (or blason) In love poetry, a blazon is a compact and systematic visual description of the beloved in terms of her (or occasionally his) physical features. It is especially prominent in the Petrarchan tradition, beginning with Petrarch's *Rime Sparse* (Scattered Rhymes, 1374). Frequently the blazon is expressed in predictable terms: eyes like stars, cheeks like damask roses (intermingling red and white), and teeth like pearls. Edmund Spenser in his *Epithalamion* (1595) describes his bride as having eyes like sapphires, cheeks like apples,

Her lips like cherries charming men to bite,
Her breast like to a bowl of cream uncrudded,
Her paps like lilies budded,
Her snowy neck like to a marble tower,
And all her body like a palace fair.

The blazon with its methodical style of praise often became the target of humor. The Countess Olivia in Shakespeare's *Twelfth Night* parodies a blazon when she mockingly says to Viola/Cesario, "I will give out diverse schedules of my beauty. It shall be inventoried and every particle and utensil labeled to my will: as, item, two lips indifferent red; item, two grey eyes, with lids to them; item, one neck, one chin, and so forth."

Bloomsbury A group of writers and intellectuals central to British modernism. Many of them attended Cambridge and later lived in the Bloomsbury section of London during the 1910s and 1920s. Among the chief Bloomsburyites were Virginia Woolf; her husband, the publisher Leonard Woolf; Lytton Strachey, the biographer; James and Alix Strachey, who translated Freud; the economist John Maynard Keynes; the art critic Clive Bell; and the philosophers G. E. Moore and Bertrand Russell. Virginia Woolf's *Moments of Being* (publ. 1976) is a lively and moving account of Bloomsbury, as is the biography of Woolf by her nephew Quentin Bell, *Virginia Woolf: A Life* (rev. ed., 1972).

blues The blues is a form of African-American literary expression, an oral tradition set to music. It usually consists of twelve bars: three four-bar phrases in 4/4 time.

The musical roots of the blues are African; its words are informed by the language of the King James Bible, particularly the Book of Psalms and the Song of Songs. The blues expresses a wry, commonplace resilience, a cool salute to bad fate, and a grim vigorous energy that make it unique among literary, and musical, forms. Its characteristic personae are the rambler, the bitter, disappointed lover, and the haunted fugitive. The continuing presence of the blues as sung poetry reminds us that poems were originally classified as songs, in both ancient Greece and ancient Israel. Among the most distinguished performers of the blues are Robert Johnson, Bessie Smith, Bukka White, Johnny Shines, Billie Holiday, Bobby "Blue" Bland, and Muddy Waters.

One common type of blues stanza consists of a refrain—a line repeated once, often with slight variation—followed by a line that "solves" or completes the refrain (in triple rhyme):

When I'm dead, bury me by the highway side.
When I'm dead and gone, people, bury me by the highway side:
So my mean old spirit, can catch a Greyhound bus, and ride.

Such a blues stanza can also be thought of as a kind of expanded couplet whose first line is roughly sketched, or tried out, twice.

Important reflections on the blues as a central form of African-American, and therefore American, culture are contained in Ralph Ellison, *Shadow and Act* (1964), Albert Murray, *Stomping the Blues* (1976), Gunther Schuller, *Early Jazz* (1968), and Greil Marcus, *Mystery Train* (1975). The Harlem Renaissance poet Langston Hughes drew on the blues in *The Weary Blues* (1926) and other volumes. See CHORUS; REFRAIN.

Blue Stockings A society of learned women and their male friends founded by Lady Mary Wortley Montague around 1750, and emulating earlier societies in Italy and France. The Blue Stockings prided themselves on their intellectual accomplishments and dedication to serious conversation, and on their neglect of the more usual "feminine accomplishments" prized by the society of the time (charming manners, musical recitals, dancing).

body theory A form of literary and social theory, prominent in the 1990s and after, that emphasized the palpable presence of the human body: the immediacy of its physical responses, its passions and sufferings. Three main inspirations were Elaine Scarry's *The Body in Pain* (1985), Caroline Walker Bynum's *Holy Feast and Holy Fast* (1987), and Judith Butler's *Bodies That Matter* (1993). See also Peter Brooks, *Body Work* (1993).

bombast Originally meant a cotton wool used for stuffing one's clothing (also known as fustian), but came to refer to the grandiose padding out of speech with heroic, bragging terms, "high swelling and heaven-disembowelling words" (in Michel de Montaigne's phrase, as translated by John Florio, 1603). In poetry and the theater, bombast is an excessively robust, scenery-chewing style of heroic declamation, used to ridiculous effect. Shakespeare's swaggerer Pistol in *Henry IV, Part 2* provides some heated examples of the style. (A later exponent of the bombastic, Yosemite Sam, appears in Chuck Jones's cartoons for Warner Brothers.)

The real name of the sixteenth-century alchemist Paracelsus was—reputedly, at least—Theophrastus Bombast von Hohenheim.

Bovarysme From the title character of Gustave Flaubert's novel *Madame Bovary* (1856), who enters upon a love affair as a result of reading novels about romantic love: these books, in their charm and excited beauty, seem more real to her than her too common, dull life. Bovarysme is similar to Quixotism in that both involve the transferring of literary responses and expectations into the arena of actual life. (Cervantes' Don Quixote, as a result of reading chivalric romances, becomes a knight, but he must ignore important aspects of the anti-chivalric reality that surrounds him in order to live out his literary dreams.)

bowdlerize Samuel Bowdler in 1815 produced *The Family Shakespeare,* an edition that expurgated from Shakespeare's works any episode or phrase Bowdler considered offensive to decency. "Those words and expressions," as he put it, "are omitted which cannot with propriety be read aloud in a family." Since then, *bowdlerize* has become a term for the mutilation of literary texts to make them conform to family values, by removing instances of undue violence, blasphemy, profanity, and grossly detailed sexuality. See Noel Perrin, *Dr. Bowdler's Legacy* (1969).

bricolage In French, a *bricoleur* is a handyman; *bricolage* is his art, which requires making inventive use of what comes to hand in the way of tools and materials. The great anthropologist Claude Lévi-Strauss sketched the definition of bricolage as a "science of the concrete" in *The Savage Mind* (1966). In *Tristes Tropiques* (1955), an inventive autobiography combined with a study of an Indian tribe in Brazil, Lévi-Strauss relies on the concept of bricolage to describe both the European investigator's method and the native culture he studies. Bricolage is also a characteristic method of much contemporary art, from Robert Rauschenberg and Joseph Beuys to Red Grooms.

Elizabeth Bishop in her poem "Crusoe in England" offers a memorable tribute to the bricoleur. Celebrating his homemade flute ("I think it had the weirdest scale on earth"), Bishop's Crusoe exults, "Home-made, home-made! But aren't we all?"

bucolics Virgil's pastoral *Eclogues* (39–38 BCE) were originally known as *Bucolica,* from the Greek *boukolos* (cowherd) and *boukolika poiemata* (pastoral poems). *Bucolics,* then, is another word for pastoral verse, though the protagonists of pastoral are usually shepherds or goatherds, rather than cowherds. Virgil's precursor in pastoral poetry, Theocritus, had used the Greek word *boukolika* in his *Idylls* (early third century BCE). See also ARCADIA; ECLOGUE; PASTORAL.

burden A burden can mean a refrain or chorus, or a theme or matter (the burden of my song = what my song is about). "Foot it featly here and there, / And, sweet sprites, the burden bear," sings Ariel in Shakespeare's *The Tempest.* Isaiah 13:1 refers to "the burden against Babylon": the Hebrew word *massa* is translated as "burden," meaning a weighty thing; a message or oracle; a lifting up of the voice in complaint.

burlesque A deliberate mismatching of style and subject matter, as in a mock epic like Alexander Pope's *Rape of the Lock* (1712–14) or his *Dunciad* (1728–42). Often, the burlesque keeps the form (in Pope's case, the elevated diction of the epic) and spoofs the content of a familiar genre. In other words, the burlesque exploits the incongruity of a low subject, like the card game in *The Rape of the Lock,* treated in a high style. In contrast to burlesque, a travesty is a high subject treated in a low style. The Mel Brooks movie *History of the World, Part II* is a distinguished recent example of travesty. See also SATIRE.

The burlesque need not be merely negative or derisive. Geoffrey Chaucer's Miller's Tale (ca. 1386) offers a burlesque of courtly love and, in the process, advocates a crude country gusto over the thin, conniving pretensions to elegance that (in Chaucer's version) characterize courtliness.

Samuel Butler in *Hudibras* (1663–78) produced a successful and influential burlesque. Here Butler describes the enormous achievements of a knight who, like the legendary folk hero Guy of Warwick, battles cows:

Right many a widow his keen blade,
And many fatherless had made.
He many a boar and huge dun cow
Did, like another Guy, o'erthrow.

caesura From a Latin word meaning "cut," a caesura is the pause or break within a line of poetry. It occurs at the end of a unit of sense, and is often indicated by a comma or period. The caesura is marked in scansion by a double vertical line (‖). Most lines of verse have at least one caesura. In Old English poetry and in the most common line of French poetry, the Alexandrine, the caesura occurs with great regularity near the middle of each line, dividing it in two. (See ALEXANDRINE.)

The placement of caesuras is essential to the rhythm of verse. In Milton's "Lycidas," the strong caesuras suggest the action of the sea as it subjects the body of Lycidas to its motions—as well as the state of the poet as he yields to the motions of his thought:

Ay me! ‖ Whilst thee the shores and sounding seas
Wash far away, ‖ where'er thy bones are hurled . . .

In John Donne's Elegy 16, the poet makes radical use of caesuras (far more frequent here than is usual in verse) to convey a desperate colloquial energy:

Oh, ‖ oh,
Nurse, ‖ O my love is slain, ‖ I saw him go
O'er the white Alps alone; ‖ I saw him, ‖ I,
Assailed, ‖ fight, ‖ taken, ‖ stabbed, ‖ fall, ‖ and die.

canon, canonical Canon comes from the Greek word *kanon,* a measuring rod used to ensure straightness. Canonical works take the measure of the reader by means of their authority: their capacity to rebuke, baffle, and thwart us, as well as surprise us with unexpected, astonishing power. Even at its most frustrating, the canonical work draws us on; in our fascination, we remain loyal to it.

"The canon" describes a body of texts that form a whole, respond to one another, and appear definitive to the culture that values them. The canon of American literature, for example, consists of the books that everyone knows, or knows about, by Emerson, Dickinson, Whitman, Hawthorne, Melville, Thoreau, Henry James, and a few others. (The priorities in such a canon can shift: some see American literature as essentially Emersonian; but one might, like Richard Brodhead in *The School of Hawthorne* [1986], recast it so that it centers on Hawthorne.)

This meaning of canon as an integrated set of writings derives from the example of religious scripture, the canon of the Old and New Testaments. The Hebrew Bible, still the original model of the canonical, contains a series of accepted texts that support and consolidate one another. The Torah (or "teaching") consists of the five books of Moses, whose authorship is traditionally ascribed to Moses himself: Genesis, Exodus, Leviticus, Numbers, and Deuteronomy. Along with the Torah, the Hebrew Bible contains the Neviim, or prophets, and the Ketuvim, or additional writings. In the first century CE the Council of Jamnia is said to have decided on the list of canonical Hebrew scriptures (though some dispute remained concerning the Song of Songs). The Jewish prophet Ezra had, according to legend, set aside seventy additional books for the wise; these were known as the "apocrypha" (literally, things hidden away). (None of Ezra's texts are extant, but a number of noncanonical Christian apocryphal works survive.)

When Christians and Muslims proclaimed their own religions, they had to deal with the canonical status of the Hebrew Bible, arguing that it presaged or provided background for their own later revelations, and their own canonical texts (the Gospels and the Quran). Christianity even included the text of the Hebrew Bible, translated into Greek, in its canon: this Greek translation is known as the Septuagint. The Christian canon was closed by Athanasius in 307 CE, producing the text of the Bible as we know it today.

In Jewish and Christian tradition, great importance has always been placed on the accurate scribal copying of the canonical books. The last few chapters of the Bible, at the end of the Book of Revelation, enforce the exactness of the canonical version in no uncertain terms, by threatening with damnation and plague anyone who would add to or subtract from this holy text.

The difference between the canonical and the noncanonical resembles, at times, the distinction between publicly available (or exoteric) teaching and hidden (esoteric) wisdom. Plato wrote a number of accepted, or canonical, dialogues, but there were also ascribed to him texts intended for adepts only, and it was rumored that the sage's real teachings were contained only in these secret writings. Here, the noncanonical constitutes the true source of knowledge.

Canonical eventually came to be a word applied to the institutionally favored or approved text, taught in schools and proclaimed as essential reading. In this sense, Shakespeare, Wordsworth, and Jane Austen are canonical; John Cowper Powys and Dorothy Richardson are not. Yet the canon changes over time, sometimes dramatically. John Donne, considered a crude and eccentric writer by most later poets and critics, was not a significant part of the poetic canon until the twentieth century; and in the mid-twentieth century T. S. Eliot attempted, with some temporary success, to eliminate Shelley from the canon. Some women and minority writers who were previously ignored, like Zora Neale Hurston, are now firmly canonical.

One way of understanding the canonical is to estimate the extent to which a work answers and revises, or measures, the already existing canon. Ralph Ellison's *Invisible Man* (1952), for example, has become canonical partly because it is constantly aware of, and places itself in challenging conversation with, the most powerful and familiar texts of American literature: among them the works of Emerson, Melville, and Poe. As a novel deeply concerned with African-American experience, *Invisible Man* also interacts with a different canon, the musical and rhetorical traditions of jazz, blues, black spirituals, and sermons. It is therefore answerable to not one but two canonical traditions, both of them crucial for contemporary American society. See Frank Kermode, "The Canon," in Robert Alter and Frank Kermode, eds., *The Literary Guide to the Bible* (1987), and Robert von Hallberg, ed., *Canons* (1984).

canzone An elaborate, wandering kind of lyric poem, often irregular in rhyme scheme. The form is associated with Provençal and Italian poets of the thirteenth and fourteenth centuries—and most of all with two great fourteenth-century Italian authors, Petrarch and Dante, who transmitted to other literatures the Italian manner of interweaving free rhyme patterns among lines of varying length. Dante discusses rules for the composition of canzoni in *De Vulgari Eloquentia* (Of Popular Eloquence, ca. 1304). The most famous canzone in English verse is Milton's elegy "Lycidas" (1637).

carnivalesque An uproarious and licentious atmosphere, as of a festival in which the crowd loudly mocks various pieties, trumpeting an enthusiastic, disorderly solidarity. Mikhail Bakhtin's *Rabelais and His World* (1965) helped introduce the term to literary and cultural study, contributing as well an emphasis on the disruptive, grotesque body as a factor in celebration. See also DIALOGIC; FESTIVE.

Caroline Age The reign of Charles I, who ruled in England from 1625 until 1649 (when he was executed, at the end of a Civil War fought between supporters of the king and the group in Parliament opposed to him). Among the major writers of this tumultuous period are John Milton, George Herbert, and Thomas Browne. A number of poets wrote lyrics of seduction and sensual indulgence during the Caroline era (see CAVALIER POETS). John Rumrich and Gregory Chaplin, eds., *Seventeenth-Century British Poetry* (2006), presents an anthology of the era's poetry along with an excellent selection of criticism; Jonathan Post, *English Lyric Poetry: The Early Seventeenth Century* (1999), is a helpful survey.

carpe diem Usually translated "seize the day"; the phrase appears in the Roman poet Horace's advice in one of his Odes (1.11; 23 BCE). *Carpe diem* actually means "pluck the day," as one might pluck a flower, rather than "seize" it: the Latin verb *carpere* evokes a delicate, transitory action.

After Horace, carpe diem becomes a major topos of lyric poetry. The carpe diem lyric is usually a poem of seduction. Frequently, the poem's speaker urges sexual enjoyment on an attractive virgin by underscoring the brevity of earthly life, and thus the desirability of present pleasures. The call to sensual indulgence is, therefore, shadowed by the knowledge of old age and death. Some of the most familiar carpe diem poems were written in the seventeenth century, by poets like Robert Herrick (who is responsible for the renowned line "Gather ye rosebuds, while ye may") and Andrew Marvell.

Marvell's "To His Coy Mistress" is a slyly impressive carpe diem poem. In it, the speaker reminds his resistant target that her virtue will be violated in the grave. So, he tells her, why not surrender now, instead of waiting for death's seduction? You will not (he continues) feel it when

> worms shall try
> That long-preserved virginity,
> And your quaint honour turn to dust,
> And into ashes all my lust:

The grave's a fine and private place,
But none, I think, do there embrace.

In the late nineteenth century, Walter Pater adapted the carpe diem theme to
aesthetic theory, writing in his conclusion to *The Renaissance* (1873), "Not to
discriminate every moment some passionate attitude in those about us, and
in the very brilliancy of their gifts some tragic dividing of forces on their
ways, is, on this short day of frost and sun, to sleep before evening." In Pater's
brilliant sentence, as in the expression *carpe diem,* life becomes a "day": and to
pluck or grasp is now to pick out, to "discriminate." Pater's idea that a knowing and diligent project shapes enjoyment, turning it to passionate recognition, was always a part of carpe diem, from Horace on.

catabasis. See KATABASIS

catalogue "Bare lists of words are found suggestive to an imaginative and excited mind," Ralph Waldo Emerson wrote in "The Poet" (1844). A catalogue
is simply a list. From Homer's epics to Cole Porter's "You're the Top," and beyond, literature and song delight in listing: a device that enjoys the separate-
ness of each item and yet suggests that an influential effect of arrangement
may come out of such a collection, however spontaneous or higgledy-pig-
gledy its shape. In Homeric epic, the lists of warriors and ships are known as
epic catalogues. The catalogue of ships in Bk. 2 of the *Iliad* is a major set
piece, serving a historical and mnemonic function for Homer's original audience. It is imitated in *Paradise Lost* (1667) by John Milton, who produces a
catalogue of devils at the end of Bk. 1.

The catalogue of trees is a feature of pastoral poetry, appearing also in epics
like Ovid's *Metamorphoses* (10.90ff.). Edmund Spenser in Bk. 1 of *The Faerie
Queene* (1590) gives a memorable example: the list of trees that cluster in his
wood of Errour includes "the Laurell, meed of mightie Conquerors / And
Poets sage," and ends with "the fruitfull Olive, and the Platane round, / The
Carver Holme, the Maple seeldom inward sound" (1.1.9). As the series of
trees fits into the intricate pattern of Spenser's rhyme, we are made to notice
the sinister implications of a declining harmony that moves from conquerors and "poets sage" to the secretly rotten maple. The catalogue surrounds
Spenser's precarious hero, Red Crosse, who is already lost in the wood.

Walt Whitman's *Leaves of Grass* (1855–92) and James Joyce's *Ulysses* (1922) offer delightful treasure troves of catalogues. Whitman's ecstatic and complex lists provide one of his chief means of savoring, and exulting in, American life. See Robert Belknap's consideration of catalogues in literature, *The List* (2004); also David Lodge's selection of novelistic lists in *The Art of Fiction* (1992).

catharsis Aristotle in the *Poetics* (ca. 330 BCE) states that tragedy "effects through pity and fear the proper catharsis of these emotions" (Ch. 6). The question for readers of the *Poetics* concerns the meaning of the word *catharsis* (in Greek, spelled *katharsis*). Catharsis might mean purging (as it does in a related passage of Aristotle's *Politics,* in which music is said to get rid of, *katharein,* disruptive emotions). But catharsis also means a purification; and, in addition, a demonstration or display. Does tragedy relieve us of emotions, or does it exhibit them? Does it educate the emotions by training them to endure extreme tragic situations? Since the Renaissance, when the *Poetics* was rediscovered, these are some of the questions that critics have raised in their efforts to explain Aristotle's use of catharsis. Beyond the issue of tragedy, catharsis involves the use of traumatic experience in any genre: see CONFESSIONAL POETRY. See Jonathan Lear, "Catharsis," in *Open Minded* (1998); Gerald Else, *Aristotle's Poetics* (1957); Martha Nussbaum, *The Fragility of Goodness* (1986). See also ARISTOTELIAN CRITICISM; TRAGEDY.

Cavalier poets The Cavalier poets of mid-seventeenth-century England were devoted to erotic themes (the carpe diem, for example) and the poetry of friendship. Most of them took the side of King Charles I (executed by order of Parliament in 1649) and opposed the party of Oliver Cromwell. (Cromwell's followers were known as Roundheads for their short haircuts, in contrast to the flowing tresses of the Cavaliers.) Richard Lovelace, Sir John Suckling, and Robert Herrick were among the chief Cavalier poets. See Gerald Hammond, *Fleeting Things* (1990), Gordon Braden, *The Classics and English Renaissance Poetry* (1978), Earl Miner, *The Cavalier Mode from Jonson to Cotton* (1971).

Celtic revival The movement of Irish writers and artists in the late nineteenth and early twentieth centuries, also known as the Irish literary renaissance. The Celtic revival may be dated from William Butler Yeats's *The Wanderings of Oisin* (1889), based on Irish mythology, and from his book of Irish stories, *The Celtic Twilight* (1893). The playwright Lady Augusta Gregory, a friend and patron of Yeats, was an important force in the revival, as were the poet AE (George Russell) and the playwright J. M. Synge. Yeats and Lady Gregory founded the Irish National Theater (the Abbey Theater) in 1903.

The Celtic revival authors wrote mostly in English rather than Irish, and their interest in Irish folklore was tempered by an emphasis on current society. Early inspirations for the Celtic revival were Ernest Renan's *The Poetry of the Celtic Races* (1854), Matthew Arnold's *On the Study of Celtic Literature* (1867), and the poems of Samuel Ferguson based on Irish legends, written in the 1860s and 1870s.

cento A Latin word meaning "patchwork"; it describes a collection of statements or sentences from a particular author, often used for parodic purposes. In ancient Greece and Rome, the *cento* was usually an amalgam of phrases from Homer or Virgil (or other authors, often used in combination). In late antiquity, authors sometimes relied on a cento from Virgil to convey Christian doctrine. In Italian the word means "a hundred": centos are sometimes exactly one hundred lines long.

chapter The standard sectional division of a prose work, analogous to the act in drama. The Hebrew Bible and the Gospels are divided by chapter and verse (as, for example, John 3:13 = the book of John, chapter 3, verse 13). (The chapter divisions of the Latin Bible translated by Saint Jerome, known as the Vulgate, were added sometime between the eleventh and the thirteenth centuries.)

We sometimes speak of chapters of our lives, which may be already closed, or still open. The end of a chapter imparts something between a pause and a finality; the next chapter often begins with a look back at the preceding one, and a summing up of its significance. Philip Stevick points to three sources of the chapter in modern prose: the book divisions of Homer's epics; the chapter divisions of the Bible; and the distinctions made in rhetoric between parts of a speech (exordium, narration, proof, and peroration). He discusses chapters with a "cadence" ending: instances where the impressions of a character at the conclusion of a chapter "become a metaphor for the relation between man and world, a cosmic cadence." See Philip Stevick, *The Chapter in Fiction* (1970).

character *Kharakter* is the Greek word for a mark or stamp: and, by extension, a distinctive feature. The character is also a genre, beginning with the

Greek author Theophrastus (ca. 372–287 BCE) and continuing into the Renaissance. Not until the mid-eighteenth century did *character* come to mean an individual, named personality, in literature or in life.

A character presents a brief sketch of a familiar social type: "A Plain Country Fellow," "A Contemplative Man," "A Drunkard." In this way, character becomes associated with type: the person depicted in a character is really just a predictable bundle of distinguishing traits. But our true character, as distinct from the literary genre of character, remains different from type, more elusive and more complete. William Collins's "Ode on the Poetical Character" (1747) and William Wordsworth's "Character of the Happy Warrior" (1807) are two later texts that diverge from the genre of the character, though they invoke this genre in their titles.

Henry James writes that "a character is interesting as it comes out, and by the process and duration of that emergence; just as a procession is effective by the way it unrolls." For James, character is plot, in contrast to the German poet Novalis, whose motto was "character is fate." Novalis's maxim suggests that the whole story of a person unfurls from the fact of that person's character. In James's argument, the unfurling itself is what makes the character interesting—even what makes it. (Aristotle's *Poetics* [ca. 330 BCE] subordinates character to plot, giving a rather blank definition of character as "that which reveals moral purposes, showing what kind of things a man chooses or avoids"—as if character could be reduced to a mere moment of a plot, the event or act of choosing.)

So character is the sign, or declaration, of a person. For Emerson, character is like an acrostic: "Read it forward, backward or across, it still spells the same thing." We are legible, exposed: showing ourselves in the smallest gesture, and even more visible when we think to disguise our character.

E. M. Forster in *Aspects of the Novel* (1927) distinguishes between flat and round characters in fiction. The flat character—one without mystery, simple, palpable, and self-contained—reassures us of our efficient grasp of reality. Obligingly fitting our understanding, flat characters dwindle into the emblematic, the typical. The round character (in Shakespeare, James, or Proust, for example) satisfies a different urge, our wish to experience as large a fictional being as there can be. As we turn pages, we pursue, inexhaustibly, a person who fascinates us, and who has not nearly finished giving away meanings. See John Hollander, "The Poetics of Character," in *Melodious Guile* (1988).

chiasmus A "crossing," or inversion, of the order of words or sounds. On the last page of "The Dead" (1914), James Joyce writes of Gabriel Conroy, "His soul swooned slowly as he heard the snow falling faintly and faintly falling, like the descent of their last end, upon all the living and the dead." "Falling faintly and faintly falling" is a gently rocking chiasmus. And from John Milton's *Paradise Lost* (1667) there is this description of Chaos: "Where all life dies, death lives."

Chiasmus can also be based on vowel sounds, as in Samuel Taylor Coleridge's line "In Xanadu did Kubla Khan . . ." (*adu/ubla*), and in the sentence above from Joyce, "swooned" and "snow" (*woo/ow*), as well as "soul" and "slow[ly]" (*oul/low*), two subtler instances of inversion. For this sort of chiasmus, see Kenneth Burke, "On Musicality in Verse," in *The Philosophy of Literary Form* (1941, rev. ed. 1957).

Chicago school A group of critics associated with the University of Chicago in the 1940s and 1950s, including R. S. Crane, Elder Olson, Richard McKeon, and others. The Chicago critics are often described as Aristotelians, though they were also influenced by the Italian philosopher Benedetto Croce (1866–1952). They resembled the New Critics in their insistence that (in Aristotle's terms) poetry is not instrumental, but final; not a means to an end, but an end in itself. (Other critics of the era like William Empson and Kenneth Burke stood at the opposite end of the spectrum, construing literary works as instrumental: as arguments for a particular view of life.)

Unlike the New Critics, the Chicago school refused to privilege lyric poetry, instead focusing on a variety of genres in order to define each one properly, in its own terms. The truest inheritor of the Chicago school's methods and attitudes is Wayne Booth; see Booth, *The Rhetoric of Fiction* (1961). R. S. Crane edited the standard collection of essays by the Chicago school, *Critics and Criticism* (1952). For a critique, see W. K. Wimsatt, "The Chicago Critics," in *The Verbal Icon* (1954).

chivalric romance A literary genre involving, characteristically, a medieval apparatus of questing knights, ladies in distress, dragons, wizards, magic spells, and tournaments. Courtly manners and the dedicated pursuit of a lady's love are major themes of chivalric romance; these features, along with its numerous forms of enchantment, distinguish chivalric romance from epic.

The genre developed first in twelfth-century France, where the most brilliant and influential French writers of chivalric romance were Marie de France and Chrétien de Troyes. Two of the main arenas for chivalric romance are the "matter of France" (stories involving Charlemagne and his knights) and the "matter of Britain" (King Arthur and his Round Table). Ludovico Ariosto, in *Orlando Furioso* (1516), combines the two. Today, of course, the prime field for chivalric romance has moved to interstellar space, with light sabers replacing lances, and an empath, rather than Merlin, playing the insightful sage or magician that the form often requires.

The two most famous chivalric romances in English are Thomas Malory's *Morte d'Arthur* (fifteenth century) and Edmund Spenser's wondrous *Faerie Queene* (1590–96). *Don Quixote* (1605–15), by Miguel de Cervantes, depends on, cherishes, and subverts the conventions of the genre.

Chivalric romance is readily parodied. Walter Scott did so with love in *Ivanhoe* (1820). Stephen Leacock, in "Guido the Gimlet of Ghent: A Romance of Chivalry," is more brutal. (Having seen the name of the willowy, goddesslike Isolde painted on a fence, Guido falls into a swoon and starts out at once for Jerusalem, swearing to kill a large Saracen for her love. See *Laugh with Leacock* [1959].) See also QUEST ROMANCE.

chorus In ancient Greece, the chorus was originally a group of fifty men who sang poems devoted to the god Dionysus: a form known as the dithyramb. A number of Greek choral poems by Bacchylides and Pindar (written 500–450 BCE), honoring gods and Olympic victors, derive from this early genre. The chorus was later reduced to a quarter of its original size and became an integral part of ancient Greek tragedy, interacting with the protagonists in the plays of Aeschylus, Sophocles, and Euripides. In later drama, the chorus can be a single actor, as in Shakespeare's *Henry V* or *The Winter's Tale* (where Time is the chorus).

The ancient Greek chorus produced a sublimely compact and intricate reflection on the tragic action. Every performance by the chorus is divided into phases alluding to the chorus's onstage movements: strophe, antistrophe, and epode (Turn, Counterturn, and Stand, as Ben Jonson translated them in his Cary-Morison Ode [1640]).

The choral odes in Greek tragedy are frequently astonishing, powerful in their riddle-like compression of syntax and abrupt imagistic leaps. But the chorus also at times becomes dull-witted, timorous, or inappropriately conventional in its attitudes, as it pursues its role of representing low-level communal opinion. A. E. Housman parodied the lumpy sententiousness of a Greek tragic chorus in his *Fragment of a Greek Tragedy* (1883, rev. 1901):

> This truth I have written deep
> In my reflective midriff
> On tablets not of wax,
> Nor with a pen did I inscribe it there,
> For many reasons: *Life,*
> I say, *is not*
> *A stranger to uncertainty.*

A chorus is also a short stanza repeated as a refrain, common in eighteenth- and nineteenth-century poetry (see Alfred, Lord Tennyson's "Mariana" [1830]). In thirty-two-bar popular song, the returning chorus (often rhymed *aaba*) comments on or frames the story told by the verse. See BLUES; REFRAIN; SONG.

chronicle Strictly speaking, a chronicle is a record of historical events arranged consecutively in list form, and largely devoid of anecdote or explanation—dependent on chronology rather than plot. Hayden White gives the following example, from the *Annals of Saint Gall,* a chronicle of Gaul in the eighth, ninth, and tenth centuries:

> 709. Hard winter. Duke Gottfried died.
> 710. Hard year and deficient in crops.
> 711.
> 712. Flood everywhere.
> 713.
> 714. Pippin, mayor of the palace, died.

Geoffrey of Monmouth's *History of the Kings of Britain* (ca. 1136), a famous English chronicle, is more expansive than such a mere list, but still terse and somberly informative. Raphael Holinshed's *Chronicles of England, Scotland, and Ireland* (1577), one of Shakespeare's major sources, presents a full-fledged narrative, and is therefore a chronicle only in a much looser sense of the word.

The *chronicle play,* which focused on English kings and the development of the nation, was popular in England from the 1580s through the 1630s. (Shakespeare's *Henry VI, Parts 1–3* are chronicle plays.)

On the chronicle as a mode of historical writing, see Hayden White, *The Content of the Form* (1987).

chronotope A term used by the Russian literary theorist Mikhail Bakhtin in his collection of essays *The Dialogic Imagination* (ed. Michael Holquist; publ. 1981, though the book was written in the 1930s). In a fictional narrative, the chronotope knits together a particular time and place, and by doing so evokes a more general union of space and time. The effect can be slightly hypnotic or sacramental: the meaning of place in the chronotope is, as it were, closer than emblematic, more intimate. Provincial estates in Chekhov where nothing ever happens; "the road" in picaresque novels, or road movies; the castle in Gothic novels; parlours and salons in Stendhal and Balzac: all are chronotopes. For more on Bakhtin, see DIALOGIC.

classic Mark Twain remarked that a classic is "something that everyone wants to have read and nobody wants to read": merely important, and therefore no fun. More neutrally defined, a "classic" is any canonical or exceptionally worthy piece of literature. As Joseph Addison wrote in the eighteenth century, a classic work is not just the product of "Graces that arise merely from the Antiquity of an Author": its importance does not result solely from an archaic flavor that makes us respect what is old. The classic incarnates, as well, a permanence that unites ancient and modern, proving continuity within change. It shows itself more truly alive and contemporary than the most recent exertions of fashionable tendency.

For the French critic Charles-Augustin Sainte-Beuve in the 1850s, Virgil represents the definitive classic because he is the poet of the capital, embodying the civility, piety, and urbane sensibility of the Roman Empire. Virgil makes an ancient subject, the fall of Troy, supremely relevant to his own historical moment. This successful effort to span the centuries persuades us of the breadth of Rome, and its continuing relevance for us. By showing the prehistory, history, and current Augustan glory of Rome as an integrated whole, the *Aeneid* proves what Frank Kermode calls "the modernity of the true classic." (T. S. Eliot draws on Sainte-Beuve in his essay "What Is a Classic?" from 1944.)

Matthew Arnold, in *Culture and Anarchy* (1869), turns to fifth-century BCE Athens, rather than Rome, in his search for the true home of the classic. Athens is the city of Plato and Sophocles: writers intent on the rational and critical, definitively modern—and therefore, according to Arnold, classics.

See Frank Kermode, *The Classic* (1975, 2nd ed. 1983), and Steven Shankman, *In Search of the Classic* (1994). See also ANCIENTS AND MODERNS (BATTLE OF THE); CANON, CANONICAL.

classical, classicism The French poet and critic Paul Valéry famously argued against relying on terms like "classicism" and "romanticism" because, he said, you can't get drunk off the labels on bottles. But such labels were, and are, important factors in literary history. Writers often think of themselves as classicists or romanticists, and we have to try to understand what they mean by these terms.

The word *classical,* in literary study, normally refers to ancient Greek and Roman writing; "classicism" designates later writing influenced by ancient models. Classicism is also counterposed to romanticism, which often replaces classical restraint, decorum, and clarity with a more spontaneous, eccentric (and therefore, it might be inferred, more authentic) manner of expression.

According to Jacques Barzun, the classical age (which Barzun dates from 1661 to 1715) follows, and with its interest in strict form attempts to compensate for, a preceding era of political disorder and disunity, the religious wars that plagued England and the Continent. Seventeenth-century classicism, according to Barzun, occupied itself with "king-worship, love-making, intrigue, etiquette, dueling": ritual forms demanding precision and loyalty. Among the names most commonly associated with classicism in England and France are Pierre Corneille, Jean Racine, John Dryden, and Alexander Pope.

Classicism is noted for its adherence to regulation, in contrast to the pleasing irregularity of pre-romantic and romantic styles. There is a tendency in classicism, most notably in Pope, to make reason and nature synonymous. The classicist emphasis on generality and abstraction argues against a later romantic sense of the odd, resonant particular: the subtle, seemingly casual, yet infinitely telling occasions that insinuate themselves into our consciousness. There is, in this respect, a vast difference between the romantic Wordsworth's "Solitary Reaper" or his "Resolution and Independence" and the classicism of Dryden and Pope. In the years 1809–11, the debate between classical and romantic as two rival kinds of literature was first proposed by Madame de Staël in France and A. W. Schlegel in Germany. (See René Wellek, "The Term and Concept of Classicism in Literary History," in *Discriminations* [1970], and "The Concept of Romanticism," in *Concepts of Criticism,* ed. Stephen Nichols [1963].)

Classicism makes an artificial unity and imposes it. Yet it may also insist that its artistic rules are, in Pope's words, "discover'd, not devis'd." Throughout, classicists base their authority on rational, considered consent between themselves and their audience: a contract that binds writer to reader.

For the classicist, then, rules ought to be reasonable; they must be justified, and publicly approved. When seventeenth-century playwrights like Corneille showed a strong interest in the unities of time, place, and action, which Aristotle was supposed to have prescribed for stage works, they defended their emphasis by claiming that observing the unities made superior sense as an artistic practice. (See NEOCLASSICISM.)

Some modernist poets, like T. S. Eliot, championed a new kind of classicism against what they saw, prejudicially, as the soggy, inaccurate diction and vaguely effusive thinking of romanticism. The critic T. E. Hulme (whose name is pronounced HUME), a strong influence on the generation of modernists that included Ezra Pound and Eliot, yearned after literary work that would be "all dry and hard, a properly classical poem." The political affiliations of such classicism were quite clearly conservative, or worse. As Hulme remarked, "Man is an extraordinarily fixed and limited animal. . . . It is only by tradition and organization that anything decent can be got out of him." (In spite of his vocal preference, shared with Hulme, for such "dry and hard" classicism, however, a poet like Eliot seems to have a greater affinity with the romanticism he scorned. His plangent and morbid moods owe much to Tennyson and Keats.)

See Jacques Barzun, *Classic, Romantic, and Modern* (1943, 2nd ed. 1961); T. E. Hulme, "Romanticism and Classicism" (1913–14), in Hazard Adams, ed., *Literary Theory Since Plato* (1971).

Clevelandism John Cleveland (1613–58) was a poet known for his extravagant, far-fetched conceits. For a volume commemorating the death of Edward King, a Cambridge student drowned at sea (1638)—a book remembered today only because one of the poems, "Lycidas" by John Milton, became the most famous elegy in English—Cleveland wrote an elegy that includes such notions as the following: King's learning was so deep that the ocean is shallow in comparison, so he cannot really be buried there; and, memorably, "our tears shall seem the Irish seas, / We floating islands, living Hebrides." This image (we are floating, like islands, in our own tears) shows the aspect of the grotesque in Clevelandism.

Cleveland was influential in his day. There is an overlap between his extreme style and some of the verbal strategies in seventeenth-century poets who have better stood the test of time. Andrew Marvell's "Upon Appleton House" and John Donne's *Anniversaries* both exhibit notable traces of Clevelandism. See CONCEIT; GROTESQUE.

close reading The discipline of careful, intricate study of a text, championed in the mid-twentieth century by the New Critics. To read closely is to investigate the specific strength of a literary work in as many of its details as possible. It also means understanding how a text works, how it creates its effects on the most minute level. As such, close reading is the necessary form of serious literary study. Any reader who wishes to avoid turning a poem or novel into a mere piece of evidence concerning society, history, or intellectual tradition, and instead wants to grasp the work's argument in its own terms, must read closely.

The institutional basis for close reading was set by Reuben Brower in Humanities 6, a team-taught course in "slow reading" that he started at Harvard in the 1950s. For a portrait of the course, see Reuben Brower, ed., *In Defense of Reading* (1962). Frank Lentricchia has edited a recent, useful anthology of criticism, *Close Reading* (2002). Brower's course at Harvard is invoked in both Richard Poirier's *Poetry and Pragmatism* (1992) and Willard Spiegelman's "'And We Will Teach Them How': But How?" *Literary Imagination* 4:1 (2002), 77–88. For some inspiring examples of close reading, see Stanley Burnshaw, *The Poem Itself* (1960); Helen Vendler, *The Odes of John Keats* (1983); Camille Paglia, *Break Blow Burn* (2005).

closet drama A dramatic work, usually in verse, that is intended not for theatrical performance but rather for solitary reading or reading aloud in a group. Some chief examples are Milton's *Samson Agonistes* (1671), Byron's *Manfred* (1817), Shelley's *The Cenci* (1819), Browning's *Pippa Passes* (1841)—and, most notable of all, Goethe's *Faust* (1808–32).

Closet drama has been called the "dreariest of literature, most second-hand and fusty of experience" (Robertson Davies). But the works named above are all lively and permanent additions to poetry. James Merrill's *The Changing Light at Sandover* (1982) revives, and revises, the tradition of the closet drama.

closure In current therapeutic language, closure has become the latter-day substitute for what the Bible refers to as peace, or rest. The association between stopping and resting goes back almost to the beginning. The Hebrew verb *sbt* means to stop: as when God stops creating on the seventh day. This word leads to the noun *shabbat,* the day of rest, of looking at creation as something that has been concluded.

There is a key difference between the therapeutic and the religious ways of looking toward a satisfying ending. In our personal lives, we are told, we ought to "achieve," or make, closure (in order to "move on" to a good new opening). The old-fashioned alternative to this brisk self-treatment was *receiving* rest: waiting for it to descend on us, as the matter is expressed in the majestic sonorities of scripture.

Literature's sense of closure resides somewhere between the current usage and the old biblical peace. A novel or poem may impose an ending on itself, and on us, achieving closure with a vengeance. Many of Shakespeare's sonnets do this, by means of a concluding couplet that can be rather disappointing in the summary way it shuts the poem up. But in verse as in prose—as well as movies, theater, and music—we generally want a fitting, rather than a merely forceful, conclusion; a work of literature is not a tennis match.

Some works just stop, rather than ending: Gertrude Stein's prose, for example, or Ezra Pound's *Cantos* (1925–69), whose incompleteness signals the author's emphatic reliance on the freedom *not* to conclude justly or properly. Other narratives seem to have been preparing their conclusions from the beginning: Samuel Beckett's *Endgame* (1958), Marcel Proust's *In Search of Lost Time* (1912–27). And then there is the ritual bang of an ending that makes a fragmentary text oddly whole, as in *The Waste Land* (1922) by T. S. Eliot.

Reading, like thinking, is free "to break itself off or to bring itself to an end" (as Stanley Cavell remarks). This is another aspect of closure: the reader's ability to start and stop at will becomes, eventually, a way of thoughtfully producing an ending. In reading, we ready ourselves for a conclusion, guiding it into position. See Frank Kermode, *The Sense of an Ending* (1967), and Barbara Herrnstein Smith, *Poetic Closure* (1968).

comedy Comedy is, along with tragedy, one of the two most familiar kinds of drama. It is associated with revelry: festive celebrations of the return of spring, carnival and folly. An acceptance of chaos and riot, of the world turned topsy-turvy, remains permanently allied to the comic spirit.

The word *comedy* comes from the Greek *komos,* a band of revelers. There is also a minor poetic divinity named Comus, who appears in a masque by Ben Jonson, *Pleasure Reconciled to Virtue* (1618), as a fat and jovial presence: the god of the belly, lavish in entertainment. "Make way, make way, for the bouncing belly, / First father of sauce, and deviser of jelly," Jonson writes, in fine comic spirit.

Aristotle in his *Poetics* (ca. 330 BCE), the most influential of the ancient works of literary criticism, writes that comedy depicts people as worse than average: that is, as more ridiculous or ugly than usual. Comic characters, we infer, may be stupid, silly, or pointedly unattractive, but not evil. There is no serious damage, no moral harm, implied by Aristotle's "worse." The comic mask is distorted, but not with pain. Moreover, the Greek word for "ugly," *aiskhron,* means "shameful" as well, testifying to an early association between comedy and the shaming or mocking of people: between the comic and public embarrassment. (See ARISTOTELIAN CRITICISM.)

The distortion inherent in comedy represents in part an infection of the human by the other-than-human, the mechanical. According to the philosopher Henri Bergson, comedy achieves its effects from the depiction of humans as strangely automatic, machinelike, in their behavior. All manner of mannerisms express us—or squeeze expressions out of us. Charlie Chaplin or Lucille Ball working at the assembly line try to accommodate themselves to the regular motions of the industrial system, and themselves become jerking, blinking machines. In comedy, we can find ourselves turned into a Rube Goldberg device. What we thought was natural (that is, *us*) suddenly looks artificial. Thus the consistent emphasis in comedy, from Aristophanes on, on the odd mechanics of the body's functions as it spurts, sluices, and twitches its way through life.

Comedy began at the ancient Greek festival of the Dionysia, about 486 BCE. Old Comedy, of which the surviving examples are the plays of Aristophanes, featured fantastic plots, the mockery of celebrities of the day, and topical satire on political issues. Aristophanes' *Frogs* (405 BCE) poked fun at his rival tragic playwrights, Sophocles, Aeschylus, and Euripides.

By the mid-fourth century BCE, Old Comedy (and its successor, Middle Comedy) had been replaced by New Comedy. New Comedy centered on domestic manners and the lives of ordinary citizens, in contrast to Old Comedy with its larger-than-life heroes and absurd plots. New Comedy also supplied a memorable collection of stock characters, like the wily slave and the foolish, irate father who finds himself outwitted by a pair of young lovers. Menander (342–290 BCE), the chief Greek exponent of New Comedy, wrote hundreds of plays, all but one of which have been lost. His Roman successors Plautus and Terence (both second century BCE) were also prolific.

Commedia dell'arte was an Italian theatrical genre, performed by traveling players who presented improvised "sketches," and widely familiar in Renaissance Europe. Commedia dell'arte used stock characters that have had a long afterlife in other literary forms: Pierrot the sad clown; Columbine, Pierrot's beloved; Pantalone the foolish old man; Harlequin the sly servant; and so on. The Punch and Judy puppet shows are derived from the Italian commedia. (On commedia dell'arte, consult Pierre-Louis Duchartre, *The Italian Comedy* [1929].)

The *comedy of manners* involves reflection on the fashionable habits of a particular social set, as in William Congreve's *Way of the World* (1700), one of the masterpieces of the form. See Charles Lamb, "On the Artificial Comedy of the Last Century" (1822).

The *comedy of humors,* most familiar in English through the plays of Shakespeare's friend and rival Ben Jonson, relies on character types firmly delineated according to the Renaissance scientific doctrine of the humors: the sanguine person is calm or blandly cheerful; the phlegmatic is sluggish; the choleric prone to anger; and the melancholic, depressed and philosophical. Comedies of humors need not rely strictly on Renaissance physiology. *The Simpsons,* for example, could be considered a comedy of humors, with Homer animated by his determination to inert relaxation, Lisa by her thirst for knowledge, and Bart by a prankster's delight.

The essence of the comedy of humors, according to Northrop Frye, is the blocking action that one character, controlled by his humor, tries to impose on the others. The obstructing character is frequently a father who attempts to stop the marriage of his son or daughter through greed, envy, or plain mean-spiritedness. He must be outwitted in his effort to "drag us backward into the tyranny of the obsession" (Frye). Instead, we move forward, at the end of a comedy, into the realm of freedom symbolized by youthful love and marriage. (See Molière's *The Miser* [1668] for an example of this sort of plot.) There are many variations: in Shakespeare's *Taming of the Shrew* and Alfred Hitchcock's *The 39 Steps* (1935), the obstructing humor belongs to the young woman, and she vanquishes it herself, with the man's help. In Howard Hawks's film version of Ernest Hemingway's *To Have and Have Not* (1945), the man is the humorous character, and he resists, for most of the story, romantic involvement—until he finally chooses the freedom offered by both romantic love and brave political risk taking. (At the conclusion of such a comic narrative, romantic freedom is the same thing as romantic, and political, commitment; it stands against the merely private inclination of the

Humphrey Bogart character earlier in the film to do as he likes, or at least avoid doing what he doesn't like.) In Hollywood screwball comedies of the 1930s and 1940s, the obstinacy is exercised by both members of a couple on the rocks, and they must overcome it themselves in order to arrive at the safe, exhilarating harbor of marriage.

Comic plots tend to end in marriage—or the promise of an offstage wedding, or the reunion of a married but estranged couple (as in Hollywood's screwball comedies: see Stanley Cavell, *Pursuits of Happiness* [1981], on the "comedy of remarriage" in movies). A wedding party connects the union of two people with a larger festive union, a high-spirited party. Comedies frequently end in marriage because marriage, with its suggestion of future children, contains the hint of human regeneration, a basic comic principle. As Benedick puts it in Shakespeare's *Much Ado About Nothing*, defending his own reluctant surrender to love, "The world must be peopled."

Comedy's emphasis on the constant presence of mistakes and foolishness offers a kind of enlightened thinking. Kenneth Burke, echoing Nietzsche, defends comedy by writing that "the progress of humane enlightenment can go no further than in picturing people not as *vicious,* but as *mistaken.* When you add that people are *necessarily* mistaken, that *all* people are exposed to situations in which they must act as fools, that *every* insight contains its own special kind of blindness, you complete the comic circle." Burke, *Attitudes Toward History* (1937, rev. ed. 1959).

One of the peculiarities of comedy is the tendency of comic performers to break the mimetic illusion, to step out of their characters and address the audience directly, as one friend to another. Even the most reflective or outrageous tragic characters (Hamlet, for example) do not puncture the theatrical illusion so bluntly. Comedy dotes on inconsistency, and its habit of switching between levels of reality (the world on the stage, the world of the spectators) fits with this inclination. Moreover, such maneuvers suggest that an even better comedy might be going on outside the theater, in the lives of the play's audience. When it makes this point, a comedy sometimes casts itself as a mere means to an end, a way of showing that *everything* is comic. Tragedy draws us in, focused on a spectacle. Comedy, at times, throws its attention around, finding itself in the strangest places.

On comedy in general, see Erich Segal, *The Death of Comedy* (2004). On Shakespearean comedy, Northrop Frye, *A Natural Perspective* (1965), and C. L. Barber, *Shakespeare's Festive Comedy* (1959), are both very useful; for a study of James that has implications for literary comedy in general, consult Richard Poirier, *The Comic Sense of Henry James* (1960). For the relation of comedy to modernism, see Hugh Kenner, *The Stoic Comedians* (1963).

commodity A key term in Marxist theory, denoting an object that is defined by its exchange value rather than its use value. If I am building a house, a hammer and nails have use value for me: I need them to do my work. But this use value is independent of the cost of hammer and nails in the marketplace—their exchange value. Under capitalism, according to Marx, exchange value tends to eclipse use value, leading to what he called *commodity fetishism*. The desirability of items comes to depend on their market price. Some substances, like gold or diamonds, are pure instances of commodity fetishism: they have astronomical exchange value, and in the case of gold can even be the basis of exchange, but they have no use value. In a broad sense, commodity fetishism is the obsessive attachment to the things of consumer culture, a phenomenon characteristic of "late capitalism."

The commodity is related to the Marxist notion of reification, the transformation of the relations among people into objects. Marx writes that a commodity is "a mysterious thing, simply because in it the social character of men's labor appears to them as an objective character stamped upon the product of that labor." A worker's labor becomes an object independent of him, "something that controls him by virtue of an autonomy alien to man" (as the Marxist critic Georg Lukács remarks). See Karl Marx, *Capital,* vol. 1 (1867), and Georg Lukács, *History and Class Consciousness* (1923). The idea of the commodity has been important to Marxist literary criticism, particularly the work of Lukács, Theodor Adorno, and Fredric Jameson. See also FRANKFURT SCHOOL; MARXIST LITERARY CRITICISM; REIFICATION.

common measure A meter often used in hymns, consisting of a quatrain (four-line stanza) usually rhymed *abab,* with the first and third lines having four beats, the second and fourth lines three beats. Common measure differs from the ballad stanza in that it rhymes all four lines of its stanza; but it resembles the ballad stanza in its alternation of three- and four-beat lines. Isaac Watts (1674–1748) used common measure in his graceful, lucid hymns, familiar to English churchgoers for centuries; and Emily Dickinson, in her poems, often relied on a variant of common measure. See Shira Wolosky, *Emily Dickinson: A Voice of War* (1984). See METER.

complaint According to the Renaissance literary critic George Puttenham (in *The Arte of English Poesie,* 1589), one of the privileges of the poet is "to lament with ease, freely to poure forth a mans inward sorrows and the griefs wherewith his minde is surcharged." The complaint is a literary genre based on seemingly interminable lamenting (in contrast to the elegy, which, after pouring out sorrow, aims at putting it in its place, mourning and then moving on). When a poet writes a complaint, he or she uses the poem to prolong the experience of loss, not, like the elegist, to frame the loss and put it in perspective. Some examples of poetic complaint are the monologue of Ariadne, abandoned by Theseus, in Poem 64 of Catullus (84–ca. 54 BCE, and in the sixteenth century, the *Complaints* of Pierre Ronsard and of Edmund Spenser. Jules Laforgue's *Complaints* (1885) represent a transformation of the genre, stirred by impulsiveness and lulling music. See John Peter, *Complaint and Satire in Early English Literature* (1956), Lawrence Lipking, *Abandoned Women and Poetic Tradition* (1988), John Kerrigan, ed., *Motives of Woe* (1991), and Mark Rasmussen, "Spenser's Plaintive Muses," in *Spenser Studies* 13 (1999), 139–64.

conceit A metaphor used to build an analogy between two things or situations not naturally, or usually, comparable. Conceits can be compact or extended. Here is a short one, from early in literary history: Aeschylus, in his *Oresteia* (458 BCE), refers to "thirsty dust, mud's twin sister." (This somewhat tortuous phrase was parodied by A. E. Housman, whose Messenger in *Fragment of a Greek Tragedy* [1883, rev. 1901] reports the weather as follows: "Mud's sister, not himself, adorns my shoes.")

A familiar example of a more elaborate conceit occurs in John Donne's "A Valediction: Forbidding Mourning." Like most conceits, this one is structural and lingering rather than momentary. Donne compares, at some length, two temporarily parted lovers to the two pointed legs of a compass, which yearn and hearken in tandem. Popular music, like poetry, is often decorated by conceits of the most pregnant and outlandish kind: to Stephin Merritt of the Magnetic Fields, a lover's kiss feels "like flying saucers landing."

It was sometimes argued in the Renaissance that the more disparate the materials of a conceit were, the higher the poet's triumph in welding them together. The rhetorician John Hoskins, in his *Directions for Speech and Style* (1600), applauds "inventing matter of agreement in things most unlike." (The word *inventing* here has the sense of "discovering": see INVENTION.)

One should note, as well, that in the Renaissance *conceit* (or *foreconceit*) usually meant "idea" (e.g., the idea for a poem). A conceited writer was one full of imagination.

K. K. Ruthven provides an excellent brief guide in *The Conceit* (1969). See also Alastair Fowler, *Conceitful Thought* (1975); and CLEVELANDISM.

concrete poetry An experimental movement inaugurated in 1953 by the Swiss writer Eugen Gomringer. Concrete poets use words as elements in visual patterns, to make us look in surprise at their sometimes dizzying texts (rather than read them sequentially, in the usual fashion). An example is the apple-shaped poem made up completely of the word *apple*—with one small interruption, the word *worm* hidden in its center. As is apparent from this instance, concrete poetry at times tends to devolve into a mere gimmick.

Concrete poems are extreme examples of *pattern poetry.* The shape of the pattern poem mimes or mimics its theme, in an act of typographical sculpture. The earliest known examples are from Greek Hellenistic poetry (third century BCE). George Herbert's "Easter Wings" resembles a pair of wings on the page, his "The Altar" an altar. At its best, as in Herbert, pattern poetry is more than a merely clever stunt. Rather, it can be the ultimate form of poetry's effort to embody its subject, to unite trope (an instance of figurative language) and scheme (the poem's overall formal pattern). (See TROPE.) The contemporary poet John Hollander has contributed some distinguished examples of pattern poetry, especially "Swan and Shadow," from his book *Types of Shape* (1969).

May Swenson's "The Shape of Death" (1970) is an advanced example of pattern poetry in which the amorphousness of both death and love are suggested. Swenson's poem begins,

What does love look like?   We know the shape of death.
death is a cloud, immense   and awesome. At first a
lid is lifted from the   eye of light. There is a
clap of sound. . . .

The pattern poem is also linked to the emblem tradition; see EMBLEM. See Mary Ellen Solt, ed., *Concrete Poetry: A World View* (1968); John Hollander, "The Poem in the Eye," in *Vision and Resonance* (1975).

concordia discors. See DISCORDIA CONCORS

confessional poetry Its source is in the American poet Robert Lowell's book *Life Studies* (1959). (The critic M. L. Rosenthal coined the term *confessional poetry* in a review of *Life Studies*.) Lowell's work was followed by that of his students, W. D. Snodgrass (b. 1926), Sylvia Plath (1932–63), and Anne Sexton (1928–74).

Confessional poetry creates an impression of revealing the naked facts of the author's life, often in its most harrowing, intimate, or traumatic aspects; it violates taboos and exposes shameful truths. Plath writes, for example,

> Dying is an art.
> I do it exceptionally well.

The blunt, extreme character of the personal revelations in confessional poetry marks its difference from an autobiographical poem like Wordsworth's *Prelude* (1805–50), which reflects from a mature distance on its subject matter. Often, as in John Berryman's *Dream Songs* (1955–69), the desperate, unachieved desire for such distance is a crucial theme of the poems. Perhaps most notable among the current inheritors of the confessional tradition is Sharon Olds.

See Paul Breslin, *The Psycho-Political Muse* (1987), and Alan Williamson, *Introspection and Contemporary Poetry* (1984). In *The Wounded Surgeon* (2005) Adam Kirsch offers a stimulating argument that Lowell and Plath should not be considered confessional poets.

constative. See SPEECH ACT

continental philosophy Post–World War II philosophy is marked by a division between two rival strains called analytic and continental (though the term *continental philosophy* was not widely used until the 1970s, after the analytic school had secured its domination of philosophy departments in England and America). Analytic philosophy, stemming from the work of Gottlob Frege, Ludwig Wittgenstein, Rudolf Carnap, and J. L. Austin, among others, consists of the attempted clarification of carefully delimited philosophical problems (for example, the definition of consciousness, of action, or of a speech act such as promising [see SPEECH ACT]). Analytic philosophy often gives logic a central place. By contrast, continental philosophy, at least since Martin Heidegger, has had little interest in logic. In distinction to the analytic manner of zeroing in on a problem defined in terms of worldly evidence, continental philosophy sometimes—though not always—casts itself as commentary on influential precursors. Working through earlier thinkers is a tradition that begins with G. W. F. Hegel (1770–1831), and flourishes in the work of Jacques Derrida (1930–2004).

The most important source of contemporary continental philosophy is phenomenology, deriving first from Hegel in *Phenomenology of Mind* (1807) and then, in the early twentieth century, from Edmund Husserl and Heidegger. The phenomenological tradition returns to the experience of the isolated consciousness in its interaction with the world (or, in the case of Maurice Merleau-Ponty, more specifically with the body). Other main influences are the existentialism of Jean-Paul Sartre; hermeneutics, the discipline that investigates the processes of interpretation and understanding, particularly across historical distances (Hans-Georg Gadamer, Paul Ricoeur); and the Frankfurt School critique of social ideology (Max Horkheimer and Theodor Adorno).

Simon Critchley's stimulating *Continental Philosophy* (2001) explains the division between analytic and continental philosophy in terms of a traditional divergence between philosophy's interest in knowledge (analytic) and its commitment to wisdom (continental). Analytic philosophy, Critchley adds, has an "empirical-scientific" attitude, as opposed to continental philosophy's "hermeneutic-romantic" bent. Often, continental philosophy concerns itself with the gap between secular reason and the fact of religious belief, whereas analytic philosophers sometimes appear indifferent to religion. Continental philosophy also engages the space between the rational advances of modernity and the mythic substratum of our experience, including artistic experience. (The continental philosopher may want to make connections across this space, or may simply lament the separation.)

Vincent Descombes, *Modern French Philosophy* (1979), provides an excellent summary of its subject; see also Richard Kearney and Mara Rainwater, eds., *The Continental Philosophy Reader* (1996); and Dermot Moran, *Introduction to Phenomenology* (2000), which includes chapters on Husserl, Heidegger, Sartre, Lévinas, Merleau-Ponty, and Derrida. See ANALYTIC PHILOSOPHY; EXISTENTIALISM; FRANKFURT SCHOOL; HERMENEUTICS; PHENOMENOLOGY; SPEECH ACT.

convention Conventions are the rules or guidelines that provide the proper framework for artistic success. This was true in the ancient world, and it is still true today. A detective story must have suspense, the solving of a crime, a narrative puzzle; a pop song requires two or three chords and (often) an evocation of the pains or rewards of love.

From the beginning, there has been an association between the conventional and the natural: conventions work because they are fitted to the world, to nature. Yet from the ancient Greeks on people have been aware that the world can be described in different, even contradictory ways, depending on the conventions one relies on. Recognition of the changing nature of artistic conventions means that they can be associated with mere custom and fashion, rather than nature. The revolution in literary history associated with Romanticism often sees conventions as artificial obstacles standing in the way of direct experience and of individuality.

Yet nature is available only through convention. It cannot be approached nakedly. Wordsworth's desired rhetoric of "a man speaking to men" is just as conventional as the artifice of a Pope satire. For all that, we still feel the intimacy of Wordsworth's speech: some conventions are closer to us than others . . .

See Lawrence Manley, *Convention* (1980). See also DECORUM.

conversation poem A mini-genre of English Romantic poetry initiated by Samuel Taylor Coleridge, notably in "The Eolian Harp" (1795) and "Frost at Midnight" (1798). The conversation poem addresses itself subtly to a friend or beloved companion, though it often, in its course, wanders away from this interlocutor. The coherence of mood that occurs between author and friend is closer than in the verse epistle (see VERSE EPISTLE). William Wordsworth adapted Coleridge's invention in "Tintern Abbey" (1798) and *The Prelude* (1805–50).

copia In Latin, "plenty." Copia is an ideal of Renaissance rhetoric, requiring the "dilation" or amplification of expressions and examples: a linguistic abundance that can be enjoyed in works like Robert Burton's *Anatomy of Melancholy* (1621) and François Rabelais's *Gargantua and Pantagruel* (1532–52). The Netherlandish humanist Desiderius Erasmus wrote a schoolbook, *De Copia* (1512), to assist students in Latin composition. There was also, at times, a backlash against copia. At the end of the sixteenth century, Francis Bacon was among those who criticized excessive "copie of speech." See Madeleine Doran, "Eloquence and 'Copy,'" in *Endeavors of Art* (1954).

coterie poetry Since the late 1980s, some critics of Renaissance literature have emphasized the fact that Renaissance verse was frequently exchanged among the members of small groups, or coteries. The most influential work for such studies is Arthur Marotti's *John Donne, Coterie Poet* (1986). Marotti's description of Donne's coterie, and its supposed responses to his poems, is partly speculative, and emphasizes Donne's political ambitions. (For two critiques of Marotti, see Christopher Ricks, "Donne After Love," in Elaine Scarry, ed., *Literature and the Body* [1988], 33–69; and Kenneth Gross, "John Donne's Lyric Skepticism: In Strange Way," *Modern Philology* 101:3 [February 2004], 371–99.)

In later eras of English literature, Romanticism and modernism might both be considered coterie phenomena, with the major writers of these movements addressing their work to one another. James Longenbach's *Stone Cottage* (1988) considers the relation between W. B. Yeats and Ezra Pound; and David Kalstone's *Becoming a Poet* (1989) describes the close relations of Elizabeth Bishop to two fellow poets, Robert Lowell and Marianne Moore.

country-house poem Popular in the seventeenth century, the country-house poem usually praises the virtues of retired existence away from the urban hubbub, with its corrupt politics and insinuating vices. (See RETIREMENT.) The best-known example of a country-house poem in English is Ben Jonson's "To Penshurst" (1616), which presents a hearty and attractive picture of the friendly society within the hospitable mansion of Penshurst, along with an idyllic view of the surrounding landscape. Other early country-house poems are "A Description of Cooke-ham" (1611) by Emilia Lanyer, Thomas Carew's "To Saxham" (1640), and Andrew Marvell's extraordinary "Upon Appleton House" (ca. 1650). Country-house poems are sometimes accused of covering up the social relations (with rural laborers, most notably) that make possible the leisured life of the house. See Raymond Williams, *The Country and the City* (1973), James W. Turner, *The Politics of Landscape* (1979), and Alastair Fowler, *The Country House Poem* (1994).

couplet A couplet is a rhymed verse form of two lines, usually composed in series, as part of a longer stanza (*aabbcc* and so on). Shakespeare's sonnets consist of three quatrains followed by a concluding couplet. From Sonnet 129:

> All this the world well knows yet none knows well
> To shun the heaven that leads men to this hell.

The *heroic couplet,* by far the commonest kind, is written in iambic pentameter. John Dryden's and Alexander Pope's versions of Virgil and Homer were written in heroic couplets, deemed the most suitable meter for high epic poetry—until 1667, when Milton published *Paradise Lost* in blank verse, in defiance of epic tradition in English.

Christopher Marlowe's couplets in his translation of Ovid's *Amores* (ca. 1590) are notably assured. The fluent, flexible lines of John Denham's "Cooper's Hill" (1642) presage the definitive ascendance of the couplet form in Dryden and Pope. Denham described the river Thames in the following terms:

> Though deep, yet clear, though gentle, yet not dull,
> Strong without rage, without ore-flowing full

—a couplet that excited much admiration in the eighteenth century. (See DISCORDIA CONCORS; PARADOX.)

The couplet is particularly well suited to the balancing or playing off of opposing terms. Here are some heroic couplets from Pope's *Essay on Criticism* (1711):

> Nature to all things fixed the limits fit,
> And wisely curbed proud man's pretending wit.
> As on the land while here the ocean gains,
> In other parts it leaves wide sandy plains;
> Thus in the soul while memory prevails,
> The solid pow'r of understanding fails;
> Where beams of warm imagination play,
> The memory's soft figures melt away.

The steadfast, daring frame of the opening couplet dramatically subordinates, or fits, human "wit" (which comes last) to a greater power: the "nature" announced in the first word of Pope's verse. The ensuing lines question such tight containment as they go on to imagine a blurry cascade of competing mental faculties, and the rhymes themselves fall off or decline, moving from *prevails* to *fails* and from *play* to *melt away.* In Pope, its most brilliant and tireless practitioner, the heroic couplet can subside, as here, from boldly pronounced antithesis to a gentle maze of words (elsewhere, Pope rises to lofty, ringing bravado).

See William Piper, *The Heroic Couplet* (1969), as well as the chapter on

Denham's "Cooper's Hill" in Earl Wasserman, *The Subtler Language* (1959); also Barbara Herrnstein Smith, "The Rhymed Couplet," in *Poetic Closure* (1968).

courtesy. See COURTLINESS

courtliness The blend of adroit, finely mannered personal display and politically minded self-promotion associated with figures surrounding the prince or monarch in a Renaissance court. The courtier must try to become (in Wayne Rebhorn's words) "the well-rounded man, the perfect amalgam of medieval knight and urbane, humanist-trained gentleman." He should be adept at dancing and ceremonial jousting, impressive in both witty conversation and meditative discussions of Plato and Augustine.

The courtier, in sum, seeks advancement at court through his capacity to produce admirable and subtle performances. His main goal is winning the favor of the prince, and defeating his competitors for that favor. But courtly love provides an important focus of his attention, as well, and he frequently devotes himself to a beloved.

The most important source for our ideas of Renaissance courtliness is Baldassare Castiglione's *The Book of the Courtier*, published in Italy in 1528. Castiglione's dialogue, which takes place among a group of men and women at the court of Urbino, authoritatively describes several courtly ideals, including a newly invented one, *sprezzatura* ("to pronounce a new word perhaps," Castiglione writes with a wink). He defines sprezzatura, best translated as "nonchalance," as a way of "conceal[ing] all art and mak[ing] whatever is done or said appear to be without effort and almost without any thought about it." Castiglione had a major influence in Elizabethan England: the idea of courtliness appears prominently in Spenser, Sidney, and Shakespeare. See Daniel Javitch, *Poetry and Courtliness in Renaissance England* (1978); Frank Whigham, *Ambition and Privilege* (1984); Wayne Rebhorn, *Courtly Performances* (1978); and Thomas M. Greene, "*Il Cortegiano* and the Choice of a Game," in *The Vulnerable Text* (1986). Kenneth Gross in *Shakespeare's Noise* (2001) offers a convincing portrait of Shakespeare's achievement set against the suspicious, double-dealing world of the Renaissance court. See also COURTLY LOVE; HUMANISM; RENAISSANCE LITERATURE.

courtly love In the eleventh and twelfth centuries, the Provençal poets, or troubadours, inaugurated the poetic celebration of the resistant beloved, who becomes in effect a muse for the male writer. The poet-lover is usually a bachelor, his beloved married. Suffering the torments inflicted by her capriciousness or coldness, he strives to prove himself through strenuous devotion to love, and pursuit of perfection in battles and courtly ceremonies.

C. S. Lewis powerfully evokes "these medieval lovers—'servants' or 'prisoners' they called themselves—who seem to be always weeping or always on their knees before ladies of inflexible cruelty." The poet-lovers were made courteous by their love. But their implication was also that only the courteous *could* love with complete and correct fervor.

The erotic ritual of "worshipping" an inaccessible lady conveyed the elegance and passion that were imagined to be at the center of court life. The lover's devotion to his lady echoes both a vassal's fealty to his lord and the worshipper's adoration of the Christian God (complete with periodic "sinning," during which the lover momentarily forgets his solemn passion).

There is no real evidence that courtly love was ever practiced. (See E. Talbot Donaldson, "The Myth of Courtly Love" in *Speaking of Chaucer* [1977] for an especially skeptical view of the subject.) But it was a prevalent literary ideal from the twelfth century on, when the wife of King Louis VII of France, Eleanor of Aquitaine, and her daughter Marie set up "courts of love." Eleanor and Marie became the patrons of poets who devoted themselves to amorous themes. In the 1180s Andreas Capellanus, influenced by Ovid, wrote a handbook explaining the principles of courtly love.

Courtly love, as described by Andreas and by the poets, subjected the lover to both torment and intense pleasure at the hands, and "eyebeams," of his lady. It sometimes culminated in nighttime encounters between the lover and his beloved, featuring rapt kisses and embraces; but the pair was obligated, at least according to the courtly ideal, to refrain from full sexual intercourse. Characteristic courtly lovers can be found in the medieval poetry of Chrétien de Troyes and Marie de France; in Dante and Petrarch; in Malory's *Morte d'Arthur* (Launcelot and Guinevere); and in Chaucer's Knight's Tale.

See Andreas Capellanus, *On Love* (1184–86), Denis de Rougemont, *Love in the Western World* (1939), C. S. Lewis, *The Allegory of Love* (1936). Roland Barthes, *A Lover's Discourse* (1977), offers a contemporary evocation of courtly love. *A Handbook of the Troubadours* (1995), ed. F. R. P. Akehurst and Judith Davis, is an invaluable compendium of sources. See FIN AMORS.

creole, creolizing A recent critical concept used to describe the mixing of different cultures. Katie Trumpener writes in *Bardic Nationalism* (1997) that the dual preoccupation of postcolonial studies has been "the indigenous and the creolized, which in some ways are collapsed into one another." Postcolonial studies associates the cosmopolitan or globalizing aspect of empire with creolizing: the mixing of foreign cultures present in, for example, the West Indies (with their blurring of African, European, and native American cultural strains).

cruel fair "Fair cruelty," sighs Cesario (Viola) in Shakespeare's *Twelfth Night*. The cruelty in question is Olivia's resistance to Orsino's amorous pleadings, and here Olivia joins a long line of fair (i.e., beautiful) Renaissance females, whose rejection of love is often called cruel by the hopeful male suitor. The concealed point of the phrase is that there is something fair, something heartening and alluring, about the supposed cruelty of the woman, and that the cruel fair is playing her proper role in a long-established drama. See also BELOVED, THE; COURTLY LOVE.

cultural capital A phrase popularized by the French sociologist Pierre Bourdieu to describe the prestige attached to a particular work of art (or, more generally, any commodity). Proust has greater cultural capital than Danielle Steele or Judy Blume, even though they have sold many more books than he ever did. See Pierre Bourdieu, *Distinction* (1979), and John Guillory, *Cultural Capital* (1993).

cultural studies A general term for much of the theoretical work practiced in humanities departments at the turn of the twenty-first century. Cultural studies focuses on "culture" as its key term, and is particularly attentive to questions of national identity, mass culture, class, race, and ethnicity. Practitioners of cultural studies insist that literature and art must be understood within a larger framework of cultural practices. For Pierre Bourdieu, a major theorist of cultural studies, questions of aesthetic preference cannot be adjudicated with reference to literary or artistic tradition, but instead must be grasped as effects of snobbery and social prejudice. (As John Frow puts it, Bourdieu shows how "differences in cultural preference become socially functional.") Theorists of cultural studies who follow Bourdieu focus on the correlation between one's social position and one's cultural practices (tastes, habits, and so on). For them, social custom tends to be linked closely to class.

Arguably, cultural studies began with the debate between Walter Benjamin and Theodor Adorno over mass culture. Adorno criticized Benjamin for his suggestion in "The Work of Art in the Age of Mechanical Reproduction" (1936) that the new technology of the cinema offered liberating imaginative possibilities. (The exchange between Adorno and Benjamin is reprinted in the collection *Aesthetics and Politics* [1977].) In *The Dialectic of Enlightenment* (1947), by Max Horkheimer and Adorno, the authors adapted Marxist analysis to show that mass culture was a means of enforcing social inequality (like the "noble lie" in Plato's *Republic*). Some later theorists opposed to the Frankfurt School see cultural practices in a different way, as offering free opportunity for individual choice, for eccentric and self-fulfilling "investments" in particular texts (see Dick Hebdige, *Subculture* [1979], and Simon Frith, *Performing Rites* [1996]).

Other significant theorists of cultural studies are Raymond Williams and Stuart Hall (both of them associated with the Birmingham School of cultural materialism), as well as Paul Gilroy, author of *The Black Atlantic* (1993). See Simon During, ed., *The Cultural Studies Reader* (1993); also John Frow, *Cultural Studies and Cultural Value* (1995), and Lawrence Grossberg, Cary Nelson, and Paula Treichler, eds., *Cultural Studies* (1992).

culture T. S. Eliot defines culture as "all the characteristic activities of a people: Derby Day, Henley Regatta, Cowes, the twelfth of August, a cup final, the dog races, the pin table, the dart board, Wensleydale cheese, boiled cabbage cut into sections, beetroot in vinegar, nineteenth-century Gothic churches and the music of Elgar." (The culture being described is, needless to say, that of Great Britain.) Eliot emphasizes the interweaving of the elite and the popular, the refined and the coarse. With its interest in food and sport, his description could stand as a presage of the current interest in culture as a many-faceted and diverse phenomenon. Under the influence of Michel Foucault, many contemporary critics have added a dose of suspicion, so that culture becomes the bearer of an ideological bias meant to defend it against the foreign, the Other. Often nowadays, culture is the key term that dictates the meaning of literary texts: an author's work becomes evidence concerning the culture of its time.

See T. S. Eliot, *Notes Toward the Definition of Culture* (1948); Eugene Goodheart, *The Reign of Ideology* (1997); Matthew S. Greenfield, "What We Talk About When We Talk About Culture," *Raritan* 19:2 (Fall 1999), 95–113, explores the influence of anthropology on the prizing of "culture" in literary studies. See also Raymond Williams, *Culture and Society* (1958).

D

dactyl. See METER

Dadaism An international artistic movement centered in Zurich and New York, and flourishing between 1915 and the early 1920s. (Its name, of uncertain derivation, has suggested to some a baby's cry; to others, an obscure French word for a rocking horse.) Dada's leaders in New York were the artists Marcel Duchamp and Francis Picabia, and in Zurich the writers Tristan Tzara and Hugo Ball and the sculptor Hans (Jean) Arp.

Dadaism construed artistic work as action, and demanded an end to the isolation of art from life. The movement was avant-garde in tenor, issuing proclamations that voiced protests against reason and logic, and demands for the freeing of the individual. (There was also a dose of nihilistic gloom. Picabia in his "Cannibal Manifesto" [1920] chanted, "DADA, as for it, it smells of nothing, it is nothing, nothing, nothing.")

At the Cabaret Voltaire in Zurich, street ballads and expressionist poetry were recited, and Ball, in formal attire, declaimed his peculiar brand of "phonetic" poetry. Here is a sample:

> gadji beri bimba
> glandridi lauli lonni cadori
> gadjama bim beri glassala.

The best-known piece of Dadaist art is probably Duchamp's *Fountain* (1917), one of his "ready-mades": a found urinal with the scrawled signature "R. Mutt." For related movements, see FUTURISM; SURREALISM; see also AVANT-GARDE. See David Hopkins, *Dada and Surrealism* (2004); Marcel Duchamp, "Painting . . . at the Service of the Mind," in Herschel Chipp, ed., *Theories of Modern Art* (1996); and Jed Perl, "A Defense of Dada," in *The New Republic,* April 17, 2006, 21–24.

daemon The particular "genius" or spirit that inhabits someone, acting as an inspirational or a blocking force. The daemon is a kind of "little man" inside the self that has its own will: a small divinity or factor of insight, telling and crucial. The best-known example is Socrates' daemon, described in Plato's *Apology* (31d) as his daimonion or "daemonic thing"—the strange inward obstruction that has prevented Socrates from entering public life. The paradox of the daemon is that it possesses me, and therefore resembles an external force: but it is still *my own* external force, revealing me even in its manipulations.

Plato's Socrates, writes Kenneth Burke, "struggled . . . to integrate the new lore of the forensic with the traditions of epic heroism surviving from the primitive period of Greece. The sophistication of the sophists was the simple negation of the earlier pieties—and Socrates tried to 'transcend' it by 'negating the negation.' He did not want to be forensic-versus-primitive, but primitive-plus-forensic. This drive for a 'higher synthesis' he named by shorthand as his 'demon.'" (Burke, *Attitudes Toward History* [1937; rev. ed. 1959].)

The Renaissance spoke of the daemon as the individual's "genius," and Emerson in his essays of the 1840s still uses the word *genius* for the daemon. There is also a less personal meaning for daemon or genius: in the mystical thought of the Renaissance, daemonic powers, both beneficent and malicious, patrol the earth, providing an ambient force field that influences human life in various directions. The Polish author Czeslaw Milosz (1911–2004) remarks in his "Ars Poetica" that "poetry is rightly said to be dictated by a *daimonion*."

débat (French, pronounced "dayBAH.") The *débat* was a literary genre of the twelfth and thirteenth centuries involving a debate or quarrel between two opposed perspectives: for example, reason versus grace, or didacticism versus pleasure in literary art. Nicholas of Guildford's *The Owl and the Nightingale* (twelfth century) is a débat centering on the alternative between poetry of moral advice and love poetry.

decadence The concept of decadence became popular in the 1890s in England, though its dark sources were mostly French. Decades earlier, Baudelaire had written his *Flowers of Evil* (1857) and Gerard de Nerval, another French writer, had walked his pet lobster on a leash. Lurid and luxuriant norms of behavior and expression began to flourish among the bohemians of Paris.

Among the decadents were figures like the English poet Algernon Charles Swinburne, the French novelist Joris-Karl Huysmans, and the English artist Aubrey Beardsley. Oscar Wilde, heir of that supreme aesthete, Walter Pater, was "the High Priest of the Decadents" and widely spoofed as a king of intellectual debauchery.

Decadence is marked by the over-subtle affectation that occurs "when thought thinks upon itself, and when emotions become entangled with the consciousness of them" (Lionel Johnson). The mood of decadence implies an attractive fatality; religious and erotic rituals valued for their gloomy, languorous glamour; an "exquisite appreciation of pain" (Johnson) and of the "strange delight [that] may lurk in self-disgust" (Arthur Symons). Often, exotic oriental landscapes are present, seen through an opiate haze.

Gustave Flaubert's *Salammbo* (1862), Wilde's *Salomé* (1892), Richard Wagner's *Parsifal* (1865–82), Thomas Mann's *Death in Venice* (1912): all are examples of decadence. Decadence also often shows a fascinated interest in decay and annihilation, and a perception of civilization's inexorable, gradual tendency toward extinction (as outlined, for example, in Oswald Spengler's *Decline of the West* [1918–23]).

See Mario Praz, *The Romantic Agony* (1933); Ellen Moers, *The Dandy* (1960); Camille Paglia, *Sexual Personae* (1990); Barbara Spackman, *Decadent Genealogies* (1989); Ian Fletcher, ed., *Decadence and the 1890s* (1979). See also ENNUI.

de casibus A poem or prose work depicting the repetitive, seemingly inevitable downfalls of great men. (*Casus* means "fall" in Latin.) The two best known examples of the genre are Boccaccio's *De Casibus Virorum Illustrium* (Concerning the Falls of Great Men, 1360–73) and Thomas Sackville's *Mirror for Magistrates* (1559).

deconstruction In current, casual usage, to deconstruct something is to analyze, to reimagine, or perhaps merely to unravel it. Deconstructing a hamburger might mean interpreting its place in our cultural life; or it might involve putting it in a pita with mango chutney, rather than on a bun with ketchup.

What I have just presented is, of course, a mere caricature of deconstruction (though it is the meaning of the word in use among the general public). The term *deconstruction* has a far different, and more rigorous, meaning. Deconstruction stems from the writings of the French philosopher Jacques Derrida, who wrote his major works in the late 1960s and early 1970s. (Derrida had in mind a similar usage by the German philosopher Martin Heidegger, *Destruktion*.) For Derrida, a philosophical or literary work contains premises contested—deconstructed—by some aspect of the work itself, which threatens to undo these premises. For example, Plato exalts speech over writing, insisting that true philosophy can take place only in the responsive, conversational situation exemplified by Socrates' questioning of his interlocutors. But Plato's dialogues are written, not spoken. The only way for Plato to claim the superiority of speech over writing is, as it turns out, in writing. This is the sort of paradox that deconstruction dotes on and devotes itself to, often with fascinating results. One of Derrida's major interests was the undermining of the self-assurance of "Western metaphysics," an assurance he located in the "voice that hears itself speak": the self-validating subject of philosophical reflection. During a detailed study of Husserl, Rousseau, Saussure, Heidegger, Freud, Nietzsche, and other thinkers, Derrida concluded that the prizing of voice and of lucid self-consciousness in philosophical and literary tradition was belied by the phenomenon of writing itself, particularly as embodied in "the trace" (an aspect of meaning that cannot be brought under control or located in a particular time and place, but that enables meaning to occur).

The other leading figure of deconstruction in the 1970s–80s, along with Derrida, was Paul de Man. Among their followers are, in literary theory, Barbara Johnson and, in religious studies, John Caputo and Mark Taylor. Johnson presents an effective example of deconstruction when she examines Herman Melville's *Billy Budd* (written 1886–87). Does Melville's story, which concludes with the execution of Billy, present a portrait of grim, tragic necessity—or a savage parody of justice? The deconstructionist will assert that this alternative is undecidable: that the text asks to be read in both ways, even though one reading renders the other impossible. The point is that our idea of tragic necessity is inwardly contaminated by gruesome, unjust violence; the two ideas cannot be separated from each other. Deconstruction, in this light, offers an ethical reflection on our values, particularly insofar as these values depend on oppositions (good versus evil, just versus unjust).

See Jacques Derrida, "Plato's Pharmacy," in *Dissemination* (1972), as well as his essay "Structure, Sign, and Play in the Discourse of the Human Sciences," in Richard Macksey and Eugenio Donato, eds., *The Structuralist Controversy* (1970); Mark C. Taylor, *Altarity* (1987); Barbara Johnson, *The*

Critical Difference (1980); and John D. Caputo, *The Prayers and Tears of Jacques Derrida* (1997). Among the critiques of deconstruction are John Ellis's *Against Deconstruction* (1989), Michael Fischer's *Does Deconstruction Make Any Difference?* (1985), and Raymond Tallis's *Not Saussure* (1995). See also DIF-FÉRANCE; LOGOCENTRIC; POSTSTRUCTURALISM.

decorum   Decorum is the standard of what is fitting or proper in literary art. It implicitly asserts a contract between author and audience, and a loyalty to the reader's expectations. The greatest characters should be treated in the highest style; tragedies ought to feature noble, famous families; shepherds usually sing of disappointed love; a single man with a fortune must be looking for a wife: these are some of the age-old insistences of decorum.

Though all the rules I have just mentioned are often violated, demonstrating that most laws of decorum are quite flexible, it is not quite true that anything goes. Sometimes, a violation of decorum can destroy the reader's pleasure, as when we discover at the end of a mystery novel that the narrator was himself the murderer, or that in reality no one was killed. We have been tricked; this is not the kind of story we wanted. The author has broken his contract with the reader.

The Roman poet Horace, in his *Ars Poetica* (Art of Poetry, ca. 20 BCE), remains the most influential spokesman of decorum. Decorum is also a prevalent ideal in the eighteenth century, among writers and critics like Alexander Pope, Joseph Addison, and Samuel Johnson.

Cicero in his *Orator* (46 BCE) remarks on the difference between the appropriate (the rule of decorum) and the right or just (the rule of law): "By 'right' we indicate the perfect line of duty which everyone must follow everywhere, but 'propriety' is what is fitting or agreeable to an occasion or person." (Cicero adds that impropriety or lack of decorum—putting silly speeches in the mouth of a wise, grave man, for example—is the worst fault a poet can commit.) Poetic judgment, because it fits itself to the setting and the moment, differs from moral judgment, which tries to make various occasions and different people conform to a standard, raising them into general truth.

In opposition to Cicero, whose ideal was to "discuss commonplace matters simply, lofty subjects impressively, and topics ranging between in a tempered style," Saint Augustine defends the manner of the Christian gospels, which sometimes treat the smallest or most trivial matters in an urgent, demanding high style. Erich Auerbach sees in Augustine's emphasis the invention of a new kind of decorum opposed to that of the classical theorists, one oriented by its lofty rhetorical purpose rather than its low or common subject matter. It is only the aim of the Christian speaker—to teach, admonish, lament—that can tell him what sort of style to employ. According to Auerbach, this admission of the most humble aspects of daily life into the precincts of Christian moral instruction has a momentous effect on literary style, generating what we now call realism.

See Erich Auerbach, *Mimesis* (1946), and J. V. Cunningham, ed., *The Problem of Style* (1966). See also CONVENTION.

defamiliarization In Russian, *ostranenie:* a term from the Russian formalist school of criticism, active in the early twentieth century. A better translation for *ostranenie* is "estrangement," and I therefore use this term rather than the more popular *defamiliarization,* both in this entry and in my discussion of formalism.

According to the Russian formalists, literary art devotes itself to the making strange (the defamiliarizing, or estranging) of our accustomed perceptions. At the same time, art exposes its own formal devices, estranging the techniques of representation. The purpose is to make life newly interesting as, or through, art: to get us to experience it as if for the first time.

A good example of estrangement comes from Jonathan Swift's *Gulliver's Travels* (1726), cited by Fredric Jameson in his account of formalism and structuralism, *The Prison-House of Language* (1971). Gulliver, finding himself stranded among the gigantic Brobdingnagians, suddenly appears tiny in comparison. Here, he confronts a female breast: "The Nipple was about the Bigness of my Head, and the Hue both of that and the Dug so varified with Spots, Pimples and Freckles, that nothing could appear more nauseous: For I had a near Sight of her, she sitting down the more conveniently to give Suck, and I standing on the table. This made me reflect upon the fair Skins of our *English* Ladies, who appear so beautiful to us, only because they are of our own Size."

See the studies by Viktor Shklovskii collected in his *Theory of Prose* (1925–29); and Charles Baxter, "On Defamiliarization," in *Burning Down the House* (1997). See also FORMALISM.

deus ex machina In Latin, the "god from the machine": the machine in question being the crane used in the ancient theater to transport deities or other superior beings and land them onstage, so that they might intervene in the action, and resolve, through divine ingenuity, various plot difficulties. An example of a deus ex machina is Athena's appearance at the end of Aeschylus's *Oresteia* (458 BCE), when she judges the case of Orestes (she approves Orestes' killing of his mother, Clytemnestra, and disciplines the Furies' vengefulness, allowing the play to conclude).

dialectic Originally, dialectic stands in contrast to rhetoric (notably, in Plato's *Phaedrus* [ca. 375–365 BCE]). Dialectic requires that we understand, through debate, a matter that is under discussion, rather than relying on mere manipulative persuasion by rhetoricians (i.e., speechmakers). Plato in the *Phaedrus* makes the case that dialectic is necessary to rhetoric. The good rhetorician ought to understand what he is arguing about: to know his theme, in order to achieve his desired effect. Aristotle remarks of dialectic that "since it is investigative, it leads the way to the first principles of all methods." The term *dialectic*, then, begins its career as the philosophical complement to the more practical-minded *rhetoric:* dialectic tries to understand what an argument is really about, rather than merely trying to win it.

In a looser and more contemporary sense of the word, calling a text or an argument dialectical implies that it places conflicting elements in productive struggle, or debate. There is also a more specific meaning to the term in modern philosophy, associated with the German idealist philosopher G. W. F. Hegel, particularly in his *Phenomenology of Spirit* (1807). For Hegel, the claims of various philosophical systems are negated by succeeding systems, but they are not abolished because of this. Instead, they take their place in a larger whole, as moments along the historical path of thought. The project of philosophical knowledge can only be completed dialectically: by an open struggle with previous ideas, and by adopting and criticizing them within one's own system (rather than by trying to show that such ideas were merely wrongheaded mistakes).

Marx's adaptation of Hegelian dialectic eventually culminated in the theories of the literary critic Georg Lukács and in the work of the Frankfurt School, especially Theodor Adorno. On Platonic dialectic, see Hans-Georg Gadamer, *Dialogue and Dialectic* (1980), and Charles Griswold, ed., *Platonic Writings, Platonic Readings* (1988); on Hegel, Alexandre Kojève, *Introduction to the Philosophy of Hegel* (2nd ed., 1947).

dialogic A critical term used in the works of the Russian literary theorist Mikhail Bakhtin, suggesting that the productive conflict of distinct voices encountering one another is definitive of social life, especially as portrayed in novels. Bakhtin remarked that "for the prose artist the world is full of the words of other people."

One of Bakhtin's first important works was *Rabelais and His World* (1965), his book on *Gargantua and Pantagruel* (1532–52), a grotesque and uproarious narrative by the French Renaissance monk François Rabelais. Bakhtin named the jostling excesses of Rabelais "carnivalesque," and saw in Rabelais's exultant and scurrilous prose style a connection to the exuberant passions of the human body. From here on, Bakhtin praised the wildly various combination of voices in literature, especially prose fiction. But Bakhtin also defined an idea of human connection at the heart of the literary works he valued: the dialogic, which invokes the meeting of different characters' voices as the ethical ideal that the novel offers.

According to Bakhtin, "the novel can be defined as a diversity of social speech types," but this diversity also puts individual voices in conjunction. For Bakhtin, a Russian Orthodox Christian influenced by the Jewish theologian Martin Buber, the fundamental unit of literature is the "utterance": "a living word exchanged between existing people" (Joseph Frank). In Bakhtin's favorite writer, Fyodor Dostoevski, the author says "thou" to each of his characters, recognizing the character's uniqueness.

In Dostoevski, Bakhtin writes, we experience a "polyphonic novel": a group of challenging, fighting voices, each of which is understood from within itself, rather than being subjected to the author's point of view. Dostoevski's people are impossibly stubborn, frustrating and perverse, intent on independence. Paradoxically, though, Dostoevski enforces the independence of his characters' voices by linking them intimately to one another, forming a magical or tyrannical bond between one character and another. One person's words become another's secret belief. Of Raskolnikov in *Crime and Punishment* (1866), Bakhtin writes, "Every person touches a sore spot in him and assumes a firm role in his inner speech." Dostoevski's characters see themselves defined through the eyes of others, but they refuse to remain in subjection: so they rise in revolt, each on his own behalf.

In Bakhtin's later work, *The Dialogic Imagination,* he develops his notion that the self is made up of a polyphony of voices: as individuals, we are the result of the endless hubbub of social life. Bakhtin argues that the novel is the genre in which this polyphony is most fully and energetically conveyed to the reader.

See Bakhtin, *Problems of Dostoevski's Poetics* (1929), and *The Dialogic Imagination* (publ. 1981, written in the 1930s); Joseph Frank, "The Voices of Mikhail Bakhtin," in Frank, *Through the Russian Prism* (1990); Caryl Emerson and Gary Saul Morson, *Mikhail Bakhtin: The Creation of a Prosaics* (1991). See also CHRONOTOPE.

didactic Since antiquity, some critics have claimed that literature is, or ought to be, a didactic form: that it should demonstrate morals, instruct us in social responsibility, or, more broadly, show us universal truth. Like the Jews' Torah, Homer's epics were originally seen as not just a collection of narratives but a guide to life. In Plato's dialogue *Ion* (ca. 390 BCE), Socrates interviews a rhapsode (a performer of Homer's poetry) who asserts that all useful knowledge can be found in Homer. According to the rhapsode Ion, the *Iliad* and the *Odyssey* provide, in effect, instruction manuals for everything from the art of war to household management to how to get ahead in political life. But if Homer knew, and taught, everything, Socrates asks Ion, why wasn't he himself a great general or politician? And why aren't the best scholars of Homer also the most adept rulers or warriors? Ion has no good answer to Socrates' question, and his silence foreshadows a centuries-long confusion about what literature might be good for.

Plato's most famous dialogue, the *Republic* (ca. 370 BCE), aims to show, among other things, why literature cannot (why it does not want to) be didactic: why it cannot teach us as philosophy can. Poems and novels do not try to improve our lives in the manner of "self-help" books; they cannot enforce moral obligations, as religion aims to do. Yet many modern critics, from Matthew Arnold to Irving Howe, have suggested that literature does support, or at least describe an arena for, moral judgment. For Lionel Trilling, the realist novel refines our moral sensibility by asking us to react in a just and nuanced way to its depictions of social life.

See Charles Baudelaire, "The Didactic Heresy" (1859–69), in Richard Ellmann and Charles Feidelson, eds., *The Modern Tradition* (1965); Matthew Arnold, "The Function of Criticism at the Present Time" (1864); Lionel Trilling, *The Liberal Imagination* (1950); Martha Nussbaum, *Love's Knowledge* (1990); Willard Spiegelman, *The Didactic Muse* (1989).

différance A term coined by the French philosopher Jacques Derrida in his essay "Différance" (1968), and intended to incorporate two meanings, "to differ" and "to defer" or postpone (both of which are implied, as well, in the French verb *différer*). Derrida in his wide-ranging essay applies the idea of différance to the works of the linguist Ferdinand de Saussure, as well as Freud, Nietzsche, and the twentieth-century philosophers Martin Heidegger, Georges Bataille, and Emmanuel Lévinas. Différance, for Derrida, suggests that there is a system behind any written or spoken utterance, which enables meaning to exist. In Saussure, who influenced Derrida, the difference between phonemes is what creates meaning; significance does not reside in any particular phoneme. This concept applies to language as a whole, appearing most audibly in puns. (A pun works only because it plays with the difference between two words.)

I have just described the spatial aspect of différance, which exists in the gap between one word and another—whether the gap is in the dictionary or in the competence of the person who speaks or writes. But difference also has a temporal aspect: it defers, in addition to differing. Only a series of uses of a word, built up over time, can create linguistic meaning. Each of the occasions of use will be related, but these occasions will also differ from one another.

Derrida takes différance to imply that there is no firm distinction between speaking and writing, though these two aspects of linguistic expression often seem opposed to each other. We assume that speech takes place on a single, present occasion, and that the speaker is in control of what is said, whereas writing sometimes comes to us from an indefinite source and raises questions about the unreliability of authorial intention. Derrida argues that both the written and the spoken word signify only by means of différance, and therefore that what we take to be the substantial presence of a speaker understanding himself and communicating a message to listeners is actually just as elusive and uncertain as a scrap of writing, full of obscure expressions, by an unknown author.

Derrida relates différance to Freud's concept of *Nachträglichkeit* (deferred action). According to Freud, the primal scene, in which an infant witnesses its parents making love, never actually took place. This original, traumatic moment is necessarily colored by later knowledge, so the primal scene cannot be said to occur at a specific moment. Instead, it is made possible by the difference between an incident and a later understanding of that incident. If the infant really did see something, it was too young to understand what was happening. The knowledge of sex, which comes later, has to be read back into the original event, which therefore no longer seems to be original. Retrospective fantasy governs our sense of our own origins; so these origins cannot be separated from what we make of them later on. See Jacques Derrida, "Différance" (1968), in *Speech and Phenomena* (English language ed., 1973). See also DECONSTRUCTION; LOGOCENTRIC; POSTSTRUCTURALISM.

difficulty Literary difficulty is often associated with modernism and the avant-garde. The issue is a more general one, however. Dr. Johnson commented on some lines of Milton's "Lycidas" (1637) that "the true meaning is so uncertain and remote, that it is never sought, because it cannot be known when it is found."

Difficulty may be a way for authors to guard themselves against the incursions of a reader: to establish the powerful chastity of their writing, and so claim their authority. Robert Frost remarked, fiercely, in a letter to the editor Louis Untermeyer, "I'm in favor of a skin and fences and tariff walls. I'm in favor of reserves and withholding." Though Frost is often seen as a plain or accessible writer, his comment suggests that difficulty can take unexpected form: the simplest statements, in poetry at least, might turn out to be the hardest. T. S. Eliot propounded a different reason for difficulty, as a response to the perceived crisis of modern culture. "Poets in our civilization, as it exists at present, must be *difficult*," Eliot wrote in his essay "The Metaphysical Poets" (1921).

George Steiner in "On Difficulty" (*On Difficulty and Other Essays* [1978]) distinguishes among four types of difficulty. The easiest kind, contingent difficulty, can be looked up and dispelled by any reader. Next is modal difficulty, present because no single reader, or community of readers, can understand all aspects of the text in question. Tactical difficulty is an author's effort to produce "rich undecidability." Finally, ontological difficulty represents a deliberate violation of norms, raising questions concerning the "nature of human speech" and the "status of significance."

Vernon Shetley's *After the Death of Poetry* (1993) reflects in stimulating fashion on difficulty in recent American poetry. See also Howard Nemerov's essay "The Difficulty of Difficult Poetry," in *Reflexions on Poetry and Poetics* (1972); John Crowe Ransom, "Poets Without Laurels," in *The World's Body* (1938); as well as AVANT-GARDE; ELLIPTICAL POETRY; LANGUAGE POETRY; MODERNISM; PARAPHRASE.

Dionysian In *The Birth of Tragedy* (1872), the young classical scholar Friedrich Nietzsche described Greek art and culture in terms of two opposed principles: the cool, poised Apollonian and the wild, dark, ecstatic Dionysian. Apollo, the sun god and patron deity of poetry, presides over the first pole; Dionysus, the god of the tragic agon and of festive madness, over the second. According to Nietzsche, the Dionysian involves a communion: a sense of oneness with universal fate that enables one to experience the sufferings imposed on other individual beings. The Dionysian ecstasy conveys a wisdom that is profound, and in its celebratory embrace of suffering, somehow violent and barbaric—a knowledge superior to that of the reasonable self. According to Nietzsche, the Apollonian Socrates, with his reliance on reason and logic, could not understand the raw Dionysian essence of tragedy. In addition to *The Birth of Tragedy*, Nietzsche also takes up the concept of the Dionysian in his *Twilight of the Idols* (1888).

James Porter discusses Nietzsche's *Birth of Tragedy* in *The Invention of Dionysus* (2000). For the inheritance of Nietzsche's concept of the Dionysian in European modernism, consult John Burt Foster, Jr., *Heirs to Dionysus* (1981). The Dionysian was an influential term in the American 1960s. See Richard Schechner, ed., *Dionysus in 69* (1970), on the Living Theatre group, which presented drama as an ecstatic ritual form. See also APOLLONIAN.

discordia concors (concordia discors) A discordant harmony (or, harmonious discord), Latin; defined by Samuel Johnson in his *Life of Cowley* (1779) as "a combination of dissimilar images, or discovery of occult resemblances in things apparently unlike."

The tempering of opposed qualities, or mixing of various contrasting elements to form a unity, was an important ideal of Renaissance thought. In his *Boke Named the Governour* (1531) Thomas Elyot describes "a man and a woman dancing together": "And the moving of the man would be more vehement, of the woman more delicate, and with less advancing of the body, signifying the courage and strength that ought to be in a man and the pleasant soberness that should be in a woman. . . . These qualities in this wise being knit together and signified in the personages of man and woman dancing do express or set out the figure of very nobility."

As the critic Harry Berger describes it, Renaissance authors preside over "the norm of a complex harmony, an equilibrium in which opposites are at once distinct and reconciled, an experience in which the mind reveals not only the ability to organize the diversity of existence into a unified whole but also the ability to fix and vividly convey this whole in the immediacy of a visual or verbal or aural image."

Visual emblems of discordia concors were popular in the Renaissance (the hermaphrodite as an image of marriage, for example; see EMBLEM). As Rosalie Colie puts it, often in Renaissance thought "each thing contains or implies its opposite; each thing refers to transcendence." By the early eighteenth century the ideal had become more placid and accessible: Pope in *Windsor Forest* speaks of a landscape "where, tho' all things differ, all agree." See Berger, *Second World and Green World* (1988); Colie, *Paradoxia Epidemica* (1966). See also PARADOX.

The eighteenth century was also attracted to discordia concors (or concordia discors) as a harmonious diversity or blend of opposites, the wholeness shown by variety. During the Augustan Age (the early eighteenth century), concordia discors was an important aesthetic and moral ideal, promising the reconciliation of contrasting aspects of humanity. See Earl Wasserman's essay on John Denham's poem "Cooper's Hill" in *The Subtler Language* (1959).

discourse A common term in recent literary and cultural criticism. A discourse is the range of social practices, customs, and institutions surrounding a given subject matter, in addition to the subject matter itself. The popularity of the term stems in part from the French philosopher and social theorist Michel Foucault (1926–84). Foucault's lecture "The Discourse on Language" (1970) proclaims that "in every society the production of discourse is at once controlled, selected, organized, and redistributed according to a certain number of procedures. . . . Disciplines constitute a system of control in the production of discourse, fixing its limits through the action of an identity taking the form of a permanent reactivation of the rules."

Current criticism has often continued Foucault's emphasis on how discourses are regulated and produced, whether officially or informally, so that the knowledge they supply is bound up with the workings of social power.

See Michel Foucault, "The Discourse on Language," in Richard Kearney and Mara Rainwater, eds., *The Continental Philosophy Reader* (1996), and Paul Rabinow, ed., *The Foucault Reader* (1985). See also Friedrich Kittler, *Discourse Networks, 1800/1900* (1985).

discursive An ideal for poetry advocated by the poet Robert Pinsky in the 1970s, in his book *The Situation of Poetry* (1977). According to Pinsky, contemporary American poetry ought to be discursive: argumentative and lucid in a sustained way. Instead, he charged, poets often prefer the pathos afforded by the easily rhapsodic, the twisted, theatrical scene of passion, or the beautiful fragment. A similar opposition between lucidity and pathos as poetic goals characterizes the criticism of Charles Altieri (see, for example, Altieri's *Self and Sensibility in Contemporary American Poetry* [1984]).

Before Pinsky, the poet A. D. Hope championed the discursive: "that form in which the uses of poetry approach closest to the uses of prose, and yet remain essentially poetry" (A. D. Hope, "The Discursive Mode," in *The Cave and the Spring* [1965]). Such an ideal goes back, in English tradition, to William Wordsworth.

disinterestedness The ideal of distanced, appreciative, critical neutrality championed by Matthew Arnold. In "The Function of Criticism at the Present Time" (1864), Arnold writes: "And how is criticism to show disinterestedness? By keeping aloof from what is called 'the practical view of things'; by resolutely following the law of its own nature, which is to be a free play of the mind on all subjects which it touches. By steadily refusing to lend itself to any of those ulterior, political, practical considerations about ideas, which plenty of people will be sure to attach to them."

Before Arnold, Immanuel Kant's *Critique of Judgment* (1790) described our appreciation of art and literature as disinterested, because it involves an elevation beyond practical use and immediate advantage. A book is not a tool, to be relied on for a concrete worldly task; nor is it consumed like a meal. Rather, literary enjoyment involves an abstraction from such concerns, satisfying neither the pleasure of one's own peculiar tastes nor the wish to prompt, through action, an effect in the world. (For Kant, aesthetic beauty differs from personal taste because calling something beautiful implies the ability to justify it to others as beautiful, whereas one's taste is allowed to be idiosyncratic and unjustifiable.) See René Wellek, "Immanuel Kant's Aesthetics and Criticism," in *Discriminations* (1970). See also BEAUTIFUL.

dissociation of sensibility A phrase invented by T. S. Eliot to describe what he saw as the shift between poets like Shakespeare, the Jacobean dramatists, and Donne, who "could devour any kind of experience" and for whom thought was immediate "as the odour of a rose," and poets of the later seventeenth century like Milton and Dryden. For Eliot, these later poets were the victims of a divorce between thinking and feeling. After the metaphysical poets, Eliot concluded, a "dissociation of sensibility" set in, severing thinking from experience in poetry: "While the language became more refined, the feeling became more crude." By the eighteenth century, poets "thought and felt by fits, unbalanced." To pass such a judgment on poems like Milton's *Paradise Lost* and Keats's Odes was highly dubious, but Eliot's prejudices proved influential for a time; his notion of the dissociation of sensibility enjoyed a vogue, especially among the New Critics. See T. S. Eliot, "The Metaphysical Poets" (1921), in Frank Kermode, ed., *Selected Prose of T. S. Eliot* (1975); as well as Kermode, *The Romantic Image* (1957).

doggerel A ready and easy kind of verse, in jerking, cloddish rhythm. Often, its rhyme words clunk with obviousness, and its meter rides roughshod, coming down hard on stressed words. For example:

> I think that I shall never see
> A poem lovely as a tree.

(Joyce Kilmer.) Here the sentiment matches the formal qualities of the verse, as frequently in doggerel. Yet doggerel has its own rules, and can rise to impressive artfulness. John Skelton, the fifteenth-century English poet, was a genius of doggerel. Samuel Butler, author of the influential mock epic *Hudibras* (1663–78), also used the energy of doggerel with adeptness (as do current performers of hip-hop and rap music).

dolce stil nuovo Italian, the "sweet new style"; term invented by Dante in his *Divine Comedy* to designate the mellifluous, subtle writing of several late-thirteenth-century love poets, including Guido Guinizelli and Guido Cavalcanti. The stilnovisti were influenced by the troubadours, courtly love conventions, Thomistic theology, and the cult of the Virgin Mary. The ecstatic spirituality that colors their praise of love influenced Dante in his *Vita Nuova* (ca. 1292–93).

double dactyl A vigorous and almost invariably comic verse form, invented by the American poet Anthony Hecht. (A dactylic foot consists of a stressed syllable followed by two unstressed ones; see METER.) The double dactyl consists of two quatrains: the last line of the first rhymes with the last line of the second, and except for these two truncated lines, there are two double dactyls per line. Here is an example by Paul Pascal, inspired by Shakespeare's *Antony and Cleopatra:*

Pattycake, pattycake,
Marcus Antonius
Whaddaya think of the
African queen?

Gubernatorial
Duties require my
Presence in Egypt. Ya
Know what I mean?

For many more, consult *Jiggery Pokery* (1967), the anthology of double
dactyls edited by Anthony Hecht and John Hollander.

drab and golden poetry. See AUREATE

drama Derives from the Greek word for "doing," *draein:* a drama is something
done onstage. The first ancient Greek drama followed in the steps of religious
ritual. The tragic contests at the festival of Dionysus, dating from the early
fifth century BCE, were implicitly a new way of worshipping the god. But there
are differences between ritual observance and dramatic action. In the ancient
world, ritual usually required animal sacrifice; in tragic drama, the hero is sac-
rificed onstage. Rituals do not involve us by way of identification with a character, as plays do, and they do not depend on surprise or suspense. It is perhaps
because ancient Greek religion strongly emphasized the power of the gods to
surprise us, to intervene in our lives and sometimes overturn them, that drama
became a chosen form for the honoring of the divine. (The religion of ancient
Israel had a similar emphasis on the surprising actions of its god, but it produced no form similar to the Greek stage drama.)

The fundamental situation of drama is the presence of an actor or actors
onstage, facing us and eliciting our response. But drama in the theater also
invokes, and seeps over into, ordinary life, which is filled with theatrical gestures and roles. For some influential reflections on these matters, see Francis
Fergusson, *The Idea of a Theatre* (1949); Erving Goffman, *Frame Analysis*
(1974); Bert States, *Irony and Drama* (1971); and Bruce Wilshire, *Role-Playing
and Identity* (1982). Michael Goldman in *On Drama* (2000) persuasively explores the themes of failed intimacy, restlessness, and identification in modern drama. The connection between theater and rituals like games and hunting is explored in Richard Schechner's *Performance Theory* (1977).

Among the major modern playwrights who have contributed to the theory of drama, both by their example and (in some cases) by their critical pronouncements, are Henrik Ibsen, August Strindberg, Anton Chekhov, Bertolt Brecht, Eugene O'Neill, Eugène Ionesco, Samuel Beckett, and Robert Wilson. The Russian Konstantin Stanislavski produced an influential theory of acting in *An Actor Prepares* (1936), emphasizing the actor's spontaneity, absorption in his role, and identification with the character being portrayed. Stanislavski had a strong impact on the Group Theater of Harold Clurman, Stella Adler, and Lee Strasberg in the late 1920s and 1930s, and on the "method acting" ethos of Strasberg's Actors' Studio, which had its heyday in the 1950s. Antonin Artaud in *The Theatre and Its Double* (1938) developed the radically avant-garde idea of a "theater of cruelty" (see THEATER OF CRUELTY).

C. L. Barber comments interestingly on the difference between religious ritual and theater in *Creating Elizabethan Tragedy* (1988). On Greek drama, consult H. D. F. Kitto, *Greek Tragedy* (1939); Cedric Whitman, *The Heroic Paradox* (1988); and John Winkler and Froma Zeitlin, eds., *Nothing to Do with Dionysus?* (1990). Finally, a good history of English-language theater during its most significant period, the Elizabethan and Jacobean years, is J. Leeds Barroll, Alexander Leggatt, Richard Hosley, and Alvin Kernan, *The Revels History of Drama in English,* vol. 3, 1576–1613 (1975).

dramatic monologue The dramatic monologue is a poem spoken by a character other than the poet: in contrast to the usual speaker of lyric, who tends to be more elusive and undefined, or a neutral representative of thought or mood. Often, but not always, a dramatic monologue directs itself to a particular audience within the poem (in addition to us, the audience without). So in Robert Browning's "My Last Duchess" (1842) the Duke of Ferrara speaks to an ambassador from a count who is offering his daughter in marriage to the duke.

Browning is the undisputed master of the dramatic monologue in English. The form reached its peak with his works and with Alfred, Lord Tennyson (e.g., "Ulysses" [1842]), but T. S. Eliot's *The Waste Land* (1922) and William Carlos Williams's *Paterson* (1946–58) contain significant fragments of dramatic monologue. There are some later distinguished practitioners of dramatic monologue, notably the American poet Richard Howard, beginning with his *Untitled Subjects* (1969).

T. S. Eliot's lecture "The Three Voices of Poetry" (1953) notes that dramatic monologues are usually delivered by characters already known to the reader, whether from history or from previous works of literature. "The poet, speaking, as Browning does, in his own voice," Eliot writes, "cannot bring a character to life: he can only mimic a character otherwise known to us. And does not the point of mimicry lie . . . in the incompleteness of the illusion?" Eliot associates the poet of the dramatic monologue with the didactic, the satirical, and the epic poet—with "the voice of the poet addressing other people," as opposed to the self-directed voice of lyric. See Herbert F. Tucker, "Dramatic Monologue and the Overhearing of Lyric," in Chaviva Hošek and Patricia Parker, eds., *Lyric Poetry* (1985); Robert Langbaum, *The Poetry of Experience* (1957).

dream vision The dream vision is a literary genre, usually in verse, and significantly related to allegory. The protagonist experiences an adventurous vision during his sleep, often involving a spiritual guide and various revelations concerning life or the cosmos. The genre was especially popular in the Middle Ages. Some well-known dream visions are the *Romance of the Rose* (ca. 1230–75) by Guillaume de Lorris and Jean de Meun, and no fewer than four poems by Chaucer: *The Book of the Duchess, The Parliament of Fowles, The House of Fame,* and the prologue to *The Legend of Good Women* (all written between about 1370 and the mid-1390s). The *Pearl* and *Piers Plowman,* from the same period as Chaucer, are also dream visions. It was also a significant Romantic form, in Keats's *Hyperion* (1818–19) and *The Fall of Hyperion* (1819) and Shelley's *The Triumph of Life* (1822). Latter-day dream visions include *Alice in Wonderland* and, in movies, *The Wizard of Oz* and David Lynch's *Mulholland Drive.* See A. C. Spearing, *Medieval Dream-Poetry* (1976).

dulce et utile In Latin, "sweet and useful": this is the Roman poet Horace's two-pronged recommendation for what a poem should offer, as outlined in his *Ars Poetica* (Art of Poetry, ca. 20 BCE). *Utile* (useful) implies didactic content; whereas *dulce* (sweet) means delightful enjoyment. Horace's tagline becomes prominent in later literary criticism, especially during the Renaissance. Philip Sidney writes that poets "imitate both to delight and teach, and delight to move men to take that goodness in hand, which without delight they would fly as from a stranger" (*Apology for Poetry* [written 1583, publ. 1595]). So, in Sidney's version, dulce is useful because it leads us to utile. Bernard Weinberg's *History of Literary Criticism in the Italian Renaissance* (1961) provides a fascinating survey of the twists and turns that Horace's formula underwent during the Renaissance. See also DIDACTIC.

early modern A currently popular replacement for the term *Renaissance,* used to describe the period of European literature and culture stretching from about 1450 to about 1650. Whereas Renaissance implies a focus on the revival of classical culture, early modern suggests a continuity with the present day. (The term was originally applied in linguistics, to cover the period between 1500 and 1700—after Middle English and before Modern English.)

Long ago, Jacob Burckhardt's wonderful and daring *The Civilization of the Renaissance in Italy* (1860) asserted that the Renaissance marked the birth of the modern individual, rather than being a look back at the ancient past, as its name would suggest (*renaissance* means "rebirth"). In some ways, Burckhardt is the (largely unacknowledged) precursor of academics who announce that they are scholars of, not the Renaissance, but the early modern period— though Burckhardt also attended to the revival of classical learning and the importance of ancient models of philosophy, art, and science in the sixteenth century. For an appreciation of Burckhardt, see William Kerrigan and Gordon Braden, *The Idea of the Renaissance* (1989). See also RENAISSANCE LITERATURE.

echo A literary echo is one way for a piece of writing to allude to earlier works. (See ALLUSION.) As some critics explain the term, an echo is evocative rather than emphatic, based in mood rather than in specific fact. Instead of just pointing to an earlier text in a particular, local way, an echo takes on the way the earlier text sounds, hearing and responding to its concerns. At the beginning of *Paradise Lost* (1667), Milton *alludes* to the story of Moses and the places associated with him (Mount Horeb and Mount Sinai), but he *echoes* the beginning of the Bible (thought to have been written by Moses):

In the beginning how the heav'ns and earth
Rose out of chaos . . .

An echo itself, properly speaking, is not written, but vocal. As John Hollander points out, the origin of the term in a sonic effect calls up an association between literary echo and "a lurking and invisible vocal presence." Pastoral poetry uses the figure of echo when shepherds, who have become their own audience, delight to hear their songs resounding among woods, caves, and mountains (as in Philip Sidney's "Ye Goatherd Gods" [1593]).

In Bk. 3 of Ovid's *Metamorphoses* (ca. 8 CE), the nymph Echo, in love with Narcissus and vainly repeating his words, dwindles to a mere voice. The crossed signals of the Echo-Narcissus story carry on into a poem like George Herbert's "Heaven," where it is unclear whether the second voice confirms, or merely repeats without grasping, the first voice (and does the first voice even hear the second?):

> Then tell me, what is the supreme delight?
> > *Echo, Light.*
> Light to the minde; what shall the will enjoy?
> > *Echo, Joy.*

The medieval interpreter Macrobius allegorized Echo as the harmony of the spheres, married to Pan (*pan* is Greek for "all"). See John Hollander, *The Figure of Echo* (1981).

eclogue A term for a pastoral poem, from Virgil's *Eclogues* (39–38 BCE). Eclogues means "selections"—though there is a suggestive false etymology stemming from the Greek word for goat, so that pastorals are also sometimes known as "goat-songs." See BUCOLICS; PASTORAL.

ecocriticism A term coined by William Rueckert in 1978 for criticism focused on writings about the natural world. The ecocritic asserts that the natural environment is a central subject matter for humanistic concern. At the same time, ecocritics tend to suggest that nature is alien to human culture. Nature, in its indifference, exposes as false human attempts to use it for our own symbolic purposes; but the naturalist who properly attends to the environment can enlist it fruitfully.

Ecocriticism can be seen as a peculiar version of pastoral. Determined to solve the complex situation of humans living in a world that is "not our own and, much more, not ourselves" (Wallace Stevens), ecocritics put their faith in the reconciling simplicity of a landscape. But they also assert, in contrast to traditional pastoral, that the landscape is essentially foreign, a scene that cannot supply us with the aesthetic and emotional satisfactions that we want. See Lawrence Buell, *The Environmental Imagination* (1995); Jonathan Bate, *Song of the Earth* (2000); and, for a critique of ecocriticism, Dana Phillips, *The Truth of Ecology* (2003). Angus Fletcher's *A New Theory for American Poetry* (2004) thoughtfully explores the issue of environmentalism in relation to American poets, especially Walt Whitman and John Ashbery. See also Bonnie Costello, *Shifting Ground* (2003); PASTORAL.

Edwardian Age The Edwardian Age was the reign of King Edward VII (1901–10). By extension, it covers the period from the death of Queen Victoria in 1901 to the beginning of the Great War, which we know as World War I (1914–18). English and Irish literature possessed a number of prominent writers during this period, among them Rudyard Kipling, Henry James (who had moved to England from America in 1876), Joseph Conrad, George Bernard Shaw, Arnold Bennett, John Galsworthy, J. M. Synge, H. G. Wells, Thomas Hardy, Ford Madox Ford, Katherine Mansfield, and W. B. Yeats. Some of these writers (Hardy, Conrad, Yeats, and James, especially) substantially influenced the modernists, and could be considered modernists themselves. Others, however (Wells, Bennett, and Galsworthy, for example), are sometimes—unfairly—seen as representing a stuffiness or moralizing naïveté, in contrast to the darker, more knowing moderns. See Virginia Woolf's essay "Mr. Bennett and Mrs. Brown" (1924); Lionel Trilling, "Rudyard Kipling" (in *The Liberal Imagination* [1950]); and Samuel Hynes, *The Edwardian Turn of Mind* (1968).

ekphrasis, ekphrastic An ekphrastic text describes a work of art, usually a painting or sculpture. *Ekphrasis* is the word for this verbal evocation of the visual: for literature's conversation with a silent counterpart.

　　John Hollander describes ekphrastic poetry as "poems addressed to silent works of art, questioning them, describing them as they could never describe—but merely present—themselves; speaking for them; making them speak out or speak up. . . . They seek to break open the self-absorption with which all images seem to be veiled."

　　One of the earliest ekphrases in literary history is the description of the shield of Achilles in Homer's *Iliad* (Bk. 18). In this instance, the shield itself provides a scheme, an organizational model of human life in its times of peace and war, celebration and lament. The shield of Achilles, as a synoptic remark on human existence in its collaborative and competitive aspects, stands apart from the *Iliad*. Inset in the poem, its wholeness frames Homer's epic, offering a perspective on the *Iliad*'s partiality, its obsession with strife. (See W. H. Auden's poem "The Shield of Achilles" [1955].)

Another famous ekphrastic moment is the episode in Bk. 1 of Virgil's *Aeneid* in which Aeneas and his men see, depicted on the murals in Dido's Carthage, an event they themselves experienced directly and traumatically: the fall of Troy. Here, the reaction of Aeneas to the story told by the murals becomes an integral part of the scene. His remark *sunt lacrimae rerum* (roughly, "here are tears for the things of the world") witnesses the power of art to sum up the meaning of an action, in a way that makes the participants themselves an audience to what they have seen and suffered.

Some later ekphrastic poems are Keats's "Ode on a Grecian Urn" (1819); Wallace Stevens's minor counterpart to the Keats poem, "Anecdote of the Jar" (1919); and Rilke's "Archaic Torso of Apollo." Rilke's two volumes of *New Poems* (1907–8) include many remarkable instances of ekphrasis. Reflections on, and examples of, ekphrastic poetry can be found in John Hollander, *The Gazer's Spirit* (1995).

elegy The term *elegy* is usually used for a poem of mourning, lamenting the death of a friend, lover, or family member. But in the ancient world an elegy was any lyric poem written in elegiac meter, a variation on the hexameter used in Greek and Roman epic. In elegiac verse, every other line is pentameter rather than hexameter, thus lacking the foot it would need to be properly epic. Ovid (43 BCE–17 CE) jokes in his *Elegies* that he was intending to write an epic, when Cupid swooped down and stole a foot from his second line, thwarting his plans and turning him into a love poet instead.

In the tradition of Ovid's *Elegies,* erotic verses in the Renaissance were sometimes called elegies as well: John Donne wrote amorous elegies, for example. But the word *elegy* was already beginning to mean a poem devoted to, and often directly addressing, a dead person. (Goethe's *Roman Elegies* [1795], however, retained the erotic meaning of *elegy*.)

Milton's "Lycidas" (1637), often regarded as the greatest elegy in English, models itself in part after ancient Greek pastoral elegies by Bion, Moschus, and Theocritus, as well as several of Virgil's eclogues (39–38 BCE). "Lycidas" represents an important subgenre of elegy, an elegy for another poet. Among other such poems are Edmund Spenser's "Astrophel," dedicated to Philip

Sidney (1595); Percy Bysshe Shelley's "Adonais," which remembers Keats (1821); and W. H. Auden's "In Memory of W. B. Yeats" (1939). In all these poems, as in Virgil's sixth eclogue, the dead poet represents the possibilities of song, and his case offers the survivor an occasion to meditate on poetic vocation: what poets are for, and how their work outlives them.

The elegiac mood, broader than elegy itself, evokes the pervasive presence of loss and the transience of the things of this world. Thomas Gray's "Elegy Written in a Country Churchyard" (1751) is an example of this more encompassing use of the term.

Other important elegies in English are Tennyson's cycle *In Memoriam* (1850); Whitman's "When Lilacs Last in the Door-yard Bloom'd" (1865–66); and Yeats's "In Memory of Major Robert Gregory" (1918). Rainer Maria Rilke's *Duino Elegies* and *Hymns to Orpheus* (1922–23) represent a momentous redefining of the elegy in its relation to vision and desire. See Peter Sacks, *The English Elegy* (1985), and R. Jahan Ramazani, *Poetry of Mourning* (1994).

Elizabethan Age The reign of Queen Elizabeth (1558–1603) was a great age of English literature, particularly remarkable for the flowering of drama in the works of Christopher Marlowe, Ben Jonson, and above all William Shakespeare. The first London public theater, called the Theatre, was established in 1576; Shakespeare's Globe was built in 1599. Among the major poetic works of the age were Edmund Spenser's *Shepheardes Calender* (1579) and *The Faerie Queene* (1590–96), and Philip Sidney's *Astrophel and Stella* (1591). The era also represented a triumph of Renaissance humanism in works by Roger Ascham, Thomas Elyot, and others. (See also EARLY MODERN; HUMANISM; RENAISSANCE LITERATURE.)

elliptical poetry A term recently made popular by the poet and critic Stephen Burt for a kind of lyric poetry popular in the 1990s and after: oblique, without a readily discernable scene (or even, at times, an identifiable speaker), and implying a cloudy, gnomic hypothesis rather than a clear argument. Frequently, epistemological uncertainty is a theme, moods shift rapidly, and the style is built on paradoxical assertions and hyperactive uses of repetition.

Burt was apparently influenced by Robert Penn Warren's essay "Pure and Impure Poetry" (1943), which uses the term *elliptical* to sum up T. S. Eliot's sense that some poets "become impatient of this 'meaning' [the explicit statement of ideas in logical order] which seems superfluous, and perceive possibilities of intensity through its elimination." The pregnancy of the elliptical mode, implying that there is a secretive wisdom concealed in the poem, differentiates it from much language poetry, which tends to be more frenetic and random in its energies. In twentieth-century American poetry, Wallace Stevens, Hart Crane, Gertrude Stein, and John Ashbery are among the ancestors of the elliptical mode. See the forum with Stephen Burt and others, "Elliptical Poetry," *American Letters and Commentary* 11 (1999), 45–76. See also CLOSURE; GNOMIC; LANGUAGE POETRY.

emblem An emblem is a pictorial version of an idea. It implies an argument: a blindfolded, because impartial, woman holding up a pair of scales is an emblem of justice—and how different than if she carried, say, a pair of handcuffs and a sword!

The emblem, also called an *impresa* or *device,* was a major Renaissance form: a pictorial representation that, like our image of justice, offered itself for decoding, with the help of a verbal tag or lines of verse appended to it. (Often there was a motto printed above the picture and a poem beneath it.) "A sweet and morall Symbole, which consists of picture and words," as it was described by Henri Estienne in 1646, the emblem was a key influence on Renaissance poets including Edmund Spenser, Ben Jonson, Richard Crashaw, and George Herbert.

The emblem resembles a diagram or miniature map of a subject; it was also called a "silent parable" (by Francis Quarles). The parabolic or riddling nature of the (in this case, purely verbal) emblem can be seen in the following passage from the Bible's book of Amos (8:2): "Thus hath the Lord GOD showed unto me: and behold a basket of summer fruit. And he said, Amos, what seest thou? And I said, A basket of summer fruit. Then said the LORD unto me, The end is come upon my people of Israel; I will not again pass by them any more. And the songs of the temple shall be howlings in that day." (For a commentary on the image from Amos, see Guy Davenport's extraordinary *Objects on a Table* [1998].)

Spenser's *The Faerie Queene* (1590–96) relies on Andrea Alciati's *Emblems* (1531) as a springboard for several of its most memorable episodes. Alciati's book was vastly popular in the Renaissance, as was Cesare Ripa's *Iconology* (1593). Geoffrey Whitney's *A Choice of Emblems* (1586) was the first English emblem book. Francis Quarles's *Emblems* (1635) was the best-known English Protestant emblem book. (For a discussion of Quarles, see Ernest Gilman, *Iconoclasm and Poetry in the English Reformation* [1986].)

Several of George Herbert's poems in *The Temple* (1633) are verbal emblems, in one way or another: "The Altar" is shaped like an altar; "Love Unknown" appears to be a commentary on a picture of a tortured heart, a popular emblem in Herbert's day. In the emblem books, the fundamental stillness of the visual image is allied to an epigrammatic fixing of meaning; but Herbert dramatizes, or moves, the meaning. William Blake's illuminated books represent a later pairing of words and vision that at times echoes the emblem book tradition, while far surpassing it in subtlety and grandeur.

There is, it could be argued, a deep relation between the compactness and coherence that visual emblems rely on and the concentration of a lyric poem. "Emblem is immeasurable—that is why it is better than fulfillment, which can be drained," wrote Emily Dickinson in one of her letters. She meant that the emblematic is, in some way, the model of a figure: that it offers itself for, and issues into, endless interpretive meditation. A Dickinson poem is often emblematic—which does not mean that it can easily be visualized, but rather that it seems to have a picture's concentric force, setting out a display of telling, strange relations. See Marjorie Donker and George Muldrow, "Emblem," in their *Dictionary of Literary-Rhetorical Conventions of the Renaissance* (1982); and Rosemary Freeman, *English Emblem Books* (1948). Northrop Frye connects the riddle to the emblem in his *Anatomy of Criticism* (1957), 300–301.

Enlightenment The "age of reason," which was determined to question prevailing customs and beliefs, particularly those associated with religion, and wished to expose human society to rational inquiry. A number of eighteenth-century thinkers are associated with the Enlightenment, including Voltaire, Denis Diderot, Gotthold Ephraim Lessing, Moses Mendelssohn, Jean-Jacques Rousseau, David Hume, and Immanuel Kant. Voltaire and Diderot relied on skeptical wit in the face of convention; an unfriendly evaluation of comfortable, habitual attitudes was a necessary part of their efforts to depend on reason rather than received ideas.

Lessing and Kant looked forward to mankind's maturity. With the ascendance of reason in enlightened minds, people would (they hoped) at last depart from childlike superstition. Freed from the bondage of custom, humanity would be released as well from the backward idea that religion must be based on experiences of revelation offered to figures like Moses or Jesus. Instead, religion would be founded in rational reflection.

All Enlightenment thinkers share a desire to appreciate the creation as if it were designed for the benefit of man's rational inquiry. The ultimate form of Enlightenment religion is deism, the reduction of God to the idea of an unmoved mover who planned and constructed the universe in a logical, sensible way. So conceived, the world can withstand the best efforts of humans to muddle this clarity with their barbarous violence and unthinking prejudice. Deism reveals the visible optimism at the heart of the Enlightenment. See Peter Gay, *The Enlightenment: An Interpretation* (1966); Isidore Schneider, ed., *The Enlightenment* (1965).

ennui A malady of great intellectual prestige in the nineteenth century, ennui is a sort of thoughtful languor, or reflective boredom. It is descended from *acedia,* the slothful lack of will stigmatized by Christian theologians in the Middle Ages. Ennui is also related to melancholia, a highly fashionable disease of inwardness in the Renaissance (epitomized in Shakespeare's Hamlet). For the man of ennui as for the melancholy man, the world's uses are stale and unprofitable, their taste bitter. As with melancholia, the exhausted lucidity of ennui (called *spleen* by one of its major proponents, or victims, the French poet Charles Baudelaire) implies a nameless woe, a disillusionment that understands itself as no one else can. In the twentieth century, Rainer Maria Rilke (in his *Notebooks of Malte Laurids Brigge* [1910]) and Thomas Mann (in *The Magic Mountain* [1924]) are among the major analysts of ennui.

We often think of ennui as the world-weary aspect of someone who has (so he or she claims) been through everything. The young Stephane Mallarmé sighed, "La chair est triste" (The flesh is sad), adding that he had read all the books. But ennui can also be an incipient mood, somewhat bleakly preparing to open itself to whatever might happen. Adam Phillips in *On Kissing, Tickling, and Being Bored* (1993) describes boredom as "that state of suspended anticipation in which things are started and nothing begins."

Ennui's cousin, important among the English Romantics, is indolence: see Willard Spiegelman, *Majestic Indolence* (1995). See Baudelaire, *Paris Spleen* (1860), and Reinhard Kuhn, *The Demon of Noontide* (1976); also Patricia Spacks, *Boredom* (1995). See also DECADENCE.

epic Epic is traditionally seen as the largest and highest literary form, a genre with the ambition to define a whole culture. (Aristotle in his *Poetics* [330 BCE] notes that the epic contains everything in the next highest genre, tragedy, but that the reverse is not true.) The epic tends to become a kind of scripture, summing up the virtues and inherited gravity of a nation: "the privileged and summary testament of a people and their epoch," as James Nohrnberg puts it. In this sense, the five books of Moses (Genesis, Exodus, Leviticus, Numbers, and Deuteronomy) are the epic of ancient Israel, as Homer's *Iliad* and *Odyssey* are the epics of archaic Greece.

Epics present narratives of sustained obligation, handed down from heaven to earth; they require the interaction of higher and lower beings, gods and mortals. The themes of Homer's two epics are Achilles' *menis*, or wrath (in the *Iliad*), and the quest of Odysseus (in the *Odyssey*). Virgil's *Aeneid* (ca. 27–19 BCE), the epic of Rome, combines the two, centering on the wrath of Juno and the quest of Aeneas. Inasmuch as Virgil is consciously belated in respect to Homer, he stands as an example of "secondary epic": a status shared by Ovid in his *Metamorphoses* (ca. 8 CE) in relation to both Homer and Virgil. John Milton's *Paradise Lost* (1667) both exploits and attempts to reverse such belatedness. Milton claims that the Greek and Roman poets, his cherished predecessors, are further from the sacred source of meaning than he himself is—since, unlike the ancients, Milton is attuned to biblical revelation.

The Roman poet Lucretius (ca. 94–50 BCE), in *On the Nature of Things,* opened a new path for epic. His intricate, and sometimes harsh, scientific poem explains the ways of the universe, life and death, from a position of godlike detachment.

The epic is comprehensive, even encyclopedic, in its scope, but it tends to start *in medias res,* "in the middle of things," rather than at the very beginning, as Horace notes in *Ars Poetica* (Art of Poetry, ca. 20 BCE). After Milton's *Paradise Lost* (1667) and Blake's major poems, verse epic in the English-speaking tradition diminished greatly—but there are some later distinguished examples, like James Merrill's *The Changing Light at Sandover* (1982), William Carlos Williams's *Paterson* (1946–58), and Ezra Pound's *Cantos* (1925–69). William Wordsworth's *Prelude* (1805–50) is a long poem drawing on epic, but it argues against the epic wish for a high subject given to the poet from above. Instead, Wordsworth's theme, the growth of the poet's mind, is generated from within. In place of the expansive, multifarious narrative characteristic of epic, the *Prelude* presents an individual, autobiographical story.

Some prose fictions have aspired to epic status. Balzac's series of novels collectively titled *The Human Comedy* (1830–50) comprises an epic of social life.

Joyce's *Ulysses* (1922) draws on Homeric situations while giving a many-sided version of a quest that involves vast, diverting fields of knowledge, from astronomy to politics to religion. Joyce's novelistic attention raises the trivia of daily life to epic status, though the epic is usually uninterested in such ephemera. Finally, Thomas Pynchon's *Gravity's Rainbow* (1973) attempts epic scope in its apocalyptic narration of World War II. Like Lucretius, Pynchon unites a panoramic vision of human motivation with theoretical physics.

See Michael Seidel and Edward Mendelson, eds., *Homer to Brecht* (1977); James Nohrnberg, *The Analogy of the Faerie Queene* (1976), on the epic traditions that inform Edmund Spenser's epic romance, *The Faerie Queene;* C. S. Lewis, *A Preface to Paradise Lost* (1941); Thomas M. Greene, *The Descent from Heaven* (1963); David Quint, *Epic and Empire* (1993); and Colin Burrow, *Epic Romance* (1993). Mark Van Doren memorably evokes Lucretius in his chapter on the poet in *The Noble Voice* (1946).

epic simile A simile (that is, a verbal comparison, usually using the words *like* or *as*) of the kind found in Homer, Virgil, Dante, Milton, and other epic poets. The epic simile frequently offers an extended set piece, characteristically invoking a scene seemingly alien to the one being described in the main narrative—but more familiar to the poem's audience than the epic subject itself. For example, in the *Iliad,* a poem occupied with exotic warfare, the matter of the epic similes is frequently pastoral: Homer's audience would have known about everyday life in the countryside. Here is the comparison of Achilles' shield to a shepherds' fire seen by sailors, from Bk. 19 of the *Iliad.* Achilles, says Homer,

> hoisted the massive shield flashing far and wide
> like a full round moon—and gleaming bright as the light
> that reaches sailors out at sea, the flare of a watchfire
> burning strong in a lonely sheepfold up some mountain slope
> when the gale-winds hurl the crew that fights against them
> far over the fish-swarming sea, far from loved ones—
> so the gleam from Achilles' well-wrought blazoned shield
> shot up and hit the skies.

(Translation by Robert Fagles.) Within the simile, the sailors wracked by winds are far removed from the "lonely shepherd," just as the ingeniously fashioned, glinting shield is removed from the ferocious and desperate *aris-*

teia, the death-dealing rampage that Achilles is about to commence. Here, the distance between the fields of action that the simile ties together makes for ominous suggestion.

There is an interesting discussion of Virgil's epic similes in Michael C. J. Putnam, *The Poetry of the Aeneid* (1965).

epic theater A form of drama associated with the German playwright Bertolt Brecht. For a description of the ideals and methods of Brechtian epic theater, see ALIENATION EFFECT.

epigram Originally, an *epigram* was an inscription on a monument, or on a made object such as a vase. During the Hellenistic period, in the third century BCE, there was a great outpouring of epigrams written in books, rather than inscribed on stone or clay. (Frequent subjects were wine, women, the love of boys, and the pleasures of song.)

The Roman poet Martial, active about 80–100 CE, was a famous and salacious author of epigrams. Martial's epigrams include praise for patrons, commemorations of public events, social satire, and cruel jokes, as well as some determined obscenity.

In the Renaissance, George Puttenham remarked that the epigram is a "short and sweete" form "in which every mery conceited man might without any long studie or tedious ambage, make his frend sport, and anger his foe, and give a prettie nip, or shew a sharpe conceit [i.e., idea] in few verses" (*The Art of English Poesy,* 1589). Epigrams of both praise and blame were a popular Renaissance genre, notably in the poetry of Ben Jonson. The critic J. C. Scaliger in his *Poetics* (1560) divided epigrams into four kinds: gall, vinegar, salt, and honey (that is, an epigram could be bitterly angry, sour, salacious, or sweet).

The epigram is, by definition, compact, pungent, and insightful: "a short, sharp saying in prose and verse," as Ambrose Bierce defined the term in *The Devil's Dictionary* (1881–1911). J. V. Cunningham (1911–85) was a distinguished modern writer of epigrams. Here is one from Cunningham, an epitaph in the form of an epigram:

Naked I came, naked I leave the scene
And naked was my pastime in between.

On the Hellenistic epigram, see Kathryn Gutzwiller, *Poetic Garlands* (1998); on the Renaissance epigram, Rosalie Colie, *The Resources of Kind* (1973), and

Joseph Summers, *The Heirs of Donne and Jonson* (1970). Geoffrey Hartman discusses the four types of epigram in his essay "Beyond Formalism" (from *Beyond Formalism* [1970]). See also APHORISM; WIT.

epistemology The philosophical study of knowledge: how and what we know. Epistemology is distinct from ontology, which occupies itself with the question of being (i.e., why and how things exist, or what existence itself is); aesthetics, the study of artistic perception; and ethics, which focuses on human character.

epistolary novel A novel composed of letters written and received by its characters. The epistolary novel was greatly popular in the eighteenth century, as witnessed by the success of Samuel Richardson's *Pamela* (1740) and *Clarissa* (1747–48).

Among the many women authors who produced epistolary novels in eighteenth-century France and England were Eliza Haywood, Maria Edgeworth, Charlotte Lennox, and Madame Beccary. Consult April Alliston, *Virtue's Faults* (1996), for an account.

Other well-known examples of epistolary novels include *Dangerous Liaisons* by Pierre Choderlos de Laclos (1782) and *Dracula* by Bram Stoker (1897), which incorporates both letters and diary entries. Nicola Watson, *Revolution and the Form of the British Novel, 1790–1825* (1994) focuses on epistolary fiction. See SENSIBILITY; SENTIMENT.

epitaph (From Greek *epi-*, "on," and *taphos,* "grave" or "tomb.") An epitaph is a poem or statement either actually inscribed on a gravestone or written as if it were so inscribed. The epitaph differs from the elegy, which also commemorates the dead, in that it characteristically refers to the deceased in the third person (rather than the second person, as frequently in elegy). Some common epitaphic motifs are the injunction to the passer-by to halt or stop, in order to read the words of the poem; the plea that the earth lie gently on the deceased; and the evocation of the deceased's virtue. There are also self-epitaphs, like this one by the seventeenth-century poet Robert Herrick:

Thus I
Passe by,
And die:

As One,
Unknown,
And gon:
I'm made
A shade,
And laid
I'th grave,
There have
My Cave.
Where tell
I dwell,
Farewell.   .

See Joshua Scodel, *The English Poetic Epitaph* (1991).

epithalamion (or epithalamium)   (The Greek word is *epithalamion;* the synonymous Latin one, *epithalamium.*) Originally, in ancient Greece, a song or
speech delivered at the door of a bridal chamber, on the occasion of the wedding night. Sappho (late seventh century BCE) was well known for her epithalamia, most of which have been lost. Catullus (ca. 84–54 BCE) wrote two
influential epithalamia, his poems 61 and 62, the latter featuring alternating
choruses of young men and young women. In the English tradition, Edmund Spenser's *Epithalamium* (1595), written for his own wedding, has been
very important for later poets.

George Puttenham in his *Arte of English Poesie* (1589) uses the epithalamion to propose an unusual defense of poetry as decorous camouflage. Describing the epithalamion as it was performed among the ancients, Puttenham writes, "The tunes of the song were very loude and shrill, to the intent
there might no noise be heard out of the bed chamber by the skreeking and
outcry of the young damosell feeling the first forces of her stiffe & rigorous
young man . . ."

epithet   An epithet is a fixed phrase attached to a god or human in Homer's
Iliad and *Odyssey,* later imitated by Virgil and other writers of epic. Athena in
the Iliad, for example, is *glaukopis Athene* (gray-green-eyed Athena), and Aeneas is *pius Aeneas* (dutiful Aeneas). In an oral epic like Homer's, epithets occur frequently because they fill, easily and predictably, a metrical gap in the
line—giving the maker of the poem a breather.

James Nohrnberg notes that, in the *Iliad,* a warrior's name and epithet adjust themselves to their fixed places in Homer's hexameter line, and that this positioning suggests a similar adaptation of each character to the heroic code, "the preordained measures on the dancing floor of the battlefield." See Nohrnberg, "The *Iliad,*" in Michael Seidel and Edward Mendelson, eds., *Homer to Brecht* (1977). The metrical function of epithets in Homer was originally discovered in the 1930s by the scholar Milman Parry: see ORAL LITERATURE.

essay From the French *essayer,* to try or attempt, *essay* became the name for a literary genre with the publication of the first two volumes of Michel de Montaigne's *Essays* (1580). The essayist tries his or her hand at observation and reflection, in an effort to convey what the world and the self feel like. Essayists characteristically combine remarks about humanity with revelations of their own ordinary lives; they shy away from both the systematic manner of the philosopher and the thorough stocktaking of the memoirist. The "familiar essay" or "personal essay" tends to be intimate and confiding in tone, while also addressing our common afflictions, blessings, and annoyances.

The essay sometimes aims at pragmatic benefits. The Roman essayist Seneca (ca. 4 BCE–65 CE) wrote on subjects like anger and friendship, hoping to provide his readers, as well as himself, with therapeutic and moral help. In the Renaissance, Francis Bacon's *Essays* (1597–1625) were crisp, economical, and intended for practical use. The lasting intersection of the essay and journalism first occurred in the early eighteenth century, when the works of Joseph Addison and Richard Steele appeared in newspapers (the *Tatler* and the *Spectator*).

Perhaps the two preeminent essayists in Western tradition are Montaigne and Ralph Waldo Emerson, whose most important writing appeared in the 1840s. Montaigne writes cheerfully and heartily about his dead father, his gallstones, his religious doubts, and his daily habits; also about cannibals, military tactics, and the sex lives of the ancients. Emerson's reach is more cosmic and less gossipy, but just as rooted in authorial personality. He balances momentously among his sentences, moving from one question, announcement, or musing to the next like (in the words of Oliver Wendell Holmes) "a cat picking her footsteps in wet weather."

Among other significant essayists are, in the Romantic Age, William Hazlitt, Charles Lamb, and Thomas De Quincey, and in the twentieth century,

Virginia Woolf, George Orwell, and Thomas Mann. For a useful anthology, consult Philip Lopate, ed., *The Art of the Personal Essay* (1994).

essentialism The belief that there is a fixed, reliable essence that determines the nature of (for instance) the human. Karl Popper in his 1957 book *The Poverty of Historicism* first used the term *essentialism* in this sense: it renames the medieval philosophical idea known as realism, which was opposed to nominalism (now called "anti-essentialism").

"Essentialist humanism" claims that the human can be defined: we strive always for certain things (happiness, for example), have certain inclinations (toward good or evil), and so on. The anti-essentialist counterargument suggests that humans have diverse desires and goals, conditioned by social and environmental factors, and that there is no common element in this variety. (Anti-essentialists usually evade the question of what we mean when we say "human," and why we so often depend on a shared, understandable idea of human nature.)

The battle between essentialists and anti-essentialists became crucial for American feminist theory in the 1980s. Is femininity the mere effect of a contingent social situation, existing over thousands of years, that tells women how to act and who to be? Or is it, instead, something that inheres in each woman (as a biological kernel, for instance—biology, in this argument, being associated with essence)?

The impact of Freudian theory on the feminist debate was considerable, since Freud's argument that the lack of the phallus is the defining fact of femininity can be turned in either an essentialist or an anti-essentialist direction. In the Freudian view as reinterpreted by Jacques Lacan, the phallus is not the penis but an associated symbol of masculine power. Every man must pretend to, or claim, the phallus. Because women do not make this claim, their power is basically different. For Freud, the difference between men and women is decisive, but not explanatory. That is, one cannot predict a man's or woman's character and behavior on the basis of his or her gender. Yet gender remains a basis: whether someone is male or female seems to be the first thing we want to know about him (her).

The most influential modern questioning of the human as an essence is Martin Heidegger's essay "Letter on Humanism" (1947), in Heidegger, *Basic Writings,* ed. David Farrell Krell (1977). Heidegger's argument was continued, in different ways, in the theories of Jacques Derrida and Michel Foucault. For commentary on the feminist debate concerning essentialism, see Diana Fuss, *Essentially Speaking* (1989), and Toril Moi, *What Is a Woman?* (1999).

eternal return The Nietzschean idea of seeing one's entire life as something that could, and should, recur, without change in any detail. The challenge of eternal return is to embrace existence without bitterness, recrimination, or desire to alter anything that has happened. In *The Gay Science* (1882–87), Nietzsche writes, "The question in each and every thing, 'Do you desire this once more and innumerable times more?' would lie upon your actions as the greatest weight. Or how well-disposed would you have to become to yourself and to life *to crave nothing more fervently* than this ultimate eternal confirmation and seal?" See AMOR FATI.

ethics From the Greek *ethos,* meaning "manner," "kind," or "character." Ethics, as a branch of philosophy, is the study of human character. Among the literary critics who have focused on ethics (on literature as a key to the character of a culture, and as a guide for refining the moral attitude of the individual reader) are William Hazlitt, Matthew Arnold, and Lionel Trilling.

There is a different sense of ethics in the French philosopher Emmanuel Lévinas. For Lévinas, ethics concerns our confrontation with the individual as a unique Other. Ethics, in Lévinas 's lexicon, stands opposed to morality, the concern with standards of behavior and normative codes of values. Instead, the Other appeals to us with an immediacy that cannot be understood by reference to moral standards. (We do not help people who are in danger because we decide they are worthy of help; our response is instinctive—ethical rather than moral.) See Sean Hand, ed., *The Lévinas Reader* (1989).

For an approach to ethics influenced by deconstruction, see J. Hillis Miller, *The Ethics of Reading* (1987). Three stimulating approaches to ethical criticism that deal with the question of the reader's identification with, and reaction to, fictional characters, are Wayne Booth, *The Company We Keep* (1988), William Monroe, *Power to Hurt* (1997), and Martha Nussbaum, *Love's Knowledge* (1990).

Euhemerism Euhemerus was a Greek writer of the fourth century BCE. He argued that the gods were originally kings and brave men who had been deified after their deaths. Euhemerism therefore means the tracing back of religion to a source in historical personages.

euphuism An elaborate and heavy-handed use of figures of speech, replete with maxims (or "sentences," as the Renaissance called them). The euphuistic style derives from a prose work by the Elizabethan playwright John Lyly, *Euphues: the Anatomy of Wit* (1578), and its sequel, *Euphues and His England* (1580). Here is a sample of Lyly's methodical extravagance, on the subject of human nature's recalcitrance in the face of attempts to change it: "It is natural for the vine to spread; the more you seek by art to alter it, the more in the end you shall augment it. It is proper for the palm tree to mount; the heavier you load it the higher it sprouteth. Though iron be made soft with fire it returneth to his hardness; though the falcon be reclaimed to the fist she retireth to her haggardness; the whelp of a mastiff will never be taught to retrieve the partridge . . ." The untamable string of similes is characteristic of Lyly's euphuism.

Shakespeare draws on euphuism during the mock trial of Prince Hal in *Henry IV, Part 1*. Falstaff, playing Hal's father, the king, judiciously reminds him that "though the chamomile, the more it is trodden, the faster it grows; yet youth, the more it is wasted, the sooner it wears. . . . There is a thing, Harry, which thou hast often heard of, and it is known to many in our land, by the name of pitch; this pitch (as ancient writers do report) doth defile; so doth the company thou keepest." See G. K. Hunter, *John Lyly* (1961).

everyday. See ORDINARY

exegesis The interpretation of a passage, frequently a biblical text, using techniques of figural or typological reading. The system of fourfold exegesis, developed in the patristic period (probably by John Cassian), claimed that one could identify literal, allegorical, tropological, and anagogical meanings in each biblical passage or phrase. Even a word like *Jerusalem* could be submitted to fourfold interpretation: on the literal level it denotes a city; on the allegorical, the church; on the tropological (or moral), the soul; and on the anagogical, man's heavenly destination. See Elizabeth Clark, "Biblical Interpretation in the Early Church," in M. Jack Suggs, ed., *The Oxford Study Bible* (1992). See also FIGURA; TYPOLOGY.

existentialism A philosophical tradition with its roots in the nineteenth-century thinkers Søren Kierkegaard and Friedrich Nietzsche, and developing in the twentieth century in works by Martin Heidegger, Karl Jaspers, Jean-Paul

Sartre, and Albert Camus. Sartre was the first to call himself an existentialist, and he is more closely associated with existentialism than any other philosopher.

For existentialists, our strange awareness of our existence challenges preconceived beliefs, forcing us to confront the fact that we are not at home in the world. The sheer fact of existence precedes any possible essence: so that life is incapable of being defined in its essential nature, as previous philosophers often tried to do.

Sartre was strongly influenced by Edmund Husserl's phenomenology, with its interest in solitary consciousness. But Sartre placed a new emphasis on *contingency:* on the unpredictability, even absurdity, of human circumstances. In Sartre, writes Iris Murdoch, "the consciousness that seeks to rise freely toward completeness and stability is continually sucked back into its past and the messy stuff of its moment-to-moment experience." People are bound to their "facticity," their concrete circumstances (body, culture, nationality, language), but they attempt freedom through their "projects" (their desires and plans). For Sartre consciousness is "for-itself" (*pour-soi*), insubstantial and strenuously desiring, whereas the world outside is immanent and substantial, "in-itself" (*en-soi*). What the pour-soi wants, and cannot have, is the thinglike stability associated with the en-soi.

Sartre sometimes insists on the utterly arbitrary character of every human action. (What does it matter what choice of action we make, a reader of Sartre might wonder, as long as we choose something?) Yet at the same time Sartre finds in each act a fateful moment of responsibility, since it testifies to an existential project.

Sartre's novel *Nausea* (1938) and Camus's *The Stranger* (1940) are the two best-known existentialist literary works. Sartre's major work is *Being and Nothingness* (1943), but his *War Diaries* (written 1939–40, published 1983) offers a better introduction to his thought. See also Sartre's *Existentialism and Human Emotions* (1957), and Iris Murdoch, *Sartre* (1953). Accounts of existentialism can be found in Albert Camus, *The Myth of Sisyphus* (1942), William Barrett, *Irrational Man* (1958), and Dermot Moran, *Introduction to Phenomenology* (2001). See also ABSURD; CONTINENTAL PHILOSOPHY; PHENOMENOLOGY.

explication de texte A step-by-step way of explaining the details of a literary text, practiced in the French school system. *Explication de texte* differs from the close reading advocated by New Criticism because it restrains itself from acts of interpretation, focusing instead on providing the information that will enable a basic understanding of the work under discussion. See CLOSE READING; NEW CRITICISM.

expressionism A form of visionary distortion in literature and art, expressionism was a recognizable style from about 1912 until the early 1920s, though there were important earlier influences, like Georg Büchner's drama *Woyzeck* (1836). Expressionism depicts the human being in a state of extremity, confronted with feverish dream states or ecstatic in nightmare. Its mannerisms are sometimes garish and shrill, its tone lurid. It is often marked by what Walter Sokel calls "a wild, anarchic yearning for 'irresponsible life' and 'pure sensation.'" Sokel interprets the wild and futile expressionist desire for life as a sign of the artist's sense of permanent exclusion from the vital center of existence. In this sense the artist stands in opposition to the complacent bourgeois, who in his stupidity and heartiness does have contact with life.

Central and northern Europe produced a number of important expressionist visual artists: Edvard Munch, Käthe Kollwitz, Emil Nolde, George Grosz, Oskar Kokoschka. For examples of expressionism in literature, consult Brecht's *Baal* (1923) and *In the Jungle of Cities* (written 1921–23), August Strindberg's *A Dream Play* (1901, performed 1907), Frank Wedekind's Lulu plays (1895–1902), and Henrik Ibsen's *When We Dead Awaken* (1899). Walter Sokel, *The Writer in Extremis* (1959), provides an overview of expressionism in literature.

F

fable The fable is one of the oldest literary genres. The Greek writer Aesop (ca. sixth century BCE) and the Roman Phaedrus (ca. 15 BCE–50 CE) were for centuries among the most universally familiar authors. Even today we still recognize some of Aesop's fables (the fox and the grapes, for example). The beast fable, originated by Aesop, is a pithy story that dramatizes human weaknesses and points a moral.

There was a great vogue for the fable in the late seventeenth and eighteenth centuries, especially in Germany. The popularity of the genre was spurred by the vast success of the French writer Jean de la Fontaine, who began publishing his fables in the 1660s.

The term *fable* is somewhat shifty: it is sometimes used to designate any pointed narrative. John Dryden's *Fables, Ancient and Modern* (1700) was not at all Aesopean, but instead presented adaptations of Homer, Ovid, Boccaccio, and Chaucer, along with some of Dryden's own poems.

For a consideration of the political uses of the Aesopean fable, see Annabel Patterson, *Fables of Power* (1991). Frank Kermode brilliantly discusses fables, parables, and other hermetic narratives in *The Genesis of Secrecy* (1979); and Mark Loveridge, *A History of Augustan Fable* (1998), discusses the fable in the Restoration and eighteenth century. See also PARABLE.

fabliau A ribald medieval verse genre (twelfth–fourteenth centuries), popular in France and England. The fabliau features conniving (and sometimes obscene) pranks, the raucous behavior of the lower classes, and, frequently, the cuckolding of a dimwitted husband. In English literature, Geoffrey Chaucer and Edmund Spenser both draw on the popular genre of the fabliau. Chaucer's Miller's Tale (ca. 1386) presents a dazzling example, told at breakneck speed. In the Renaissance, Spenser adapts the fabliau in his delightful tale of Paridell and Hellenore, who succeed in cuckolding Hellenore's jealous husband Malbecco (*The Faerie Queene,* 3.10).

fairy tale and folk tale The fairy tale develops out of the wider genre of the folk tale: the latter being a story told by both literate and illiterate cultures, and often addressing the wishes and needs of its audience through mythic themes of heroism, imperilment, and adventure. In German the folk tale is known as the *Märchen* or *Volksmärchen* (the word *Märchen* originally meant "news" or "gossip"). Folk tales, like all oral narratives, often give evidence of the collective desires and circumstances of the communities that create them and pass them on. (See ORAL LITERATURE.)

The fairy tale is a specific literary form, frequently featuring magical transformations, giants and dwarves, young women suffering cruel captivity or placed under spells, and heroic rituals of initiation. The end of the seventeenth century in France witnessed a craze for fairy tales written by aristocratic women, like the collection by Mme Marie-Catherine d'Aulnoy (1697). Charles Perrault's *Stories or Tales of Times Past* (1697) was a strong influence on later fairy tales, as was the monumental collection by the Brothers Grimm, whose first version appeared in 1812. See Jack Zipes, *Breaking the Magic Spell* (1979, rev. ed. 2002), and Zipes, ed., *The Oxford Companion to Fairy Tales* (2000); also FOLKLORE.

fame Eternal fame, otherwise known as secular immortality (from Latin *saeculum,* age or era), has long been a literary ideal. The Greek poet Theognis (sixth century BCE) speaks of immortalizing his beloved in his poetry. And the Roman Horace (65–8 BCE) promises his friend Lollius unending fame (Odes 4.9). Horace also declares, "Exegi monumentum aere perennius" (I have built a monument more lasting than bronze [Odes 3.30]): his poetry will outlive even the proud architecture of the Roman Empire. This theme of the poem's longevity also appears in Ovid's *Amores* (16 BCE), 1.15.

The idea of secular immortality is most familiar to the English-speaking reader from Shakespeare's sonnets: for example, Sonnet 65, Sonnet 55 ("Not marble, nor the gilded monuments / Of princes, shall outlive this powerful rhyme"), and Sonnet 18 ("So long as men can breathe, or eyes can see, / So long lives this, and this gives life to thee").

See J. B. Leishman, "Shakespeare and the Roman Poets," in his *Themes and Variations in Shakespeare's Sonnets* (1961). For a broader investigation of fame in the arts, see Leo Braudy, *Fame: The Frenzy of Renown* (1986).

fancy Samuel Taylor Coleridge, in *Biographia Literaria* (1817), distinguishes fancy from imagination. Fancy is like "ordinary memory," writes Coleridge, in that it "receive[s] all its materials ready made from the law of association," and then plays with, or manipulates, these materials. Imagination, by contrast, is a higher power: "It dissolves, diffuses, dissipates, in order to recreate . . . it struggles to idealize and to unify."

Fancy, then, according to Coleridge, relies on and rearranges images received by the senses, in rather mechanical fashion: whereas imagination is organic and vital, and echoes God's own creative power. See I. A. Richards, *Coleridge on Imagination* (1934); M. H. Abrams, *The Mirror and the Lamp* (1953).

fantastic The fantastic is a literary genre characterized by a hesitation between the real and the supernatural: the reader finds it hard to decide between a magical and a reasonable explanation of events. Henry James's *The Turn of the Screw* (1898), for example, is either a ghost story or else a psychological thriller in which the ghosts are merely delusory, figments of the narrator's imagination. This effect of mysterious, suspenseful uncertainty between a reasonable and a supernatural explanation of events is also called *uncanny*. See Sigmund Freud's essay of 1919, "The Uncanny," in Freud, *Character and Culture*, Philip Rieff, ed. (1963); also the standard work on the genre, Tzvetan Todorov's *The Fantastic* (1970), and Dorothea von Mücke, *The Seduction of the Occult and the Rise of the Fantastic Tale* (2003).

feminist theory An important influence on literary study since the 1970s. Feminist approaches to literature have taken two main forms: the recovery of writing by women, including many texts that were lost or neglected; and the study of the image of woman in literature and culture.

Feminist critics study the ways women have written, and read, literature through the centuries, in an effort to recover this history. Such a project must battle against the force of patriarchy, which has so often proved determined to repress or destroy the evidence of women's writing and reading.

The historically oriented feminist critic wants to recover the way that women's life experience, as wives, mothers, and oppressed members of society, intertwines with their literary experience. But as Elaine Showalter points out, feminism also produces the "*hypothesis* of a female reader": a reader who would properly identify with the women in a book (as male readers, and some female readers too, often do not). Even within the responses of women themselves, patriarchy does its work, making them prefer independent male heroes and scorn mothers. Judith Fetterly proclaimed in *The Resisting Reader* (1978) that women readers must "begin the process of exorcising the male mind that has been implanted in us." "To read as a woman" becomes, as Jonathan Culler puts it, "to avoid reading as a man." (Culler, "Reading as a Woman," in *On Deconstruction* [1982].) The spurning of sentimental fiction is one chief way of reading as a man, argues Jane Tompkins in *Sensational Designs* (1986). For the other side—the case against sentimentality—see Ann Douglas, *The Feminization of American Culture* (1977).

Modern feminist criticism dates from Virginia Woolf's landmark essay, *A Room of One's Own* (1929). Woolf is searching, rather than merely celebratory, in her examination of earlier women writers. She insists that women must attain financial and intellectual independence—a room of their own—in order to create a thriving literature. Simone de Beauvoir in *The Second Sex* (1949) pioneered the study of women's images in society. De Beauvoir concludes that the mythology sponsored by patriarchal society, according to which femininity implies self-sacrifice and narcissism, and women are identified with the biological fact of their sex, works to sustain masculine privilege. Such patriarchal bias stands in the way of women constituting themselves as a "we": as a collective, independent subject. Following de Beauvoir, one early book of feminist criticism, *The Madwoman in the Attic* by Sandra Gilbert and Susan Gubar (1979), focused on the crippling influence of Victorian stereotypes (for example, the woman as "angel in the house," or spirit of perfect, placid domesticity). Gilbert and Gubar analyze "the suicidal passivity implicit in Victorian femininity." Margaret Homans, *Women Writers and Poetic Identity* (1980), offered another approach to some of these concerns. Kate Millett in *Sexual Politics* (1970) aggressively criticized the versions of women present in the fictions of some male authors.

Feminist theory influenced by psychoanalysis has been an important strain, beginning with Juliet Mitchell, *Psychoanalysis and Feminism* (1974)—though feminists have also abundantly criticized Freud for his patriarchal inclinations. In the 1970s and 1980s, two French thinkers, Luce Irigaray and Hélène Cixous, took feminism in a direction informed by poststructuralism (especially the theories of Jacques Derrida and Jacques Lacan), and by their close study, both admiring and antagonistic, of Freud and Nietzsche. For a good summary of the developments in French feminist theory, particularly during the 1970s, see Alice Jardine, *Gynesis* (1985).

Feminist theory has often occupied itself with the question of essential-ism: is "woman" an identifiable, stable entity; a shifting concept without pre-dictable boundaries; or can "she" be located somewhere between these two poles? The question is related to the effort on the part of many feminist thinkers to develop ideals of "woman" or of "feminine writing" that go be-yond actual women or their literary works. Toril Moi in *What Is a Woman?* (1999) makes a persuasive effort to resolve the essentialist/anti-essentialist de-bate. See ESSENTIALISM.

In film study, feminist theory has been especially influential. Laura Mul-vey's well-known essay "Visual Pleasure in Narrative Cinema" (in *Visual and Other Pleasures* [1988]), which accused film of positioning women as the ob-ject of the "male gaze," was answered by a number of critiques, ranging from William Rothman's *The "I" of the Camera* (2nd ed., 2004) to Carol Clover's study of horror films, *Men, Women, and Chainsaws* (1992). Also relevant to the theory of the male gaze is Tania Modleski's book on Alfred Hitchcock, *The Women Who Knew Too Much* (1988), Linda Williams's study of pornogra-phy, *Hard Core* (1989), and Stanley Cavell's work on melodrama, *Contesting Tears* (1996).

Feminist literary study has lately played a role in creating the allied fields of gay studies, queer theory, and gender studies. Ann Brooks, *Postfeminisms* (1997), is a useful overview of recent developments; the encyclopedic *Com-panion to Feminist Philosophy* (1998), ed. Alison Jaggar and Iris Marion Young, is also valuable. See GAY STUDIES; GENDER STUDIES; QUEER THEORY.

festive Introduced as a critical term by C. L. Barber in *Shakespeare's Festive Comedy* (1959). Renaissance England, Barber explained, was much occupied with rural festivities involving the overturning of established social order, the mocking of pieties, and the celebration of absurdity. Barber writes, "Mirth took form in morris-dances, sword-dances, wassailings, mock ceremonies of summer kings and queens and of lords of misrule, mummings, disguisings, masques—and a bewildering variety of sports, games, shows, and pageants."

Shakespeare in his comedies draws on such festive rituals, which exult in a topsy-turvy world and provide a temporary release, or relief, from everyday existence. In later works, Barber reflected on the difference, as well as the sim-ilarity, between social ritual and theater; his sense of the resemblance between these two phenomena strongly influenced new historicism. See also GREEN WORLD; NEW HISTORICISM.

fetishism In current theory, fetishism often means the hyperbolic, obsessive cherishing of a particular commodity (that is, an object of consumption) as if it were a thing bearing great spiritual value. The term derives in part from Freud's examination of sexual fetishism, but mostly from the Marxist idea of "commodity fetishism." As Marx explains it in *Capital,* vol. 3 (1894), in capitalism the commodity becomes virtually animate, replete with the kind of significance usually given to human beings.

Literary critics with demystifying tendencies are sometimes inclined to criticize the fetishizing of certain ideas: that is, the treatment of these ideas with undue reverence ("Critic X fetishizes humanist ideals").

fiction *Fiction* derives from the Latin *fingere:* "to mold" or "to shape to a design," but also "to fake." By the end of the fourteenth century, Raymond Williams notes in *Keywords* (1976), one of the meanings of *fiction* was "an imaginative work"—still its main meaning today. But a fiction also meant a lie or an act of feigning (as it still does now, too).

John Hollander remarks that "fictions *are,* after all, like lies (the kind we tell ourselves, for example)." Fiction seems happily to evade the rhetorical category of the lie; we would not call a novel false in the same way, or with the same vehemence, that we assail the lying speeches of a lover or a politician. Yet fiction-making does seem to be like lying, and specifically like lying to oneself. (We are not as hard on our own lies as we are on the lies of others; it even seems unfair to accuse ourselves of lying. We were just applying some useful distortion, increasing our imaginative strength; or maybe we experienced an interesting, and therefore pardonable, lapse into untruth.)

Incapable of being defeated through the direct application of facts, a fictional narrative sets itself against what we know to be the case: as an answer to, a transfiguring of, this case. "The poet never affirmeth, and therefore never lieth," wrote Philip Sidney in his *Apology for Poetry* (written 1583, publ. 1595).

It is interesting to note that historical writing began before the difference between history and fiction was established, in the works of Herodotus and Thucydides (both fifth century BCE). Thucydides invents his politicians' speeches, arguing that they represent what these figures could, or ought to, have said. This primal interweaving of fiction and history yields eventually to the separation of the two: historians now try to adhere to the facts, and refrain from making it all up. Aristotle argues in his *Poetics* (ca. 330 BCE) that

FIGURA 121

poetry (by which Aristotle means fiction, in verse form) is superior to history because poetry narrates what is probable rather than what is necessary. That is, poetry generates a suitable and satisfying fiction, something better expressing the spirit of events than the mere recital, bound by necessity, of what actually did happen.

The word *novel,* derived from the French word for news, suggests journalism rather than make-believe; Daniel Defoe, who was perhaps the first English novelist, deliberately obscured the difference between fiction and journalistic account. Defoe presents his *Moll Flanders* (1722), for example, as a true story, rather than the fable it is.

In the novelistic tradition, there are several ways of suggesting that "all is true" (the subtitle of Honoré de Balzac's *Père Goriot* [1835]). One way is what Samuel Richardson, in the eighteenth century, called "writing to the moment." Richardson composed epistolary novels, consisting of letters produced by his characters. Writing to the moment, for him, meant composing fiction that conveys a breathless involvement, often by making characters narrate events that have just happened, or that overtake them in the course of their letter writing. (Fielding mocks this Richardsonian habit to hilarious effect in his parody of Richardson, *Shamela* [1741].) Another way for fiction to claim that all is true is for it to present a comprehensive vision of the social world as a totality, so that every possibility of life seems present: the vision of realism. (See REALISM.)

David Lodge in *The Art of Fiction* (1992) presents an entertaining anthology of various fictional devices (dialogue, the list, place description, etc.). See EPISTOLARY NOVEL; FABLE; MIMESIS; NOVEL; SHORT STORY.

figura The interpretive process, especially in scripture, in which a prototype is fulfilled by a later event or character. In Romans 5:14, Saint Paul describes Adam as "the figure of him that was to come": that is, Jesus. (In the original Greek text, Adam is said to be the *tupos,* or type, of the savior; the study of figura is also known as typology.) Similarly, in 1 Peter 3:20–21, baptism becomes the antitype (*antitupos*), or answering fulfillment, of Noah's flood. (The Greek prefix *anti-* here means completing, rather than opposing.)

For the Christian reader, the events of the New Testament must be prefigured in the Old; what was obscure in the scripture of the Jews has now been revealed. The mysterious "man of sorrows" of Isaiah 53 prefigures the Son of the passion story. The binding of Isaac (Genesis 22) similarly becomes an early version of the crucifixion. The method has its ridiculous excesses: as Nietzsche grumpily noted (in *Daybreak* [1881]), Christians seem to take every tree, every plank or bit of wood mentioned in the Hebrew Bible as an awesome presage of the cross. But figura, when taken up by a writer like Dante, also offers a serious theory of history, pressing us to read forward in search of fulfilled meaning: something that will finally make sense of the whole of sacred, and human, time.

A classic treatment of figural interpretation is Erich Auerbach's essay "Figura" in *Scenes from the Drama of European Literature* (1959). Northrop Frye in *The Great Code* (1982) provides an updated and sophisticated figural reading of the Bible. See ALLEGORY; ANAGOGIC; TYPOLOGY.

film theory Cinema studies has been an important arena for theoretical speculation, especially in the 1960s and 1970s. In some ways, current debates in the study of film can be traced back to the division between the writings of Sergei Eisenstein and those of André Bazin. Eisenstein, the great Russian director, singled out the "extraordinary plasticity" of cinematic effects. In his essay "Dickens, Griffith, and the Film Today" (1944), he compared the cumulative, quickening action of film to the literary lightning of Dickens, Shakespeare, and Greek tragedy. In keeping with this emphasis on mobile power, Eisenstein championed the shock of montage, the dynamic combination of shots, as the basic unit of meaning in film. Bazin, by contrast (in *What Is Cinema?* [1958]), exalted the long take, the slow, expansive movement of the camera, as the basic way in which film creates a seamless and total world. According to Bazin, the aim of the movies is "a recreation of the world in its own image."

Some significant later developments in film criticism are the sharp-eyed individualism of Manny Farber, who valued attractive imperfection in movies ("termite art," as he called it); the *auteur* theory advocated by Andrew Sarris, the notion that each remarkable film can be ascribed to the guiding hand of its director; the psychoanalytically informed approach of the theorists writing for the French journal *Cahiers du cinéma* in the 1960s; feminist theories of the spectator's gaze, expounded in the 1970s and 1980s by Laura Mulvey, Linda Williams, and others; and the exploration of film as a reflection on the spectator's responsibility and freedom, in the writings of Stanley Cavell and William Rothman. For a good anthology on these and other subjects, consult Gerald Mast and Marshall Cohen, eds., *Film Theory and Criticism* (1985). See also Rothman, *The "I" of the Camera* (2nd ed., 2004).

fin amors (Pronounced FEEN aMORS.) Provençal for "refined (or advanced) ways of loving": the method of the troubadours, who in the twelfth and thirteenth centuries, in southern France, presented themselves as the loyal servants of their ladies, striving to win grace in their eyes. *Amor de longh* (love across distance) is a central aspect of fin amors. Characteristically, the poet-singer's desire is excruciating, his suffering intensely pleasurable, like ice gripped so hard in the hand that it burns (a simile probably derived from medieval Arabic verse, and later taken over by the Italian poet Petrarch). The poet's beloved, usually a woman married to another man, is only rarely and partially attainable. The excited frustration of the troubadour mode carries over into later European poetry, which often exults in erotic pangs. See *A Handbook of the Troubadours* (1995), ed. F. R. P. Akehurst and Judith Davis. See also COURTLY LOVE.

fin de siècle French (pronounced FAHN deh seeAYKleh): "end of the century." A term applied to the literature and art of the final years of the nineteenth century, and associated with a mood of decadence. See DECADENCE.

flyting A poetic showdown in which two rival bards hurl put-downs at each other; originally a Scottish tradition. William Dunbar (ca. 1460–1520) is probably the best-known exponent of the flyting match: the record of his competition with his rival Walter Kennedy survives. The form lives on, and thrives, in the adversarial boasting of contemporary hip-hop MCs. (Flyting resembles the game of "playing the dozens" in African-American tradition: see Henry Louis Gates, *The Signifying Monkey* [1988].)

focalization A term made popular by the narratological theorist Gérard Genette in his *Narrative Discourse* (1972). Genette distinguished between "zero focalization," in which a narrator maintains a distance from the fictional world he depicts, giving a commentary on this world, and "internal focalization," in which the events of a narrative appear to us through the experience of one of the narrative's characters, with the narrator reduced to a minimal presence. See Dorrit Cohn's discussion of focalization in *The Distinction of Fiction* (1999), as well as Shlomith Rimmon-Kenan's comments in *Narrative Fiction* (2nd ed., 2002); and see POINT OF VIEW.

folio A large book consisting of sheets folded only once, into halves. By contrast, a quarto is made from sheets folded twice, into quarters, and is therefore much smaller. (The octavo, another small volume, is folded three times.) Many of Shakespeare's plays were issued during his lifetime as quartos; the First Folio of his work, edited by his fellow actors John Heminges and Henry Condell, appeared in 1623, seven years after his death.

There is also a less technical meaning for *folio,* one familiar for centuries. A folio is the name for any very large, oblong-shaped book (i.e., taller than it is wide). A quarto designates a smaller, squarish volume, and an octavo, a still smaller, oblong book, either standard bestseller-sized or pocket-sized. For more on these terms, consult John Carter, *ABC for Book Collectors* (1952).

folklore The realm of rituals, songs, stories, legends, and popular practices handed down orally from one person to another, rather than through written transmission. It is most remarkably present in the countryside, but urban folklore has now become an object of academic study in its own right. Among the major subjects of folklore studies are the nature of oral tradition, the purpose and definition of festive social interaction, the prevalence of spontaneous or improvised forms, and the often antagonistic relation between popular cultural expression and the official powers that be.

Folklore research as an academic discipline is less than a hundred years old. In the 1930s and later, John Lomax and his son Alan Lomax traveled through the American South and Southwest collecting folk songs, blues, and cowboy ballads. Stith Thompson completed the monumental *Motif-Index of Folk-Literature* in six large volumes (1932–37). The study of folklore was also influenced by anthropologists like Melville Herskovits and Clifford Geertz and sociologists like Erving Goffman. For more on folklore, see Dan Ben-Amos, ed., *Folklore Genres* (1976); Linda Degh, *Legend and Belief* (2001). Roger Abrahams in *Everyday Life* (2005) focuses on "enactments of community" involving playful competition, ecstatic celebration, or sly one-upsmanship, as well as the concepts of diaspora and creolization, both of them important to folklore studies. See also CREOLE, CREOLIZING; FAIRY TALE AND FOLK TALE; FESTIVE; ORAL LITERATURE.

folk tale. See FAIRY TALE AND FOLK TALE

formalism In the religious debates of the Reformation, a formalist was someone who adhered to mere show, to the performing of ritual acts rather than their spiritual meaning: just going through the motions of faith. This religious designation of formalism as a trust in superficial appearances differs from the notion of form in Aristotle's *Poetics* (ca. 330 BCE). For Aristotle form is a fundamentally deep apparatus, the organizing principle of a literary text. Just as, in Aristotle's biological theory, the form of a rodent or a tree can be understood as its shaping motive—sharp teeth to gnaw, long branches to reach for the sun—so the formal features of a tragedy, its reliance on *anagnorisis* (recognition) and *peripeteia* (reversal), show its essence. (See RECOGNITION; REVERSAL.)

The use of the term *formalism* in literary study hovers between the two senses just outlined: the Protestant religious idea that form may be merely superficial, in contrast to the inward, invisible motions of the heart, and the Aristotelian sense that form is essential and generative. "Formalist" is sometimes used as a slur, in the Protestant manner, by literary critics: particularly those of the Marxist variety, who deride formalism for sticking to the surface and failing to see the ideological content, the hidden agenda, of a piece of literature.

But form is all we can see of a text. The attraction of the Aristotelian point of view is that it tries to explain what a literary work (or a literary genre) *is* by understanding its only apparent, or available, features: its form.

In the twentieth century, the Russian Formalists, beginning around 1914 and ending in 1930 due to Stalin's opposition, set themselves the task of understanding what makes a text literary: the study not of literature but of literariness. For the Formalists, literariness was achieved through the deformation of everyday linguistic usage; they called such deformation the defamiliarization, or "estrangement," of language. (See DEFAMILIARIZATION.)

Such estrangement means describing familiar things as if they were unfamiliar. James Joyce's *Ulysses* (1922), for example, practices estrangement in its Sirens chapter, with its depiction of two barmaids at work:

Bronze by gold heard the hoofirons, steelyringing.
Imperthnthn thnthnthn.
Chips, picking chips off rocky thumbnail, chips.
Horrid! And gold flushed more.
A husky fifenote blew
Blue. Blue bloom is on the.
Goldpinnacled hair.

There are other kinds of estrangement effects. A sentence from one of the later novels of Henry James might suggest that what is being described is not just the physical scene and the characters, but the author's movement of thought, apparent in the careful, varying sway of the sentence itself. "Art removes objects from the automatism of perception," wrote the formalist Viktor Shklovskii. Estrangement impedes, and by doing so deepens, the reader's perceptions. The author creates a special kind of perception, a way for the reader to *see,* rather than merely recognize, the things of the world.

In addition to their study of estrangement on the level of discrete passages and sentences, the Formalists described an estrangement that occurs when a work exposes its own structure. They drew a distinction between story (*fabula* in Russian, *histoire* in French) and plot (*sjuzet* in Russian, *récit* in French). Plot orders events in a significant way, and tells them to us one by one. Plot, then, is the sequence of events as they are presented, in the order that the author decides on (a writer may, for example, start with the end of a love affair and then go back to recount its beginning). Story, by contrast, makes up the mass of events that plot draws on, the "material" of a narrative (e.g., the love affair in its actual sequence). The Formalists particularly prized novels like Miguel de Cervantes' *Don Quixote* (1605–15) and Laurence Sterne's *Tristram Shandy* (1759–67) that uncover the struggle between story and plot, revealing with enthusiasm the artificiality of literary procedure. For some of the Formalists, at least, literary history would be nothing but the repeated surfacing of such artificiality. Yet making an object artistic also, for them, coincides with making it newly real: bringing it to life.

At its best, formalism looks for the caress of words, the artistic rubbing that irritates, stimulates, and takes its proper time. Here is Shklovskii in his *Theory of Prose:* "Why does Ovid, who made an *Art of Love* out of love itself, advise us to take our pleasure in leisurely fashion? The path of art is a tortuous path, on which your feet feel each stone, a path that winds back and forth. Word goes together with word, one word rubs against the other like a cheek against another's cheek."

The formalist idea of the conspicuous friction that constitutes literariness would influence the linguist Roman Jakobson, who declared in 1923 that verse is "an organized violence of poetic form over language": the "violence" being audible, according to Jakobson, in particularly marked phonemic features (phonemes are the sound units of language). The sharp repetitions in Poe's "The Raven," one of Jakobson's favorite poems, assault the ear.

See Viktor Shklovskii, "Art as Technique," and Boris Eichenbaum, "The Theory of the Formal Method," both in Lee Lemon and Marion Reis, eds., *Russian Formalist Criticism* (1965); as well as Roman Jakobson, "The Metaphoric and Metonymic Poles" (1956), in Hazard Adams, ed., *Critical Theory Since Plato* (1971), and Fredric Jameson's assessment of formalism and structuralism, *The Prison-House of Language* (1971). Stephen Cushman in *Fictions of Form in American Poetry* (1993) adroitly explores the attachment to form as a vehicle of meaning. See also PLOT; STRUCTURALISM.

Frankfurt School A group of social and cultural theorists first located at the University of Frankfurt and then, after the advent of Nazism, at the New School in New York City. Its most prominent members were Theodor Adorno and Max Horkheimer; among others associated, to different degrees, with the Frankfurt School were Walter Benjamin, Leo Lowenthal, Siegfried Kracauer, and Herbert Marcuse. The Frankfurt School thinkers, who tended to be pessimists rather than revolutionaries, nevertheless adapted Marxist analysis in order to understand modernity. They studied the rationalized social relations characteristic of "late capitalism," along with the dominance of the commodity form and what they called the "culture industry." In *The Dialectic of Enlightenment* (1947), Adorno and Horkheimer presented a critique of scientific knowledge and progressive opinion under capitalism. In capitalist modernity, they argued, enlightenment becomes a self-congratulatory myth, dominating society and obstructing truly independent thought. The contemporary philosopher Jürgen Habermas is the heir of the Frankfurt School; see Habermas, *The Philosophical Discourse of Modernity* (1985). *Aesthetics and Politics* (1977) is an excellent collection of essays by members of the Frankfurt School and related figures (Adorno, Benjamin, Ernst Bloch, and Georg Lukács). See also COMMODITY; MARXIST LITERARY CRITICISM.

free indirect style. See POINT OF VIEW

free verse (vers libre) Free verse (in French, *vers libre*) is verse that has been liberated from the regular constraints of meter. It has sometimes been perceived as a revolutionary achievement: "to break the pentameter, that was the first heave," Ezra Pound strenuously declared. Yet free verse is never wholly free. It is shaped by the rhythms of speech, and therefore can be described in terms of traditional metrical feet. The difference is that, while traditional verse follows a predictable pattern (so that iambic pentameter consists mostly of iambs, for example), free verse may juxtapose any kind of foot with any other.

Free verse is mostly devoid of rhyme, but there are exceptions in the work of Jules Laforgue (1860–87) and T. S. Eliot (1888–1965). (Rhyme in Laforgue plays a chiming rather than the more traditional timekeeping role.) Walt Whitman, the best-known writer of free verse, was superbly attentive to meter. (For an example of how a Whitman line can be scanned, see METER.)

The question of free verse played a role in modernist polemics concerning whether authors ought to pursue freedom of expression or, on the contrary, order and severe organization. In March 1917, T. S. Eliot published in *The New Statesman* his "Reflections on Vers Libre," which concluded, "The division between Conservative Verse and free verse does not exist, for there is only good verse, bad verse, and chaos." "Any verse," he added, "is called 'free' by people whose ears are not accustomed to it." By this point both Eliot and Pound were ready to strike out against what Pound later called "the dilutation of *vers libre*, Amygism, Lee Mastersism, general floppiness." (Pound was referring to Amy Lowell, one of the main poets of Imagism, and Edgar Lee Masters, author of the folksy *Spoon River Anthology* [1914–15]; see IMAGISM.) See Michael Levenson, *A Genealogy of Modernism* (1984).

Freudian literary criticism. See PSYCHOANALYTIC CRITICISM

Futurism The Italian writer Filippo Tommaso Marinetti was the leader of the Futurist movement, a radical wing of early-twentieth-century modernism. The Futurist Manifesto of 1909 invoked the brutal power of the machine age to abolish the past, and advocated setting fire to the libraries and flooding the museums. Futurism made war on the classics, proclaiming that "a roaring car that seems to be driving under shrapnel is more beautiful than the Victory of Samothrace." The Futurists complained that "immobility, ecstasy, and sleep" had been prized in literature up until their own day, and trumpeted their intention to instead "exalt the aggressive gesture, the feverish insomnia, the athletic step."

Marinetti's outrageous celebrations of violence, war, and rebellion, his attacks on high culture, and his scorning of hypocrisy were influenced by the turn-of-the-century French playwright Alfred Jarry. Marinetti added an insistence on the modern age as a meshing of the human and the machine, and he attributed to modernity a transfiguring and unifying force akin to radioactivity or electricity.

The two main Italian Futurist artists, Gino Severini and Umberto Boccioni, produced forceful, disturbing works. In 1912, Severini was instrumental (with Pablo Picasso and Guillaume Apollinaire) in the development of the collage technique used by Picasso, Georges Braque, Hannah Höch, and many others.

The Russian Futurists, in addition to the artists Kasimir Malevich and Vladimir Tatlin, included the poets Velimir Khlebnikov, Alexei Kruchenykh, and Vladimir Mayakovsky. Roman Jakobson in *The New Russian Poets* (1922) called Khlebnikov "the greatest world poet of our century." Khlebnikov's practice of *zaum*, a dynamic combination of sounds that was meant to affect the reader directly, led to striking poems. (Zaum, a term coined by Kruchenykh, is derived from the Russian *za*, "before" or "beyond," and *um*, "mind": this poetry transcends, or occurs prior to, the mind's sense-making.)

Not all have loved the Futurists. In his assault on them, the critic Kenneth Burke comments: "Marinetti contrived to attain 'yea-saying,' at whatever cost. . . . Like a cruel caricature of Whitman, he would be the omnivorous appetite. . . . Futurism, so cast, could provide the most rudimentary kind of solace. Were the streets noisy? It could counter by advocating an uncritical cult of noise. . . . *Apparently* active, it was in essence the most passive of frames, an elaborate method for feeling *assertive* by a resolve to drift with the current." (See Kenneth Burke, *Attitudes Toward History* [1937, rev. ed. 1959].)

The Futurists were influential for later artistic movements, especially Vorticism, led by Wyndham Lewis and Ezra Pound, but also Dadaism and Surrealism (see DADAISM; SURREALISM; VORTICISM). Consult "A Manifesto of Italian Futurism" in Irving Howe, ed., *The Idea of the Modern* (1967); and Marjorie Perloff, *The Futurist Moment* (1986). Also Günter Berghaus, ed., *International Futurism in Art and Literature* (2000), and Guy Davenport, *Tatlin!* (1982).

G

gay studies A rapidly growing field of cultural and literary study in the 1980s and the following decades, gay studies investigates the relation between the sexuality of individuals and how they describe and understand themselves. One of gay studies' key interests is the fact that *straight* and *gay* are terms that depend upon, or implicate, each other, and that *straight* is the "invisible" or unmarked term. Some of the main points made by gay studies are: straightness is ensured by being unlike gayness; social oppression leads to the secretive or "closeted" status of homosexuality, which then becomes a telling fact about persons (in a way that straightness is not); at times, gayness, like femininity, alternates between hiding itself and declaring itself in theatrical fashion.

Gay studies draws much from the French philosopher Michel Foucault. In his *History of Sexuality* (1976), Foucault observed that sex, a biological fact, is different from sexuality, a shifting rubric of identity that may change over historical time. Gay studies has at times dedicated itself to the "outing" of authors whose homosexuality is somehow concealed, oblique, or in dispute (Henry James and Willa Cather, for example). Queer theory, in contrast, is less concerned with the definition of sexual identity and more with the way that unusual or unofficial sexuality pervades social and cultural life.

Three useful anthologies are Henry Abelove, Michèle Barale, and David Halperin, eds., *The Lesbian and Gay Studies Reader* (1993); Diana Fuss, ed., *Inside/Out: Lesbian Theories, Gay Theories* (1991); and George Haggerty and Bonnie Zimmerman, eds., *Professions of Desire* (1995). (More bibliography is listed under GENDER STUDIES.) See also GENDER STUDIES; QUEER THEORY.

Geisteswissenschaft A German word that covers the disciplines of the "human sciences": everything from philosophy, history, and sociology to literary study and art history. (*Geist* means spirit; *Wissenschaft,* the studious pursuit of knowledge.) Among the German philosophers who have contributed to the understanding of the Geisteswissenschaften are Friedrich Schleiermacher (1768–1834) and Wilhelm Dilthey (1833–1911).

gender studies Gender studies sees itself as the successor to feminist literary study. It shifts the study of gender away from its earlier, exclusive focus on women and addresses questions of masculinity, transvestism ("cross-dress-ing"), and male and female homosexuality (gay studies). Among the cur-rently influential texts in gender studies are Michel Foucault, *The History of Sexuality* (1976); Marjorie Garber, *Vested Interests* (1992); and Eve Kosofsky Sedgwick, *Between Men* (1985) and *Epistemology of the Closet* (1990). The theme of performing one's identity is important in the works of Judith But-ler, including *Gender Trouble* (1990) and *Bodies that Matter* (1993). Male friendship and its intersection with homosexuality is a common subject, es-pecially since John Boswell, *Christianity, Social Tolerance, and Homosexuality* (1980). Also significant are John Winkler, *Constraints of Desire* (1990), and James Saslow's authoritative *Ganymede in the Renaissance* (1986). Tim Dean presents an interesting evaluation of gender studies, along with a critique of Sedgwick, in *Beyond Sexuality* (2000). See also GAY STUDIES; QUEER THEORY.

genealogy A term stemming from Friedrich Nietzsche's *Toward a Genealogy of Morals* (1887). In this shocking, fascinating book, Nietzsche wrestles with questions of historical origin and development that have shaped our souls and our values: How did Christianity, with its belief in the virtue of being punished by one's conscience, arise? How did Christian asceticism manage to transform the meanings of "good" and "bad" from their Roman, aristocratic sense to a newer one, so that the meek, rather than the brave and warlike, now become the worthy ones?

In his intriguing, rhapsodic essay "Nietzsche, Genealogy, History" (1971), Michel Foucault reinterprets Nietzschean genealogy, reading it as a mode of historical inquiry that "seeks to reestablish . . . the hazardous play of domina-tions." For the genealogist, Foucault writes, the world is not an "ultimately simple configuration where events are reduced to accentuate their essential traits, their final meaning, or their initial and final value. On the contrary, it is a profusion of entangled events."

Instead of trying to sum up the meaning of historical processes as a story of progress, enlightenment, or the emergence of truth, the genealogist sees in history a conflicting array of forces both afflicting us and enabling our flourishing, from moment to moment (and even, according to Foucault, seeing in affliction a kind of flourishing). See Michel Foucault, "Nietzsche, Genealogy, History," in James Faubion, ed., *Essential Works of Foucault,* vol. 2: *Aesthetics, Method, and Epistemology* (1998).

genre The word *genre* means kind: a genre is a kind of literature. Among the more familiar genres are epic, romance, comedy, tragedy, melodrama, lyric, satire, and elegy. Genres can be contained within one another: an elegy is one sort of lyric poem. They can also overlap. Spenser's *The Faerie Queene* (1590–96) is an epic romance, or romance epic.

Aristotle's *Poetics* (ca. 330 BCE) presents the first systematic reflection on genre. It focuses mostly on tragedy (another section of Aristotle's treatise, on comedy, was lost). Ancient and Renaissance literary theory conceived a hierarchy of genres, with epic at the top, since the epic poem was the most comprehensive literary text. Epic had encyclopedic breadth and national import. A poem like Virgil's *Aeneid* was the epic of Rome; Homer's *Iliad* and *Odyssey,* some ancients claimed, contained all the information one might require in life, from the art of war to household management. Tragedy was considered the next highest genre, since it treats a complete and resonant action in high style, concerns itself with noble or great characters, and aims at eliciting a profound, impressive emotional response.

Renaissance literary critics debated whether *mixta genera,* mixed genres, conformed to standards of literary decorum, or whether genres ought to be pure instead. Was it proper to write what Polonius in *Hamlet* (2.2) calls a "tragical-comical-historical-pastoral," even a "poem unlimited"? A work like Ludovico Ariosto's *Orlando Furioso* (1516), a comic epic romance with pastoral, satirical, and tragic episodes, affords an excellent example of a work that mixes genres. Ariosto's melting pot approach to literature prompted serious battles among Renaissance critics. (See Daniel Javitch's book on the canonizing of Ariosto, *Proclaiming a Classic* [1991].)

The opponents of mixta genera were forced to yield before the plain fact that authors like to combine different kinds together. The quarrel raised the question, though, of what readers expect and want from a kind, or type, of literature. Sometimes we do like our genres straight up. A pure detective story can be more satisfying than an example of the genre that aims at the sort of social commentary and breadth of depiction that the full-fledged realist novel trades in.

Northrop Frye, in a major section of his magisterial *Anatomy of Criticism* (1957), presents a theory of genres. Frye's four genres (comedy, tragedy, irony, romance) are keyed to the seasons; romance is the genre of genres since it is identified with springtime, enabling revival from the bitter chill of irony. (See QUEST ROMANCE.)

Alastair Fowler lists a variety of criteria for determining genre: external features (novels are divided into chapters, plays into acts and scenes); size or scope (epics are long, lyrics short); mood (the shuddery creepiness of the Gothic novel); style (high, low, or in between); the reader's task (in the detective story, trying to solve the puzzle); and occasion (an epithalamium is a poem composed for a marriage). See Alastair Fowler, *Kinds of Literature* (1982).

Georgian Age In literary study, the Georgian period usually means the reign of King George V (1910–36) of England. (It can also designate the reigns of George I through George IV [1714–1830].) Georgian poetry of the early twentieth century, by writers like Walter De la Mare and Rupert Brooke, was often effusive and delicate, with a limpid, rhapsodic quality, and enwrapped in what is still thought of as characteristically "poetic" diction. Reacting against this style, the modernist poets, especially Ezra Pound, took aim at the mellifluous Georgian diction, replacing it with a far rougher, stranger and more varied manner.

Five anthologies entitled *Georgian Poetry* were issued between 1912 and 1922, all of them edited by Edward Marsh and published by Harold Monro. In addition to the poems of Brooke and De la Mare, *Georgian Poetry* also included work by John Masefield, Edmund Blunden, Siegfried Sassoon, D. H. Lawrence, and Robert Graves (the last two would certainly not be considered typically "Georgian").

Georgic A poem devoted to the farming life (from the Greek *georgein,* to till the earth). The most influential example of the genre is Virgil's *Georgics* (ca. 29 BCE). Often esteemed as Virgil's most perfect poems, these works run the gamut from viniculture to beekeeping, and express the human struggle with the forces of nature in noble terms. Joseph Addison, in his Preface (1697) to John Dryden's translation of the *Georgics,* comments that Virgil "breaks the clods and tosses the dung about with an air of gracefulness." Addison concludes by calling the *Georgics* "the most complete, elaborate and finished piece in all antiquity."

Georgic poetry presents a celebration of an ordinary, laboring heroism intended to contrast with the warlike valor or brave cunning of the epic hero (Achilles or Odysseus, say). The georgic also distinguishes itself from the pastoral, whose shepherds usually live a life of relaxed singing contests and amorous dispute, very unlike the hard work of the farmer.

In Virgil's *Georgics,* human culture, beginning with the cultivation of the fields, does violence to nature (including human nature). "The poet's task," David Quint writes, "is both to partake in and to celebrate the work of culture *and* to register and to mourn its casualties, to take on the voice of nature." There is an integrity and even-handedness involved in Virgil's work that helps make the georgic the foundation for later political ideals (those of Thomas Jefferson, most notably).

Milton's Eden, in *Paradise Lost,* combines elements of the pastoral and the georgic; see Anthony Low, *The Georgic Revolution* (1985). A prominent later georgic poem is James Thomson's *The Seasons* (1726–30, rev. 1746), with its celebration of rural virtue. See Dwight Durling, *Georgic Tradition in English Poetry* (1935), and David Quint, "The Farmer as Hero," *New Republic,* March 20 and 27, 2006, 33–37.

ghazal The ghazal (pronounced GHUZZ-l, with the *gh* somewhere between the French *r* and the Hebrew or Scottish *ch*) is a classical verse form from the Near East. It has recently become a popular verse form in English, largely through the effort of the poet Agha Shahid Ali (1949–2001). The ghazal derives from seventh-century Arabia, was transmitted to Persian (Farsi) tradition, and exists in Turkish, Urdu, Pashtun, and Hindi. Two of its great masters are the Persian poets Sa'di (d. 1291) and Hafiz (d. 1389). The ghazal entered European poetry through Goethe's *Westöstlicher Divan* (1819).

The ghazal is made of couplets. The first and second lines of the opening couplet end in the same phrase, and the second line of each subsequent couplet repeats the phrase (and rhyme). (In the classical Persian ghazal, the poet signs his name in the concluding line.) Here are some stanzas from a contemporary ghazal by Agha Shahid Ali:

Where are you now? Who lies beneath your spell tonight
Before you agonize him in farewell tonight?

Pale hands that once loved me beside the Shalimar
Whom else from rapture's road will you expel tonight?

Those "fabrics of Cashmere—" "to make Me beautiful—"
"Trinket"—to gem—"Me to adorn—How—tell"—tonight?

I beg for haven: Prisons, let open your gates—
A refugee from Belief seeks a cell tonight.

(The quotations in the third stanza are from a poem by Emily Dickinson [no. 473].) The resonant satisfaction of the ghazal's repetitions makes it sound similar to another form, the blues. See Agha Shahid Ali, *Ravishing DisUnities* (2000).

gnomic From the Greek *gnome,* a memorable, deliberately fashioned sentiment having general application (the Latin equivalent is *sententia*). *Gnomic* as it is currently used, however, implies less the force of a maxim than that of a strange obliqueness: the gnome enigmatically claims its own truth, bristling against the reader. The Greek thinker Heraclitus (ca. 535–475 BCE) is the first writer of gnomic sentences in this strong sense of the word. He proclaims, to give one instance, "The way up and the way down are the same." In poetry, the Old English gnomes are short verse riddles, frequently in first person. The reader must deduce from the clues given what entity is speaking (a thunderstorm, a shield).

Here are some gnomic lines by Wallace Stevens, from "Thirteen Ways of Looking at a Blackbird" (1917):

A man and a woman
Are one.
A man and a woman and a blackbird
Are one.

These lines present something that asks to be figured out, or grasped, but at the same time they prevent such understanding. (In this way Stevens's passage distinguishes itself from allegory, which can be decoded.) Does the blackbird cast an ominous shadow over the union of man and woman, becoming part of this union like a foreign object lodged in it, adulterating it? Or does the blackbird secure the union, through the addition of a refreshing eccentricity or oddness to the familiar Edenic couple? Does the blackbird suggest, in its darkness, the death that haunts human things? Or the fleetingness of a winged, momentary presence, in contrast to the permanence of marriage?

According to Angus Fletcher, the gnomic utterance involves "our need to discover what, in nature, we can be part of, to what order we can belong." See Angus Fletcher, "Stevens and the Influential Gnome," in *Colors of the Mind* (1991); also Eleanor Cook, *Enigmas and Riddles in Literature* (2006). Guy Davenport collects his translations of two remarkable gnomic Greek writers in *Herakleitos and Diogenes* (1976).

gnosis, Gnosticism In Greek *gnosis* means, simply, "knowledge." Gnosis became the aim of a group of ancient mystical sects, dating from the second century CE, who were interested in knowledge as illumination of one's secret, true self: the self that is usually obscured by our conventional thoughts and activities. Somewhere deep beneath everyday life, they insisted, lies the authentic spark or *pneuma,* imprisoned in matter.

The aim of gnosis is to see one's life as it has never been properly seen before. In setting this goal, Gnosticism distinguishes itself from classical Greek philosophy, according to which objects are more definitive the more general they are. In Plato and Aristotle, the exemplary, generally applicable idea— the concept of the just or the good, say—is more significant than a specific person or thing. In Gnosticism, by contrast, the object of knowledge remains particular: indeed, it is transcendent *because* it is so particular. Gnosis is thus an event in one's personal history, rather than an aspect of universally available knowledge.

According to Harold Bloom, two aspects that gnosis shares with the much later Romantic movement are evasion (a will to escape or refute one's fate, one's destiny in the universe of death and limitation) and the sublime (an encounter with near- or pseudo-annihilation, followed by a recovery). For Bloom, such later writers as Emerson may profitably be considered Gnostics. See Hans Jonas, *The Gnostic Religion* (1934), Harold Bloom, *Omens of Millennium* (1996), Elaine Pagels, *The Gnostic Paul* (1994), and Karen King, *What Is Gnosticism?* (2003).

Gothic The word *Gothic* derives from the Goths, the northern European tribe that warred against the Roman Empire. As a critical term, it was used by the art historian Giorgio Vasari in 1550 to signify the "monstrous, barbarous, and disorderly" in visual art, a style that departs from the Greco-Roman tradition. (The irregularities and fantastic exuberance of the Gothic style were later celebrated by art historians, most famously John Ruskin in *The Stones of Venice* [1851–53].) In 1765 Horace Walpole chose "gothic" as a descriptive term for his *Castle of Otranto,* a wildly popular novel that depicted the super-natural events occurring in a decrepit, hideous castle. From Walpole on, Gothic becomes a name for the literary genre trading in terror and fantasy—and for the ghostly, ruined, and morbid settings chosen by its writers. Two of the major Gothic novels are Ann Radcliffe's *Mysteries of Udolpho* (1794) and Matthew Lewis's *The Monk* (1796), featuring a depraved clergyman. Edward Young's book of poems *Night Thoughts* (1742) was an important precursor for the Gothic interest in crypts and corpses.

Daniel Cottom outlines some of the characteristic happenings of early Gothic: "Portraits stir and look back at their beholders, statues bleed, suits of armor walk . . . picturesque scenes open themselves to nightmares." Often, the reader enjoys an "imaginative imprisonment in extravagantly hostile sit-uations."

The Gothic is often darkly medieval. Bishop Richard Hurd's *Letters on Chivalry and Romance* (1762) championed the Middle Ages for "the superior solemnity of their superstitions," and for their appreciation of sublime and enjoyably terrifying horrors. Hugh Blair in 1763 described the sort of "wild and romantic" landscape preferred by Gothic writers: "The extended heath by the seashore; the mountains shrouded with mist; the torrent rushing through a solitary valley; the scattered oaks, and the tombs of warriors over-grown with moss, all produce a solemn attention in the mind, and prepare it for great and extraordinary events."

In the nineteenth century the Gothic tradition flourished in stories and novels by Edgar Allan Poe, Bram Stoker, Sheridan Le Fanu, and many others. Jane Austen's *Northanger Abbey* (written 1798–99, publ. 1818) parodies the Gothic novel. The continuing popularity of the Gothic is witnessed by works as various as William Faulkner's "A Rose for Emily," Alfred Hitchcock's movie *Psycho,* and Joss Whedon's television series *Buffy the Vampire Slayer.* See Anna Wittmann, "Gothic *Trivialliteratur,*" in Gerhart Hoffmeister, ed., *European Romanticism* (1990). Mark Edmundson, *Nightmare on Main Street* (1997), considers contemporary American Gothic in stimulating fashion. Kenneth Clark's *The Gothic Revival* (1928) is still essential reading.

grand style Defined by Matthew Arnold in his essays on translating Homer (1861–62), the grand style is exemplified when a writer, "poetically gifted, treats with simplicity and severity a serious subject." The grand style is not spare or austere; neither is it frivolous or unduly ornamented. See also Christopher Ricks, *Milton's Grand Style* (1963); and for an important discussion of levels of style in literary tradition, Ernst Robert Curtius, *European Literature and the Latin Middle Ages* (1948). Friedrich Nietzsche discusses the grand style in *The Gay Science* (1882–87). See CLASSICAL, CLASSICISM; DECORUM.

Great Chain of Being   A concept made popular by Arthur O. Lovejoy in *The Great Chain of Being* (1936) and by E. M. W. Tillyard in *The Elizabethan World Picture* (1943). The model for the image is a passage in the *Iliad* (Bk. 8) in which Zeus pictures himself dangling a golden chain from Olympus. In medieval and Renaissance thought, the Great Chain of Being extends from God in his heaven to the angels, then to humans, all the way down to the lower animals, plants, and inanimate matter. This cosmology generates a hierarchical picture infinite in its variety, a universe full of every possible degree of existence. Ulysses' famous speech on order in Shakespeare's *Troilus and Cressida* is a shrewd, underhanded use of the concept of the Great Chain of Being.

green world   A pastoral haven away from the city: a refuge from tyrannical urban business and the obsessive, controlled behavior that occupies life in the metropolis. The green world lives by its own rules, which oppose themselves to uptight workaday regulations: highjinks based on mistaken identity are strongly encouraged, as are amorous foolishness and careless lounging in the embowered space of the *locus amoenus* (or "pleasant place"). In Shakespeare's *A Midsummer Night's Dream,* the wood that the young lovers steal away to represents the green world: a place of freedom and rollicking confusion set against Athens, which is controlled by Theseus and the oppressive father Egeus. Stanley Cavell observes that, in Hollywood screwball comedies of the 1930s and '40s, the green world usually appears to be located in Connecticut.

   Northrop Frye's book on Shakespeare *A Natural Perspective* (1965) made the green world a fruitful critical concept. See Cavell, *Pursuits of Happiness* (1971), and Harry Berger, *Second World and Green World* (1988). See also LOCUS AMOENUS.

grotesque   The grotesque is an artistic style that audaciously rouses disgust and astonishment in the viewer or reader. It can become a form of monstrous play, entangled in its own encumbrances. In visual art, Pieter Brueghel, Hieronymus Bosch, and David Lynch might all be considered purveyors of the grotesque; in literature, one thinks of E. T. A Hoffmann or Poe, or Patrick Süskind's *Perfume* (1985).

The word *grotesque* derives from *grotto,* a picturesque cave. In antiquity and in the Renaissance, the grotto was the characteristic place for revelations from the lower world, contorted and terrifying phantoms. (On the continuing connection between underground caves and the grotesque, see Victoria Nelson's fascinating *Secret Life of Puppets* [2001].)

Baudelaire commented on the "frenzy and ferment" of the English illustrator George Cruikshank: "An extravagant violence of gesture and movement, and a kind of explosion, so to speak, within the expression." Robert Browning's poetry, according to G. K. Chesterton, communicates a similar grotesque energy. "The same sense of the uproarious force in things which makes Browning dwell on the oddity of a fungus or a jellyfish makes him dwell on the oddity of a philosophical idea," Chesterton wrote.

The critic Geoffrey Harpham writes that the grotesque subjects us to a kind of aesthetic overcrowding, arresting our attention and taunting our understanding. Another commentator, Hugh Kenner, defends the grotesque as an effective stab at classical proportions when he remarks, "A dwarf may be nature's critique of the tailor's dummy."

Vitruvius's *On Architecture* (27 BCE) and Horace's *Art of Poetry* (ca. 20 BCE) condemns the grotesque as a fantastic excrescence of style. In the Renaissance, Giorgio Vasari's *Lives of the Artists* (1550–68) mentions the grotto style, associated with the rediscovery of sites like the Golden House of Nero. (The Golden House was ornamented with fantastic pagan details, satyrs and cyclopes: sometimes luxurious and morbid, with intertwining foliage sprouting sex organs, lizards, and death's heads.)

In Plato's *Symposium* (ca. 385–378 BCE), the image of Socrates as a Silenus, or foul satyr, is a grotesque. And the traditional figure of the fool offers a defense of the grotesque, signaled by a deformed physique and the distorted perspective that goes along with it, but allied to wisdom. See Justus Möser's *Harlequin, or Defense of the Grotesque Comic* (1761). Also Wolfgang Kayser, *The Grotesque* (1957); Geoffrey Harpham, *On the Grotesque* (1982); and Frederick Burwick, "The Grotesque in the Romantic Movement," in Gerhart Hoffmeister, ed., *European Romanticism* (1990).

haiku A classic Japanese verse form that has been popular and influential among English-language poets, notably the Imagists. A haiku has three lines, the first and third consisting of five syllables and the second of seven syllables, for a total of seventeen syllables. Haiku began as the *hokku* or "opening part" of the *renga,* a linked verse form composed by two or more poets, and consisting of units of three lines (5-7-5 syllables) and two lines (5-5 syllables). Here is a haiku by Basho (1644–94; translated by David Lehman):

> At the ancient pond
> A solitary frog leaps—
> The sound of water.

There is a related thirty-one syllable Japanese form known as *tanka.* See Harold Henderson, *An Introduction to Haiku* (1958); see also IMAGISM.

Harlem Renaissance The name for the outpouring of literature, art, and music among African-American citizens of Harlem, chiefly in the 1920s. The sociologist and cultural critic W. E. B. DuBois was one of the main inspirations for the Harlem Renaissance, especially in his book *The Souls of Black Folk* (1903), which argued for a distinctive tradition of self-expression in black American life. Among the main writers of the Harlem Renaissance were, in poetry, Langston Hughes, Countee Cullen, Claude McKay, and Sterling Brown, and in prose, James Weldon Johnson, George Schuyler, Nella Larson, and Zora Neale Hurston. Two richly detailed accounts are Nathan Huggins, *Harlem Renaissance* (1971), and David Levering Lewis, *When Harlem Was in Vogue* (1981). Ann Douglas's *Terrible Honesty* (1995), on Manhattan in the 1920s, also contains a worthwhile discussion of the Harlem Renaissance.

hegemony A concept developed by the Italian Marxist Antonio Gramsci (pronounced GRAHMshee; 1891–1937). Hegemony means domination, not merely through instruments of violence (the police, the army), but also through the control of knowledge and culture. For example, it is sometimes argued that capitalism has attained hegemonic dominion in American society by instilling in the masses an unquestioning belief in free enterprise and the ability of the individual to achieve financial success. These ideals are demonstrated in many television programs and movies (the cultural productions controlled by capitalism). See Gramsci's *Prison Notebooks* (written 1929–35).

Hellenistic. See ALEXANDRIAN

hermeneutics From the Greek messenger god Hermes (the Roman Mercury). Hermeneutics is the study of interpretation, thought of both as reading and as dialogue: the conversation that occurs between readers and texts. It has been of crucial importance not just in literary study, but also in theology (where it originated) and in law. The discipline began around 1819 with the writings of Friedrich Schleiermacher, and was further developed by Wilhelm Dilthey (1833–1911). Hermeneutics, Schleiermacher and Dilthey explained, sees human experience, which appears most permanently and significantly in written texts, as an object of interpretation. Their goal was to establish a proper foundation for the discipline, or science, of such interpretation. For Schleiermacher, this effort meant trying to recover the original intention of an author by investigating the author's psychology and historical circumstances.

The philosopher Hans-Georg Gadamer in *Truth and Method* (1960) departed from Schleiermacher's attempt to recover an original meaning by suggesting that the early text and the later reader's expectations interpenetrate. Gadamerian hermeneutics requires that we make an effort to grasp our position in relation to the subject matter we are trying to understand: such positioning precedes, and forms the basis for, understanding. Interpreting the human world differs from interpreting the natural world because in the former case the interpreter's prejudices and preconceptions interact with the attitudes displayed in the text. Such conversation between interpreter and text contrasts with the natural scientist's effort to explain an inert, natural object, which cannot respond.

Gadamer called this interaction of reader and text the melding of horizons (in German, *Horizontverschmelzung*). The reader and the book that he studies question each other and modify each other's understanding. Gadamer's definition of hermeneutics as "the bridging of personal or historical distance between minds" turns interpretation into a dialogue between the reader and the literary work (or the work's author)—a conversation modeled in some ways on the Platonic dialogues.

For Gadamer, *prejudice* means the prior inclination and knowledge that we bring to our experience of a work of art. Such prejudice is necessary for our participation in this work. (Gadamer's provocative anti-Enlightenment stance is that prejudice—in German, *Vorurteil*—is a *good* thing.) We become conscious of our prejudice when we grapple with a text, and we modify this prejudice in accord with our sense of the text's authority, its traditional force. This force is not to be coldly evaluated, and even combated, in the name of reason, as the Enlightenment advocated, but rather accepted. We then reach an "agreement," similar to what occurs in human negotiation and dialogue, between ourselves and the text, between its past and our present.

Gadamer sees interpretation as a game. We are not set "over against" the work of art, as subjects contemplating an object. Instead, we engage in a form of play that transforms both us and the work.

Gadamer's ideas were based in part on Martin Heidegger's claim in *Being and Time* (1927) concerning *Dasein,* or being-in-the-world. For Heidegger dasein is distinguished by the fact that it attempts to understand itself; and this self-understanding occurs as a process, an emergence of meaning. (Truth, for Heidegger, is not a property of statements about the world: not a matter of correct description, but rather a revealing of the world in language. Heidegger calls this revealing an event.)

Just as it connects past and present, so hermeneutics bridges the distance between familiar and strange meanings, and between the parts and the whole of a text. The *hermeneutic circle* is an important concept developed by Schleiermacher and Dilthey: a reader cannot understand the whole of a work without grasping its parts; but the reader must have an idea of the whole before beginning to read any part of it.

In addition to Gadamer, the other major twentieth-century philosopher of hermeneutics is Paul Ricoeur. In *The Symbolism of Evil* (1960), Ricoeur explores the implications of the mythic images and symbols that we find necessary to our thinking. He draws a contrast between the "hermeneutics of suspicion," which demystifies the symbols that we fear or revere with the aim of decreasing their power, and a hermeneutics that attends to and appreciates symbols. Ricoeur's late work involves the concepts of temporality, metaphor, and narrative, and links hermeneutics to phenomenology's interest in self-reflection. See Ricoeur, *The Rule of Metaphor* (1975).

See Hans-Georg Gadamer, *Philosophical Hermeneutics* (1976) and *Truth and Method* (1960); E. D. Hirsch, *Validity in Interpretation* (1967); Gerald Bruns, *Hermeneutics Ancient and Modern* (1992); Joel Weinsheimer, *Philosophical Hermeneutics and Literary Theory* (1991); and, on biblical hermeneutics, Hans Frei, *The Eclipse of Biblical Narrative* (1974). Peter Szondi presents a critique of Gadamer in his *Introduction to Literary Hermeneutics* (1975).

hermetic The origins of the word *hermetic* lie in mysticism. It is derived from the fabulous magical theorist Hermes Trismegistus, a legendary ancient author associated with the Greek god Hermes and the Egyptian Thoth. The corpus of hermetic writings includes works on astrology, alchemy, and philosophy, but much has been lost or exists only as rumor.

The scholar Frances Yates, in *Giordano Bruno and the Hermetic Tradition* (1964), considers the influence of the hermetic tract *Koré Kosmou* (1591) on the great Renaissance magus and philosopher Giordano Bruno (1548–1600).

heroic couplet. See COUPLET

historicism In his influential book *The Poverty of Historicism* (1957), the philosopher of science Karl Popper described historicism as the search for laws controlling social development and change.

The historicist effort has, according to Popper, two basic aspects, anti-naturalist and naturalist. The anti-naturalistic aspect of historicism emphasizes the differences among historical periods and the emergence of revolutionary newness, and celebrates the distinctive spirit of a nation or an age. The naturalistic aspect, by contrast, looks for principles that govern the unfolding of history from one age to another, rules that would make the future predictable. (Naturalism believes that there exist stable and certain laws of human nature, discernable in the course of events.) The historicist defers to the differences among distinct ages and cultures (anti-naturalism), but also insists on a universal, naturalist law of development—a tendency toward greater freedom or enlightenment over the course of time, for example (the so-called Whig version of history). Historicism, then, is both relativist (i.e., anti-naturalist) and anti-relativist (i.e., naturalist).

Popper argues that historicism responds to a real need, the desire for an explanation of history that would be more profound, sensible, and intrinsic than the "great man theory," which sees historical events as the effects of powerful individuals. But Popper argues against historicism because it turns historical trends into inexorable laws, much as the Fascist and Communist states did. The opposition to historicism (more or less in Popper's sense of the term) plays an important role in the theories of Leo Strauss and his students; see Strauss, *The City and Man* (1964). And Martin Buber, who influenced Strauss, presents a powerful argument against historicism, strongly influenced by Nietzsche's "On the Use and Disadvantage of History for Life" (from his *Untimely Meditations* [1873–76]). See Buber, "The Man of Today and the Jewish Bible," in *The Writings of Martin Buber,* ed. Will Herberg (1956).

In contemporary literary study, *historicism* tends to have a looser meaning, one that emphasizes its anti-naturalistic, or relativistic, character, and which has little to do with questions of historical development. The historicist critic emphasizes the qualities of a specific era or cultural situation, often by describing customary beliefs and daily habits in a particular place and time. The historicist's validating term of reference is usually national. He or she will rely on a broad definition of, say, "the America of the 1950s" in order to characterize individual works that were written in this place and time. One obvious limitation of the historicist method for literary study is that works that are less useful in contributing to a picture of social life in the chosen period and country tend to be less often discussed. Lyric poetry is sometimes ignored, and realist novels exalted, by historicist critics. Shakespeare has been and will be read infinitely more, and more deeply, than playwrights like Thomas Dekker and John Marston; yet these minor dramatists might tell us more about the historical spirit of Renaissance England than Shakespeare can. See also NEW HISTORICISM.

hortus conclusus Latin, "sealed garden." The hortus conclusus is a central image in the Bible's Song of Songs (also called the Song of Solomon): "A garden inclosed is my sister, my spouse; a spring shut up, a fountain sealed" (Song 4:12).

In his Merchant's Tale, from *The Canterbury Tales* (ca. 1386–1400), Geoffrey Chaucer terrifyingly makes an old man court his much younger beloved with images from the Song of Songs. This grotesque suitor degrades even the beautiful source of his words: "Swich olde lewed verses used he." (*Lewed,* or *lewd,* meant ignorant before it meant crudely lustful.)

The gardens of Adonis of antiquity were another sort of *horti conclusi:* usually small bowls in which women would plant herbs for a brief period, and then toss them into the sea at the conclusion of the festival of Adonis (thus the definition of Garden of Adonis in *Brewer's Dictionary of Phrase and Fable:* "a worthless toy, very perishable goods"). The practice is discussed by James Frazer in *The Golden Bough* (1922) and Marcel Detienne in *Gardens of Adonis* (1972). Spenser's splendid, lavish garden of Adonis, in Bk. 3 of *The Faerie Queene* (1590), draws on this tradition: the beauty of Adonis is bound up with fading, perishing humanity; it is kept alive only artificially.

The hortus conclusus tradition, as Stanley Stewart points out, often draws on erotic imagery to convey a vision of the spiritual life. See Stanley Stewart, *The Enclosed Garden* (1966), A. Bartlett Giamatti, *The Earthly Paradise and the Renaissance Epic* (1966), and Noam Flinker, *The Song of Songs in English Renaissance Literature* (2000).

humanism A new concept of human individuality, originating in the city-states of fourteenth- and fifteenth-century Italy, that was based on desire for excellence in scholarship, creative work, and education. The humanist movement spread to northern Europe, France, England, and elsewhere, and continued to flourish until the mid-seventeenth century. Among its more familiar literary figures are, in Italy, Dante Alighieri, Francesco Petrarca (known as Petrarch), Giovanni Boccaccio, Baldassare Castiglione, and Niccolò Machiavelli; in England, Thomas More, Francis Bacon, and John Milton; in France, François Rabelais and Michel de Montaigne. Books setting forth an ideal of the well-formed individual, ruler, or commonwealth are a major aspect of the humanist movement, from Leonardo Bruni's *Dialogues* (1401–6) to Roger Ascham's *Schoolmaster* (1570), Machiavelli's *The Prince* (1513, publ. 1532), Castiglione's *The Courtier* (ca. 1516, publ. 1528), and More's *Utopia* (1516).

During the Renaissance the term *humanista* meant nothing more than a teacher of Latin. But the Latin classics proved to be the key to the era's renewed understanding of the individual's goals and ideas. Latin authors addressed issues like the dignity of man, the role of fate, and the strength of human will: the factors in life that make for human happiness, or flourishing.

(Greek was somewhat less familiar, at least at first, among the humanists; Petrarch and Dante could not read it.)

The Renaissance's new *studia humanitatis* contrasts with the earlier medieval version of education, which consisted of the *trivium* (grammar, rhetoric, and dialectic) and the *quadrivium* (arithmetic, music, geometry, and astronomy). In the medieval scheme, there was little room for the study of history or moral philosophy. Now, though, education could be based on the ethical ideas suggested by the ancients in their literary and philosophical speculations.

The key terms of the Italian humanists are fame, fortune, glory, and virtue. They see creative achievement and knowledge as heroic tasks, analogous to the brave deeds of conquerors and emperors. In the Middle Ages, prior to the humanist revolution, the sense of history was providential, based on the sacred narrative of the Bible, and moving from creation to revelation and redemption. (Saint Augustine's *City of God* [413–426/27 CE] was the major commentary on this narrative.) In the Italian Renaissance, with political life controlled by rivalrous city-states, history became a matter of daring strategy, not scriptural validation. Providential history did not disappear, of course; it was a significant influence in the Reformation. But it had been challenged.

Another aspect of the humanist movement was its sense of intimacy with the classical past. Petrarch wrote a series of familiar letters addressed to Homer, Virgil, Cicero, Livy, and others. Allied to this closeness with antiquity was a desire to correct the distortions of ancient texts, to recover them in their original fullness. The ambition to search for the source characterized the humanist attitude toward religious texts and ideas. The great Netherlandish humanist Desiderius Erasmus translated the New Testament into Latin (1516), saving the sacred text from the errors committed in the Vulgate (the medieval Latin Bible, in the universally read version produced by Saint Jerome). In an effort analogous to his philological study of the original text of the Bible, Erasmus in his *Colloquies* (1518) reacted against the medieval corruptions of church hierarchy. Through his description in the *Colloquies* of friendly, egalitarian conversation on both spiritual and worldly matters, he tried to regain the original ethical ideal of Christian community and decency: a humorous, liberal-minded fellowship.

For humanists like Castiglione in *The Courtier,* the self became a work of art, with the individual's "knowledge and skill informed by proportion and grace" (Joseph Mazzeo). The Swiss historian Jacob Burckhardt, in his great *Civilization of the Renaissance in Italy* (1860), first described the ambition of figures like Leonardo da Vinci and the architect Leon Battista Alberti to become the *uomo universale,* or universal man. Here Burckhardt evokes the supremely well-rounded, eccentrically talented Alberti (who became world-famous as the inventor of the laws of perspective): "In all by which praise is won, Leon Battista was from childhood the first: . . . with his feet together, he could spring over a man's head; . . . in the cathedral, he threw a coin in the air till it was heard to ring against the distant roof. . . . He acquired every sort of accomplishment and dexterity, cross-examining artists, scholars and artisans of all descriptions, down to the cobblers, about the secrets and peculiarities of their craft. . . . He also wrote an Italian treatise on domestic life in four books; and even a funeral oration on his dog. . . . And all that he had and knew he imparted, as rich natures always do, without the least reserve, giving away his chief discoveries for nothing." Burckhardt concludes by remarking, of this godlike *lusus naturae,* that "an iron will pervaded and sustained his whole personality." Alberti proved that the individual can do anything, and with perfect style.

The humanist was an intellectual hero and adventurer. His interest in magic and mystical lore, like Francis Bacon's devotion to science, was a way to achieve power over the secret sources of nature. For Pico della Mirandola, author of the *Oration on the Dignity of Man* (1486), the human self was distinguished by flexibility and aspiration, and was capable of raising itself almost to divine level: wrestling successfully with the Protean, the endlessly various, character of God's creation.

The Renaissance is the real home of humanism. But Victorian sages like Matthew Arnold, Thomas Carlyle, and John Ruskin shared the humanist belief in individual aspiration and excellence, necessarily grounded in the strength of the surrounding culture. Their concerns lived on in the works of American critics a hundred years later: for example, Lionel Trilling and Irving Howe.

In the early twentieth century, a "new humanism" was promoted by the literary critics Irving Babbitt and Paul Elmer More, who reacted against the overly specialized aspects of philology as it was then practiced. But Babbitt and More were felt to be too vaguely emotive, their moralizing too glib. When critics like Robert Penn Warren and Cleanth Brooks turned, in the 1940s, toward a stricter consideration of the technical aspects of poetic language, they were in fact promoting another version of the humanist ideal: man as the hero of articulation, expressing his precarious and uniquely complicated existence, and fighting with the weapons of skilled ambiguity, irony, and paradox (see NEW CRITICISM).

Humanism can be a pejorative term in current literary and cultural criticism, especially in the disciplines of cultural studies and new historicism. This turn began with the philosopher Martin Heidegger, whose "Letter on Humanism" (1947) criticized Jean-Paul Sartre for his humanist existentialism. Heidegger asserted that man, Sartre's focus, was a limited concept and should be superseded by the notion of Being (in German, *Sein* or *Dasein,* two distinct but related terms). Later philosophers like Michel Foucault and Jacques Derrida, both highly influential in literary studies, followed Heidegger's lead in questioning the centrality of the human. But humanism always seems to return, if humanism is understood as the commitment to asking whether particular goals, practices, and ideas serve or damage the hope for human excellence and happiness. The definition of humanist ideals remains a constant concern of philosophy and cultural commentary, as seen recently in the works of thinkers like Martha Nussbaum and Tzvetan Todorov.

On Renaissance ideas of humanism, see Joseph Mazzeo, *Renaissance and Revolution* (1967); Paul Oskar Kristeller, *Renaissance Thought* (1955); Hans Baron, *The Crisis of the Early Italian Renaissance* (1955); Eugenio Garin, *Italian Humanism* (1947); and Thomas M. Greene, *The Vulnerable Text* (1986). Constance Jordan provides an interesting account of Renaissance humanism in its attitude toward women in *Renaissance Feminism* (1990). Rebecca Bushnell in *A Culture of Teaching* (1996) connects Renaissance ideals with contemporary American debates over education.

humors, comedy of. See COMEDY

iambic. See METER

iconography From the Greek *eikon* (image), and *graphe* (writing). Iconography is the study of the discursive content of images: the symbolic meanings that they express. The art historian Erwin Panofsky (1892–1968) was, along with Aby Warburg (1866–1929), one of the founders of the modern discipline of iconography. According to Panofsky, iconography tries to understand the symbolic aspect of images: the aspect of the visual that is meant to be read. Consider some of the puzzles we find ourselves confronted by on a visit to a museum of Renaissance or medieval art. Why does the baby Jesus hold a pomegranate? Why does Father Time carry a sickle? Iconography aims to answer such questions. (For the answer to the question about Father Time, see MYTHOGRAPHY.)

All eras carry a rich load of iconographical meaning. Understanding the iconography of the 1960s would mean knowing the significance of the Mao jacket, love beads, and the peace sign.

The iconographical associations in earlier art frequently involve material taken from religion and mythology. Often, pagan figures bear a Christian theme. So a painting of Hercules mastering Cerberus, the fierce, monstrous dog that guards Hades, can be read as Christ harrowing hell. Grasping iconography often requires recognizing in paintings, drawings, and statues arguments derived from the intellectual orientation of the artist's era. So, to give one instance, in Renaissance and Baroque art, through the influence of philosophy, nakedness becomes a figure for truth, and for ideal or inherent beauty. Such intellectual themes sometimes ally themselves to the formal qualities of the artist's work. Michelangelo's adherence to the Neoplatonic idea of the body as an earthly prison appears in his sculptures, which depict figures struggling mightily, and vainly, to escape from the stone that incarnates them.

Iconographical effect clearly depends on the cultural literacy of the viewer. Panofsky writes that someone unfamiliar with the Christian Gospels (his example is an Australian bushman) "would be unable to recognize the theme of a Last Supper; to him, it would only convey the idea of an excited dinner party." (Panofsky wittily posits that bushmen have dinner parties.) But a true iconographical sense requires more than the knowledge of basic plots and scenes: it also demands that we engage with a hidden meaning. Many a visitor to the Sistine Chapel, while recognizing Michelangelo's biblical stories, may be bewildered by the mystical significance of God's naked backside being displayed to Moses (and to us, the viewers of the painting). (See Exodus 33:23.)

Among Panofsky's virtuoso treatments of iconography are his studies of blind Cupid and Father Time, both in *Studies in Iconology* (1939); see also his *Idea* (1924) and *Meaning in the Visual Arts* (1955). For a fascinating account of the iconographical afterlife of the Greek and Roman gods, consult Jean Seznec, *The Survival of the Pagan Gods* (1940). And for some especially fervent and impressive iconographical detective work, see Leo Steinberg, *The Sexuality of Christ in Renaissance Art and Modern Oblivion* (1984).

idyll (Often pronounced "IHdill" rather than "EYEdill"; both ways are acceptable.) The word applied by the Greek poet Theocritus (third century BCE) to his pastoral poems: in Greek, *eidyllion,* meaning a little *eidos* (picture, appearance). More common names for pastoral poems are eclogues (meaning selections or, fancifully, goat-songs) and bucolics (from *boukolos,* "herdsman"). The term was used in the Victorian era by Alfred, Lord Tennyson, for his Arthurian verse romance, *Idylls of the King* (1859–85). See also ECLOGUE; PASTORAL.

imagination The word *imagination* originally meant, rather simply, the faculty that forms mental images (similar to the Renaissance term *phantasy*). The imagination could be scheming, anticipatory in a merely practical way, or frightened. (Chaucer writes in his Miller's Tale [ca. 1386], "Men may dyen of ymaginacioun / So depe may impression be take.") But beginning in the Renaissance, imagination also began to attain its current grand status as a power of the mind that informs and humanizes us.

One of the key moments in the linking of these two senses of imagination, the low or practical one and the high, poetic one, occurs in Shakespeare's *Midsummer Night's Dream:*

And as imagination bodies forth
The forms of things unknown, the poet's pen
Turns them to shapes, and gives to airy nothing
A local habitation, and a name.

Shakespeare here proposes an analogy between the humdrum, everyday sense of imagination (picturing or "bodying forth" unknown things) and the high poetic one: a fitting analogy, since in *A Midsummer Night's Dream* the everyday is transformed into the high magic of poetry.

Joseph Addison in his *Spectator* essay no. 411 (1712) defines the imagination as the mind's ability to picture scenes, whether these scenes are literally present or not. For Addison, imagination is a faculty midway between the senses (which aim at consuming and possessing the world) and understanding (which reasons about the world). The imagination offers enjoyments that are easier than those of the understanding, with its bent for hard philosophizing, but not so crude or gross as those of the senses (which would want to own the landscape, or eat the animals in it, rather than merely look at it appreciatively). "A man of a polite imagination . . . can converse with a picture, and find an agreeable companion in a statue," Addison suavely writes, endowing cultivated seeing with a refined capacity for dialogue.

For Addison, defense of imaginative seeing leads to an advocacy of fiction's "splendid and illustrious objects" over the "knotty and subtle disquisitions" of philosophy. Ever since Plato, the relation between imagination on one hand and theory or philosophy on the other has always been peculiarly worried. Should philosophy draw on imagination for its examples, or must it guard itself against the overly imaginative?

Mark Akenside in *The Pleasures of the Imagination* (1744) writes that the disposition of our "moral powers" is similar to that of our imagination: "Those who are most inclined to admire prodigious and sublime objects in the physical world, are also most inclined to applaud examples of fortitude and heroic virtue in the moral. While those who are charmed rather with the delicacy and the sweetness of colours, and forms, and sounds, never fail in like manner to yield the preference to the softer scenes of virtue and the sympathies of a domestic life."

Critics have sometimes distinguished between greater and lesser kinds of imagining. Samuel Taylor Coleridge in his *Biographia Literaria* (1817) describes the imagination as a power that "dissolves, diffuses, dissipates, in order to recreate; or where this process is rendered impossible, yet still at all events it struggles to idealize and to unify." The contrasting power to the imagination is, for Coleridge, the fancy, which "receive[s] all its materials ready made from the law of association," and which merely rearranges what already exists. Characteristically, imagination unifies; fancy merely assembles. Coleridge also draws a distinction between primary imagination ("the living power and prime agent of all human perception") and secondary imagination ("an echo of the former, co-existing with the conscious will").

Frederic Bogel persuasively describes the anxieties attending imagination in the eighteenth century and after, the "uncertainty . . . whether an energetic exercise of modern imagining can be distinguished from the willfulness of mere fancy or the vain projection of neurotic fantasy." William Collins's "Ode to Fear" (1746) is a case in point noted by Bogel. On the association of fancy with cheating or delusion and the difficulty of distinguishing it from the nobler, more secure form of imagination, see Bogel's *Literature and Insubstantiality in Later Eighteenth Century England* (1984), and Geoffrey Hartman, "False Themes and Gentle Minds," in *Beyond Formalism* (1970).

On Coleridge, consult I. A. Richards, *Coleridge on Imagination* (1934). This book was familiar to the poet Wallace Stevens, whose own writing on imagination is essential: see Stevens, "Imagination as Value," in *The Necessary Angel* (1951). For an account of eighteenth-century debates over the nature of the imagination, see Thomas McFarland, *Originality and Imagination* (1985).

Imagism Imagism was an avant-garde movement in poetry during the early twentieth century, especially between the years 1913 and 1917. The original stimulus for the movement was a series of essays by the critic T. E. Hulme (pronounced HUME; 1883–1917), who protested against the "messy" and sentimental manner of Georgian poetry, and called for the production of colder, harder verse.

Imagism espoused an evocative, laconic directness, and trusted in strict verbal economy. Pound, in his essay "A Few Don'ts by an Imagiste" (1913), expressed the Imagist credo in the following starkly negative terms: "Use no superfluous word, no adjective, which does not reveal something." Pound quarreled two years later with the poet Amy Lowell over leadership of the Imagists: a fight she won, whereupon Pound derisively named the movement "Amygism."

Imagist poems were usually written in free verse. Among the movement's adherents were, in addition to Pound, H.D. (the nom de plume of Hilda Doolittle) and William Carlos Williams. The best-known Imagist poem is probably Pound's "In a Station of the Metro" (1916):

The apparition of these faces in the crowd;
Petals on a wet, black bough.

Pound's poem embodies a major feature of Imagism: the unexpected encompassing power hidden in its spare focus. The poem's restriction, aiming at the current instant, the merely physical world and the naked response of the eye, paradoxically conjures up vast echoes of literary tradition (here, the image of dead souls as leaves from Homer's *Odyssey,* Dante's *Inferno,* and other epics). (See TROPE.)

Hugh Kenner defines the goal of Imagism as "elevating the glimpse into the vision": devising a fixed, memorable equivalent for the visual moment, rendering this moment "reduced, intensified." From the point of view of a Pound, the preceding era, ruled by the spirits of Alfred, Lord Tennyson, Walter Pater, the French Symbolists, and the pre-Raphaelite poets, had traded in gauzy glimpses rather than the concentrated, self-sufficient image.

On Imagism, see Hugh Kenner, "Imagism," in *The Pound Era* (1971); John T. Gage, *In the Arresting Eye* (1981); T. E. Hulme, "Lecture on Modern Poetry" (1908–9) in *Speculations* (1924); and Michael Levenson, *A Genealogy of Modernism* (1984).

imitation Imitation (in Latin, *imitatio*) is, in literature, the art of modeling one's writing on a distinguished source. In the Renaissance, for example, apprentice poets fashioned their work on the basis of prestigious Roman models like Virgil, Horace, and Ovid.

The theory of imitation is itself Roman in its origins. In his Odes (4.2), Horace (65–8 BCE) writes that the Greek poet Pindar, his sublime predecessor, resembles a rushing torrent; to imitate Pindar's vast power would be disastrous. Horace compares himself, in contrast, to the industrious bee that gathers thyme from various sources. Like the bee, he carefully and modestly makes up his poems. Seneca the Younger (ca. 4 BCE–65 CE), in his Epistle 84, takes up Horace's image of the bee as an exemplary figure for the author. As Seneca puts it, the bee, after sampling various texts by earlier writers, "so blend[s] those several flavors into one delicious compound" that the final product, the honey, "is clearly a different thing from that whence it came." The Renaissance humanist Desiderius Erasmus in *Ciceronianus* (1528) further expands the bee topos derived from Horace and Seneca. Erasmus insists that, as a young writer, one must gather and digest earlier literature to make one's own: "So that your mind crammed with every kind of food may give birth to a style which smells not of any flower, shrub, or grass but of your own native talent and feeling; so that he who reads may not recognize fragments from Cicero but the reflection of a well-stored mind."

In John Dryden's *Preface to Fables* (1700) and in T. S. Eliot's "Reflections on Contemporary Poetry" (1919) there are stirring evocations of imitation as a kinship between authors. Eliot's more famous essay "Tradition and the Individual Talent" (1917) celebrates imitation as an impersonal connection between a writer and the tradition that precedes him. "Reflections on Contemporary Poetry" strikes a different note. Eliot here describes the "peculiar personal intimacy" a writer may experience "with another, probably a dead author." "We may not be great lovers," he continues, "but if we had a genuine affair with a real poet of any degree . . . we do not imitate; we are changed; and our work is the work of the changed man; we have not borrowed, we have been quickened, and we become bearers of a tradition." (See also INFLUENCE.) On Renaissance imitation, see Thomas Greene, *The Light in Troy* (1982); Richard Peterson, *Imitation and Praise in the Poetry of Ben Jonson* (1982).

impersonality Along with the notions of the objective correlative and the dissociation of sensibility, T. S. Eliot (1888–1965) is best known for his idea of impersonality. Eliot wrote in "Tradition and the Individual Talent" (1917) that "poetry is not a turning loose of emotion, but an escape from emotion; it is not the expression of personality, but an escape from personality. But, of course, only those who have personality and emotions know what it means to want to escape from these things."

In a canny and fascinating way, Eliot in this passage gestures toward the half-hidden psychodrama of those who want to escape their emotions. Rather than underlining the success of the escape, he draws our attention to the motives for it. Eliot's emphasis on the impersonality of artistic creation is largely derived from Walter Pater's essay "Style" (1888), although Pater the late-Victorian aesthete was a writer scorned by Eliot. See also ASCETICISM; MODERNISM; NOUVEAU ROMAN; OBJECTIVISM; PARNASSIANS.

implied author/implied reader The concept of the implied author—a surrogate figure designed by a book's author, with whom the reader identifies as he or she reads—was developed by the American critic Wayne Booth. Booth writes in *The Rhetoric of Fiction* (1961) that "as I read . . . I become the self whose beliefs must coincide with the author's. . . . The author creates, in short, an image of himself and another image of his reader; he makes his reader, as he makes his second self, and the most successful reading is one in which the created selves, author and reader, can find complete agreement." Booth agrees with a traditional emphasis of hermeneutics: in the words of the eighteenth-century scholar J. J. Rambach, "The interpreter needs to take on the spirit of the author to such an extent that he slowly becomes like a second I." See Hans-Georg Gadamer, "Rhetoric and Hermeneutics," in Walter Jost and Michael Hyde, eds., *Rhetoric and Hermeneutics in Our Time* (1997); and see HERMENEUTICS.

Wolfgang Iser in *The Implied Reader* (1972), departing from Booth's emphasis on an agreement between the author and the reader, examines cases in which "a subtly instituted opposition" between them impels the narrative. For Iser, a strong divergence between author and reader often occurs in nineteenth- and twentieth-century novels, whose authors "explicitly refrain from telling [the reader] what to do."

impressionism A short-lived literary movement during the decade beginning in 1910, based in the ideas of the novelists Ford Madox Ford and Joseph Conrad. Ford remarked that "life [does] not narrate, but [makes] impressions on our brains." The impressionist author does not let his personality appear in his work; but, Ford added, "his whole book . . . is the impression of his personality." (For a comparable concept evoked in T. S. Eliot's essay "Tradition and the Individual Talent," see IMPERSONALITY.)

Impressionism, which draws on the philosophical tradition of skepticism, may require the dismantling of conventional narration in an effort to give what Ford calls "the impression not the corrected chronicle": "the sort of odd vibration that scenes in real life really have." It is the image or sense of life itself that impressionism aims for: an ambition often stated in the critical writings of Virginia Woolf and other modernists.

See Ford Madox Ford, "Impressionism and Fiction" and "On Impressionism" (1914), in *Critical Writings of Ford Madox Ford*, ed. Frank MacShane (1964), John Peters, *Conrad and Impressionism* (2001); Jesse Matz, *Literary Impressionism and Modernist Aesthetics* (2001); Mark Wollaeger, *Joseph Conrad and the Fictions of Skepticism* (1990).

inexpressibility topos (A *topos,* in Greek "place," signifies a literary commonplace; the plural is *topoi.*) The claim that a particular experience, person, or object is beyond verbal description, usually because of its excellence. The inexpressibility topos often carries with it an automatic paradox. When a poet says that his love is inexpressible because incomparable, deeper than that of any previous poet-lover, such a poet knowingly courts comparison with all the others who have announced that *their* love is (also) beyond words. The best-worn verbal paths are frequently the ones that deny their own strategies—in a strategic way. See Ernst Robert Curtius, "Inexpressibility Topoi," in *European Literature and the Latin Middle Ages* (1948). See also TOPOS.

influence The effect that an earlier writer has on a later one, visible in the later writer's stance, style, and imaginative identity. John Dryden in his preface to *Fables* (1700) writes, "Spenser more than once insinuates that the soul of Chaucer was transfused into his body; and that he was begotten by him two hundred years after his decease." As Dryden suggests, the affiliations between writers often take the form of a familial inheritance: the later author is "begotten" by the earlier, the "great original" who survives within him. This family romance may take severe or contentious form; or it may be amiable and fairly untroubled.

For more on the drama of influence, see ANXIETY OF INFLUENCE.

inspiration Inspiration is the Latin *afflatus,* the breath of the god that fills a poet or an oracular sage. The prophetic Sibyl's ecstatic "Deus ecce deus" (The god is here!) in Bk. 6 of Virgil's *Aeneid* offers a palpably tremendous instance of inspiration, the breathing in of divinity.

An invocation of the Muse is a familiar part of the apparatus of poetic inspiration. "Andra moi ennepe, Mousa," begins Homer in his *Odyssey:* "Sing in (or to) me, Muse . . . the man"—Odysseus. Later poets claimed to be inspired by a beloved, who takes the place of the Muse as a poetic source. Wordsworth finds inspiration (or, rather, it finds him) in his own mind's casual encounters with the world, especially the natural landscape.

Milton gives a homely, moving version of inspiration, in his early "At a Vacation Exercise" (1628): "I have some naked thoughts that rove about, / And loudly knock to have their passage out . . ." Keats's "Ode to Psyche" (1819) carries inspiration to such rhapsodic height that the poet discards all outside sources in favor of his own powers of sight: "I see, and sing, by my own eyes inspired." Wallace Stevens echoes Keats's passionate isolated selfhood in his "Tea at the Palaz of Hoon" (1921):

> I was the world in which I walked, and what I saw
> Or heard or felt came not but from myself;
> And there I found myself more truly and more strange.

See Ernst Robert Curtius, "The Poet's Divine Frenzy," in *European Literature and the Latin Middle Ages* (1948).

intentional fallacy The notion that a piece of literature can be adequately interpreted by understanding the intentions of its author. W. K. Wimsatt and Monroe Beardsley argue against such reliance on authorial intention in their essay "The Intentional Fallacy" (1946; reprinted in *The Verbal Icon* [1954]). Wimsatt and Beardsley assert that the author's intent is the cause of a piece of literature, but cannot be a standard by which the work may be understood or judged. Unlike a "practical message," whose meaning depends on the reader's inference concerning the writer's (or speaker's) intent, a literary text, they write, "is detached from the author at birth and goes about the world beyond his power to intend it or control it." Wimsatt and Beardsley here adapt an image from Plato's dialogue *Phaedrus* (ca. 375–365 BCE) concerning the helplessness of writing, which Plato sees as an orphan deprived of its parent, the author. But for Wimsatt and Beardsley, in contrast to Plato, the author, not the text, is the abandoned one.

Wimsatt and Beardsley in "The Intentional Fallacy" accept some uses of biographical evidence, but they caution that the use of such evidence runs the risk of substituting for the book's own interests the mere circumstances of the author's life—thereby distracting the reader from how a poem or novel works, how it achieves its effects. As "The Intentional Fallacy" continues, the issue for Wimsatt and Beardsley becomes the dangerous potential for the reader's knowledge of a work's context (whether intellectual, biographical, or literary) to overwhelm his sense of the work itself. In truth, the work may or may not be interested in a particular context. The evidence for the interest can be tested only by seeing how a specific literary text functions, rather than by citing the supposedly pressing character of external facts like the author's life and times, or the weight of literary tradition. The Wimsatt-Beardsley critique of intention comes down to a polemic against careless uses of historicism and philology, when such methods fail to attend to the literary work as a discrete object: an object that can, in effect, itself decide on the relevance of its contexts. See also AFFECTIVE FALLACY.

interior monologue In fiction, an extensive and articulate reflection that becomes an episode in itself, consisting of the thoughts that a character speaks (or would speak) to himself or herself. James Joyce and Virginia Woolf are two notable practitioners of the interior monologue.

The Hungarian Marxist critic Georg Lukács, in *Realism in Our Time* (1958), distinguishes between the interior monologue in Thomas Mann and in Joyce's *Ulysses* (1922). For Mann, whom Lukács prefers to Joyce, the interior monologue is merely a way of exploring a character's thinking; it keeps its proper, limited status. For Joyce, though (in Molly Bloom's soliloquy, for example), interior monologue takes on a higher profile, becoming an emblem of Joyce's world as composed of "powerfully charged—but aimless and directionless—fields of force." (See also STREAM OF CONSCIOUSNESS.)

interlude A common medieval and Renaissance word that sometimes means any play or dramatic performance, and sometimes a short, comic dialogue performed between courses at a banquet. Thus Goneril's scornful interjection to her husband Albany when he confronts Edmund in *King Lear* (5.3): "An interlude!"

invention The hard-boiled American detective novelist Raymond Chandler, explaining the rules of literary creation, remarked, "When in doubt have a man come through a door with a gun in his hand." As Chandler hints, literary invention sometimes requires an author's excited ingenuity, or contrivance. At bottom, though, invention describes an act of making that is also a sudden finding, or discovery. The author happens upon his moment, rather than merely manipulating it. (It should be noted, however, that invention, in Latin *inventio,* is also the part of rhetoric concerned with finding and deploying arguments, and as such is a rule-bound discipline, one that does not rely on spontaneity or inspiration.)

Invention is the reader's work, not just the author's. Faced with a book, we must be ready to find the new: to make something useful, turn it to hand.

"One must be an inventor to read well," Ralph Waldo Emerson writes in "The American Scholar" (1837).

To invent, then, is to come upon something. It is therefore appropriate that A. E. Housman images poetic discovery, or invention, as occurring unexpectedly during the act of walking. Housman remembers that "having drunk a pint of beer at luncheon—beer is a sedative to the brain, and my afternoons are the least intellectual portion of my life—I would go out for a walk of two or three hours. As I went along, thinking of nothing in particular . . . there would flow into my mind, with sudden and unaccountable emotion, sometimes a line or two of verse, sometimes a whole stanza at once." (Housman, *The Name and Nature of Poetry* [1933].)

Housman's version of invention is allied to the "free association" of Freudian psychoanalysis; it also pays tribute to the traditional alliance between poetry and walking (on this subject, see Roger Gilbert, *Walks in the World* [1991]). At the bottom of the potentially slippery Housmanian slope lies the anti-art of the poetry slam, which unites the moment of performance with that of invention. When a poet's first invention, the initiating instant of the poem, takes the place of the poem itself, literature can become mere "improv."

Wordsworth's formula that poetry is "emotion recollected in tranquility" invests invention with more prestige than Housman gives it, by adding a procedure: the gathering and composition of thoughts (Wordsworth, "Preface to *Lyrical Ballads*" [1800]). Wordsworth, through his interest in recollection, is closer than Housman to the traditional way of defining invention, which remains associated from the Renaissance on with the careful process of literary work known as imitation. (See IMITATION.)

invocation The traditional calling of, or to, the Muse, which is also the Muse's calling of the poet, at the beginning of an epic. Homer's *Iliad* begins with the command to sing a warlike subject, the anger of Achilles. The *Odyssey* starts, by contrast, by invoking the Greek word for man, *aner*: "The man sing in me, Muse, the one of many devices . . ." Virgil's *Aeneid* combines the two: "Arma virumque cano" (Arms and the man I sing).

Milton's *Paradise Lost* (1667) contains the most famous invocations in English verse, at the beginnings of Bks. 1, 3, 7, and 9. The invocation to Bk. 3, beginning "Hail heavenly light," with its reference to the poet's own blindness, provides perhaps the most memorable and affecting section of Milton's epic. Wordsworth's *Prelude* (1805–50) continues the tradition of the invocation by welcoming, in its opening pages, the "gentle breeze" that stirs the poet's thinking: the intimate breath of inspiration derived from a surrounding landscape.

Byron's *Don Juan* (1818–23) supplies the quickest and funniest invocation in English poetry:

Hail Muse! etcetera . . .

And there is this, from the contemporary American poet Gjertrud Schnackenberg:

Sing, Heav'nly Muse, and give me lyric flight,
Give me special effects, give me defiance
To challenge the Academy of Science
On fundamental points, and get them right . . .

(Gjertrud Schnackenberg, "Cadenza," from *The Lamplit Answer* [1985].)

Irish literary renaissance. See CELTIC REVIVAL

irony Irony in its simplest form is a trope that consists of saying one thing while meaning something opposite. Antony, by repeatedly telling the crowd in Shakespeare's *Julius Caesar* that "Brutus is an honorable man," clearly means to show them that Brutus is in fact dishonorable, the murderer of Caesar. As the critic Christopher Ricks notes, irony differs from its annoying kid brother sarcasm, with his one-track mind. Unlike sarcasm, irony entertains the idea that there might be truth in what someone is saying, even if he or she is, strictly speaking, lying.

Aristotle remarks that the ironic man tells a joke for his own amusement, the buffoon for another's. There is a self-indulgent, or at least self-regarding, aspect of irony: it enjoys itself. (This self-reflective, self-experiencing aspect of irony is emphasized by German Romantics like Friedrich Schlegel.)

At times these days, the word *ironic* is used to mean "surprising and incongruous, but strangely fitting." It should be restored to its earlier sense of a speech act that says one thing but means another (or, sometimes, means two contrary things at once).

Here are a few interesting cases of ironic statements. My first example of irony is a familiar one. Oedipus, near the beginning of Sophocles' *Oedipus*

Rex, speaks to the people of Thebes, who are afflicted by plague, and stresses his sympathy for their plight. He says that no one is sicker than he, Oedipus himself. Oedipus has no idea (but the play, of course, does) that he himself will be revealed as the sickest one of all, the monstrous case of incest that has caused the plague.

Another well-known instance of irony is committed by the Roman soldiers who crucify Jesus: "And they clothed him with purple, and platted a crown of thorns, and put it about his head, And began to salute him, Hail, King of the Jews!" (Mark 15:17–18). The soldiers clearly intend their coronation of Jesus to be ironic. Their point is that a miserable, powerless person like Jesus is certainly no "king," despite the rumors to that effect. But Mark's irony actually plays against the soldiers, since Jesus will be a king of a kind that has never been known before: the soldiers are merely demonstrating their blindness to this new, truer sense of the word *king.* (See Wayne Booth's *The Rhetoric of Irony* [1974] for a discussion of this and many other examples.)

In ancient Greek comedy the *eiron* is a character, frequently a slave, who consistently, and strategically, understates his own claims and achievements, in contrast to the boastful *alazon.* And yet (ironically enough) the eiron is in fact more intelligent and successful, and more truly ambitious, than the grandstanding alazon. Northrop Frye describes these two types in his *Anatomy of Criticism* (1957). Plato's Socrates was an eiron: constantly proclaiming his own confusion and tentativeness, while exemplifying a relentless, aggressive intellectual drive.

Romantic irony is another thing altogether. Friedrich Schlegel, called by G. W. F. Hegel the "father of irony," supplied much of the theory of Romantic irony. Schlegel, in the years 1798–1800, championed a kind of thinking that would "raise reflection to ever-higher powers" and "multiply it in an endless row of mirrors" (so the ironist becomes a god lost in a funhouse). The infinite freedom of speculation and invention associated with irony by Schlegel and other German Romantic writers found heroic examples in Shakespeare's Hamlet and Plato's Socrates. (Søren Kierkegaard's *The Concept of Irony* [1841] presents a notable version of Romantic irony centered on Socrates.)

The true heights of Romantic irony can be glimpsed in statements like the following (loosely paraphrased from Schlegel and others): everything worthwhile is both itself and its contrary; the world is paradoxical and therefore only an ambivalent consciousness can grasp it fully; experience constantly deceives us, and therefore we must be willing to be fooled in order to know its truth. Romantic irony sees detachment as the path to freedom. But it implies at the same time that freedom may be mere detachment, nothing more: and so the free man feels a disappointment bordering on despair. This harsh let-down can make the ironist restive, even cruelly aggressive. In Denis Diderot's *Rameau's Nephew* (1762), irony "pour[s] scornful laughter on existence, on the confusion pervading the whole, and on itself as well" (Lionel Trilling, *Sincerity and Authenticity* [1972]).

Despite the flowering of Romantic irony during the early nineteenth century, it is hard to confine irony to a particular period of literature. Eager spectators of their own passions, writers like Michel de Montaigne (1533–92) and Heinrich Heine (1797–1856) hover between a naive appetite for experience and an inclination to dissect it, and retain a fine sense of the ways that reflection and immediate feeling stumble against each other. Henry James, Jane Austen, and Vladimir Nabokov expose the ironies of their characters' lives, sometimes lovingly, sometimes brutally.

In the America of the 1940s, the New Critics rescued irony from the dizzying extremes of Romanticism, and redefined it in sober fashion as a functional principle of literature, especially lyric poems. Irony in their sense of the word had a far more workmanlike face than it did for the Romantics. For the New Critics, irony was simply the balancing or playing off of opposed elements in a literary work. "The bringing in of the opposite, the complementary impulse," was the definition of I. A. Richards (who influenced the New Critics). See AMBIGUITY; NEW CRITICISM.

See Cleanth Brooks, "Irony as a Principle of Structure" (1949), in Hazard Adams, ed., *Literary Theory Since Plato* (1971); also Bert States, *Irony and Drama* (1971). On Romantic irony, consult Ernst Behler, "The Theory of Irony in German Romanticism," in *Romantic Irony*, ed. Frederick Garber (1988). On Socratic—and Platonic—irony, see Alexander Nehamas, *The Art of Living* (1998).

Jacobean Age The reign of King James I, who succeeded Queen Elizabeth I on the throne of England and ruled from 1603 to 1625. The era's drama was often dark and violent, in the works of Cyril Tourneur, John Ford, John Webster, and Thomas Middleton, as well as Shakespeare's *Macbeth* and *King Lear.* Ford's *'Tis Pity She's a Whore* (1633), Webster's *The Duchess of Malfi* (ca. 1612, publ. 1623), and *The Changeling* (1622, publ. 1653) by Middleton and William Rowley are typical of the bloody and ominous Jacobean stage style. There were also heroic dramatists like George Chapman, however, and the court masque was an important form in the hands of Ben Jonson and his collaborator Inigo Jones. (See MASQUE.) Some important prose works of the age are Thomas Browne's *Religio Medici* (1642), Francis Bacon's *Essays* (1597–1625), and Robert Burton's *Anatomy of Melancholy* (1621). The King James Bible, a collaborative effort, was produced during the period. In poetry, the Jacobean era was dominated by the metaphysical poets and the group around Ben Jonson known as the "sons of Ben."

For various approaches to the idea of Jacobean literature, consult T. S. Eliot's essays on Jacobean drama in *Selected Prose of T. S. Eliot,* ed. Frank Kermode (1975); Jonathan Goldberg, *James I and the Politics of Literature* (1983), and Joseph Summers, *The Heirs of Donne and Jonson* (1970). See also META-PHYSICAL POETS; SONS OF BEN.

jeremiad From the book of Jeremiah in the Hebrew Bible: a fierce denunciation of the depravities and backsliding of one's own people. The term entered literary criticism with Perry Miller's chapter "The Jeremiad" in *The New England Mind* (1953), a study of early American puritanism. Numerous early American preachers produced jeremiads describing the failures of their communities in the sight of God. Miller finds, in the wailing, monotonous laments and recriminations of these sermons, indication of puritanism's declining sense of mission: the weakening of religious rule in New England, even as early as the 1670s. By contrast, Sacvan Bercovitch in *The American Jeremiad* (1978) understands the jeremiad as a mode that continues past the end of early New England theocracy and informs the rest of American history. For Bercovitch, the jeremiad, which calls on America to become what it ought to be and at the same time criticizes it for its current failures, characteristically combines vehement self-castigation with a "promise of ultimate success." This combination is linked to the sense of America as a promised land whose people have an exalted "peculiar mission." The idea of America as an elect or chosen nation, following the model of the ancient Israelites, is an example of typology or figura: the embodiment of biblical prototypes in later history (or in texts sacred or secular, beginning with the Christian gospels). See FIGURA; TYPOLOGY.

judgment Immanuel Kant's third critique, concerned with aesthetics, is his *Critique of Judgment* (1790). For Kant, as for earlier eighteenth-century critics like David Hume (1711–76) and Edmund Burke (1729–97), judgment is superior to mere invention or poetic imagining because it relies on generally persuasive, objective standards. Hume and Burke agree, David Bromwich writes, that "through judgment alone we detach ourselves from a particular state of mind, humor, culture, and history, everything which permits us to be 'influenced by prejudice' and prevents us from enlarging our comprehension. 'Cleared of all prejudice,' we may acquire delicacy of taste."

For Hume and Burke, a necessary detachment from prejudice must precede accurate readerly judgment. In the Victorian era, Matthew Arnold (1822–88) carried forward this emphasis on the objectivity required and instilled by judgment, so that we can (in Arnold's well-known formulation) "see the object as in itself it really is." For Romantic and post-Romantic critics like William Hazlitt (1778–1830), Walter Pater (1839–94), and John Ruskin (1819–1900), by contrast, we draw on, reevaluate, and refine our prejudices when we confront a work of art or literature, rather than attempting to free ourselves of them. By doing so, we reach a considered judgment that is fully conscious of its partiality. (Prejudice in this sense does not mean the crude ideologies generally distributed in mass society, but rather the leanings of the self that prepare for articulated judgment.) This Romantic tradition involves the self's strongest inclinations, and aspires toward a more intimate form of persuasion than exists in Kant, Burke, Hume, or Arnold. See

Matthew Arnold, "The Function of Criticism at the Present Time" (1864) and "The Study of Poetry" (1880), in Hazard Adams, ed., *Critical Theory Since Plato* (1971); Harold Bloom, ed., *Selected Writings of Walter Pater* (1974); David Bromwich, *Hazlitt* (1983); and on Ruskin, John D. Rosenberg, *The Darkening Glass* (1961).

Juvenalian satire. See SATIRE

K

kabbalah (Hebrew for "reception" or "welcoming.") In Jewish tradition, the esoteric or mystical study of God's universe.

The origins of kabbalah occurred in the south of France, in the thirteenth century; kabbalistic study then spread to the Jews of Spain. The Zohar, the first important kabbalistic book, was written by Moses de Leon in the thirteenth century in Spain. Isaac Luria, a scholar who lived in sixteenth-century Palestine, then decisively developed kabbalistic thinking, giving it the form in which we know it today.

Kabbalah has a theory of emanations, the radiating of the divine substance outward into the created universe. (It was influenced by Neoplatonism in this respect; see NEOPLATONISM.) In Kabbalah the emanations are called *sefirot*. The sefirot are the expressions of God, his form of language; they are also described as his tools, his vessels, his mirrors, his faces, his names, his garments, and his limbs. In kabbalistic mystical practice, the student meditates on the relations among the sefirot, their emergence and interaction.

Kabbalah resembles Gnosticism in its concern with the problem of evil, which it sees as resulting from God's concentration on *din* (strict justice) and his separation of himself from *hesed* (acts of kindness). In a complex vision, Luria's kabbalah claims that God's creative rigor led to a catastrophe-creation in which his sefirot, the vessels for his creativity, could not hold the light he filled them with. The vessels burst apart. In this way, flawed, fallen life was born. Redemption from evil takes the form of tikkun, mending the broken vessels through meditation.

Kabbalah remains perpetually popular in its various diluted versions, hawked by enterprising pop stars, among others. But it is also a substantial branch of knowledge.

Harold Bloom, most prominently, has applied kabbalistic ideas to literary study, in lively fashion. The two great scholars of the kabbalistic tradition are Gershom Scholem, who revived the serious study of kabbalah, and Moshe Idel. See Gershom Scholem, *Kabbalah* (1974); Harold Bloom, *Kabbalah and Criticism* (1975); Moshe Idel, *Kabbalah* (1988).

katabasis A descent to the underworld, especially in epic poetry: examples are Bk. 11 of Homer's *Odyssey,* Bk. 6 of Virgil's *Aeneid,* and the whole of Dante's *Inferno.* Pope's Cave of Spleen, in *The Rape of the Lock* (1712–14), is a loving parody of a katabasis.

kenning In Old Norse and Old English poetry, a clever circumlocution taking the form of a compound noun: a "whale-road" is the ocean; "bone-house," the human body. In Old Norse, kennings consisting of up to five nouns have been attested. The kenning has an affinity to the riddle, a popular form in Old English verse (see GNOMIC).

Kunstlerroman (German, "artist novel.") A novel centered on the struggles or strivings of an artist or writer. (The term is modeled on *Bildungsroman,* "novel of education.") Some examples are James Joyce, *Portrait of the Artist as a Young Man* (1916), Thomas Mann, *Tonio Kröger* (1903), D. H. Lawrence, *Sons and Lovers* (1913), and Willa Cather, *The Song of the Lark* (1915). See also BILDUNGSROMAN.

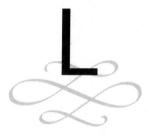

lai (Also *lay.*) The Breton lai is a genre involving tales of love and battle, and adventures with deep implication for the character of the knightly hero. Its stories stem from folkloric sources in Brittany (Bretagne), in northern France. The lai sometimes resembles the raucous fabliau, but is at other times solemn and stately. (See FABLIAU.) E. Talbot Donaldson writes that the Breton lai is marked by "brevity, simplicity, concern with love and the inviolability of promise, use of the supernatural, and a predominantly optimistic spirit." The most renowned author of lais is Marie de France (twelfth century). Geoffrey Chaucer's Franklin's Tale (from *The Canterbury Tales* [ca. 1386–1400]) is a Breton lai. In later eras, the word *lai* (or lay) was used by Walter Scott, in his *Lay of the Last Minstrel* (1805).

See Mortimer Donovan, *The Breton Lay* (1969); Thomas Rumble, ed., *The Breton Lays in Middle English* (1965); E. Talbot Donaldson, commentary on the Franklin's Tale in his *Chaucer's Poetry* (1958; rev. ed., 1975).

Lake Poets Name applied to William Wordsworth, Samuel Taylor Coleridge, and Robert Southey, who lived in the Lake District in the northwest of England at the beginning of the nineteenth century. Francis Jeffrey described them as "Lakers" in an unfavorable article in the *Edinburgh Review* (August 1817); the appellation was later taken up by Lord Byron, in similarly mocking fashion. Thomas De Quincey's *Recollections of the Lake Poets* (1834–40) is a fascinating firsthand account.

language poetry A school of poetic practice whose program is to disrupt our usual agendas of sense making, and upset our search for comfortable meanings, by relying on language that is, often, extremely hard to decipher. Language poets introduce a risky liveliness of linguistic expression that enables the reader to appreciate language's sounds and gestures as such, in all their concrete actuality. The champions of language poetry frequently claim a democratizing agenda: though their work may seem obscure, even at times impenetrable, it does not require scholarly interpretation. Instead, its purpose is to show, quite simply, that language is at once extraordinary and common, something shared by all.

Language poetry might be seen as a riposte to the modernist prizing of difficulty: language poets claim that they are not difficult at all, even when they appear most opaque. One might also consider language poetry an extended (or perhaps diluted) Romanticism in which the poet's sympathy for humankind, a deep tendency of the Romantic poets, transmits itself automatically, through the mere fact of writing and speaking.

Language poetry distinguishes itself from elliptical poetry because the elliptical poet's poem is a puzzle, something that teases and challenges the reader's understanding. The language poet, by contrast, wants to shock us into reevaluating the very concept of understanding—and make us decide that non-understanding may be a more immediate, and therefore a superior, mode.

Some major theoretical documents of language poetry are contained in Bruce Andrews and Charles Bernstein, eds., *The L=A=N=G=U=A=G=E Book* (1984). Charles Bernstein, *Content's Dream* (1986), is a stimulating book of essays by one of the main practitioners of language poetry. See DIFFICULTY; ELLIPTICAL POETRY; MODERNISM; SURREALISM.

lectio difficilior (Latin, "the more difficult reading.") A principle of editing suggesting that the easier interpretation of a textual problem is the one more likely to be transmitted in print, and therefore more likely to be wrong: since individual scribes tend to correct unusual readings and substitute more facile alternatives. An example is the punning phrase of Costard from Shakespeare's *Love's Labour's Lost* I.I: "Such is the sinplicitie of man to harken after the flesh." In later editions the phrase is usually corrected to "the simplicity of man," but especially in a play of such inventiveness and verbal extravagance, "sinplicitie"—the more difficult choice—is probably right.

light verse Light verse begins with the ancient genre of the epigram, which shows economy, finish, and a skillful surface. Sometimes, it tells us things that most poetry is uninterested in grasping, as in Dorothy Parker's well-known "News Item":

Men seldom make passes
At girls who wear glasses.

This kind of verse has an ambivalent relation to "serious" poetry, making light of it (as its name suggests) but also, often, correcting it or calling it to account. Metrical adroitness, a distinct spring in the step, seems necessary to the wit of light verse—which is almost always in strict metrical forms, though Don Marquis (1878–1937) wrote distinguished light free verse.

Kingsley Amis, in his introduction to *The New Oxford Book of Light Verse* (1977), argues that light verse in English is a historically circumscribed phenomenon. One of its main inspirations was the poetry of the seventeenth century, when John Dryden and John Milton introduced a somber gravity, and at times solemnity, into poetic speech. This new poetic style, Amis writes, was "asking to be made to look odd or obscure or pompous or exclusive." (The light verse of John Taylor the Water Poet [1580–1653], however, precedes the seventeenth-century poets mentioned above.) In the Romantic period, the light verse of Byron (*Beppo, Don Juan, The Vision of Judgment*) and of Shelley (*Peter Bell the Third*) distinguished itself from the sober coloring of Wordsworth—and from the poignance or gravity of Byron's and Shelley's own songs and odes.

Amis is correct in suggesting that light verse measures itself, much as parody does, against a prevailing poetic manner. Lewis Carroll's "You Are Old, Father William," from *Alice's Adventures in Wonderland* (1865), a delightful piece of light verse, parodies the then-famous style of Robert Southey (1774–1843).

Nonsense verse and nursery rhymes are other kinds of light verse with, frequently, a parodic connection to a familiar style. For example, Carroll's "Jabberwocky" (written 1855, publ. 1871) pokes fun at ballads that use archaic words; and the rhymes of Edward Lear (1812–88) often spoof the self-congratulatory cleverness of the verse riddle.

W. H. Auden, author of one of the most widely reflective works of light verse, *Letter to Lord Byron* (1936), also edited an *Oxford Book of Light Verse* (1938).

Lightness sometimes attaches to poetry's subject matter. *Vers de societé* like that of Dorothy Parker (1893–1967) or W. M. Praed (1802–39) must always be, to some degree, light, to match the shining surfaces of the balls or cocktail parties these writers habitually describe.

Light verse is not the same as satirical verse. As Amis mentions, Byron's *Vision of Judgment* (1822) succeeds best when it is most light and least satirical (that is, least pointed or polemical).

locus amoenus (Pronounced "LOkus aMEENus"; in Latin, "pleasant place.") The literary topos depicting an idyllic scene in nature, often featuring a meadow, a rustling stream, singing birds, and a fresh breeze. The description of the garden of Alcinous in Homer's *Odyssey* (Bk. 7) is an early, and influential, example of the locus amoenus. The chittering cicadas and restful landscape of Plato's *Phaedrus* (ca. 375–365 BCE) provide another famous instance. Edmund Spenser, with his Bower of Bliss in Bk. 2 of *The Faerie Queene* (1590–96), draws a picture of a deceptive locus amoenus, ready to seduce an unwary knight into languorous, soul-killing illusion. Here, in "the most daintie Paradise on ground," Spenser's hero Guyon sees

The painted flowers, the trees vpshooting hye,
The dales for shade, the hilles for breathing space,
The trembling groues, the Christall running by;
And that, which all faire workes doth most aggrace,
The art, which all that wrought, appeared in no place.

See E. R. Curtius, "The Ideal Landscape," in *European Literature and the Latin Middle Ages* (1948); Michael O'Loughlin, *The Garlands of Repose* (1978). See also TOPOS.

logocentric A word popularized in the theories of the French philosopher Jacques Derrida, particularly his works of the late 1960s and 1970s. Derrida charges that "Western metaphysics," the centuries-long tradition of reflection practiced by Europeans and their cultural heirs, depends on a belief in the word (Greek *logos*) as something clear and present to itself. Just as the gospels claim that Jesus is the Word, that his life and his utterances have divine authority, so, according to Derrida, Western thought trusts in the authority of its own word: the lucid statement, stemming from self-conscious reflection, that is capable of determining its meaning for, and by, itself.

Ever since Plato, Derrida writes, philosophy has prided itself on its construction of a true world based on ultimate clarity of expression and thought. For example, Plato imagines that Socrates, responding to his interlocutors, controls his words perfectly. Socrates speaks, he knows exactly what he is saying, and he attends with complete insight to each person's responses. But, Derrida writes, the model is false: the conversational utopia depicted by Plato differs fundamentally from what happens to Plato's dialogues themselves as they circulate among readers. These dialogues, like all philosophical works, are pieces of text, physical artifacts adrift in the world, to be read in partial and perhaps distorted fashion by anyone who happens to take them up. So the word may be ignored or put to strange, perverse uses. Writing escapes from the mastery of the philosopher, who wants to define and limit its meaning.

Derrida further explains that the clarity sought by the philosopher is unavailable, not just in writing, but even in oral conversation or silent meditation. We tend to think of solitary thought and face-to-face dialogue as primary: as immediate experience, whereas reading is subject to greater uncertainty (we cannot ask a book what it means, as we can ask a person). But for Derrida thinking and speaking are always infected by the drifting or scattered character of writing, which for him becomes a primal fact about language. So for Derrida no statement, whether oral or written, is reliable; it cannot be pinned down or made to bear responsibility for what interpreters make of it.

Variations on logocentric, also used by Derrida, are phonocentric (which implies the central role of the voice, the *phōnē*), and phallologocentric. This last term ties male dominance of society and the self-confidence of men's speech to the supposed obviousness of gender division. With the strength of words, men assert their possession of the phallus, the symbol of self-confident authority.

See Derrida, "Plato's Pharmacy" in *Dissemination* (1972), and *Of Grammatology* (1967). Two interesting critiques of Derrida's idea of logocentrism are Stanley Cavell, *A Pitch of Philosophy* (1994), and Diane Michelfelder and Richard Palmer, eds., *Dialogue and Deconstruction* (1989). See also DECONSTRUCTION.

long eighteenth century The current name in literary studies for the period encompassing the Restoration (1660–1700), the eighteenth century, and the Romantic era (ca. 1789–1832).

lyric poetry It is difficult to give a definition of lyric poetry. The lyric poem can be contrasted to the narrative poem, which tells a more elaborate story;

or it can be defined on the basis of its length (short enough to fit into an anthology without being excerpted). But these definitions seem insufficiently essential.

Lyric in a more proper sense appears to mean something like a pure or true poem, one removed from more worldly rhetorical uses. J. S. Mill (in "What Is Poetry?" [1833]) wrote: "Eloquence is *heard*, poetry *overheard*. Eloquence supposes an audience; the peculiarity of poetry appears to lie in the poet's utter unconsciousness of a listener. Poetry is feeling confessing itself to itself, in moments of solitude."

Mill captures something of the aura of lyric, the lucid, indrawn security that results from its apparent freedom to disregard the reactions of an audience. (Though it can be argued, contra Mill, that many lyrics do imagine a listener, and contend with this listener's reactions.) In a similar vein, the critic Sharon Cameron writes, "The lyric is a departure not only from time but also from the finite constrictions of identity." For Helen Vendler, a lyric poem is a "script written for performance by the reader—who, as soon as he enters the lyric, is no longer a reader but rather an utterer, saying the words of the poem *in propria persona,* internally and with proprietary feeling."

These definitions of lyric are in accord with the fact that in ancient Greece a lyric was a poem sung to the accompaniment of the lyre, a small stringed instrument, in contrast to the large kithara used for choral odes and tragedy. The lyric was, therefore, a relatively private genre. Horace's odes are often intimate, in contrast to the more public and sublime odes of Pindar. During the Romantic period, the lyric devolves to the "song," a light expression of pathos, as opposed to the sublime ode in the Pindaric tradition.

Northrop Frye sees lyric as combining the functions of riddle and charm (the old Roman word for poem, *carmen,* means originally "charm" or "magic spell," and then "song"). Some of the earliest Anglo-Saxon poems are riddles; many lyrics retain an enigmatic profile (asking the reader to solve them? or respect their impenetrability?). And magic inheres in the lyric's power to persuade or influence a listener, or reader. Seduction is an age-old function of lyric: casting a spell over the person addressed by the poem, to get her to respond with loving kindness. Poets may perform an immortalizing alchemy on the beloved (or themselves, or their poems).

The lyric seems an inherently modest or circumscribed form, one that keeps itself separate from the greater expanses of history and social action, and the vast sweep of a culture's grand narratives. Yet many lyric poets strive to attune themselves to history, politics, and the language of their time and place. Often, the paradoxical character of this effort makes for its integrity: the poet's desire to reach beyond the limits of lyric into a wider world still relies on the lyric's role as a precise, contained vehicle for meaning, a "little room" (as Donne puts it). See also POETRY; PURE POETRY; SONG.

On lyric, see Northrop Frye, "Approaching the Lyric," and the other essays in Chaviva Hošek and Patricia Parker, eds., *Lyric Poetry* (1985); Sharon Cameron, *Lyric Time* (1979); James Rolleston, *Narratives of Ecstasy* (1987); Allen Grossman, *The Long Schoolroom* (1997) and *The Sighted Singer* (1992); W. R. Johnson, *The Idea of Lyric* (1982); Paul de Man, "Lyric and Modernity," in *Blindness and Insight* (rev. ed., 1983); and William Waters, *Poetry's Touch* (2003).

mannerism A mannerist art work is marked by refinement and grace, polished high style, and (often) a courtly reserve. In the visual arts, its usual home, mannerism succeeds the pure, classical Renaissance mode of Raphael; it can be seen in the paintings of Bronzino and Parmigianino, and in much of Michelangelo. James Mirollo in *Mannerism and Renaissance Poetry* (1984), following E. R. Curtius, *European Literature and the Latin Middle Ages* (1948), makes a case for the usefulness of mannerism as a literary category, to describe works of elegant artificiality. An excellent general study of the subject is John Shearman's *Mannerism* (1967). See also S. J. Freedberg's magisterial *Painting in Italy, 1500–1600* (1971). For a related concept, see BAROQUE.

Marxist literary criticism The tradition of Marxist literary criticism begins in a minor way with Karl Marx and Friedrich Engels themselves. In their book *The Holy Family* (1844–45), Marx and Engels ridiculed the melodramatic French novelist Eugène Sue (1804–57) as a spokesman for bourgeois ideology. But, as Edmund Wilson notes, Marx loved and admired great poetry, from Aeschylus to Shakespeare to Heine, and he had very little interest in reducing it to an expression of socioeconomic forces. The tradition of Marxist literary criticism proper begins long after Marx and Engels, with figures like Leon Trotsky (1879–1940), Theodor Adorno (1903–69), and Bertolt Brecht (1898–1956).

There are two major tendencies in Marxist literary criticism. First is the idea that a society's literature and art can be understood as a result, or reflection, of its economic and class-based arrangements (its "relations of production"). Second is the assertion that literature should be evaluated in terms of its effectiveness as a weapon of class struggle.

The latter notion, of books as a kind of working-class propaganda, was popular among intellectuals in the United States during the 1930s, when Stalinism was a substantial influence. Periodicals like the *New Masses* judged writers according to whether they were more, or less, useful for the coming revolution. In Soviet Russia, the doctrine of socialist realism held sway, with its insistence on the need to represent workers in heroic terms. But such views of literature as a mere weapon in a propaganda war now seem quaint and repulsive. (See AGITPROP; SOCIALIST REALISM.)

In *Literature and Revolution* (1924), Trotsky, one of the leaders of the Russian Revolution, expressed skepticism about the idea of a proletarian literature that would replace bourgeois forms. Yet Trotsky, in the same book, also scorned formal experimentation for its own sake, and underlined the need for writers to be committed to the revolution in their work. (Trotsky was not unfriendly to the avant-garde; in 1938, while in exile in Mexico, he coauthored a pamphlet with the Surrealist André Breton.) The playwright Bertolt Brecht, like Trotsky, argued that a Marxist author should dedicate himself, before all else, to representing class struggle.

Theodor Adorno and Georg Lukács (1885–1971), the two preeminent Marxist critics of the twentieth century, were less interested in finding in literature signs of the author's political commitments. Rather, Adorno and Lukács, in their different ways, emphasized that literary forms mediate social relations: as they put it, there is a "dialectical" relation between literature and society. Adorno and Lukács are grouped with other Marxist thinkers like Ernst Bloch (1885–1977) and Herbert Marcuse (1898–1979) in a school often called "Western Marxism," since most of these writers were diffident about or resistant to professing loyalty to the Soviet Union. Western Marxism builds on Marx's early notion of alienation to criticize "instrumental reason": a term for the technologizing of society, and even of thinking itself. Instrumental reason, in the view of these critics, tends to corrode social relations. Our lives together become analogous to the buying and selling, and the "fetishizing," of commodities. Compared with these thinkers, Walter Benjamin (1892–1940), who often invoked Marxist terms in his work, was far less pessimistic about—he was even appreciative of—the effects on the imagination of modern technology and the commodity form. (See Miriam Hansen, "Of Mice and Ducks: Benjamin and Adorno on Disney," *South Atlantic Quarterly* 92:1 [Winter 1993], 27–61.) See also FRANKFURT SCHOOL.

Writers in the Western Marxist tradition often assume a distance from the prospect of actual political revolution—and (necessarily) from the reality of life in Communist society. (For Adorno, revolution was both impossible and undesirable.) The most prominent heir of Western Marxism is probably

Fredric Jameson, who in the 1980s developed theories that focus on Marx's notion of the commodity, and on artistic perception as both an alternative to and an expression of commodity fetishism.

Edmund Wilson's "Marxism and Literature" (1937) is an early assessment of Marxist criticism (see Wilson, *The Triple Thinkers* [1938]). For an instructive collection of statements by Adorno, Brecht, Bloch, Lukács, and Walter Benjamin, the reader should consult the collection edited by Fredric Jameson, *Aesthetics and Politics* (1977). See also Theodor Adorno and Max Horkheimer, *The Dialectic of Enlightenment* (1944), Lukács, *The Historical Novel* (written 1936–37), as well as Jameson's monumental *The Political Unconscious* (1981) and his *Marxism and Form* (1974). The most important English Marxist critic was Raymond Williams, author of *Culture and Society* (1958) and *The Country and the City* (1973). Also in the English-speaking tradition, Kenneth Burke (in *The Philosophy of Literary Form* [1941]) and William Empson (in *Some Versions of Pastoral* [1935]) have an ambivalent but productive relation to Marxism. Terry Eagleton's *The Ideology of the Aesthetic* (1990) is a Marxist treatment of aesthetic theory; Andrew Bowie presents a critique of Eagleton in *From Romanticism to Critical Theory* (1996).

masque The masque is a Renaissance form, a brief poetic entertainment usually performed at court and incorporating music, dance, and visual spectacle. Its lavishness points in the direction of idealization. Messages concerning virtue and vice are often prominent; these qualities seem directly incarnated onstage. Moral features emanate from the masque's characters and are displayed to the audience; such display marks the masque as an allegorical form. (See ALLEGORY.) Masques also empower the audience as a source of judgment, openly appealed to by the characters onstage.

The masque was especially popular in the first half of the seventeenth century in the courts of the English monarchs James I (ruled 1603–25) and Charles I (ruled 1625–49). The plots of masques are frequently mythological and outlandish, featuring pygmies, amazons, fairies, or other exotic beings. The anti-masque is a section of the masque in which misrule (i.e., unruly revelry) comes to the fore—to be corrected by the winning forces of order, who comprise a more decorous party. Robert Adams writes that the conflict between the masque's forces of good and the anti-masque's rowdy badness is "heraldic, not dramatic; good appears, declaring itself, and the figures of evil withdraw like the shades of night when the sun rises."

Masques depend on luxurious visual imagery and ravishing music for their effects. This reliance on sensuous, show-stopping sights and sounds was a source of annoyance for Ben Jonson, the most famous Jacobean writer of masques. Jonson quarreled with his collaborator, Inigo Jones, over whether words or spectacular visual design should take precedence in the court masque. (Jonson's masques remain amply beautiful without the assistance of lavish stage sets, costumes, and special effects.)

The masque was the Hollywood blockbuster of its day, highly expensive due to its elaborate staging and splendid costumes. It was performed with the monarch (or ranking patron) at the center of the audience, and the line between spectator and actor was often blurred. At the end of the masque, the audience was customarily invited onstage to dance with the performers.

In addition to Jonson's masques, there is a memorable masque by Milton: the work known as *Comus* (1634), performed for the Earl of Bridgewater and featuring the earl's children as actors. Peculiarly, Milton's masque celebrates chastity, a virtue antithetical to the masquing culture of revelry and good party spirits. Milton inherited his character Comus from Jonson's *Pleasure Reconciled to Virtue* (1618), but instead of reconciling pleasure and virtue, Milton opposes them. Comus, with his broad devotion to sensual enjoyment, glowers threateningly over the chastity of Milton's heroine, the Lady. (Traditionally, Comus is the minor divinity dedicated to sociable intoxication and the rollicking feast. In Jonson, he enters exulting as the "bouncing belly.")

See D. J. Gordon, *The Renaissance Imagination* (1975); David Lindley, ed., *The Court Masque* (1984); Stephen Orgel, *The Jonsonian Masque* (1965) and *The Illusion of Power* (1975); and Robert M. Adams, ed., *Ben Jonson's Plays and Masques* (1979).

medieval literature Medieval literature stretches from approximately the fourth century to the beginning of the fifteenth century—an enormous span, and a various one. In the early part of this period, Latin poetry took the form of hymns, saints' lives, and poems written by scholars ranging from historical chronicles to light verse. Vernacular poetry in northern Europe consisted of riddles, charms, drinking songs, and (prominently in Iceland) heroic epics, known as sagas. Beginning in the twelfth century, medieval romance was a significant literary presence, especially in France. Also in France, the troubadours and trouvères influenced much later love poetry, including the work of Dante and Petrarch. Among the central works of medieval poetry are the Old English *Beowulf* (early eighth century), the Old French *Song of Roland* (twelfth century), the *Romance of the Rose,* begun by Guillaume de Lorris (fl. ca. 1230) and continued by Jean de Meun (ca. 1250–1305), and the Spanish *Poem of the Cid* (twelfth century). Finally, Dante's *Divine Comedy* (ca. 1308–21) and Geoffrey Chaucer's *Canterbury Tales* (ca. 1386–1400) are monumental presences in European literature.

The religious and philosophical prose of Saint Augustine's *Confessions* (ca. 397) and Boethius's *Consolation of Philosophy* (524) became central to literary tradition, as did the writings of Thomas Aquinas. See J. B. Trapp, Douglas Gray, and Julia Boffey, eds., *Medieval English Literature* (2002); J. Huizinga, *The Waning of the Middle Ages* (1919); Lorraine K. Stock, "Medieval Literature," in John B. Friedman and Kristen Figg, eds., *Arts and Humanities Through the Ages: Medieval Europe, 814–1450* (2005). See CHIVALRIC ROMANCE; COURTLY LOVE; FIN AMORS; SAGA; TROUBADOURS.

melodrama As with pornography, so with melodrama: we all feel we know it when we see it. Depending on one's age and experience, one might think of the panicked Lillian Gish threatened by a surly brute, and helplessly clutching her fair little head, in D. W. Griffith's *Broken Blossoms* (1919); of a dozen breathless and pathetic scenes in Charles Dickens; of Douglas Sirk, Joan Crawford, and Bette Davis; or of any number of currently desperate housewives on the television screen. The genre gained popularity in the mid-nineteenth century with books like Eugène Sue's *The Mysteries of Paris* (1842–43), and on the Victorian stage, and its appeal has not ebbed since.

Melodrama is among the most frequently maligned and condescended to of narrative forms. Often, unfriendly critics describe melodrama as a face-off between virtue and vice painted in the most lurid colors, with (male) evil twirling its moustaches and (female) innocence dissolving in frightened shrieks. But there is also the melodrama of the heroic, rebellious woman who cannot be understood by the world around her, and who defies that world. This is the genre that Stanley Cavell has called "the melodrama of the unknown woman." The woman in certain Hollywood melodramas, Cavell claims—films like *Stella Dallas* (1937) or *Now, Voyager* (1942)—achieves the power to remain isolated, unintelligible to her society. She learns "to live without, the frightening capacity to wait." Her self-sacrifice in such films is, according to Cavell, in reality a sign of ascending privilege: she can judge the world and find it wanting.

In an evocative passage, Cavell writes about melodrama's apparent desire to express everything, all at once, in the most fervent and extreme way possible. Melodramatic hyperbole is at once "a terror of absolute inexpressiveness, suffocation," and a "terror of absolute expressiveness, unconditioned exposure." The naked, exposed self and the smothered, hidden self are the twin nightmares spawned by melodrama. Both are intense, distorting, but fully justified allegories of the perilous conditions in which humans voice their desires.

See Peter Brooks, *The Melodramatic Imagination* (1976); Miriam Hansen, *Babel and Babylon* (1994); Stanley Cavell, *Contesting Tears* (1996).

memoir. See BIOGRAPHY

Menippean satire. See SATIRE

metafiction Metafiction is fiction that is about fiction: drawing attention to its own artifice, announcing its status as fable rather than reality, or exposing, in a systematic way, the writer's process of tale-telling. The term was popular in the 1970s and often applied to the American writers John Barth, Donald Barthelme, Robert Coover, William Gass, and others. (The term may have originated in a critical book by Gass, *Fiction and the Figures of Life* [1970].) Earlier writers from Miguel de Cervantes and Laurence Sterne to Samuel Beckett and Jorge Luis Borges were substantial influences on the genre.

The concerns of metafiction extend into broader territory, insofar as such narratives reflect on how people create meaning for themselves by self-consciously inventing roles and stories. There can be a desperately self-amusing aspect to this invention, as in Beckett, or a liberating one. The avant-gardist Ronald Sukenick in "The Death of the Novel" (1969) asks the reader to join in the author's fun, commenting that "what we need is not great works but playful ones . . . a story is a game someone has played so you can play it too." Barth's short-story collection *Lost in the Funhouse* (1968) contains some classic examples of metafiction, as does Daniel Stern's *Twice-Told Tales* (1989). On the tradition of the "self-conscious novel," consult Robert Alter's deeply reflective *Partial Magic* (1975); also Patricia Waugh, *Metafiction* (1984).

metaphor In classical Greek, "a carrying or bearing across" (in present-day Greece, *metaphora* designates a moving van!). In the succinct definition of Donald Davidson, metaphor is a figure of thought and of speech that "makes us see one thing as another." Time is a river, God is love: these are seemingly essential (if well-worn) metaphors, which we would find it hard to live without. The literal is often counterposed to the metaphorical. The biblical statement that faith can move mountains cannot be meant literally; if it were, it would be telling us which personal qualities are best suited to manipulating masses of rock and dirt. In this sense, then, the mountains must be metaphorical rather than literal. But there is always a certain literalistic charge to a metaphor, unless it is totally dead. We are meant to think of—to picture— mountains in order to understand the enormous, unprecedented achievement of faith.

Samuel Johnson commented that metaphor gives you two ideas for the price of one. Its compactness makes it both profitable and thrifty; it seems to offer the reader a bonus of meaning. Angus Fletcher, following Johnson's insight into metaphor's efficiency, remarks that it is "the fastest-thinking linguistic form." In a flash, a metaphor transfigures, makes one thing into something else while at the same time keeping the two separate. "Death is the mother of beauty," Wallace Stevens writes in "Sunday Morning" (1915): and we instantly know that death is in fact maternal, that it gives birth to, or nurtures, beauty—at least the kind of beauty that exists as memory, constituted by the lostness of the object. Keats speaks of "beauty that must die"; for Poe the death of a beautiful woman was the greatest theme in literature. Like them, Stevens sees the beauty that is born to, borne by, death.

Contrast Stevens's line with Milton's allegory in *Paradise Lost*, Bk. 2 (1667), of Satan giving birth to Death through sexual intercourse with Sin. Milton uses allegory rather than metaphor, and so his argument takes the form of a deliberately artificial, spelled-out sequence rather than an intuitive, insightful moment.

A *dead metaphor* is one that has become so familiar that we are no longer tempted to visualize (or to see literally) the action that the metaphor refers to. The phrase "life sucks" is a fine example, since it does not evoke the image of life as a sucking thing. Yet even a dead metaphor can come momentarily back to life, showing a bit of verve as it flirts with the literal. ("Being a vampire *sucks*.")

Sometimes one metaphor answers another. So "love stinks," which implies an image of love as a rotten, reeking thing, responds to the more predictable picture of love the sweet-smelling rose.

Structuralist literary critics contrasted the metaphorical with the metonymic, describing them as opposing poles of literary language. (See Roman

Jakobson, "The Metaphoric and Metonymic Poles," in Hazard Adams, ed., *Critical Theory Since Plato* [1971].) Often, metaphor is identified with poetry, while metonymy is aligned with the habit of describing the details of events and scenes in realist prose. For some stimulating discussions of metaphor, see Sheldon Sacks, ed., *On Metaphor* (1979); Francis Sparshott, "'As,' or the Limits of Metaphor," in *New Literary History* 6:1 (Autumn 1974), 75–94; Paul de Man, "Image and Emblem in Yeats" (1961), in de Man, *The Rhetoric of Romanticism* (1984); and Jacques Derrida, "White Mythology," on the central metaphors of Western philosophy (in his *Margins of Philosophy* [1972]). See also ALLEGORY; METONYMY; SYMBOL; TROPE.

metaphysical poets A group of poets from the early decades of the seventeenth century, including John Donne, George Herbert, Abraham Cowley, Henry Vaughan, Andrew Marvell, Thomas Carew, and Richard Crashaw.

John Dryden, at the end of the seventeenth century, apparently gave birth to the term *metaphysical poetry* when he remarked that Donne "affects the metaphysics . . . not only in his satires, but in his amorous verses, where only nature should reign." Later, Samuel Johnson in his *Life of Cowley* (1779) famously designated Donne and other early-seventeenth-century poets as metaphysical. (When Johnson wrote, Donne had not been reprinted for more than half a century and was largely unknown to readers.)

Dr. Johnson's description of the metaphysical poets is largely negative. Anxious to display their learning, he writes, "they neither copied nature nor life. . . . Their thoughts are often new, but seldom natural; they are not obvious, but neither are they just." For Johnson, the metaphysical poets' pursuit of the singular and the unusual proves deficient when compared with true wit. Wit should strike the reader with surprise and deliver the just and fitting, rather than (in Johnson's charge) the metaphysicals' "combinations of confused magnificence." Johnson concludes that, in this poetry, "the most heterogeneous ideas are yoked by violence together; nature and art are ransacked for illustrations, comparisons, and allusions; their learning instructs, and their subtilty surprises; but the reader commonly thinks his improvement dearly bought, and, though he sometimes admires, is seldom pleased."

Johnson's denunciation of the metaphysical poets, though profoundly unjust, hit its target. They were largely neglected until the 1890s and the first decades of the twentieth century, which saw Herbert Grierson's edition of Donne (1912) and his anthology *Metaphysical Lyrics and Poems of the Seven-*

teenth Century (1921). T. S. Eliot's essay "The Metaphysical Poets" (1921) played the crucial role in making Donne, in particular, a central object for literary study for decades to come. Donne was adopted in the 1940s and 1950s by New Critics like Cleanth Brooks and Robert Penn Warren, who recommended him for classroom use in the teaching of poetry.

Eliot reverses Johnson's account. Instead of being mired in mere ingenuity and divorced from life, Donne, according to Eliot, could "feel [his] thought as immediately as the odour of a rose. A thought to Donne was an experience; it modified his sensibility." Eliot found in the metaphysicals "a direct sensuous apprehension of thought, or a recreation of thought into feeling." (See also DISSOCIATION OF SENSIBILITY.)

J. B. Leishman notes the influence of Ben Jonson's "serious and intellectual kind of 'wit'" on the metaphysicals, and the "hard, satirical, and rather bitter" stance that they found in the works of Jonson (1572–1637). They play with knowledge "much as the Elizabethans had played with words," Leishman writes, "to allow their imagination to suggest subtle analogies and resemblances."

See Gerald Hammond, ed., *The Metaphysical Poets: A Casebook* (1974); J. B. Leishman, *The Metaphysical Poets* (1934); Rosemond Tuve, *Elizabethan and Metaphysical Imagery* (1947); Earl Miner, *The Metaphysical Mode from Donne to Cowley* (1969). Helen Gardner's anthology of 1957, *The Metaphysical Poets,* is still a worthy collection. The recently published lectures given by T. S. Eliot in 1926 and 1933, collected under the title *The Varieties of Metaphysical Poetry* (1993), are also fascinating.

meter The pattern of emphasis, or rhythm, in a line of verse. In every kind of verse except *free verse* the metrical pattern is recurrent and, to some degree, predictable.

In the Renaissance, some poets tried to write in *quantitative* meter, in imitation of Greek and Latin verse, which accents syllables purely on the basis of their duration, as in a song. For the most part, though, English and the other modern European languages are inimical to quantitative forms. Instead, they base their meters on the number of accents and syllables in a line.

English poetry was originally purely *accentual;* that is, it counted a certain number of accents per line without regard to the number of syllables. (The Old English *Beowulf* is in accentual verse.) In modern times, some poets, notably W. H. Auden and Marianne Moore, wrote *syllabic* verse, which often sounds conspicuously prosy in English. A syllabic line counts the number of syllables without regard to accent (haiku is syllabic, as is French verse, since the French language lacks accent).

Most English-language poetry is neither purely accentual nor purely syllabic, but rather *accentual-syllabic,* which means that a reader or listener can determine the verse form by counting both the number of syllables and the number of accents (also called stresses or beats) in a line. (Free verse, by contrast, is not written in forms; the free verse line has no predetermined number of accents or syllables.) Describing poetry by using these technical terms is known as *scansion;* one *scans* a line or a passage.

The rhythmic units that make up a line are called feet. A foot combines a particular number of accents with a particular number of syllables. In scansion, the accented or stressed syllables are marked by ´, the unstressed syllables usually by ˘. The division between feet is indicated by a ǀ. The most important feet in English verse are

> iamb (adj. iambic): ˘ ´ (e.g., sŭbmít)
> trochee (adj. trochaic): ´ ˘ (métĕr)
> spondee: ´ ´ (óne, twó)
> dactyl: ´ ˘ ˘ (súffĕrĭng)
> anapest: ˘ ˘ ´ (tŏ ă tée)

(The *pyrrhic* foot, consisting of two unstressed syllables (˘ ˘), is very rare in poetry.)

> Sŭbmít, ǀ súbtlĕ ǀ pérsŏn, tŏ ǀ súităblĕ ǀ métĕrs!
> Óne, twó: ǀ yŏu căn sée ǀ hŏw ĭt fíts . . .

A *caesura* is a sharp break between words in a line, indicated by a ǁ—as in Tennyson's "Bréak, ǁ Bréak, ǁ bréak, / On thy cóld ǀ gréy stónes, ǁ Ó séa!" (In scansion, the ˘ can be omitted.) See CAESURA.

Lines of verse are either end-stopped or enjambed: that is, the syntax either concludes at the end of the line (an end-stop), or else it carries over from one line to the next (an enjambment). Here are two enjambed lines by Louise Bogan: "No stone, slate, metal under or above / Earth is so ponderous, so dull, so cold." We could convert them into end-stopped lines by punctuating them differently, with an exclamation point at the end of the first one: "No stone, slate, metal under or above! / Earth is so ponderous, so dull, so cold." In this example by Bogan (and frequently in a writer like Milton), there is a "ghost" of the sense that the enjambed lines would have if they were end-stopped instead of running on. A line with a *masculine* ending finishes with an accented syllable ("New Yórk"), a *feminine* ending with an unaccented one ("Califórnia").

We can characterize a line of verse by describing the kind of foot it contains along with the number of feet in the line. A line with five feet, most of them iambs, is iambic pentameter; a line with four feet, most of them trochees, is trochaic tetrameter. Iambic pentameter, also called *blank verse,* is the most common meter in English. The trochaic tetrameter is often used for a rapid, dazzling effect, as when Shakespeare's Ariel in *The Tempest* (1.2) sings "Fóot it | féatly | hére and | thére." (As here, the final trochee in a line often drops its unaccented syllable.) Anapests can produce a toppling, tripping motion; or they can waltz dizzily and rapidly, as in Swinburne's evocation of how "fate is a sea without shore":

> And bít|ter as blóod | is the spráy; | and the crésts |
>   are as fángs | that devóur
> And its vá|pour and stórm | of its stéam | as the sígh|ing of spir|
>   its to bé

Very few lines of verse are perfectly iambic, trochaic, or anapestic. Instead, metrical variation usually occurs, for the sake of fluency and surprise. When the meter is perfectly regular, it can sound blunt, even primitive, as it rocks into place. Here are some assertively iambic (and end-stopped) lines by Philip Larkin:

> They fúck | you úp, || your Múm | and Dád.
> They máy | not méan | to, || bút | they dó.

The meter conveys Larkin's theme: a dull, unavoidable, and endlessly repeated law. (The caesuras in Larkin's poem are also remarkably apt; the second halves of the lines drop in with a heavy grunt.) Strict iambic pentameter can also produce a herky-jerky feel, as in this line from Fielding's burlesque drama *Tom Thumb* (1730), in which the tiny hero sighs for his giant girlfriend, Huncamunca: "Oh, Húnclamúncla, Húnclamúncla, óh!"

A spondee slows down a line, giving it more weight. It is often used for thematic effect, as when Shakespeare's Theseus, in *A Midsummer Night's Dream* (1.1), laments, "But Ó, | methínks | how slów / This óld | móon wánes!"

In poetry as in common conversation, there are frequently several alternative possibilities for the placing of accent, depending on what we want to mean. (What vast differences there are between "Í love you," "I lóve you," and "I love yóu"!) In the line from Shakespeare's sonnet 18, "Sháll I | compáre | thee tó | a súm|mer's dáy," the accent could go on either "thee" or "to." But the end of Shakespeare's line could not be accented "summér's day" (as it could in a rendition by a jazz singer, for example), because this would violate the normal stress we give to the word *summer.* When such a violation does occur (rarely, and most often in ballads), it is called a *wrenched accent:* "She cáme | from a fár | countrée."

Conversational speech and written prose have metrical patterns, just as verse does, but the patterns are not fixed. Any sort of foot can follow any other, so that it is usually hard to characterize a stretch of speech or prose as predominantly iambic, dactylic, anapestic, or trochaic. Iambs are, however, the most prevalent meter in everyday speech.

In free verse, a line can be as long or as short as it likes, without regard to the other lines that surround it. The greatest free-verse poet, Walt Whitman, makes use of this expansiveness to achieve a liberating effect: the line stretches out like America itself. (But then, often, it snaps in, with a stinging decisiveness: for a discussion, see Guy Davenport's essay on Whitman in *The Hunter Gracchus* [1996].) Whitman, like other writers of free verse, often draws on the feel of particular meters. His poetry is not actually "free" of metrical constraint, but rather enabled by the rhythm of meter, only in a more fluid and unpredictable way than occurs in formal verse. This line by Whitman, from "Crossing Brooklyn Ferry," shifts from a dactylic and trochaic first half to an iambic second half, so that the swaying openness of the line's beginning is completed by the tight, rapping ending: "Flóod-tide be|lów me! | I sée | you fáce | to fáce!"

On meter, see Derek Attridge, *The Rhythms of English Poetry* (1982); John Hollander, *Rhyme's Reason* (1981); Paul Fussell, *Poetic Meter and Poetic Form* (1965); and John Thompson, *The Founding of English Meter* (1961). Mary Kinzie, *A Poet's Guide to Poetry* (1999), contains some rewarding remarks on meter. Jacques Barzun, *An Essay on French Verse* (1991), is an excellent introduction to technical aspects of French poetry from the Renaissance to the present; on ancient verse, see James Halporn, Martin Ostwald, and T. G. Rosenmeyer, *The Meters of Greek and Latin Poetry* (rev. ed., 1980).

metonymy A figure of speech that involves the substitution of an adjacent item or an attribute of a thing for the thing itself. So "a bunch of hardhats" denotes the workmen wearing the hardhats; and "the deep" stands in for "the sea" (since depth is an attribute of the sea). Metonymy is closely associated with synecdoche, the substitution of a part for the whole ("she's the best nose in the business").

Ferdinand de Saussure in his *Course in General Linguistics* (1916) contrasts metonymy with metaphor, casting them as two rival poles of language. The opposition was taken up about ten years later, with influential results, by Roman Jakobson (and, briefly, by another Russian critic of the 1920s, Viktor Zirmunskij). René Wellek and Austin Warren refer to the opposition in their *Theory of Literature* (1948). Finally, Jakobson's classic statement of the metaphor-metonymy distinction appeared in "Two Aspects of Language and Two Types of Aphasic Disturbances," first published in his and Morris Halle's book *Fundamentals of Language* (1956).

As Jakobson explains it, metonymy is fundamentally prosaic; metaphor, by contrast, is allied to poetry. Metonymy works on the axis of combination (or contiguity), metaphor on the axis of selection (or comparison). The realist novel characteristically engages in metonymy: an essential form of distraction that proves its commitment to the world. As Jakobson notes, "In the scene of Anna Karenina's suicide Tolstoy's artistic attention is focused on the heroine's handbag." If Tolstoy were to make the purse a symbol of Anna, his attention would be metaphoric, but it is not—the purse is simply metonymic, part of an indifferent reality. See David Lodge, *The Modes of Modern Writing* (1977).

mimesis *Mimesis* is a Greek word usually translated as "imitation." (Imitation, though, has another meaning in the Renaissance: the modeling of one's work after that of an earlier writer; see IMITATION.) Arts are said to be mimetic when they represent or copy reality. "A novel is a mirror carried along a high road," Stendhal wrote in *The Red and the Black* (1830). And much earlier, Philip Sidney in his *Apology for Poetry* (1583, publ. 1595) remarked, "Poesy . . . is an art of imitation, for so Aristotle termeth it in the word mimesis—that is to say, a representing, counterfeiting, or figuring forth—to speak metaphorically, a speaking picture." Sidney here mentions a familiar idea: literature is a picture of reality that makes us realize it is a mere picture. A book gives us a representation rather than a piece of reality: but it is nevertheless based on, or modeled after, or somehow close to, reality (it is hard to know which formulation to choose).

The mimetic image, then, demands that we know it as an image, rather than the real thing. According to legend, the ancient Greek painter Apelles created a picture of Alexander the Great's horse so realistic that other horses neighed at it; and Zeuxis, another Greek artist, made a painting of grapes that birds pecked at. But we are not like these horses or birds. We want a gap between the thing and its image. (See ANTITHEATRICAL, though, for the traditional worry that representations will be taken for realities.)

Gregory Nagy defines the original, archaic Greek sense of *mimesis* as "the reenactment, through ritual, of the events of myth." The main rituals in question were the Greek theatrical festivals, both tragic and comic, that took place from the late sixth century BCE on. Homer's epics were performed by solo rhapsodes (talented actors of poetry). These mimetic practices come under scrutiny in the dialogues of Plato, especially the *Ion* (ca. 390 BCE) and the *Republic* (ca. 370 BCE). Plato worries about the bad moral effects of a tragic mimesis intended to "keep sorrow fresh" (as Edward Snow puts it) instead of reconciling us to loss, and instead of making us attend to reasoned argument as Plato himself does. In effect, Plato proposes his dialogues as a superior form of mimesis to that of Homer and the tragic poets, and Socrates as a greater hero than can be found in these earlier writers.

There are some peculiarities in the ancient use of the term *mimesis*. Aristotle in his *Poetics* (ca. 330 BCE), for example, describes dance as a mimetic art. Apparently, he does not mean that dancers mime the specific gestures that we perform in ordinary life, but rather that they present human feeling or character in a more abstract, and therefore truly representative, way.

At one point in the *Poetics,* Aristotle defines the pleasure of mimetic art in a rather simple fashion: mimesis pleases because representation itself is a source of enjoyment. He notes that we admire pictures of things that we don't like to see in real life, "the lowest animals, for example, or corpses." Finally, though, Aristotle's idea of mimesis in the *Poetics* is a complicated one: the complete picture of a human action offered by tragic drama convinces because it involves the spectator as the hero's judge and fellow sufferer. Dramatic representation requires more than mere accuracy of detail or avoidance of implausibility (though Aristotle considers these aspects too). Rather, the evocative power of the work, its capacity to raise a fitting and thoughtful response in the audience, is what marks the successful mimesis. These questions about the relation of mimesis to audience response, and the ways literary representation may monitor or inflect our ideas of the just and the fitting, were later pursued by critics like John Dryden (1631–1700), Samuel Johnson

(1709–84), and William Hazlitt (1778–1830). (See also DECORUM; POETIC JUSTICE.)

The breadth of literary mimesis, its encompassing quality, is a traditional argument in its favor. Roger Ascham in his *Schoolmaster* (1570) writes that "the whole doctrine of Comedies and Tragedies is a perfite *imitation,* or faire lively painted picture of the life of everie degree of man." Ascham implies the kind of argument that, centuries later, will prize the realist novel over the lyric poem, because realism presents a wider, more various picture of life. (There is a contrary argument to be made, of course: lyric focus and intensity may sometimes be a truer route to the hidden life of individuals than the dispersed panorama that nineteenth-century realism, with its divided attentions, can offer. See Ralph Freedman, *The Lyrical Novel* [1963].)

Erich Auerbach's *Mimesis* (1946) is a grandly inspiring, irreplaceable survey of "the representation of reality in Western literature," from Homer and the Hebrew Bible to Virginia Woolf. Particularly influential is Auerbach's contrast between the representation of human action and character in the Bible, on one hand, and ancient Greek epic on the other. Robert Alter, like Auerbach, locates the profound insights of biblical mimesis in what it leaves out, forcing the reader to speculate about, and judge, characters whose emotions are often concealed or omitted by the narrative (Alter, *The Art of Biblical Narrative* [1981]).

On mimesis as ritual, see Gregory Nagy, "Early Greek Views of Poets and Poetry," in George A. Kennedy, ed., *The Cambridge History of Literary Criticism,* vol. 1 (1989). A. D. Nuttall's *A New Mimesis* (1983) is a stimulating study. See also UT PICTURA POESIS.

mock epic For John Dryden, "mock heroic" was a distinguished form of literature, exemplified by Dryden's own *MacFlecknoe* (1682). Mock heroic, or mock epic, dates back to archaic Greece: a poem concerning the battle of the frogs and the mice was even attributed to Homer himself. Mock epic relies on the grand conventions of Homeric and Virgilian poetry, using them in an incongruous and amusing way. For example, in Alexander Pope's *Rape of the Lock* (1712–14), warfare takes place in the salon, and the traditional epic voyage to the underworld is matched by a descent to the Cave of Spleen. Earlier examples of mock epic in English literature include Ben Jonson's "On the Famous Voyage" (1612), Samuel Butler's *Hudibras* (1663–78), and Milton's War in Heaven, recounted in Bks. 5 and 6 of *Paradise Lost* (1667).

In the work of its greatest practitioners, Dryden and Pope, mock epic balances nobility with triviality, rather than reducing the noble to the trivial. The sylphs in Canto 2 of *The Rape of the Lock* are exquisite, and delicately drawn: Pope enhances the action of his poem by diminishing it. Martin Price notes that Pope hovers between the "trivial fragility of mere play" and "the preciousness of a life ordered with grace." And Pope's *Dunciad* (1728–42), as it mimics *Paradise Lost* (1667), attains real loftiness, evoking the power of Milton's chaos and his creation. Mock epic, then, at least as Dryden and Pope perform it, is far from derisory in its attitude toward its epic models; instead, it draws on epic variously and brilliantly.

See Martin Price, *To the Palace of Wisdom* (1964), Ian Jack, *Augustan Satire* (1952), and John Sitter, *The Poetry of Pope's Dunciad* (1971). Ruth Nevo's commentary on Butler's *Hudibras* in *The Dial of Virtue* (1963) is also helpful.

modernism   The term *modernité* was first applied to literature in 1849, by the French writer François René de Chateaubriand. Charles Baudelaire, in the course of his writings on modern art in the 1860s, reflected continually on the revolutionary character of modern life: its speed, confusion, and reckless, sensational moods. But modernism is normally associated with the years from about 1910 through the 1920s, and (frequently) the following few decades. High modernism, as it is sometimes called, includes the other arts as well as literature: the achievements of Stravinsky, Schoenberg, Picasso, and Giacometti as well as Marcel Proust, Thomas Mann, James Joyce, Franz Kafka, T. S. Eliot, Wallace Stevens, and Virginia Woolf.

Woolf, in her essays "Modern Fiction" (1925) and "Poetry, Fiction, and the Future" (1927), proclaimed that modernist novelists "attempt to come closer to life" by showing that "everything is the proper stuff of fiction, every feeling, every thought . . . no perception comes amiss." Of Joyce's *Ulysses* (1922), she remarked, "If we want life itself, here surely we have it." Woolf's comments demonstrate that modernism justified itself by its revolutionary ambition for truth to life: for a greater, more complete realism. Joyce had accomplished a mimesis encompassing dreams and unconscious thoughts, as well as the most minute details of waking existence. This was global grasp, not mere capricious or random exploration.

Modernism aimed to supply a greater intensity, too, to match the bewildering energies of contemporary life. Woolf celebrated the extremism and wildness of Russian novels, in contrast to the Edwardian fictions that directly preceded modernism: what she saw as the overly decorous work of John

Galsworthy, Arnold Bennett, and H. G. Wells. The poet Hart Crane wrote in his essay "General Aims and Theories" (1926) of the need for "fresh concepts, more inclusive evaluations, . . . added consciousness and increased perceptions." (Or, as one of Crane's poems put it, "new thresholds, new anatomies.") Such a program needed to discard the heavily adjectival, gorgeous diction of the Georgian poets in favor of a newly harsh and strange dialect.

The measuring of the modern age often involved the use of (mostly Greek) myth. T. S. Eliot wrote a famous essay on Joyce's "mythic method" in *Ulysses* ("Ulysses, Order, and Myth" [1923]). And Crane remarked, of his poem "For the Marriage of Faustus and Helen" (1926), "So I found 'Helen' sitting in a street car . . . and the katharsis of the fall of Troy I saw approximated in the recent World War."

Modernists often had a belief in the crisis of twentieth-century civilization: the world's fall into chaos, decadence, or other dismal, yet dramatically exciting, straits. But such inclinations, fostered by books like Oswald Spengler's *Decline of the West* (1918–23), were not universal. Richard Poirier in *Robert Frost* (1977) gives a portrait of one modern poet who resisted the cultural crisis aspect of modernism.

Modernism frequently exalted difficulty. The works of writers like Joyce, Ezra Pound, and Gertrude Stein resist the reader, relying on the discordant, the dispersed, and the esoteric. Joyce's intricacies, especially, have kept scholars busy for generations. Modernist difficulty often becomes a way of testing the idea of the work and its tradition: asking us to define anew what a novel or a poem is, or might be. (See DIFFICULTY.)

Two useful anthologies are Richard Ellmann and Charles Feidelson, eds., *The Modern Tradition* (1965), and Irving Howe, ed., *Literary Modernism* (1967). Hugh Kenner's *The Pound Era* (1971) supplies a commanding depiction of the group of modernist writers associated with Pound. Lionel Trilling's essays, especially those collected in *Beyond Culture* (1965), offer a sustained reflection on modernism as a response to cultural crisis, as does the book by Marshall Berman, *All That Is Solid Melts into Air* (1982). Two very helpful general studies are Michael Levenson's *A Genealogy of Modernism* (1984) and Sanford Schwartz's *The Matrix of Modernism* (1985). See also F. R. Leavis's pioneering *New Bearings in English Poetry* (1932).

For modernism as inheritor of romanticism, see Erich Heller, *The Disinherited Mind* (1952); Harold Bloom, *Yeats* (1970); Perry Meisel, *The Myth of the Modern* (1987). On Woolf, consult Maria DiBattista, *Virginia Woolf's*

Major Novels (1980); on Joyce, S. L. Goldberg, *Joyce* (1962). Three recent examinations of poetic modernism are Charles Altieri, *Painterly Abstraction in Modernist American Poetry* (1989), Langdon Hammer, *Hart Crane and Allen Tate* (1993), and David Bromwich, *Skeptical Music* (2001). On the afterlife of modernism in American poetry, see James Longenbach, *Modern Poetry After Modernism* (1997).

morality play A dramatic form popular in fifteenth-century England, in which a representative protagonist (such as Mankind or Everyman) is tempted and persecuted by various allegorical figures and, frequently, saved by heavenly grace in the end. The morality plays generally present a picture of human life from birth to death, in which outside forces struggle for the soul of the hero. In *Mankind*, Mankind encounters Nought, Newguise, and Now-a-days, is temporarily defeated by the comic Titivillus, and finally is saved by Mercy. Morality plays tend to be somber and raucous by turns, often including some colorful obscenity. The best-known of them are *Mankind* (ca. 1471–75), *Everyman* (ca. 1509), and *The Castle of Perseverance* (ca. 1405). David Bevington's *From Mankind to Marlowe* (1962) describes the influence of the morality play on later English drama. See also Hardin Craig, *English Religious Drama of the Middle Ages* (1955).

multum in parvo The Latin *multum in parvo* means "much in little": the capacity of a literary work to express an enormous theme in a small space. Consider Andrew Marvell's summary of the subject of *Paradise Lost* (1667), by his friend John Milton:

> When I beheld the poet blind, yet bold,
> In slender book his vast design unfold,
> Messiah crowned, God's reconciled decree,
> Rebelling Angels, the Forbidden Tree,
> Heaven, Hell, Earth, Chaos, all . . .

In modernist poetics, Imagism provides a significant case of multum in parvo aesthetics. (See IMAGISM.)

There is a variation on multum in parvo that might be called *parvum in parvo,* or little in little. Consider the sparkling, peculiar, and proudly contained modesty of Robert Herrick, another seventeenth-century poet, in "A Ternary of Littles, Upon a Pipkin of Jelly Sent to a Lady" (1648; a pipkin is a tiny jar):

A little stream best fits a little boat,
A little lead best fits a little float;
As my small pipe best fits my little note.

A little meat best fits a little belly,
As sweetly, lady, give me leave to tell ye,
This little pipkin fits this little jelly.

(From Herrick, *Hesperides* [1648].) See Rosalie Colie, *The Resources of Kind* (1973).

mummers' plays The mummers' play was a traditional and often rudimentary form of drama in rural England, flourishing in the Middle Ages and the Renaissance. Such plays usually center on a fight between two brave antagonists; the hero "dies" and then revives, aided by a clownish, fumbling doctor who is also something of a bragging huckster, touting his medicinal remedies. A mummers' play normally consists of an Introduction, a Battle, a Lament over the fallen hero, a Cure, and—last but certainly not least—a Quete, in which the players wend their way through the audience asking for money.

The mummers' plays frequently depict the battle between the chivalric warrior Saint George, the patron saint of England, and a fearsome dragon. Old King Cole, Merry Andrew, and other folkloric figures often appear, too, accompanied by raucous morris dancers.

There are other traditional plots for mummers' plays: the wooing play, in which a lady's soldier-lover, gone off to war, is replaced in her bed by a fool; and the sword play, in which a man is surrounded by swordsmen, cut to pieces, and then miraculously revived.

It is possible that the mummers' plays are entwined, in their origin, with folk rituals celebrating the resurrection of the year in spring after its death in winter. (Saint George's Day is April 23—incidentally also, by tradition, the day of Shakespeare's birth—and Saint George, as noted, is frequently central to the mummers' plays.) See Arthur Kinney, "The Oxfordshire Saint George Play," in Kinney, ed., *Renaissance Drama* (2000); Alan Brody, *The English Mummers and Their Plays* (1970); Alex Helm, *The English Mummers' Play* (1980). Modern drama sometimes draws on the mummers' plays (notably W. H. Auden's *Paid on Both Sides* [1930]).

muses In the ancient world, the nine female figures who inspire and guide the different forms of imaginative creation: Calliope (epic or heroic poetry),

Clio (history), Terpsichore (dance), Thalia (comedy, pastoral poetry), Erato (erotic poetry), Melpomene (tragedy), Polyhymnia (religious dancing, lyric poetry), Euterpe (Dionysiac music), and Urania (astrology). (Sappho, the greatest woman poet of antiquity, was often called "the tenth muse.") The muses are routinely invoked, especially in epic, as sources of information and power, often at difficult or crucial moments.

Even in the ancient world the muses sometimes seemed tired. They are invoked parodically by Horace in his *Satires* (ca. 38–30 BCE) and with playful irony by Ovid in his *Art of Love* (ca. 1 BCE). Other Roman poets, Tibullus and Propertius (both first century BCE), call on a beloved or a friend for inspiration rather than the muses. In English poetry, the most famous invocation of a muse is Milton's calling on Urania in Bk. 7 of *Paradise Lost* (1667). For Milton, Urania is no mere patroness of astrology, but the "heav'nly Muse," Wisdom's sister. See Ernst Robert Curtius, "The Muses," in *European Literature and the Latin Middle Ages* (1948).

mystery play Mystery plays, performed throughout the fifteenth century and well into the sixteenth, narrate the mysteries of scriptural history: especially creation, judgment, and Christ's incarnation. They were also produced by craftsmen's guilds, which were called mysteries—the trades of shoemakers or carpenters, for example. (The original etymology behind *mystery play* is probably the late Latin *ministerium,* meaning "church service.")

There was an element of self-advertisement in the mystery plays' tradition of sponsorship by guilds. Carpenters celebrated their importance through a play depicting the building of Noah's ark; bakers put on a play in which Jesus provides bread for the masses. The mystery plays, associated with particular towns in England (Towneley, Chester, York), were usually performed as a cycle on a specific day (or several successive days) of the Christian calendar, either Corpus Christi or Pentecost. A cycle, often consisting of dozens of brief plays, extended from the fall of Lucifer and the creation to the Last Judgment. The plays were presented on stationary scaffolds or on wagons that traveled through the town's streets, stopping to entertain the crowds.

The surviving mystery plays are often colloquial, brusque, and funny. In *Noah,* from the Chester cycle, Noah's bickering wife refuses to enter the ark. In the wonderful *Second Shepherds' Play,* the pastoral characters, oppressed by the rich, complain of their hardscrabble existence. (They are, they say, "hammed, / Fortaxed and rammed [i.e., crippled, taxed, and crushed], /

With these gentlery-men.") But these works also give off a somber magic. Mystery plays stand at the intersection of the everyday with sacred history, as the familiar stories of the Bible join the equally common experience of the audience. In this way, they evoke the meditative, spellcasting mood that the scriptural narrative still exerted over the audience's lives. Commenting on the mystery play, Northrop Frye notes their atmosphere of pensiveness, implying the spectators' "continuing imaginative subjection to the story" (Frye, *The Anatomy of Criticism* [1957]). See Arthur Kinney, "The Cycle Plays," in Kinney, ed., *Renaissance Drama* (2000); V. A. Kolve, *The Play Called Corpus Christi* (1966); O. B. Hardison, Jr., *Christian Rite and Christian Drama in the Middle Ages* (1965); Sarah Beckwith, *Signifying God* (2001).

myth Myth comes from the Greek *muthos:* simply, something that is said. The opposing term to *muthos* is *logos,* which might be translated as "account" or "discourse," and which implies a reasoned basis for what is said. Muthos, by contrast to logos, dwells in the realm of rumor and speculation, of fancy.

Yet, in our cultural lives, myth often seems to have greater authority than reasoned explanation. For the French anthropologist Claude Lévi-Strauss, who has had a large influence on literary and cultural theory, myths are the building blocks or governing thought structures of collective human existence. Lévi-Strauss argues that myths are based on oppositions (cultivated versus primitive, human versus divine). (See Lévi-Strauss, *The Raw and the Cooked* [1964], and "The Structural Study of Myth," in his *Structural Anthropology* [1958]; see also STRUCTURALISM.)

Several major writers in the English tradition invented their own mythic systems, notably William Blake (1757–1827) and W. B. Yeats (1865–1939) in their poems and James Joyce in *Finnegans Wake* (1939).

Myths are central to the literary criticism of Northrop Frye (who began as a student of Blake). Frye, drawing on the theories of C. G. Jung, emphasized the symbolic weight of certain mythic patterns and topoi: in the Bible, for example, themes of ascent and descent, as well as places like the garden, the tower, and the wilderness. Frye in fact defines literature as "conscious mythology," and adds, "it creates an autonomous world that gives us an imaginative perspective on the real one." See Frye's *Anatomy of Criticism* (1957) and *The Great Code* (1982). K. K. Ruthven's *Myth* (1976) is a wry and informative commentary on the fashion for myth criticism that developed in the wake of Frye's work. For a stimulating application of mythic criticism to literary tradition, indebted to Frye as well as to the anthropologists Jane Harrison and Mary Douglas, see Camille Paglia, *Sexual Personae* (1990). Frank Kermode draws a persuasive distinction between myth and fiction in *The Sense of an Ending* (1967). Finally, Roland Barthes in his pathbreaking book *Mythologies* (1957) sees myths as the ideological forms that organize and direct social life. See ARCHETYPE; MYTHOGRAPHY.

mythography Mythography, a fundamental activity in the medieval period and especially the Renaissance, is the imaginative interpreting of myths, often to moralizing ends. This way of reading myth begins in the ancient world, with the allegorizing of stories of the gods in terms of the virtues or the physical elements. In the Middle Ages, such reading becomes centrally important. In the *Mythologies* of Fulgentius (sixth century CE), the three goddesses who stand before Paris's judgment become symbols of the active, the contemplative, and the voluptuous life. The early-fourteenth-century *Ovide Moralisé* (Ovid Moralized), an edition of and commentary on Ovid's *Metamorphoses* (ca. 8 CE), decodes the story of Ceres searching for her daughter Proserpina as the Church looking for believers who have strayed. Such harmonizing of paganism and Christianity (called *syncretism*) was natural in the intellectual climate of the Middle Ages and the Renaissance, in which Plato's *Timaeus* was thought to agree with Moses' Pentateuch, and Socrates to confirm the truth of Christ.

In the Middle Ages, the gods and antique heroes were often depicted in contemporary dress, even as they carried their familiar attributes: Jove his lightning, Hercules his club. The ancient deities had wandered down into a later era and remained there, somewhat stranded amid the unfamiliar bustle of life.

The Renaissance departed from the medieval syncretic mode. In recovering a new sense of the ancient world, Renaissance writers also attained a consciousness of the Greek and Roman divinities as inhabiting a foreign, lost realm, rather than a current one. The contention of the old gods with the damaging passage of time becomes the theme of Edmund Spenser's Mutabilitie Cantos (1596) and John Milton's Nativity Ode (1629). (This Renaissance theme was adapted, much later, by Richard Wagner in his *Ring of the Nibelungen* [1876].)

Erwin Panofsky supplies an example of mythographic deciphering when he explains the figure of Father Time with his sickle. Time is the descendant of the Greek god Kronos (the Roman Saturn)—thus our word *chronology.* The sickle, writes Panofsky, which had often been explained as a farming tool (since Kronos or Saturn was associated with agriculture) or an instrument of castration (since he had castrated his father, the sky god Ouranos), gradually became a symbol of the temporal cycle, time returning upon itself. The myth that Saturn had eaten his own children was then illustrated by the Latin motto *tempus edax rerum,* "Time is the devourer of things."

Among the chief Renaissance mythographic manuals are Andrea Alciati's *Emblemata* (1531), the *Mythology* by Natale Conti (Natalis Comes; 1551), Cesare Ripa's *Iconologia* (1593), and Vincenzo Cartari's *Images of the Gods* (1556). These books are especially relevant to Edmund Spenser's *Faerie Queene* (1590–96); see James Nohrnberg, *The Analogy of the Faerie Queene* (1976), and Thomas P. Roche, *The Kindly Flame* (1964).

On mythography, see Jean Seznec, *The Survival of the Pagan Gods* (1940), and Erwin Panofsky, "Father Time" and "Blind Cupid," in *Studies in Iconology* (1939). See also EMBLEM; ICONOGRAPHY.

N

naive and sentimental Friedrich Schiller, in *On Naive and Sentimental Poetry* (1795–96), writes that primitive man enjoys a correspondence between feeling and thought. In later, more civilized stages, this correspondence becomes an unfulfilled ideal only. In the early, primitive phase of culture, poetry is naive: it need only mimic the actual world around it, especially the natural landscape.

Schiller remarks, admiringly rather than disparagingly, that Homer is a naive poet, a heroic child who simply imitates nature and his own feelings. In later times—our times, which began, according to Schiller, with the Roman poet Horace (65–8 BCE)—poetry becomes sentimental. The sentimental poet evokes an ideal to create a contrast with the hard limits of the reality that we see and feel every day. Sentimental poetry, Schiller writes, tends toward either the satiric (excoriating the inconvenient actuality that surrounds us) or the elegiac (expressing pleasure in the unachievable ideal, at the expense of a sense of actuality).

Schiller is ambivalent about the sentimental. On one hand he favors it as "a beautiful, elevating fiction": the idyllic imagination that offers a critique of, and an alternative to, present-day reality. But on the other hand, he warns against the weakness and backward-looking character of the sentimental poet's nostalgia. The sentimental wish for a unity of thought and experience that belonged to the childhood of the race (that is, the wish for the naive!) can seem a dead end.

Paul Alpers, in *What Is Pastoral?* (1996), discusses the application of Schiller's dichotomy to theories of pastoral. Specifically, Alpers contrasts the rigidity of Schiller's division between naive and sentimental to William Empson's more flexible use of the terms *simple* and *complex* in *Some Versions of Pastoral* (1935). Complex and simple (related, respectively, to Schiller's sentimental and naive poles) infiltrate, undermine, and aid each other in Empson's reading. So the naive and the sentimental cannot be kept apart, as Schiller tries to do. See Thomas G. Rosenmeyer, *The Green Cabinet* (1969).

narratology Originally an outgrowth of structuralist studies of narrative, perhaps most significantly Vladimir Propp's *Morphology of the Folktale* (1928). In a sense, Propp was developing Aristotle's idea that tragic plot centers on a moment of recognition and one of reversal. (See ARISTOTELIAN CRITICISM; RECOGNITION; REVERSAL.) Describing a different genre than Aristotle, Propp multiplies the number of structural features. In the folktale, we have not just recognition (exposure of truth) and reversal (from one state of things to its opposite), but also the hero's departure, the villain's trickery, the chase or pursuit, the rescue, and so on. Propp's ideas were developed and altered by A. J. Greimas, who in his *Structural Semantics* (1966) developed a theory centered on six actants, or basic roles. These actants, Greimas claimed, characterize narrative structures: Subject, Object, Sender (who sends the Subject questing for the Object), Helper, Opponent, and Receiver (who guards the Object that the Sender is looking for). One of Greimas's rather whimsical illustrations of his scheme is Marx's *Capital,* as follows:

Subject: man
Object: classless society
Sender: history
Receiver: humanity
Helper: proletariat
Opponent: bourgeoisie

One can see from this example that narratological reductions share some of the allure, and some of the disadvantages, of reductions in general. They can be both alarming and lucid, reframing matters in an aggressively simplifying way. Narratologists frequently study the nature of plot (how and to what extent it recapitulates or circles back on itself, for example); or of setting (which may be, in given instances, merely incidental or instead symbolically central). They are engaged in a search for the essence of storytelling through an examination of the rules that govern, in any story, questions of problem and solution, beginning and ending, progress and obstruction.

Later landmarks in narratology are Tzvetan Todorov's *The Poetics of Prose* (1971); Roland Barthes's essay "Introduction to the Structural Analysis of Narratives" in his *Image/Music/Text* (1977); Gérard Genette's *Figures of Liter-*

ary Discourse (1966–72; selected English ed. 1982); Seymour Chatman's *Story and Discourse* (1978); and Mieke Bal's *Narratology* (rev. ed., 1997). Dorrit Cohn's *Transparent Minds* (1978) draws on narratological categories, and Clare Kinney's *Strategies of Poetic Narrative* (1992) applies narrative theory to poetry. For two interesting and thoughtful critiques of narratology, see Peter Brooks, *Reading for the Plot* (1984), and Ross Chambers, *Story and Situation* (1984). John Winkler's *Auctor and Actor* (1985) is a wonderful narratological reading of an ancient novel, *The Golden Ass* of Lucius Apuleius.

narrator Most works of fiction have a narrator, whether conspicuous or not. (Not all. In William Faulkner's *As I Lay Dying* [1930], for example, we have only the monologues of Faulkner's characters, and the "implied author," in Wayne Booth's term, who has arranged them; see IMPLIED AUTHOR / IMPLIED READER.)

There are some remarkable examples of books with noticeable narrators. In Laurence Sterne's *Tristram Shandy* (1759–67), the narrator constantly obstructs the tale with low gags and learned diversions; in Chaucer's *Troilus and Criseyde* (ca. 1385), he agonizes and yearns, in frustrated or companionable solidarity with the characters. But most narrators make cameo appearances only, pulling the reader's sleeve from time to time. Booth in *The Rhetoric of Fiction* (1961) writes that the narrator may be more or less distant from the author, from the characters in the story, or from the reader's norms. The narrator, unlike the author, may not know how a narrative turns out. Even when narrators are not characters in the work, they may have a distinctive personality, as in the case of *Troilus and Criseyde*.

The unreliable narrator is a particularly radical example of separation between narrator on the one hand and author and reader on the other. In Henry James's *Turn of the Screw* (1898), we are meant to doubt the narrator's ability to evaluate the other characters' actions (and her own).

naturalism A harsh form of realist fiction most often identified with the works of novelists from the late nineteenth and early twentieth centuries: Émile Zola, Theodore Dreiser, Frank Norris, and, later, Richard Wright, whose *Native Son* (1940) may be the last full-fledged naturalist novel. The naturalist writer frequently depicts a hero who is at the mercy of larger social forces, which represent a cruel, overmastering fate. And the forces of character often seem just as implacable as those of society. The doctrine of Social

Darwinism, which saw life as a brutal struggle for survival, had a strong influence on the naturalists.

For naturalist writers, as Lee Clark Mitchell puts it, "When everything required for an action is present, determined characters cannot refrain. Because they always choose to act as their strongest desires dictate, their choices always seem predictable and outside their control. . . . All we now need to explain any action [is] a set of conditions, not a responsible self."

Naturalism presents, therefore, a powerful and distorting reduction of our usual idea of human character. But the reduction has some basis in what we feel about ourselves, since as readers we respond to it so strongly. Naturalism, rather than being allied to realism, in fact casts itself on the side of melodrama and romance, genres in which characters incarnate certain irresistible tendencies. (On this point, see Richard Chase, "Norris and Naturalism," in *The American Novel and Its Tradition* [1957].) Irving Howe notes that naturalism is frequently determined to explore, and connect, two senses of lowness: the lower classes, and low manners and morals (Irving Howe, "Naturalism and Taste," in *A Critic's Notebook* [1994]).

The Marxist critic Georg Lukács in *Realism in Our Time* (1958) contrasts realism to naturalism, to naturalism's disadvantage. Perhaps oddly, Lukács aligns modernism and naturalism. Lukács describes modernism as a form of naturalism lacking the "hierarchy of significance" among situations and characters that distinguishes realism. See also Walter Benn Michaels, *The Gold Standard and the Logic of Naturalism* (1987); Lee Clark Mitchell, *Determined Fictions* (1989); David Baguley, *Naturalist Fiction* (1990).

negative capability A phrase invented and defined by the poet John Keats, in a letter from December 1817. Keats wrote of the capacity that "Shakespeare possessed so enormously—I mean *Negative Capability,* that is, when a man is capable of being in uncertainties, mysteries, doubts, without any irritable reaching after fact and reason." Negative capability is often thought to be a desirable quality in a poet, since it implies a judicious self-assurance, as well as the power to refrain from adhering to customary standards of fact, evidence, and knowledge. See Walter Jackson Bate, *John Keats* (1963).

neoclassicism Neoclassicism is associated most of all with the French writers of the late seventeenth century: notably, the playwright Pierre Corneille (1606–84), who championed the notion of the three unities. Taking Aristotle's *Poetics* (ca. 330 BCE) as a prescriptive rather than a descriptive text, a handbook meant to guide all future dramatists, Corneille writes that plays ought to observe the unity of time (with the plot's action covering as brief a period as possible, ideally somewhere between two and twenty-four hours), unity of place (no shifts of location), and unity of action (a seamless plot tied together by suspense). Corneille acknowledged that his rules were not always present in Aristotle (who does not mention unity of place, for example).

The Art of Poetry (1674) by Nicolas Boileau-Despréaux is a more flexible document of neoclassicism than Corneille's writings. One of Boileau's maxims, "Never deviate from nature," embodies a chief tenet of neoclassical theory: the emphasis on rules is meant to serve the natural, the just, and the true. For Alexander Pope in his *Essay on Criticism* (1711), artistic rules are "nature methodized." "Learn hence for ancient rules a just esteem," Pope writes: "To copy nature is to copy them." In England, during the Restoration and early eighteenth century, neoclassical critics like Thomas Rymer (1641–1713) and John Dennis (1657–1734) combined the wish for accurate representation, for a just mimesis, with the wish for literary effectiveness through the producing of appropriate emotional responses in the audience.

The greatest critic of the Restoration, John Dryden, in his *Essay of Dramatic Poesy* (1668) criticizes (through his character Neander) the rigid, regular forms of French neoclassicism. Dryden writes that "those beauties of the French-poesie . . . are indeed the Beauties of a Statue, but not of a Man, because not animated with the Soul of Poesie, which is imitation of humour and passions." As Joseph Addison (1672–1719) does later, Dryden challenges neoclassicism by identifying what is natural and right in literature with the writer's capacity to evoke certain responses in the reader (through the representation of "humour and passions"), rather than with the writer's conformity to rules. See Lawrence Manley, *Convention* (1980); Pierre Corneille, "Of the Three Unities" (1660), in Hazard Adams, ed., *Critical Theory Since Plato* (1971).

Neoplatonism A doctrine of great prestige in European intellectual tradition, first formulated by a Greek philosopher of Alexandria, Egypt, named Plotinus (205–70 CE). Plotinus in his *Enneads* propounded the theory of three "hypostases": the One, the Intelligences, and the Soul (Psyche). (We might translate these three levels as, respectively, God, the Ideas, and Us.)

Plotinus's problem was to bridge the gap between divine perfection and the very imperfect universe that we experience. He addressed this problem through his theory of emanations. The goodness of the One spills over, or emanates into, first the Intelligences (analogous to Plato's ideas, the abstract forms that organize all existence), then our Souls, and then, finally, the realm of body or matter. This last region touched by emanation, the material world, is felt by us as imperfect only because it is so distant from the One, not because it is inherently flawed or evil. In this way, Plotinus's monistic vision combats the dualist idea of Gnosticism. (The Gnostics thought that existence is fundamentally fallen, and that the divine remains antithetical to the corrupt, temporal world that we know. See GNOSIS, GNOSTICISM.) The American pragmatist William James disdained Plotinus's One as embodying "the stagnant felicity of absolute perfection," useless for any practical purposes.

In the late fifteenth century, Florentine Neoplatonists, most prominent among them Marsilio Ficino (1433–99) and his follower Pico della Mirandola (1463–94), combined the study of Plato with an interest in mysticism and occult knowledge. They were syncretic in their attempt to reconcile Plato with other esoteric masters, and relied on the works of magical lore and cosmological theory attributed to such legendary, maguslike authors as Hermes Trismegistus and Pythagoras. (See HERMETIC.) Ficino's *On Love* was an influential commentary on Plato's *Symposium;* and Pico's *Oration on the Dignity of Man,* an astounding document of Renaissance intellectual ambition, claimed the godlike capacities of human thought and imagination.

In the Renaissance, Neoplatonism furnished a rich variety of themes for writers and visual artists: for an introduction see Erwin Panofsky's essay on Michelangelo in his *Studies in Iconology* (1939). See "Platonism and Neoplatonism," in Isabel Rivers, *Classical and Christian Ideas in English Renaissance Poetry* (1979, 2nd ed. 1994), C. B. Schmitt et al., eds., *The Cambridge History of Renaissance Philosophy* (1988), and Paul Oskar Kristeller, *Renaissance Thought and Its Sources* (1979).

New Criticism The New Critics were a group of writers and intellectuals from the American South: most prominent among them Robert Penn Warren, Cleanth Brooks, Allen Tate, and John Crowe Ransom. This group revolutionized the academic study of literature in the 1940s. (They were soon joined by other important figures like W. K. Wimsatt and Earl Wasserman.) Before the New Criticism, literature departments were dominated by research into the literary sources and historical contexts of literature, by literary biography, and by the (often vague and effusive) "appreciation" of great writers. Such appreciation was frequently stated in emotional and moralizing terms that paid scant attention to how literary works actually achieve their effects. Influenced by I. A. Richards, William Empson, R. P. Blackmur, and Kenneth Burke, among others, the New Critics introduced the practice of *close reading:* looking at a piece of literature as an intricate and precisely functional object, whose parts interact with one another, and whose words bear an exact connotative weight. For New Criticism, the primary question to be asked about a poem or story is *how it works* (rather than, for example, the previous literary works it draws on, the historical situation of the writer, or the moral statement that the author intended to make).

The New Critics rebelled against the distinction, often made by philology, between a reader's subjective or emotional responses and the certifiable facts of literary history (the latter being the philologist's proper subject). Instead, for them, subjective responses were an essential proof that a reader was giving the text sufficient attention: the closer the attention, the more interesting and accurate the responses. Literary history, like a text's social and political references, was relevant only insofar as the text put it to use in order to make the reader react.

The New Critics offered a humanistic defense of literature along the following lines. In opposition to the Marxist criticism popular in the 1930s, they valued not the sheer statement or position voiced by a piece of literature, but rather the (often playful or paradoxical) manner in which literature, if it is interesting at all, manages such statements. Writers use ideas ironically rather than straightforwardly, the New Critics argued, because they subject these ideas to literary form, and to the texture or resonance of words. In this way, the literary author differs from the mere rhetorician. The polemical journalist or advertising man aims, through rhetoric, at persuading the audience to a course of action (voting a certain way, buying a certain product). By contrast, the only action demanded of the reader of literature is a reflection on the complex nature of our situations and attitudes. For a New Critical reader, the point of reading a book was not to decide on its political leanings—what "statement" it was making (the frequent obsession of the left-leaning New York intellectual establishment in the 1930s). Instead, such a reader wanted to see how any statement the book made was inflected and qualified by the artfulness that marked it as a piece of literature (rather than a newspaper editorial).

Since the 1980s, New Criticism has often been maligned for what its opponents claim is an indifference to political ideology and social history. There
is some truth to the charge. But in general, the New Critics showed intelligent wariness of political and historicizing readings, rather than indifference.
And the techniques of close reading that the New Critics pioneered, especially in *Understanding Poetry* (1938), the great classroom text by Brooks and
Warren, are now an integral part of all literary study.

See W. K. Wimsatt, *The Verbal Icon* (1954); Cleanth Brooks and Robert
Penn Warren, "The Reading of Modern Poetry" (1937); Cleanth Brooks, *The
Well Wrought Urn* (1947); and John Crowe Ransom, *The New Criticism*
(1941). Geoffrey Hartman in his essay "Beyond Formalism" (from *Beyond
Formalism* [1970]) sees in New Criticism a neglect of the historical transitions
from one literary style to the next, and a failure to take into account the effect
these transitions have on poetic meaning. Two helpful overviews are Mark
Jancovich, "The Southern New Critics," in Walton Litz, Louis Menand, and
Lawrence Rainey, eds., *The Cambridge History of Literary Criticism*, vol. 7
(2000); and Jennifer Lewin and Stephen Burt, "Poetry and the New Criticism," in Neil Roberts, ed., *The Blackwell Companion to Twentieth-Century
Poetry* (2001). See also CLOSE READING; PARADOX; PARAPHRASE; PHILOLOGY.

new historicism An academic movement of the 1980s and the following
decades emphasizing the intersection of literature with historical anecdote,
and with the cultural practices of ordinary people. The history that new historicists focus on is sometimes of a strange or lurid sort: for Renaissance studies, witch trials, cannibals, and exorcisms became significant, especially in the
work of the movement's central figure, Stephen Greenblatt. One ancestor of
new historicism is C. L. Barber's fascinating *Shakespeare's Festive Comedy*
(1959), which connects Shakespearean revelry with popular practices like
maypole dancing and rural festivals of "misrule," during which authority was
vigorously parodied. (See also FESTIVE.) Another influence is the histories of
everyday life written by Fernand Braudel (1902–70) and the other historians
of the French Annales school.

Catherine Gallagher writes that new historicism "entails reading literary
and nonliterary texts as constituents of historical discourses that are both inside and outside of texts." New historicists, she continues, "generally posit no
fixed hierarchy of cause and effect as they trace the connections among texts,
discourses, power, and the constitution of subjectivity." These quotations

from Gallagher give a sense of the favored new historicist terms (discourse, text, power, subjectivity), as well as the movement's determination to avoid deciding on the exact role of literature in relation to political and intellectual history. Instead, literature is associated with politics, with ideas, and with social life, all these things being fluidly interconnected.

Gallagher's formulation bears witness to this group's insistence on history as a "God-term" (Kenneth Burke), an all-encompassing power that operates "both inside and outside of texts." Often, in new historicism, history somewhat resembles the police, exercising surveillance and stifling freedom. This aspect of the new historicism was heavily influenced by the French philosopher Michel Foucault, especially his *Discipline and Punish* (1975). At other times, though, the new historicist takes a more freewheeling approach to history, inspecting unaccustomed regions for clues to human experience in past eras. A new historicist might write an essay on mirrors or cosmetics in the Renaissance as a key to understanding the status of the individual during this age: combining a study of the material objects a culture uses with a reading of the culture's literary products.

In American Studies, new historicism was inspired by works like Walter Benn Michaels, *The Gold Standard and the Logic of Naturalism* (1987), and David Reynolds, *Beneath the American Renaissance* (1988). It addressed the British novel in D. A. Miller's *The Novel and the Police* (1988). In Renaissance studies, see Stephen Greenblatt's *Renaissance Self-Fashioning* (1980) and the essays collected in his *Shakespearean Negotiations* (1988). (This bibliography could be vastly expanded given the quantity of new historicist work; I list only especially influential books.)

For more general treatments one may consult the book Greenblatt wrote with Catherine Gallagher, *Practicing New Historicism* (2000), as well as H. Aram Veeser, ed., *The New Historicism* (1989).

Some critiques of new historicism are (in Renaissance Studies) Richard Strier, *Resistant Structures* (1995); Graham Bradshaw, *Misrepresentations* (1993); Stanley Cavell, "Macbeth Appalled," in *Disowning Knowledge in Six Plays of Shakespeare* (rev. ed., 2002); and David Mikics, "Poetry and Politics in *A Midsummer Night's Dream*," *Raritan* 18:2 (Fall 1998), 99–119. For a critique focusing on American Studies, see Andrew Delbanco, *Required Reading* (1997).

A more general criticism of how new historicism avoids the style and stance of the literary works it studies is contained in Timothy Peltason's "The Uncommon Pursuit," *Literary Imagination* 6:3 (2004), 499–515.

New York school A group of poets including Frank O'Hara (1926–66), John Ashbery (b. 1927), Kenneth Koch (1925–2002), James Schuyler (1923–91), and others. Ashbery and O'Hara, especially, have been influential on later poets. Many of the New York school poets were connected to the visual arts; both O'Hara and Ashbery wrote art reviews. Influenced particularly by the French writer Guillaume Apollinaire (1880–1918), the New York school poets introduced a new casualness and immediacy into poetry. O'Hara's poems, for example, prominently featured the names of friends, slices of chance conversation, and odd details of daily life. The New York school poets can make silliness and melancholy interact with each other, or entertain, almost simultaneously, feelings of the sublime and the tedious. They may joke, get evasive or confused, change the subject, or otherwise play hard to get. (See also ELLIPTICAL POETRY.)

Tongue half in cheek, O'Hara wrote a manifesto for "Personism" in 1959, in which he aimed to both combat and revise the modernist notion of impersonality (see IMPERSONALITY): "Personism has nothing to do with philosophy, it's all art! It does not have to do with personality or intimacy, far from it! . . . The poem is at last between two persons instead of two pages. In all modesty, I confess that it may be the death of literature as we know it."

On the New York school poets, see David Lehman, *The Last Avant Garde* (1999), as well as the collection edited by David Shapiro and Ron Padgett, *An Anthology of New York Poets* (1970).

nihilism The term *nihilist* was first applied in the 1860s to fierce critics of the Czarist regime in Russia, haters of bourgeois hypocrisy who were sometimes linked to what we would now call terrorist groups. Violence was used for its own sake, and to provoke the czar into a brutal crackdown. The movement culminated in 1881, with the assassination of Czar Alexander II.

Nihilism practices violent extremism for extremism's sake: spurred by cynicism and disillusionment, the nihilist believes in nothing. Humiliation of the bourgeois enemy, the sowing of fear and panic, the use of violence for the momentary achievement of fame or personal power—all these motives play a strong role. For Friedrich Nietzsche (1844–1900), nihilism is an important moment in European intellectual history, one that must be passed through so that a new consciousness can emerge on the other side.

The character Bazarov in Ivan Turgenev's *Fathers and Sons* (1862), though he is fatalistic rather than violent, is called a nihilist. The main literary treatment of nihilism is Fyodor Dostoevski's terrifying, exciting *The Possessed* (more accurately translated as *The Demons* or *The Devils* [1871]). Joseph Conrad's *The Secret Agent* (1907) also portrays nihilism. Conrad's character the Professor, Michael Ignatieff writes, is "fascinated with the invulnerability that his own willingness to die confers on him."

For a wide-ranging and provocative study of nihilism up to the present day, see Michael Ignatieff, *The Lesser Evil* (2004). For philosophical treatments of nihilism, consult Michael Gillespie, *Nihilism Before Nietzsche* (1995), and Stanley Rosen, *The Question of Being* (1993).

nonfiction novel A form pioneered by Truman Capote's *In Cold Blood* (1965) and continued by Norman Mailer in his impressive *The Executioner's Song* (1979). The nonfiction novel uses fictional techniques of characterization and interior monologue, but bases its story on real events. These two books by Capote and Mailer, both of them accounts of violent criminals, are probably responsible for the "true crime" category in bookstores. Mailer had earlier written *Armies of the Night* (1968), an account of the countercultural assault on the Pentagon featuring Mailer himself. The book's slogan was "history as a novel/the novel as history."

Many biographies could be considered nonfiction novels, since they necessarily invent the thoughts of their protagonists. (This has been a theme in historical writing since Thucydides [ca. 460—ca. 395 BCE], who cheerfully made up the speeches of his generals and politicians.) The freedom of such invention may seem like mere license, or an underhanded way of claiming authority: note the furor over Edmund Morris's *Dutch* (1999), an imaginative biography of former president Ronald Reagan.

The nonfiction novel is distinct from the *roman à clef* (French *roman*, "novel," and *clef* [pronounced CLAY], "key"). The roman à clef is a thinly disguised tale asking the savvy reader to recognize the real identity of the characters, who travel under assumed names. One recent popular example is *Primary Colors* (1996). See ROMAN À CLEF.

No play (Also spelled "Noh" or "Nō.") A brief Japanese dramatic form drawing on poetry, prose, dance, and music. Elaborate, nobly styled and slow in tempo, the No drama, like ancient Greek tragedy, uses masks, as well as a chorus that comments on the action. It reached its peak in the fourteenth century and later.

No theater has made its mark on twentieth-century European and American drama. It was particularly influential on the poets Ezra Pound, who published Ernest Fenellosa's translations of No plays in 1916, and W. B. Yeats. Yeats even named some of his poetic dramas No plays. See Yeats's introduction to *Certain Noble Plays of Japan* (1916), Earl Miner, *The Japanese Tradition in British and American Literature* (1958), Donald Keene, *Nō, the Classical Theatre of Japan* (1966), and K. Yasuda, *Masterworks of the Nō Theater* (1989).

nouveau roman French, "new novel." The innovative form of writing associated especially with the works of Alain Robbe-Grillet, frequently involving a stripped-down fictional surface, an ascetic purity of style, and the attempt to eliminate signs of the author's presence, in order to depict an objective, solid, neutral world. Robbe-Grillet's major novels are *The Voyeur* (1955), *The Erasers* (1953), *Jealousy* (1957), and *In the Labyrinth* (1959). Nathalie Sarraute's *The Planetarium* (1959), Claude Simon's *The Wind* (1957), Michel Butor's *The Modification* (1957), and Marguerite Duras's *Moderato Cantabile* (1958) were also important to the nouveau roman movement. (Duras, it should be noted, always denied that she was part of the nouveau roman trend.) Robbe-Grillet's manifesto is entitled *For the New Novel* (1963); in it, he protested against writers who "adopt the *humanist* point of view" that "man is everywhere." The nouveau roman influenced the style of several filmmakers of the 1960s, notably Jean-Luc Godard and Michelangelo Antonioni.

The style of the new novel is spare, astringent, and at times baffling to the reader in its imperturbable evenness. As such, it is a form of modernist impersonality; see AVANT-GARDE; IMPERSONALITY; MODERNISM.

novel A word derived from the Italian *novello,* meaning "a small new thing": a modest enough etymology for the novel, quantitatively the most substantial genre of literature. (A novella is a prose fiction between a short story and a novel in length: that is, about seventy to a hundred pages. A novel, like an epic or a prizefighter, has to have a certain mass to qualify for the title.) Competing meanings of the word *novel* also survived: in the Renaissance, *novel* means "news"; and it also signifies something innovative and inventive. The novel promises us news of the world, and advertises itself as a new thing under the literary sun.

In French and German, the name for the novel suggests the genre of romance: *le roman, der Roman.* But the novel and the romance have historically been rivals. Romance is fantastic, full of marvels, often involving extravagant adventures, wizardry, and oracles; in it, as Northrop Frye remarks, the favored means of transportation seems to be by shipwreck. (See CHIVALRIC ROMANCE; QUEST ROMANCE.) The novel, by contrast, frequently offers a sober, realistic portrait of society and focuses on such issues as inheriting property and getting married. The contrast between romance and novel finds support in comments like those in Samuel Johnson's *Rambler* no. 4 (1750; see REALISM). *Don Quixote* (1605–15) by Miguel de Cervantes is probably the best-known instance of a novel that takes up a contrast between its own seriously adventurous consciousness and the narrower enjoyments of chivalric romance (represented for Cervantes by the anonymous *Amadis of Gaul* from the thirteenth–fourteenth century).

But romance and novel are also close relatives. Recently Margaret Doody, following Frye, has outlined the concerns that romance shares with the novel. Both novel and prose romance often show a chaste, virtuous protagonist at risk, contending with threats of rape, imprisonment, or torture (as in the Joseph story in the Bible, or Samuel Richardson's *Clarissa* [1747–48]). Many novels portray the fortunes of an enterprising young man down on his luck, or seeking his chance in the world (as in Honoré de Balzac's *Lost Illusions* [1837–43], Charles Dickens's *Great Expectations* [1861], or Saul Bellow's *The Adventures of Augie March* [1953]). Others focus on the search for the right marriage partner, which brings with it the discovery of one's own true self (Jane Austen's *Pride and Prejudice* [1813], George Eliot's *Middlemarch* [1871–72]). Whether in self-criticism or self-promotion, novels frequently reflect on the capacity of fiction reading to take over one's life. Don Quixote reads chivalric romances and himself becomes a character in one; Flaubert's Emma Bovary is profoundly, disastrously influenced by the romantic novels she reads.

As I have suggested, there is an early association between the novel and the news (*nouvelles*): recent events reported in exciting fashion. The line between reportage and fiction was originally rather unclear (and may be so still, at times). Early English novelists like Daniel Defoe sometimes claimed that their books were actual journalistic reports, fact not fiction. Introducing his *Robinson Crusoe* (1719), Defoe assured his readers that Crusoe's story was plain truth, solid and verifiable. But Defoe's preface to *Moll Flanders* (1722) strikes a more coyly ambiguous note: "The world is so taken up of late with novels and romances, that it will be hard for a private history to be taken for genuine, where the names and other circumstances of the person are concealed; and on this account we must be content to leave the reader to pass his own opinion upon the ensuing sheets and take it just as he pleases."

Usually, though, the novel is the opponent of history, instead of aspiring after journalistic fact. One Austen character (in *Northanger Abbey* [written 1798–99, publ. 1818]) condemns books of history "with wars or pestilences, in every page; the men all so good for nothing, and hardly any women at all—it is very tiresome." The novel has usually been, by definition, a *popular* genre, its audience not esoteric and peculiarly learned, but a representative section of society (middle-class women, for example, or, in the Victorian era, newspaper readers).

The novel's representative nature gets stressed in other ways as well. The novel is often described as *the* literary form of the modern age, the genre that has superseded and taken over the privileges of some earlier one (most often, epic or romance). Socially minded critics often point out that the novel's dominion over the reading public is linked to the flourishing of capitalism or the rise of the middle class: so the novel's fortunes become society's as well.

Epistolary novels, composed entirely of letters exchanged among the characters, were popular in the eighteenth century. Among the most famous examples are Samuel Richardson's *Pamela* (1740) and *Clarissa,* Madeleine de Scudéry's *Amorous Letters* (1641), and *Les liaisons dangereuses* by Choderlos de Laclos (1782). Richardson's successor, Henry Fielding, parodied Richardson's epistolary technique of "writing to the moment" in *Shamela* (1741). Epistolary novels by women were greatly popular in late-eighteenth-century France. Another product of French tradition, Madame de la Fayette's *Princesse de Cleves* (1678), is an early example of the historical novel. Among the most notable examples of novels from the non-Western world are two monumental works, Lady Murasaki's *Tale of Genji,* written in eleventh-century Japan, and the Chinese novel *The Story of the Stone* (also called *The Dream of the Red Chamber,* eighteenth century), by Cao Xueqin (Ts'ao Hsueh-ch'in).

The novel of sentiment (or sensibility) appeared in the later eighteenth century (Henry Mackenzie's *The Man of Feeling* [1771], Laurence Sterne's *A Sentimental Journey* [1768]), as did the Bildungsroman or novel of education (Goethe's *Wilhelm Meister's Apprenticeship* [1795–96]). The Gothic novel was very important as well in the late eighteenth and early nineteenth centuries, beginning with works like Horace Walpole's *The Castle of Otranto* (1764), Ann Radcliffe's *The Mysteries of Udolpho* (1794), and Matthew Lewis's *The*

Monk (1796). Jane Austen reflected on both the Gothic and the novel of sensibility in (respectively) *Northanger Abbey* and *Sense and Sensibility* (1811).

In the Victorian Age, realist novels (by Dickens, most famously) were serialized in newspapers, a format that encouraged the ingenuities of week-to-week suspense. Authors like Wilkie Collins perfected the "sensation novel," which relied on abundant cliffhanging and nailbiting effects. Closer to the end of the nineteenth century, the naturalist novels of Émile Zola and Theodore Dreiser depicted the harsh, oppressive facts of capitalist society, in all its destructive effect on innocent or hopeful protagonists.

Novels have traditionally been outposts of bizarre and stimulating literary experiment, from Lucius Apuleius's *Golden Ass* (second century CE) to Sterne's *Tristram Shandy* (1759–67) to twentieth-century works by James Joyce (1882–1941), Virginia Woolf (1882–1941), and Gertrude Stein (1874–1946). The novel sometimes appears as an extended or involuted parable, or fable, as in the works of Franz Kafka (1883–1924). Such modernist experiments were succeeded by the spare, parabolic nouveau roman ("new novel") practiced in France by Alain Robbe-Grillet (b. 1922) and others.

The encyclopedic ambition of the novel has often been commented on. Novels sometimes aim to encompass the entire world of their characters, down to the smallest, but perhaps most significant, details: what Woolf called the "orts, scraps and fragments" of their existence. The most successful example of such a total, encyclopedic fiction is probably Joyce's *Ulysses* (1922). The careful tracking of a character's memories, thoughts, and sensations takes on a new expansiveness in the late novels of Henry James (1843–1916) and Marcel Proust's *In Search of Lost Time* (1912–27). Novels may attempt to tell everything about a historical moment, a family, or a culture, as in Anthony Trollope's *The Way We Live Now* (1875), Thomas Mann's *Buddenbrooks* (1900) and *The Magic Mountain* (1924), or Thomas Pynchon's *Gravity's Rainbow* (1973).

For the origins and background of the novel form, see Ian Watt, *The Rise of the Novel* (1957), Michael McKeon, *The Origins of the English Novel, 1600–1740* (1987), and Margaret Anne Doody, *The True Story of the Novel* (1996). Some influential studies of the realist novel are Georg Lukács, *The Historical Novel* (written 1936–37); Irving Howe, *Politics and the Novel* (1962); and René Girard, *Deceit, Desire, and the Novel* (1961). Mikhail Bakhtin in *Some Problems of Dostoevski's Poetics* (1929) and *The Dialogic Imagination* (publ. 1981, written in the 1930s) proposes a "dialogical" theory of the novel, based on the polyphonic, various character of social life. On the American novel, Richard Chase's *The American Novel and Its Tradition* (1957) is still very useful. James Wood's *The Broken Estate* (1999) and *The Irresponsible Self* (2004) are two superb collections analyzing, respectively, questions of belief and comedy in the novel. Finally, Philip Stevick, ed., *The Theory of the Novel* (1967), is an immensely useful anthology.

See also CHIVALRIC ROMANCE; DIALOGIC; EPISTOLARY NOVEL; GOTHIC; MODERNISM; NATURALISM; NOUVEAU ROMAN; QUEST ROMANCE; REALISM; SENSATION NOVEL.

objective correlative T. S. Eliot in his essay "Hamlet and His Problems" (1919) wrote that "the only way of expressing emotion in the form of art is by finding an objective correlative," that is, "a set of objects, a situation, a chain of events which shall be the formula of that *particular* emotion." The objective correlative stands in contrast to what Eliot calls the "intense feeling, ecstatic or terrible, without an object or exceeding its object."

Eliot's essay is a somewhat covert assault on what he regarded as the extreme, disconnected effusions of Romanticism, its production of "intense feeling . . . without an object." But such intensity is also a facet of Eliot's own poetry, which is at times (often at its most brilliant and authoritative moments) remarkably high-strung, even hysterical. See Louis Menand's essay on Eliot in *The Cambridge History of Literary Criticism,* vol. 7 (2000).

objectivism The objectivists were a group of poets gathered together by Louis Zukofsky (1904–78) for an issue of Harriet Monroe's *Poetry* magazine in 1931. The most significant objectivist poets were George Oppen (1908–84), Charles Reznikoff (1894–1976), and Carl Rakosi (1903–2004), as well as Lorine Niedecker (1903–70), who was not represented in Zukofsky's issue but corresponded with him extensively after its appearance. Two of the main influences on the objectivists were Ezra Pound (1885–1972) and William Carlos Williams (1883–1963). Following Williams's dictum "no ideas but in things," the objectivists found, at their best, a flatness that illuminates, along with a sometimes dour, sometimes lively attachment to the details of the everyday. They adhered to the rigor of visible evidence, often found in hard urban landscapes—their form of modernist impersonality. See also IMPERSONALITY.

ode A form of lyric poetry, by turns heroic and intimate. The most influential ancient authors of the ode are the Greek poet Pindar (518–438 BCE) and the Roman Horace (65–8 BCE). Pindar's poems celebrate the victors in the

Olympic games. Horace, unlike Pindar, and in contrast to Homeric and Virgilian epic, reflects on heroism from a distance, as he invokes his life in the country, the bittersweetness of love, and the choice among kinds of life. He has retreated from the life of politics and war, into the pleasures of poetry and secluded, thoughtful relaxation. (See RETIREMENT.) In Horace, the ode is deliberately removed from historical greatness, fitted to the smaller scale of a private man expressing his own satisfactions and frustrations.

The ode underwent a long eclipse in literary history. In his *Dictionary of the English Language* (1755), Samuel Johnson wrote of the ode, "It is not very suitable to the English language, and has not been used by any man of eminence since Milton." But the 1740s were marked by significant collections of odes by poets like Joseph Warton, Mark Akenside, and William Collins. These writers relied on the ode to charge poetry with the lofty inventions of a solitary imagination, in contrast to the moralizing, socially specific interests of Augustan verse. In the hands of these writers, the ode was a various form, displaying sudden shifts of mood and subject.

Writing of lyric poetry in 1783, Robert Potter clearly had in mind the sublime ode, a form of "composition [that] not only allowed, but even required sudden and bold transitions, and the highest flights of imagination to which even the Epic Muse dared not aspire. . . . The Lyric is a Muse of fire that rises on the wings of Extasy, and follows her Hero or her God from one glorious action to another, from earth to heaven."

During this eighteenth-century revival, the ode was thought to be related to the psalm and the hymn. In his *Lectures on the Sacred Poetry of the Hebrews* (1753), Bishop Robert Lowth wrote that "the origin of the ode may be traced into that of poetry itself, and appears to be coeval with the commencement of religion, or more properly to the creation of man."

Some significant later odes are John Dryden's "Song for Saint Cecilia's Day" (1687), William Wordsworth's "Intimations of Immortality" and "Ode to Duty" (both 1807), and perhaps above all, Keats's Odes (1819). Few poets of the twentieth century called their works odes, but the category is still useful in the interpretation of works like Paul Valéry's "Le cimetière marin" (The Cemetery by the Sea, 1920), W. H. Auden's "The Shield of Achilles" (1955), and Robert Lowell's "For the Union Dead" (1964). The twentieth-century poets Pablo Neruda and Kenneth Koch wrote odes to everyday objects and common preoccupations, in order to play, less derisively than affectionately, on the traditionally high ambition of the ode.

See Ralph Cohen, "The Return of the Ode," in John Sitter, ed., *The Cam-*

bridge Companion to Eighteenth-Century Poetry (2001); Norman Maclean, "From Action to Image: Theories of the Lyric in the Eighteenth Century," in R. S. Crane, ed., *Critics and Criticism* (1952); Geoffrey Hartman, "Evening Star and Evening Land" in *The Fate of Reading* (1975); Paul Fry, *The Poet's Calling in the English Ode* (1980); Helen Vendler, *The Odes of John Keats* (1983).

oral literature Oral literature seems a contradiction in terms, since by definition literature requires (written) letters, and oral cultures do not possess writing. But beginning with the classicist Milman Parry's trips to the Balkans in the 1930s, during which he investigated how contemporary oral bards might throw light on Homer, oral literature has defined itself as a distinct field. After Parry died in 1935, Albert Lord continued his work, showing that epic singers do not memorize but rather recreate their work differently in each performance. The oral poet relies on a repertoire of episodes and themes, as well as epithets and phrases that fill up spaces in the verse line. (See EPITHET.) Albert Lord's *The Singer of Tales* (1960) considered Homer's epics alongside those of the current Yugoslavian bards known as goslars. For an influential meditation on the difference between the oral and the literate, consult Walter Ong, *Orality and Literacy* (1982). See also FOLKLORE.

ordinary Nick Halpern in his book *Everyday and Prophetic* (2003) remarks that the ordinary differs from the everyday: it seems to be more lucid and concentrated, presenting a distilled sense of what everydayness might mean. Halpern derives his discussion from the sense of the ordinary in twentieth-century philosophy, particularly in the works of Ludwig Wittgenstein and J. L. Austin. Wittgenstein and Austin aimed to lead philosophical discussion back to a concern with what we really think and do. Their wish was to turn philosophy away from its traditional distractions of scholastic definition-making, and make it attentive to common life.

In literature, William Wordsworth (1770–1850) is the great poet of the ordinary. For Wordsworth the ordinary, the voice of what is most universal and general, bespeaks a consistent, sheltering dignity. And the great American sage Ralph Waldo Emerson, in "Self-Reliance" (1841), turns an eye to the ordinary world as a place of more interest than mystical passions and dreams: "What would we really know the meaning of?" Emerson asks: "the milk in the firkin, the meal in the pan . . ." It is not so much what lies within or behind the ordinary that fascinates, as what the fact of it betokens: what it means turns out to be what we mean.

For an interesting exploration of "ordinary language criticism," partly inspired by the works of Stanley Cavell, Richard Rorty, and others, see Kenneth Dauber and Walter Jost, eds., *Ordinary Language Criticism* (2003).

originality Originality is one of the oldest tropes in the writer's book. It is a tricky one, too. Often, there is no quicker way for an author to slump into the predictable than by trying to be original. The Book of Genesis, John Hollander notes, forms a meditation on original composition: God makes his peculiar new creature much as an artist would, shaping it from dirt and clay. But how convincingly can we imitate God in this respect?

The older view of originality, prior to the mid-eighteenth century, is that it is often merely raw and eccentric, a fledgling. Francis Bacon emphasizes such awkwardness in his essay "Of Innovations" (1625): "As the births of living creatures at first are ill-shapen, so are all Innovations, which are the births of time." As time passes, Bacon continues, the original work will fortunately be smoothed out into acceptability, its promise honed by imitators.

Originality also means wanting to be one's own origin, the situation of Satan in Milton's *Paradise Lost* (1667) and of many a later romantic rebel. As time went on, originality became a prized virtue, until it is now nearly synonymous with inventive achievement. One originates oneself, as well as one's work, by doing something truly new.

In his "Conjectures on Original Composition" (1759), Edward Young applauds the flourishes of the original, asking, "Who listens to a twice-told tale: our spirits rouse at an original; that is a perfect stranger, and all throng to learn what news from a foreign land. . . . Thus every telescope is lifted at a new-discovered star; it makes a hundred astronomers in a moment, and denies equal notice to the sun." "Imitators," Young decides, "only give us a sort of duplicates of what we had, possibly much better, before; increasing the mere drug of books." But "the pen of an original writer," he concludes, "out of a barren waste calls a blooming spring." There is a bold paradox hidden in Young's advocacy of newness, as he himself notes: "For may not this paradox pass into a maxim? viz. 'The less we copy the renowned ancients, we shall resemble them the more.'"

See Thomas MacFarland, *Originality and Imagination* (1985); also John Hollander, "Originality," in *The Work of Poetry* (1997), and Gerald Bruns,

"The Originality of Texts in a Manuscript Culture," in *Inventions* (1982). (According to Bruns, in the manuscript cultures of the ancient and medieval world, "originality is a sort of happy accident that disrupts imitation.")

ottava rima A stanza of eight iambic pentameter lines, rhyming *abababcc*. Much of its popularity in England was due to the example of two Italian epics: Ludovico Ariosto's *Orlando Furioso* (1516) and, later, Torquato Tasso's *Jerusalem Delivered* (1575). John Harington in his translation of Ariosto (1591) announced that ottava rima was "English heroical verse." The Renaissance poets Samuel Daniel and Michael Drayton both wrote long poems in ottava rima. In its solidity and expanse ottava rima competed with a native English form, rhyme royal, as well as the Spenserian stanza developed by Edmund Spenser in his epic *The Faerie Queene* (1590–96). (See RHYME ROYAL; SPENSERIAN STANZA.) The form was used by Byron in three of his greatest poems, *Beppo* (1818), *The Vision of Judgment* (1822), and *Don Juan* (1819–24), and by W. B. Yeats in two major poems, "Among School Children" (1927) and "The Circus Animals' Desertion" (1939).

Oulipo Short for Ouvroir de Littérature Potentielle (Workshop of Potential Literature). Starting at the beginning of the 1960s, the Oulipo group, whose best-known members were Raymond Queneau, Jacques Roubaud, and Georges Perec, set themselves the task of searching for new forms and structures for the making of literary works. As a way of trying to free themselves from influence, from the burden of past tradition, they cultivated "systematic artifices": the productive constraints and experimental schemes that define writing "as practice, as work, as play." One example of an Oulipo-influenced work is Walter Abish's novel *Alphabetical Africa* (1974), whose first chapter uses only words that begin with the letter *a;* the second chapter, words that begin with *a* or *b;* the third, *a, b,* or *c;* and so on. And Perec, one of the original members of the group, wrote a three-hundred-page novel in which no word containing the letter *e* appears.

The Oulipo group's experiments raise some questions. How do the constraints they invent differ from other literary conventions? Such games appear in fact to parody the traditional literary laws centering on form and genre. Oulipan playfulness seems to be, then, a way of claiming that the powers due to conventional means have been exhausted, and that convention itself can be replaced by rules derived from a liberating randomness. See

Leland de la Durantaye's essay on Oulipo, "The Cratylic Impulse," *Literary Imagination* 7:1 (2005), 121–34; see also AVANT-GARDE; CONVENTION.

oxymoron A conjoining of opposites or stark contrasts, as in Edmund Spenser's line from *The Faerie Queene* 1.1 (1590), "The Mirrhe sweet bleeding in the bitter wound," or the Renaissance concept of the beloved as a "cruel fair" (see CRUEL FAIR). The oxymoron is related to the paradox (see PARADOX).

P

paleface and redskin The literary and cultural critic Philip Rahv, in "Paleface and Redskin" (1938), made a distinction between two kinds of American authors. The first kind "glories in his Americanism" (the "redskins" Walt Whitman, Mark Twain, and James Fenimore Cooper, for example); the second regards being American with ambivalence, as "the source of endless ambiguities" (the "palefaces" T. S. Eliot, Henry James, and Nathaniel Hawthorne). In the twentieth century, Rahv concludes on rather flimsy evidence, the palefaces have been overthrown by the redskins. Rahv's essay is reprinted in *Image and Idea* (1948).

palinode In Greek, "singing back": a poetic retraction. The most famous palinode was the one produced by the poet Stesichorus (sixth century BCE), after he was blinded for claiming (following Homer) that Helen had deserted Menelaus for Paris and Troy. Here is the palinode of Stesichorus, as reported by Plato in the *Phaedrus* (243a):

> The story is not true,
> She never went in the well-decked ships,
> She didn't travel to the towers of Troy.

panegyric A poem or oration in praise of some great person or momentous achievement. Important models can be found in the Hebrew Bible: Psalm 45, for example, with its celebration of a famous king and hero, and the striking victory ode known as the Song of Deborah (Judges 5:2–31). The Greek poet Pindar (518–438 BCE) wrote a series of odes celebrating the victories of Olympic athletes, godlike in their strength. In English, one of the best-known panegyrics is Andrew Marvell's Horatian Ode on Cromwell's return from Ireland (1650).

Panegyric is related to epideictic, the division of oratory devoted to praise (as distinguished from the other two branches of oratory, deliberative [i.e., political] and forensic [i.e., legal]). (See RHETORIC.) Medieval panegyric poetry and oratory often followed an elaborate step-by-step scheme. E. R. Curtius gives an example: "In a Lombard rhythm on Milan the following are eulogized: 1. Its site in a fruitful plain; 2. towers, walls, and gates; 3. forum, paved streets, baths; 4. churches; 5. the piety of the inhabitants; 6. saints' tombs; 7. Ambrose and later bishops; 8. cultivation of science, art, and liturgy; 9. wealth and charity of the citizens; 10. the rule of King Liutprand (d. 744); 11. Archbishop Theodore II (d. 735); 12. achievements of the citizens in the war against infidelity."

Thomas Love Peacock offers a disillusioned perspective on the panegyric (as well as the Virgilian epic) when he remarks in *The Four Ages of Poetry* (1820) that peoples, in their "traditionary songs," "magnify their founder through the mists of distance and tradition, and perceive him achieving wonders with a god or goddess always at his elbow."

The panegyric is distantly related to the epithalamium, or marriage poem, which characteristically praises the happy couple; and also, more closely, to the festive anthems that a community sings to itself ("America the Beautiful," for instance). See "Judicial, Political, and Panegyrical Oratory in Medieval Poetry," in Ernst Robert Curtius, *European Literature and the Latin Middle Ages* (1948).

pantoum The pantoum has its origins in Malay poetry, where it is a central verse form (in Malay it is called the *pantun; pantoum* is French). It is made up of quatrains in which the second and fourth lines of a stanza return as the first and third lines of the following stanza. In the final stanza, the first and third lines of the first stanza return in reverse order (sometimes in a concluding four-line stanza and sometimes as a couplet envoi—a two-line send-off). In some pantoums, the second half of each stanza concerns a different subject than the first half. As John Hollander notes, such stanzas can have the character of a riddle (see Hollander, *Rhyme's Reason* [1981]).

Here is the beginning of a pantoum by David Lehman ("Amnesia," from *An Alternative to Speech* [1986]):

Neither the actors nor the audience knew what was coming next.
That's when the assassination must have taken place.
The car pulled up and the driver said, "Get in."
"Wolves don't criticize sheep," Cage grinned. "They eat them."

That's when the assassination must have taken place.
The wedding dress in the window had vanished.
"Wolves don't criticize sheep," Cage grinned. "They eat them."
This announcement will not be repeated.

The wedding dress in the window had vanished
At dawn, the perfect time for an execution.
This announcement will not be repeated:
The only victory in love is retreat. So we retreated . . .

parable The parable, by definition, is a simple, fable-like story that points beyond itself, showing us a lesson. "The only kind of literature which has gospel authority is the parable, and parables are secular stories with no overt religious reference," the poet W. H. Auden remarked in *The Dyer's Hand* (1963). As Auden suggests, the parable is a literary genre basic to the Christian gospels, which contain the best-known parables.

In the parable, a precept or allegorical kernel, often an enigmatic one, lies hidden under the tale. Franz Kafka, expert at such concealment, is one of the most attractive and most distancing masters of the genre. Here is one of Kafka's parables: "Leopards break into the temple and drink to the dregs what is in the sacrificial pitchers; this is repeated over and over again; finally it can be calculated in advance, and it becomes part of the ceremony."

The parable also exists abundantly in non-European traditions: in the works of the thirteenth-century Tibetan sage Sakya Pandita (collected in *Ordinary Wisdom,* trans. John Davenport [2000]); in the Sanskrit *Panchatantra* (third to fifth century CE), and in the lore attached to the thirteenth-century Sufi sage Nasruddin. See ALLEGORY; GNOMIC.

paradox A paradox is a contradiction that somehow proves fitting or true. As such, it is a central device of seventeenth-century literature, in the work of writers like John Donne, Andrew Marvell, George Herbert, and Thomas Browne. The most efficiently speculative paradoxical poem in English is probably Shakespeare's "The Phoenix and the Turtle."

In her book on paradox in the Renaissance, *Paradoxia Epidemica* (1966), Rosalie Colie writes that paradoxes exploit "the fact of relative, or competing, value systems." Paradoxes are characteristically impelled beyond their own limitations: so that a logical paradox, for example, is not *merely* logical, but a telling observation about the world.

Paradox, along with ambiguity and irony, was a key word for the New Critics. (See AMBIGUITY; IRONY; NEW CRITICISM.) In a poem like Marvell's "The Definition of Love," the New Critics valued the poet's cool, adroit balancing of thought: his equilibrium, achieved through paradox. (The speaker in "The Definition of Love" argues that his love is more valuable because it can never be consummated.) Cleanth Brooks and Robert Penn Warren, *Understanding Poetry* (4th ed., 1976 [1938]), 222–25; see also Cleanth Brooks, *The Well-Wrought Urn* (1947).

paraphrase Cleanth Brooks's famous essay "The Heresy of Paraphrase" (from *The Well-Wrought Urn* [1947]) is rather mislabeled. For Brooks did not reject paraphrase. Instead, he made the case that "paraphrase is not the real core of meaning which constitutes the essence of the poem." (Although, Brooks remarked, "We can very properly use paraphrases as pointers and as shorthand references.") A poem's images and its rhythms, Brooks stated, do not merely make up an ornamental surface. Instead, these specifically poetic features constitute the poem's argument. As one tries to adequately report what a poem "says," one must describe its poetic devices. So form becomes content; trope turns into theme.

Brooks was reacting in part to the poet and critic Yvor Winters, who wrote that much twentieth-century poetry, because of its obscurity, cannot be paraphrased, and that this is a defect. Modern poets, Winters added, often make us feel that we know what they mean, but leave us unable to explain this knowledge in a lucid or definitive way. So for Winters the paraphrasability of a poem was its essence or core, the proof of its value.

The poet Hart Crane took Winters's criticism as a challenge when he wrote a letter (1926) to Harriet Monroe, the editor of *Poetry* magazine. Crane offered this explanation of the phrase "adagios of islands," from his poem "Voyages (II)": "The reference is to the motion of a boat through islands clustered thickly, the rhythm of the motion, etc. And it seems a much more direct and creative statement than any more logical employment of words such as 'coasting slowly through the islands,' besides ushering in a whole world of music."

There are several kinds of paraphrase. Crane offers an account of how his phrase works poetically. But one might also paraphrase a poem's argument, taking the poem as a statement about what the world is like (or what it looks like from one angle). Helen Vendler in *Poems Poets Poetry* (2002) asserts that we should focus on how a poem works, not on its argument about the world.

(That is, how it uses assonance, rhyme, and meter; how it structures itself; how it guides or teases the reader.) This is especially true, Vendler adds, when we are first learning to read poetry. But other critics, like William Empson, characteristically paraphrase a poem's perspective on the world, as well as its strategies or poetic manner. For Empson, each literary work makes a case: it has an opinion about what life is like (see Empson's account of Shakespeare's Sonnet 94 in "They That Have Power," from *Some Versions of Pastoral* [1935]).

See Hart Crane, *Complete Poems and Selected Letters,* Langdon Hammer, ed. (2006). Stanley Cavell's essay "Aesthetic Problems of Modern Philosophy" (1965) in *Must We Mean What We Say?* (1969) offers an important argument about paraphrase. See also Yvor Winters, *In Defense of Reason* (1947), for the defense of paraphrase that Brooks reacted against.

Parnassians (From Mount Parnassus, associated with the muses in ancient Greek tradition.) From 1866 on, the Parisian periodical *Le Parnasse contemporain* (The Contemporary Parnassus) published poets who dedicated themselves to ideals of objectivity: to keeping their emotions out of their poems. These writers, the most prominent among them Charles-Marie Leconte de Lisle, were known as the Parnassians; they represented a reaction against the Romanticism of Victor Hugo and Alfred de Musset. See Jacques Barzun, *An Essay on French Verse* (1991).

parody Parody began as a term for antiphony, a musical form in which two or more singers would sing contradictory lines at once. It then shifted its meaning. In the current sense of the word, parodies mock the style and stance of particular authors, works, or genres.

A good parody can be a perverse act of homage or a declaration of artistic purpose, rather than a vulgar mocking. An example is Anthony Hecht's "The Dover Bitch: A Criticism of Life" (1967), which responds to Matthew Arnold's "Dover Beach" (1851). Henry Fielding's *Shamela* (1741), a parody of Samuel Richardson's *Pamela* (1740), becomes a statement of the distance between Richardson and Fielding, as makers of opposing worlds that require drastically different fictional techniques. And Jane Austen's *Northanger Abbey* (written 1798–99, publ. 1818), offers a parody of the Gothic novel.

Max Beerbohm is perhaps the most distinguished parodist of the twentieth century, targeting Henry James, Joseph Conrad, and others. See Beerbohm, *A Christmas Garland* (1912).

The parodist goes to work on form as well as substance—as in Beerbohm's brilliant send-up of James's winding sentences, or this parody of Longfellow's "Hiawatha" (sometimes attributed to George Strong):

He killed the noble Mudjokivis.
Of their skin he made him mittens.
Made them with the fur side inside,
Made them with the skin side outside.
He, to get the warm side inside,
Put the inside skin side outside.
He, to get the cold side outside,
Put the warm side fur side inside.
That's why he put the fur side inside,
Why he put the skin side outside,
Why he turned them inside outside.

And Algernon Charles Swinburne preempted the critical opposition by parodying his own style in "Nephelidia":

From the depth of the dreamy decline of the dawn through a notable
    nimbus of nebulous noonshine,
Pallid and pink as the palm of the flag-flower that flickers with fear of
    the flies as they float,
Are the looks of our lovers that lustrously lean from a marvel of mystic
    miraculous moonshine,
These that we feel in the blood of our blushes that thicken and
    threaten with throbs through the throat?

William Zaranka, ed., *The Brand X Anthology* (1981), offers an enjoyable collection of poetic parodies; even better is Dwight Macdonald, ed., *Parodies* (1965).

pastoral (From the Latin *pastor,* meaning "shepherd.") Pastoral has been one of the kinds, or genres, of literature since the Greek poet Theocritus, who lived in sophisticated Alexandria in the third century BCE, but wrote about Sicilian rustics. Shepherds and goatherds make up the characteristic population of pastoral poetry, though cowherds and even fishermen occasionally appear. Pastoral poems are often known as eclogues (Virgil's name for his pastorals [ca. 39–38 BCE]), bucolics, or idylls. The landscape of pastoral is some-

times identified as Arcadia, a region of the Peloponnesus suitable for sheep-
and goat-herding, and associated with a legendary race of simple, honest folk
(see ARCADIA).

The most common activity of pastoral is the reciting of verse: sometimes
solitary, and sometimes in the form of the singing contest, characteristically
performed by two herdsmen on panpipes cut from wild reeds. (See AMOE-
BEAN SONG.) The pastoral characters enjoy a life of *otium* (Latin for "leisure"),
with plenty of time for composing poetry, though they are also subject to the
pains and scarcity of country life. The lament for a dead beloved or friend, often another poet-shepherd, makes up the subgenre of the pastoral elegy,
which culminates in English with Milton's *Lycidas* (1637).

Pastoral often evokes the Golden Age, a legendary time before the dep-
redations and conniving of civilized existence set in. In the words of the
chorus from Torquato Tasso's *Aminta* (publ. 1581), put into English by Henry
Reynolds in 1628, this was the "happy Age of Gould" when "with milke the
rivers ranne, / And hunny dropt from ev'ry tree"—and before "Honour"
(i.e., the strategic withholding of sexual favors) began to tyrannize over disappointed lovers.

The figures of pastoral poetry in the Renaissance are often courtiers in disguise, mere masks for the expression of the artificial, urbane conceits that poets are so inclined toward. But the pastoral landscape, once the courtier puts
himself in it, often seems capable of healing his pangs of self-consciousness,
bringing him out of his restless, corrupt sophistication. The most famous examples of this pastoral theme, in which the court invades the countryside and
finds there an antidote for the city's ills, are Shakespeare's *As You Like It* and
Bk. 6 of Spenser's *Faerie Queene* (1590–96). "The Passionate Shepherd to His
Love" by Christopher Marlowe (1564–93) and many of the poems of Andrew
Marvell (1621–78) are also in this line. They use the pastoral setting as a way
to reflect on the poet's devices, which stem from a world far more compro-
mised, or sullied, than the soothing, healthy one of woods, streams, and
meadows. As Frank Kermode dryly observes, "Living in his city garden with
its sophisticated philosophies, its exotic plants, its cultivated music, the poet
contemplates the life he has rejected, the life of the healthy countryside, with
its simple manners, natural flowers, and rude pipings."

Pastoral relies on the kinship often felt to exist between poetic composition and the beauties of nature. "WOODS induce revery: well-suited to the
composition of verse," wrote Gustave Flaubert in his *Dictionary of Received*

Ideas. Pastoral also harks back to a pagan naïveté that finds, living in the landscape, well-intentioned divinities providing joys both amorous and sociable. Samuel Johnson gracefully outlines this naive aspect of pastoral when he remarks, "The shepherd in Virgil grew at last acquainted with Love, and found him a native of the rocks."

For later poets, too, the pastoral realm appeared simple and blessedly ordinary, in contrast to the vexed corruptions of urban life. William Wordsworth in his preface to *Lyrical Ballads* (1798–1800) writes of choosing "low and rustic life" for the setting of his poems because "in that situation our elementary feelings exist in a state of greater simplicity." In rural life, Wordsworth remarks, "the passions of men are incorporated with the beautiful and permanent forms of nature." These passions are therefore "less under the action of social vanity," Wordsworth concludes, than in the city.

The most wide-ranging twentieth-century reflection on the pastoral genre is William Empson's *Some Versions of Pastoral* (1935), which extends the category of the pastoral to include socialist realism, Lewis Carroll's *Alice in Wonderland* (1865), and other unexpected examples. The books that Empson discusses develop, in their different ways, an image of a simple or pure life: designed to contrast with, but also to clarify, the complexity of our own existence. Empson says that pastoral "put[s] the complex into the simple." (Harry Berger persuasively develops Empson's theme in the essays collected in his *Second World and Green World* [1988], especially "The Renaissance Imagination.")

The Renaissance was in many ways the real home of pastoral. Renaissance pastoral is often infused with a freshness and delight, and a delicate sympathy between humans and nature, that remains profoundly enjoyable. Richard Barnfield says of a pastoral singer in *The Shepherd's Content* (1594):

He sits all Day lowd-piping on a Hill,
    The whilst his flocke about him daunce apace,
His hart with joy, his eares with Musique fill:
    Anon a bleating Wether beares the Bass,
    A Lambe the Treble . . .

Frank Kermode's anthology, *English Pastoral Poetry* (1952), is a wonderful place to begin exploring pastoral verse, as is the Elizabethan collection titled *England's Helicon* (1600); also, Michael O'Loughlin, *The Garlands of Repose*

(1978); Thomas G. Rosenmeyer, *The Green Cabinet* (1969); David M. Halperin, *Before Pastoral* (1983); and Renato Poggioli, *The Oaten Flute* (1975).

pathetic fallacy John Ruskin (1819–1900), the great Victorian critic of art, literature, and society, invented the idea of the pathetic fallacy, which he defined as the "extraordinary, or false appearances" taken on by objects in the world "when we are under the influence of emotion, or contemplative fancy." Though Ruskin named this phenomenon a fallacy, it is not necessarily, in his view, something avoidable or undesirable. Ruskin cites as an instance of the pathetic fallacy Charles Kingsley's *Alton Locke* (1850):

> They rowed her in across the rolling foam—
> The cruel, crawling foam.

Ruskin comments, "The foam is not cruel, neither does it crawl. The state of mind which attributes to it these characters of a living creature is one in which the reason is unhinged by grief." (The ocean is, of course, famously poetic. In 1712, Joseph Addison wrote [in *Spectator* no. 489] that "I cannot see the heavings of this prodigious bulk of waters, even in a calm, without a very pleasing astonishment." Over two centuries later, Wallace Stevens, in a letter, remarked on the poet's habit of investing the ocean with sublime or terrifying powers, and added, "Seen up close, it is dirty, wobbly and wet.")

Ruskin writes (in *Modern Painters,* vol. 3 [1856]), "The temperament which admits the poetic fallacy, is . . . that of a mind and body in some sort too weak to deal fully with what is before them or upon them; borne away, or over-clouded, or over-dazzled by emotion; and it is a more or less noble state, according to the force of the emotion which has induced it."

Ruskin presents both an appreciation and a wary critique of the pathetic fallacy. His wariness stems from his knowledge of the human cost of what Wordsworth and other Romantic poets achieved when they made our perception susceptible to over-strong colors. In the wake of the Romantics, we submit ourselves to the wayward career of the emotional life, which is charged with strange significance, and out of our control. The Romantic poets remain "subdued by the feelings under which they write," Ruskin comments. But a higher order of creative poets (Dante, Homer) "receives feeling and watches it, as it were, from far off." Steadfast and true-seeing, this latter group—the strongest poets—harbors no inclination toward the pathetic fallacy. See Harold Bloom, ed., *The Literary Criticism of John Ruskin* (1969).

pathos   In Greek, emotion or affect. The word is often counterposed to *ethos* (character). In his *Rhetoric* (ca. 350 BCE), Aristotle remarks that an orator can try to convince his audience by appealing to its reasoning power, its trust in character—or its emotions. Whereas Aristotle prefers an argument based on logos, a reasonable account, rather than pathos, Roman rhetorical writers were not so particular, having a more pragmatic attitude to persuasive technique. On pathos in literature, see Adela Pinch, *Strange Fits of Passion* (1996).

perfectionism   The ascent, moved by intellectual inquiry, toward an onward-reaching, better state of the soul and of the world in which it exists. Martin Buber rapidly summarizes Plato's *Republic* (ca. 370 BCE) in his essay "Plato and Isaiah": "The soul wishes to infuse the idea of justice with the breath of life and establish it in the human world in the living form of a just state. The spirit is in possession of truth; it offers truth to reality; truth becomes reality through the spirit." Buber captures a central motif in Plato's perfectionism: the desire to move from a state of the soul that quests after justice to a just civic order.

Plato's perfectionism often involves the presence of an older, more knowing friend who converts the soul of a younger man, turning him toward new interest in the good and the true. The same guiding motion can occur between an author and a reader—even now. Mark Edmundson offers a strong argument for perfectionist literary education—for reading as "the crafting of souls"—in *Why Read?* (2004). For Edmundson, as you read seriously, you "dream of changing your current state": re-creating yourself in a new image, one yet unreached; and you are assisted by what you have read. See Martin Buber, "Plato and Isaiah," in Nahum Glatzer, ed., *Martin Buber on the Bible* (1968, 2nd ed. 1982); also relevant are Stanley Cavell, *Cities of Words* (2004), and Martha Nussbaum, *Love's Knowledge* (1990).

performativity   A term originally derived from J. L. Austin's study of the "performative utterance" in *How to Do Things with Words* (1955, publ. 1962), but later given a far different emphasis from Austin's. (See SPEECH ACT.) Performativity, as the critic Judith Butler develops the concept, suggests that one's gender and social identity result from acts that bear decisive symbolic weight. As people perform everyday actions, what they do identifies them as male or female, heterosexual or homosexual. Butler combines this basic point with the idea of *interpellation,* derived from the French Marxist Louis Althusser (1918–90). According to Althusser, individuals lack status, and therefore identity, until they identify themselves as members of a socially approved category. This emphasis, in Butler and Althusser, on the emptiness of the self until it is slotted (interpellated) into an official role controlled by the social power structure, is shared by Michel Foucault (1926–84), an influential thinker for new historicism and cultural studies. (See CULTURAL STUDIES; NEW HISTORICISM.) See Althusser's well-known essay on "ideological state apparatuses" in *Lenin and Philosophy* (1969), as well as Judith Butler, *Bodies that Matter* (1993).

peripeteia. See REVERSAL

persona In Latin, the word *persona* means "mask," as well as "character" and "role." The reference is to the masks invariably worn by actors on the ancient comic and tragic stage. *Persona* later came to designate the "mask" worn by authors who impersonate characters in their books (i.e., who create, and thus speak for, these characters). Aristotle in his *Rhetoric* (ca. 350 BCE) pays great attention to the character that an orator should present to his audience in order to get them to believe him. Aristotle's concern carries over to the later practice of writers, from Michel de Montaigne to Walt Whitman to Sylvia Plath, whose authorial personalities are relatively conspicuous.

Persona is sometimes contrasted to authentic selfhood. But such authenticity, in literature as in life, is itself a construct. Some confessional poets of the 1960s and 1970s claimed to espouse an authentic self rather than a constructed one. (See CONFESSIONAL POETRY.) Lionel Trilling, writing in 1972 in *Sincerity and Authenticity*, notes that "within the last two decades English and American poets have programmatically scuttled the sacred doctrine of the persona." See Robert C. Elliott, *The Literary Persona* (1982).

phenomenology Phenomenological inquiry in philosophy dates back to G. W. F. Hegel's *Phenomenology of Mind* (1807), with its drama of a single consciousness encountering itself (and therefore the world). A century after Hegel, modern phenomenology, with its emphasis on the connection between appearance (Greek *phainomein*) and mental reflection, was initiated by Edmund Husserl (1859–1938). In Husserl's account, the phenomenologist tries to establish philosophy's intellectual privilege by distinguishing it both from the sciences (which unlike philosophy are based on the results of empirical investigation) and from the tradition of humanist moral reflection (which seems too vague or undisciplined to attain philosophical rigor).

Husserl argued that philosophy, in order to make its claim, must differentiate itself from natural science, from common sense, and from mere thoughtful moralism as well. From the year 1900, when he published his *Logical Investigations,* Husserl reacted against two prevailing trends of his era: naturalism and psychologism. For naturalism, all things are part of the physical world, so that even thinking can be explained on the basis of biological processes. For psychologism, all thinking, including the forms of logic and mathematical calculation, is simply an aspect of our mental disposition, or psychic makeup. In the twentieth century especially, Husserl saw, our experience has often been described by means of scientific explanations (whether of brain chemistry or socioeconomics) and by means of psychological categories like Freud's. Husserl was determined to place knowledge on an absolute basis, rather than surrendering it to the shifting realm of scientific opinion. Explaining experience through scientific or psychological theories was equivalent, for him, to a surrender to what Plato disparagingly called the *doxa,* the realm of common opinion that opposes true philosophy.

Husserl grounds philosophy's authority by describing a reduction, or *epoché* (pronounced ehpoKAY). (There are actually several reductions in Husserl; this is a simplified account.) We experience the reduction when our ongoing, unreflective involvement with the world, our daily routine, suddenly comes into relief: when we begin to wonder about what we are doing, or what we mean. Husserl argues that the reduction is the originary moment of philosophy; it lets us know what philosophy is for. Phenomenology attempts to reproduce this stimulating and momentary experience of wonder, and inquires into its meaning. For Husserl, exploring the significance of the reduction helps us understand consciousness, ordinary experience, and human interaction; and such understanding makes a firm basis for philosophy.

Husserl's inheritors departed from his emphasis on solitary consciousness, but retained his interest in exploring the relations between phenomenal appearances, thinking, and day-to-day existence. Martin Heidegger's phenomenology attempted to place the self within a context of continual, practical interaction with the world. Maurice Merleau-Ponty, influenced by Jean-Paul Sartre, developed an "existential phenomenology" that defined man as an incomplete being, and also attempted to account for the role of the body in thinking and perceiving. Finally, Emmanuel Lévinas described our encounters with other human beings (the Other) in phenomenological terms.

Among Husserl's central works, in addition to the *Logical Investigations,* are *Ideas* (1913) and *The Crisis of the European Sciences and Transcendental Phe-*

nomenology (1953). Maurice Natanson in *Edmund Husserl* (1973) offers a highly readable introduction to Husserl.

For the phenomenological study of literature, see Roman Ingarden, *The Literary Work of Art* (1931), Georges Poulet, *The Interior Distance* (1952), and J. Hillis Miller, *Poets of Reality* (1965). Sharon Cameron's *Thinking in Henry James* (1989) draws inventively on phenomenology.

philology Philology is literary scholarship based on the inquiry into a text's sources, both literary and cultural, and into the original meaning of its words. As such, philology attained prominence in the Renaissance, especially in Desiderius Erasmus's translation of and commentary on the New Testament (1516). In nineteenth-century Germany, philology became a systematic discipline, spurred largely by the work of the brothers Grimm, who studied both grammar and national folkloric tradition (their *German Grammar* appeared in 1819–37). Nineteenth-century philology aimed to make the study of literature truly comprehensive, careful, and searchingly oriented toward details.

In classical studies, the main arena of nineteenth-century philology, the work of Ulrich von Wilamowitz-Moellendorff (1848–1931) was exemplary. Wilamowitz produced dozens of definitive editions of the Greek classics. He would commit himself to deciding the precise meaning of a line in a tragedy; he explored the Greek text's relation to historical events, or its parallels with other moments in other ancient literary works. For this school of reading, discerning the conventions of ancient literature was necessary preparation for interpreting particular passages. Wilamowitz mobilized his enormous learning in order to discover the contexts, and thereby the meaning, of each classical work he studied.

The decisive nature of the nineteenth-century philologist's claim to know the meaning of the text under examination can seem like hauteur; later critical stylists often find such manners irritating. But many philologists did learn, and teach, the essential critical practice of relying on a deep, thoughtful caution when trying to understand a book. Friedrich Nietzsche in his *Daybreak* (1881) produced a moving tribute to the true possibilities of philology, centered in its habit of slow reading and its "connoisseurship of the *word*": "For philology is that venerable art which demands of its votaries one thing above all: to go aside, to take time, to become still, to become slow. . . . It teaches to read well, that is, to read slowly, deeply, looking cautiously before and aft."

The final flowering of philological study in the twentieth century was achieved in the works of Erich Auerbach, Ernst Robert Curtius, and Leo

Spitzer. These scholars had each mastered a good handful of literary traditions, both ancient and modern. A work like Auerbach's *Mimesis* (1946) is supremely attentive to what a literary language tells us about the social world of its day. To this end, Auerbach considers the minute particulars of vocabulary and phrasing: the genre affiliations of words, their status as "high" or "low" diction, the ways they both reflect and express the world around them. See E. R. Curtius, *European Literature and the Latin Middle Ages* (1948); Erich Auerbach, *Mimesis* (1946); Leo Spitzer, *Linguistics and Literary History* (1948). In *Professing Literature* (1987), Gerald Graff outlines the debate, in American education of the 1870s and after, between detailed philological analysis and a more general humanistic focus on literature as the source of values or great ideas: the division that is healed in later work like Auerbach's.

picaresque The picaresque derives its name from the Spanish *pícaro,* meaning "rogue," a word that may in turn be derived from *pico* or *picante* (sharp, biting). The picaresque is often a kind of biting satire, centered on the career of a hero who lives by his quick wits. Usually he is sly, wary, and not without malice. Often an urchin or urban castaway, as morally obtuse as he is savvy with respect to his own survival, the picaresque protagonist both suffers and administers violent and memorable punishments. He gets along by (in Ronald Paulson's words) "mingling naiveté and awareness, simplicity and cunning." In the first work of the genre, the anonymous Spanish novel *Lazarillo de Tormes* (1554), the hero Lázaro alternately suffers and thrives under a series of masters (a beggar, a priest, a nobleman). The character of the pícaro (or his female equivalent, the *pícara*) can vary from a rather hapless, though clever, bumpkin to a trickster who manipulates others with cruelty and finesse. The picaresque story is usually serial and episodic. Some examples are Thomas Nashe's *The Unfortunate Traveller* (1594), Daniel Defoe's *Moll Flanders* (1722), and, in the twentieth century, Thomas Mann's *Confessions of Felix Krull* (1954). See Ronald Paulson, *The Fictions of Satire* (1967).

picturesque A highly fashionable concept in the 1790s and for several decades afterward, especially in England. The picturesque finds both charm and strength in wildly overgrown, craggy, and irregular landscapes—though it may also prize a gently consoling, idyllic scene. The soothing, idealized landscapes of three seventeenth-century artists, Salvator Rosa, Claude Lorraine, and Nicolas Poussin, were notable influences on the picturesque.

William Gilpin in his *Three Essays* (1792) provided influential formulations of the picturesque aesthetic, as did Richard Payne Knight in *An Analytical Inquiry into the Principles of Taste* (1805). One of the main advocates of the picturesque was a landscape architect: Uvedale Price, who wrote *An Essay on the Picturesque, as Compared with the Sublime and Beautiful* in 1794. The picturesque, wrote Price, "holds a station between beauty and sublimity," the two major terms opposed in Edmund Burke's *Philosophical Enquiry into the Origin of Our Ideas of the Sublime and Beautiful* (1757). The beautiful is uniform, and softly contoured; the sublime irregular, and terrible. The picturesque brings neither the cool satisfactions of beauty nor the terrors of the sublime, but rather a lively curiosity: an enjoyment of the rough, varied, and playful, shown in "intricacy" and "partial concealments." In his landscaping work, Price tried to preserve winding lanes, ruined cottages, and decaying copses, as stimulating ornaments for the observer.

Travelers on walking tours went in search of the picturesque, outfitted with sketchbooks and Claude glasses (named after Claude Lorraine, the Claude glass was a lens designed to bathe the landscape in a becoming haze). Richard Payne Knight, perhaps thinking of Lorraine's landscapes, described the picturesque as "a blending and melting of objects together with a playful, airy lightness, a sort of loose, sketchy indistinctness." These tourists' prizing of eccentric vistas was sometimes mocked, as in this passage from James Plumptre's *The Lakers* (1798), spoken by the sublimely pretentious Miss Beccabunga Veronique: "How frigidly frozen! What illusions of vision! The effect is inexpressibly interesting. The amphitheatrical perspective of the long landscape; the peeping points of the many colored crags of the head-long mountains, looking out most interestingly from the picturesque luxuriance of the bowery foliage, margining their ruggedness, and feathering the fells; the delightful differences of the heterogeneous masses; the horrific mountains, such scenes of ruin and privation . . . I must take a sketch." This gets across something of the preening manner, the caressing of one's own impressions, that often went along with an enthusiasm for the picturesque.

John Ruskin's "Of the Turnerian Picturesque," from his masterpiece *Modern Painters,* vol. 4 (1856), rescues the picturesque from the faddish superficiality satirized in Plumptre's passage. In his essay, Ruskin underlines the bleak sympathy and the steady, noble, scarred character conveyed by the true picturesque.

The fashion for the picturesque clearly influenced literature. Consider the inclination toward dark, dreary, and excessively interesting landscape in

Gothic fiction; or the Romantic preference for a lonely heath and a hermit's fire in the distance. Martin Price, "The Picturesque Moment," in Frederick Hilles and Harold Bloom, eds., *From Sensibility to Romanticism* (1965), brilliantly explores the critique of the picturesque in some poems of Wordsworth. Christopher Hussey's *The Picturesque* (1927) is still an informative delight. More recent studies are collected in Stephen Copley and Peter Garside, eds., *The Politics of the Picturesque* (1994).

plain style   Cicero in his *Orator* (46 BCE) remarks on the "Attic" style, used by the speaker who "is restrained and plain" and who "follows the ordinary usage": so that "the audience, even if they are no speakers themselves, are sure they can speak in that fashion." Cicero goes on to remark that the speaker of the plain style, who avoids overly fancy locutions and elaborate, periodic sentences, nevertheless shows artfulness, even in his seeming casual manner. "There is such a thing as a careful negligence," Cicero writes: "Just as some women are said to be handsomer when unadorned—this very lack of ornament becomes them—so the plain style gives pleasure even when unembellished . . . all noticeable ornament, pearls as it were, will be excluded; not even curling-irons will be used; all cosmetics, artificial white and red, will be rejected; only elegance and neatness will remain. The language will be pure Latin, plain and clear; propriety will always be the chief aim."

The plain speaker, then, eschews verbal cosmetics, what Claudius in *Hamlet* calls the "painted word." Instead, words become a way to declare oneself. "Language best shows a man," wrote Ben Jonson (1572–1637): "Speak that I may see thee."

The plain style was a major mode in the Renaissance, for example in the prose of Francis Bacon (1561–1626). It was often associated with the Stoic ideals of self-sufficiency and independence. See Morris Croll, "'Attic Prose' in the Seventeenth Century" (1921), in *Style, Rhetoric, and Rhythm* (1966), and, for the plain style in seventeenth-century America, Perry Miller, *The New England Mind* (1954). See also ATTIC.

plot   We can usually anticipate the plots of most fictional narratives, with their trademark ways of possessing a reader's interest. Here is Samuel Johnson, in his *Preface to Shakespeare* (1765), summarizing with a lively sneer the plot of the typical modern drama: "To bring a lover, a lady and a rival into the fable; to entangle them in contradictory obligations, perplex them with oppositions of interest, and harass them with violence of desires inconsistent with each other; to make them meet in rapture and part in agony; to fill their mouths with hyperbolical joy and outrageous sorrow; to distress them as nothing human ever was delivered . . ."

More soberly, the French philosopher Paul Ricoeur (1913–2005) defined plot as "the intelligible whole that governs the succession of events." In the early twentieth century, the Russian formalists distinguished plot from story (in Russian, *sjuzet* from *fabula;* in French, *récit* from *histoire*). Plot orders events so that they go somewhere, make significance; it is the narrative sequence presented by a book as we read it from first page to last. Often, the plot begins at a later chronological point and doubles back to an earlier one. Story, by contrast, is the raw material that precedes (so to speak) the making of the plot sequence: the reservoir of happenings that the author chooses from, and that gets referred to or used, at some point, by the plot.

Some novels (Joyce's *Ulysses* [1922], for instance) get as much of the story into the plot as they can: in Joyce's case, by introducing the reader to a vast number of details and perceptions from Leopold Bloom's long day in Dublin. Usually, though, plot is very selective, and excludes more items than it admits. Cleanth Brooks remarked that the plot goes over the ground of the story like a detective. In fact, detective fiction is one of the most judicious genres, carefully presenting only what might prove significant for the plot.

Peter Brooks notes that the apparent priority of story to plot is an illusion, since the reader knows only the plot. Plot (*récit*) seems to turn events into a shaped and fashioned reality, while still giving us the impression that the amorphous mass of happenings (story, or *histoire*) came first: this basis in the "reality" of histoire is fiction's claim to authority.

One of the most memorable experiments in the relation of story to plot is Laurence Sterne's *Tristram Shandy* (1759–67). The infinitely amusing Sterne takes up hundreds of pages to get through the first few hours of his hero's existence: the author wading his way through story, trying to find the plot.

See Robert Caserio, *Plot, Story, and the Novel* (1979); Peter Brooks, *Reading for the Plot* (1984); Paul Ricoeur, "Narrative Time," in *On Narrative* (1981); Thomas Pavel, *The Poetics of Plot* (1985); Seymour Chatman, *Story and Discourse* (1979). See also NARRATOLOGY.

poetic justice John Dryden in his *Essay of Dramatic Poesy* (1668) writes that "a Play ought to be, A just and lively image of Humane nature." Representation must be not merely "lively" (that is, lifelike) but also "just." *Just* in Dryden's usage means fitting, both plausible and satisfying. (See DECORUM.) And, undeniably, one aspect of the reader's satisfaction is enjoyment of the rewards and punishments distributed by the godlike author of a narrative: what we call poetic justice.

Aristotle in his *Poetics* (330 BCE) worries that audiences will be turned off, and aesthetic effects ruined, if a tragedy depicts the success of a bad man. Poetic justice as Aristotle conceived it is mostly negative: it means that the author must avoid treating characters in ways that will shock or alienate the audience. (The Hollywood rule that one must never kill a baby on screen is properly Aristotelian.) In later eras, though, poetic justice inclines toward the positive, the benefits that an author bestows. The notion arises that a satisfying fiction depends on (as Henry James disparagingly put it) "a 'happy ending' . . . a distribution at the last of prizes, pensions, husbands, wives, babies, millions, appended paragraphs, and cheerful remarks."

According to the Restoration critic Thomas Rymer, commenting on stage plays, "*poetical Justice*" requires "that the satisfaction be compleat and full, e're the *Malefactor* goes off the *Stage,* and nothing left to God Almighty, and another World. Nor will it suffer that the Spectators trust the *Poet* for a *Hell* behind the *Scenes;* the fire must roar in the conscience of the *Criminal,* the *fiends* and *furies* be conjur'd up to their faces, with a world of *machine* and horrid spectacles; and yet the *Criminal* could never move *pitty.*"

More than any other critic, Rymer is responsible for the popularity of the phrase "poetic justice." But his fervent, not to say hysterical, desire for an ironclad moral effect in the theater protests too much. Such insistence bears witness to the artificiality, even illegitimacy, of the devices required to punish and reward (mostly punish) characters properly.

In the Augustan era, satire, in the works of Pope, Swift, and others, sometimes seems to embody a poetic justice gone wild, with the satirist as all-powerful judge and executioner. See Susan Staves, *Players' Scepters* (1979); Curt Zimansky, ed., *The Critical Works of Thomas Rymer* (1956); John Dryden, "Grounds of Criticism in Tragedy" (1679) and "Heads of an Answer to Rymer" (ca. 1678), in John Conaghan, ed., *Dryden: A Selection* (1978); and Henry James, "The Art of Fiction" (1884), in Hazard Adams, ed., *Critical Theory Since Plato* (1971). See also Kathy Eden, *Poetic and Legal Fiction in the Aristotelian Tradition* (1986).

poetry From Greek *poiein,* to make. The poet is traditionally seen as a maker, compared at times to a smith, or a potter at his wheel. Eberhardus Bethuniensis in his *Graecismus* (ca. 1212) remarked, "Arte poetica fungor dum fingo poema" (While I make a poem, I am being made by poetry). The idea that poetic making returns upon the author is inherited in very different ways by Ben Jonson, W. B. Yeats, and T. S. Eliot, among others.

Poetry originally meant imaginative literature in general. As Philip Sidney puts it in his *Apology for Poetry* (written 1583, publ. 1595), "Verse [is] but an ornament and no cause to Poetry: sith there have beene many most excellent Poets, that never versified."

In a different vein, Immanuel Kant in his *Critique of Judgment* (1790) remarks that "rhetoric is the art of carrying on a serious business of the understanding as if it were a free play of the imagination; poetry, the art of conducting a free play of the imagination as if it were a serious business of the understanding." Whether one accepts Kant's axiom or not, poetry frequently does position itself between *negotium* and *otium,* between worldly business and the leisure of imagining and playing.

At least six distinct (though sometimes combined) traditions can be identified behind European and American poetry: the lyric or private song, descending from classical poets such as Sappho and Horace; the sharp epigrammatic and satirical verse of the Greeks and Romans (Martial, Catullus); the epic (Homer, Virgil, Lucretius); the psalms of the Hebrew Bible; the love song or canzone derived from Provençal, and then Italian, tradition; the sublime ode, adopted by the eighteenth century and the Romantics from the Greek poet Pindar.

See James Longenbach, *The Resistance to Poetry* (2004); Allen Grossman, *The Long Schoolroom* (1997); Stephen Cushman, *Fictions of Form in American Poetry* (1993); Mary Kinzie, *A Poet's Guide to Poetry* (1999); Helen Vendler, *Poets Thinking* (2004); and Tony Hoagland, *Real Sofistikashun* (2006). Some anthologies of poems with helpful commentary are Stanley Burnshaw, *The Poem Itself* (1960); Hugh Kenner, *The Art of Poetry* (1959); Cleanth Brooks and Robert Penn Warren, *Understanding Poetry* (1938); and Camille Paglia, *Break Blow Burn* (2005). See also LYRIC POETRY; SONG.

point of view A term applied to fictional narrative (and, of course, to cinema, with its point-of-view shot). At given moments in a narrative, we may see through the eyes of a character: from his or her point of view—just as a cinematic point-of-view shot gives us a character's perspective.

At the beginning of Dostoevski's *The Double* (1846), the author presents, and corrects, the main character's point of view (in fact, he offers his correction first): "Though the sleepy, short-sighted countenance and rather bald head reflected in the looking-glass were of such an insignificant type that at first sight they would certainly not have attracted particular attention in any one, yet the owner of the countenance was satisfied with all that he saw in the looking-glass."

As we can see from the Dostoevski example, the author or narrator, in addition to a fictional work's characters, also has a point of view. In *The Craft of Fiction* (1921), Percy Lubbock distinguishes between the author who fashions his fiction and gives it to the reader, "leaving him alone with it," and the author who acts as the reader's confidant, inducting him into the author's point of view. In this latter case, Lubbock writes, "the reader faces towards the storyteller and listens to him, in the other he turns towards the story and watches it." (Lubbock is here discussing what narratology was later to call focalization.)

Lubbock's model is the late novels of Henry James: but not all authors have so advanced a position in relation to their fictions. Irving Howe notes that, in Defoe's *Moll Flanders* (1722), "What is missing is an inflected narrative voice or even a shadowy authorial presence which, at need, can move closer to or farther away from Moll."

The novels of Gustave Flaubert (1821–80) are associated with the term *style indirect libre,* "free indirect style." In free indirect style, even though there may be no overt indication that a passage belongs to the consciousness of a given character (no "he thought" or "it seemed to her"), we can detect that the passage is colored by the character's attitude and feelings. The subtlety imparted by free indirect style has been used by authors virtually since the beginnings of prose fiction, but Flaubert turns it into a system or method (as does James Joyce [1882–1941]: see Hugh Kenner, *Joyce's Voices* [1978]).

Henry James's prefaces to the New York edition of his novels are essential for the study of point of view in fiction. See also Wayne Booth, *The Rhetoric of Fiction* (1961); Irving Howe, "Obscurity in the Novel," in *A Critic's Notebook* (1994); and Dorrit Cohn, *Transparent Minds* (1978). Two excellent studies of cinematic point of view are William Rothman's *Hitchcock: The Murderous Gaze* (1982) and *The "I" of the Camera* (rev. ed., 2004). See also FOCALIZATION; IMPLIED AUTHOR / IMPLIED READER; NARRATOLOGY.

postcolonial studies A new academic field, increasingly popular in the 1980s and 1990s, that concentrates on the effects that Western European and American colonialism have had on the rest of the world. The area of the former British Empire is a particular focus.

The reigning definition of a postcolonial society is that it must itself be non-European and non–North American, and that it must have been invaded or occupied by Europeans or North Americans, or both. (A partial exception is Ireland: though European, it is now often discussed as a postcolonial state.) In other words, the dominion of Arab conquerors and then of the Ottoman Empire over the Middle East, the Japanese colonization of China, and the Soviet Union's control over its ethnic populations are not generally considered the subject matter of postcolonial studies. Moreover, Eastern European countries are almost never described as postcolonial societies, despite their long subjection under the Soviet empire. Palestinians, but not Israeli Jews, are considered postcolonial subjects, though both groups experienced British political domination.

There is a logic behind these exclusions. According to the customary definition, a postcolonial society has undergone not merely foreign political rule but a forcible modernization associated with such rule, and the attendant upheavals of traditional life. Postcolonial societies are generally rural or peasant cultures that have been violently transformed by their invaders (mostly for ill, in the postcolonial critics' version, although they also emphasize one positive result of empire: the cosmopolitan character of the postcolonial world).

Postcolonial studies began when Western-educated intellectuals from colonial societies, like Frantz Fanon and C. L. R. James, became increasingly attentive to the influence of Western racism on their own consciousness, and to the need to combat this influence. See Fanon, *Black Skin, White Masks* (1952), and O. Mannoni, *Prospero and Caliban* (1950). Some currently influential books in postcolonial studies are Edward Said's *Orientalism* (1978) and *Culture and Imperialism* (1993); *Nation and Narration* (1990), edited by Homi Bhabha; Gayatri Spivak, *The Post-Colonial Critic* (1990); and Robert Young, *Postcolonialism* (2001). For a significant critique of Said, see Bernard Lewis, *Islam and the West* (1993); as well as Aijaz Ahmad, *In Theory* (1992).

postmodernism An increasingly general term for the literature and art that succeeded high modernism. In literature, the monumental figures from the years of World War I and the 1920s and 1930s epitomize modernism: Marcel Proust, James Joyce, Thomas Mann, Wallace Stevens, W. B. Yeats, and others. Postmodernists, aware of this vast legacy, distinguish themselves from their precursors by claiming their difference. (See MODERNISM.)

Postmodernism first achieved popularity as a term applied to architecture and visual art. Postmodern artists deviate from the monolithic purity incarnated by the International Style in architecture and Abstract Expressionism in painting (both popular in the mid-twentieth century). Frequently, they use a mixture of styles, contaminate the visual with the verbal, or play jokes on the idea of artistic greatness that modernism took so seriously.

Alan Wilde writes that, while the defining feature of modernism is its urge to repair, or else rise above, a disjointed, fragmented world, "postmodernism, more radical in its perceptions, derives instead from a vision of randomness, multiplicity, and contingency: in short, a world in need of mending is superseded by one beyond repair. Modernism, spurred by an anxiety to recuperate a lost wholeness in self-sustaining orders of art or in the unselfconscious depths of the self . . . reaches toward the heroic in the intensity of its desire and of its disillusion. Postmodernism, skeptical of such efforts, presents itself as deliberately, consciously antiheroic."

In other words, postmodernism is tolerant of, and even revels in, the waste land of contemporary chaos that Eliot, Yeats, and Pound protested against. For this reason, postmodernism is sometimes accused of being merely "affirmative" rather than "critical": aping the trends of the surrounding culture in a piecemeal, unreflective way. (The debate over the critical intelligence of postmodernism is best pursued through a reading of Hal Foster's anthology *The Anti-Aesthetic* [1983], which contains essays by Jürgen Habermas, Fredric Jameson, and others.)

The literature about postmodernism is by now vast. Some useful sources are Eyal Amiran and John Unsworth, eds., *Essays in Postmodern Culture* (1994); David Mikics, "Postmodern Fiction," in Josephine Hendin, ed., *A Concise Companion to Postwar American Literature and Culture* (2004); Ihab Hassan, "Toward a Concept of Postmodernism," in *The Postmodern Turn* (1987); Alan Wilde, *Horizons of Assent* (1981); Andreas Huyssen, *After the Great Divide* (1987); Fredric Jameson, *Postmodernism* (1991); Margaret Rose, *The Post-Modern and the Post-Industrial* (1991). Jean-François Lyotard's *The Postmodern Condition* (1979) is a crucial work, often cited by theorists of the postmodern. For an early critique of postmodernism see Irving Howe, "Mass Society and Postmodern Fiction" (1959), reprinted in *Decline of the New* (1970).

poststructuralism Poststructuralism was born at some point in the mid-1960s in France: between the climactic revelations of high structuralism in Claude

Lévi-Strauss's *The Savage Mind* (1962) and the full-fledged poststructuralism of Jacques Lacan's *Écrits* (1966–67) and Jacques Derrida's *Speech and Phenomena, Of Grammatology,* and *Writing and Difference* (all three published in 1967). Lévi-Strauss was an anthropologist, Lacan a psychoanalyst, and Derrida a philosopher; but each of them had an inestimable impact on the discipline of literary studies.

Whereas the structuralist Lévi-Strauss, influenced by the linguist Ferdinand de Saussure, had suggested it was possible to map a symbolic system fully (and so to describe, for example, the myths that stand behind the behavior of a particular tribe or culture), the poststructuralists Lacan and Derrida emphasized the idea that such completeness is merely a wishful fantasy. In their view, a system is both accomplished and undone by what it wants to master, but cannot. So, for Derrida, philosophy's dream of being totally present to itself, and totally lucid, is contaminated (but, strangely, also made possible in the first place) by a factor that always escapes philosophy. Derrida calls this factor *writing* or the *trace*. Philosophy conceives itself as a voice that understands itself perfectly. But, Derrida points out, in fact books of philosophy are handed down, unpredictably, from one reader to another: the fate of writing is necessarily chancy, circumstantial.

Lacan's critique of self-assurance was similar to Derrida's. Freud, by showing that the ego is not master in its own house, also shows that consciousness can never be fully secure, that it is always haunted, even invaded, by the unconscious. We always mistake ourselves and others, Lacan asserted, and by doing so we involuntarily give the lie to our strident claims of truthfulness and self-knowledge.

Josué V. Harari, ed., *Textual Strategies* (1979), is a useful anthology of poststructuralist texts. For other poststructuralist thinkers, in addition to those mentioned, see Roland Barthes, *The Pleasure of the Text* (1973); Julia Kristeva, *Desire in Language* (1980); and Michel Foucault, *Language, Counter-Memory, Practice* (1977). Paul de Man, Jean Baudrillard, Jean-François Lyotard, Gilles Deleuze, and Slavoj Zizek have also been influential. There are a number of substantial critiques of poststructuralist thought. Among the most worthwhile are Vincent Descombes, *Modern French Philosophy* (1979), Tzvetan Todorov, *Literature and Its Theorists* (1987), and Eugene Goodheart, *The Skeptic Disposition in Contemporary Criticism* (1984). See also DECONSTRUCTION; DIFFÉRANCE; LOGOCENTRIC; STRUCTURALISM.

pragmatism Pragmatism, invented at Harvard around the year 1898, identifies the meaning of an idea with its results, or practical consequences: its "cash value." The founder of pragmatism was the Harvard philosopher Charles Sanders Peirce (pronounced PERSE; 1839–1914). The greatest pragmatist thinker was William James (1842–1910), who also taught at Harvard. (Pragmatism seems peculiarly a product of the new world; its third influential figure was also an American, John Dewey [1859–1952].)

James writes that pragmatism is an outgrowth of the "empiricist temper" in philosophy, the inclination to look at facts and reality rather than proposing ideal solutions. But the pragmatist differs from the empiricist. While empiricism "sticks to the external senses," pragmatism takes seriously the influence of ideas on the world. For James, pragmatism is a way of "settling metaphysical disputes that might otherwise be interminable." Each of our "thought distinctions," he argues, can be reduced to the difference in practice that would result from thinking one way rather than another. The pragmatist, James remarks, turns his back on "verbal solutions, bad a priori reasons . . . fixed principles, closed systems, and pretended absolutes and origins." Theories should be seen as tools, ways of doing things, *"not answers to enigmas, in which we can rest."*

Among the American literary figures notably influenced by pragmatism, and especially by James's work, are Robert Frost, Wallace Stevens, and Gertrude Stein. For an economical definition of pragmatism, see William James, "What Pragmatism Means," in *Pragmatism* (1907). Richard Poirier is one of the best examples of a literary critic inspired by pragmatism: see his *Poetry and Pragmatism* (1992). David Bromwich usefully estimates the influence of James's pragmatism on Wallace Stevens in "Stevens and the Idea of the Hero," in *Skeptical Music* (2001). Louis Menand, in *The Metaphysical Club* (2001), offers a stimulating account of the birth of pragmatism at Harvard. On William James's intellectual relation to his brother Henry, see Ross Posnock, *The Trial of Curiosity* (1991); also on James, Harvey Cormier, *The Truth Is What Works* (2001). The most distinguished recent advocate of pragmatism is Richard Rorty: see his *Consequences of Pragmatism* (1982) and *Contingency, Irony, and Solidarity* (1989).

pre-Raphaelites The Pre-Raphaelite Brotherhood was formed around 1848 by some English poets and painters, most prominently William Holman Hunt, John Everett Millais, and Dante Gabriel Rossetti. They were later joined by William Morris and Edward Burne-Jones. The pre-Raphaelites were distinguished by their medievalism, their interest in rural life, and their precise observation of natural detail, inspired in part by their reading of the great art critic John Ruskin (1819–1900). Ruskin became an advocate of the pre-Raphaelites, praising "the frankness and honesty of their touch."

The pre-Raphaelites' name harked back to Italian painters of the fifteenth century, the age preceding Raphael, who were admired for their rude and innocent spirituality. See Ruskin's commentaries on the pre-Raphaelites in *The Art Criticism of John Ruskin,* ed. Robert L. Herbert (1964).

proem   The prelude or prefatory exhortation to a longer work of poetry. Tennyson's *In Memoriam* (1850) has a proem, as does James B. V. Thomson's *City of Dreadful Night* (1870–74). As a subgenre, it is related to the invocation, but it often has the additional job of giving a plan or prospect of the work, or describing its origins (see Wordsworth's *Prelude* [1805–50] and his *Recluse* fragment). The best-known proem in modern poetry is Hart Crane's "Proem: To Brooklyn Bridge," the opening section of *The Bridge* (1930). See INVOCATION.

prose   Conventionally and casually speaking, prose is the default or unmarked term posed against poetry, which is thought to be more fashioned, more strange, and more intense than prose. Yet much English prose shares the characteristics of poetry. Consider this passage from Melville's *Moby-Dick* (1851), which, as Anthony Hecht points out, rises to iambic meter as it echoes the grandeurs of Shakespeare. (An iamb is a foot that follows an unstressed with a stressed syllable: see METER.) Melville's Ishmael, confronting Ahab, exclaims, "My soul is more than matched; she's overmanned; and by a madman! Insufferable sting, that sanity should ground arms on such a field! But he drilled deep down, and blasted all my reason out of me . . ."

For William Wordsworth in his preface to *Lyrical Ballads* (1798–1800), "the language of every good poem can in no respect differ from that of good prose. . . . [T]here neither is, nor can be, any *essential* difference between the language of prose and metrical composition." Poetry, Wordsworth continues, "can boast of no celestial ichor that distinguishes her vital juices from those of prose; the same human blood circulates through the veins of them both."

See Wordsworth, preface to *Lyrical Ballads,* in Hazard Adams, ed., *Criti-*

cal Theory Since Plato (1971); Anthony Hecht, "Blank Verse," in Annie Finch and Kathrine Varnes, eds., *An Exaltation of Forms* (2002). For an interesting stylistic study of English prose, see George Williamson, *The Senecan Amble* (1951). Also notable is Tzvetan Todorov's wide-ranging *Poetics of Prose* (1971).

prose poem A poem written in prose rather than verse, distinct from short prose forms like the vignette or parable. The prose poem is an elusive creature. Frequently, what makes it a poem is its impressionistic or meditative character, its indolent resistance to the pressures of fiction. Unlike a story, the prose poem does not (usually) wish to develop a plot, point a moral, or portray a social scene. It characteristically has more room than short fiction for puzzled elaboration and rhapsodic flight, and less room for tale-telling.

The best-known prose poems in literary history are those by Charles Baudelaire (1821–67). In American modernism, two books of prose poems, Gertrude Stein's *Tender Buttons* (1914) and William Carlos Williams's *Kora in Hell* (1918), played a significant role. A spectacular example of the expansive poem in prose is John Ashbery's *Three Poems* (1972). See Steven Monte's book on the prose poem, *Invisible Fences* (2000); also Michael Benedikt's anthology, *The Prose Poem* (1976), and David Lehman, ed., *Great American Prose Poems* (2003).

proverb Whether tricky, homespun, or banal, proverbs represent the common coin of literary experience. Humble yet assertive, they give poetic speech to trivial, casual, and telling moments of social encounter. They have played a motivating role in literary history, dramatically embedded in works by authors ranging from Geoffrey Chaucer to Robert Frost and W. H. Auden.

Archer Taylor presents an invaluable guide in *The Proverb* (1962). F. P. Wilson's *Oxford Dictionary of English Proverbs* (3rd ed., 1970) is authoritative; many of the most fascinating proverbs are discussed in *Brewer's Dictionary of Phrase and Fable* (rev. by Ivor Evans, 1969). See also APHORISM; EPIGRAM; FABLE; PARABLE.

psychoanalytic criticism The literary critic Erich Heller writes that "if a writer today speaks of fathers or sons, of mothers or dreams, of lovers or rivals, of accidents that determine destinies or destinies rooted in character, of the will to live or the longing for death—and what else is it that poets and writers talk about?—how can he remain untouched by Freudian thoughts even if he has never read a line by Freud?" Heller testifies to the pervasive effect of Sigmund Freud's thinking on an area, literature, where (as Freud himself remarked) the poets and writers were there before him, anticipating his discoveries.

Psychoanalytic literary criticism began in the writings of Freud (1856–1939), the founder of psychoanalysis. In his *Interpretation of Dreams* (1900), Freud commented briefly on Sophocles' *Oedipus Rex* as the source for his theory of the Oedipus complex. In "Creative Writers and Daydreaming" (1908), he addressed the connection between writing fictions and fantasizing. And "The Uncanny" (1919) presents a substantial reading of "The Sandman," a short story by the German author E. T. A. Hoffmann. Two other significant essays by Freud on literature are "Jensen's *Gradiva*" (1907) and "Dostoevski and Parricide" (1928). Freud's most resonant, moving, and convincing treatment of literature is "The Theme of the Three Caskets" (1913), on Shakespeare's *King Lear.*

In most of these essays and remarks on literature Freud displayed a tendency toward reductiveness. For example, in "The Uncanny" he claims that the impact of Hoffmann's tale is due solely to the castration anxiety that it evokes in the reader. Similarly, Freud locates the power of Sophocles' *Oedipus* in its reference to our supposed universal wish and dread, the Oedipus complex, rather than in any nuanced aspect of the play's plot or its characters.

Hamlet and Oedipus (1949), by Freud's English disciple Ernest Jones, is similarly reductive. Jones offers a somewhat rigid, though fascinating, piece of detective work, single-minded in its effort to pin an Oedipus complex on Shakespeare's most elusive hero. More persuasive than Jones's strategy would have been a focus on Oedipus's self-assured mastery, his pride in his knowingness. As Adam Phillips puts it, "Freud clearly was not merely showing us how irrational we are: he was showing us how irrational rationality is; that we are at our maddest when we are at our most plausible (to ourselves)."

The importance of Freud's work for literary study spread far beyond his own rather preliminary attempts at analyzing works of literature. Freud saw the psyche as imagination: a place of fiction-making and heated interpretation. And this meant that psychoanalysis itself was in some respect literary. Psychoanalysis invented useful, sometimes sublime myths (the Oedipus complex, the death drive, the trauma of birth). It also recognized, as writers like Jonathan Lear and Adam Phillips have emphasized, that psychic health consists in being able to tell an interested, sufficiently individual story of oneself: to articulate one's desire. In Freud's universe, everyone is an author (and at times a bad one).

From the beginning, writers and critics felt compelled to respond to Freud's enormous achievement. At times, they bore a grudge produced by their impression that Freud stands for a ruthless modernity: that he suspects the high, traditional claims of art. Vladimir Nabokov in his autobiography, *Speak, Memory* (1951), disdained the "vulgar, shabby, fundamentally medieval world" of Freud (called by Nabokov "the Viennese quack"). In a more accepting vein, Kenneth Burke and Lionel Trilling considered, with due ambivalence, the implications of Freud's demystifying inclinations, and his new way of valuing desire, for our sense of art and culture. And Harold Bloom inquired into the connection between Freud's theory of the drives and the literary sublime. (The essays by Burke, Trilling, and Bloom are all contained in the collection edited by Perry Meisel listed below.) Freud's own writings, especially the Dora and the Wolf Man case studies, themselves became objects of literary interpretation.

Psychoanalytic criticism has often been concerned with the issue of idealizing or (in Freudian terms) splitting: the division of the world into good and evil opposites. According to writers like Shakespeare and Dostoevski, our passionate attachments to images of the admirable or the corrupt lead us to create idols worthy of our extreme love or total hatred. Shakespeare's Hamlet, as William Kerrigan notes, inhabits a mental universe in which the innocent and pure seem forever staged against the unimaginably corrupt; and Kerrigan, in his study of Milton, *The Sacred Complex* (1983), makes powerful connections between Freudian theory and Reformation religious psychology. The death drive, Freud's grimmest theoretical device, has proved central to Leo Bersani's accounts of Baudelaire and other writers. Feminist critics, too, have made abundant use of Freud, finding his own troubled relation to femininity to be a useful source for their own speculations. See Juliet Mitchell's *Psychoanalysis and Feminism* (1974), Alice Jardine, *Gynesis* (1985), and Peter Rudnytsky and Andrew Gordon, eds., *Psychoanalyses/Feminism* (2000).

Psychoanalytic thought does not begin and end with Freud. Other important psychoanalysts have been inspirations for literary criticism, perhaps most prominently Jacques Lacan. Lacan underlined the idea of narcissism, the linguistic nature of the unconscious, and the intransigent presence of the death drive. Lacan stands behind the work of the cultural critic Slavoj Zizek; earlier, he inspired the feminist theories of Jane Gallop, Jacqueline Rose, Ju-

dith Butler, and others. Melanie Klein has been a limited but significant influence, cited by Lacan and others, due to her emphasis on the death drive.
The English psychoanalyst D. W. Winnicott has recently become a more often cited presence in literary circles. Winnicott emphasized playfulness, illusion, and the collaborative nature of the relation between our desire and the
reality we encounter: a realm of attunement, prompting, and excited manip-
ulation that extends into the making of literature and art. Finally, Freud's
heretical disciple C. G. Jung provided a source for the mythic archetypal criticism of Northrop Frye, a central literary critic of the postwar era (see ARCHE-
TYPE).

Two very useful anthologies are Edith Kurzweil and William Phillips, ed.,
Literature and Psychoanalysis (1983), and Perry Meisel's collection in the
Twentieth-Century Views series titled *Freud* (1981). (The Kurzweil-Phillips
anthology contains Erich Heller's "Observations on Psychoanalysis and
Modern Literature" [1976]; Meisel's volume includes Burke's "Freud—and
the Analysis of Poetry," Trilling's "Freud and Literature," and Bloom's "Freud
and the Poetic Sublime.") *In Dora's Case* (1985), edited by Charles Bern-
heimer and Clare Kahane, assembles some striking readings of Freud's case
study of Dora. Harold Bloom's "Freud—A Shakespearean Reading," in *The
Western Canon* (1994), offers an intriguing take on Freud's apparent envy of
Shakespeare's literary resources. And William Empson's chapter on *Alice in
Wonderland,* in *Some Versions of Pastoral* (1935), remains one of the most genial and stimulating uses of Freud in literary criticism.

See also Freud, *Character and Culture,* ed. Philip Rieff (1963); Peter Rudnytsky, *Freud and Oedipus* (1987); William Kerrigan, *Hamlet's Perfection*
(1994); Norman Holland, *The Dynamics of Literary Response* (1968); Meredith Skura, *The Literary Use of the Psychoanalytic Process* (1981); Leo Bersani,
Baudelaire and Freud (1977); Shoshana Felman, ed., *Literature and Psychoanalysis* (1977); Slavoj Zizek, *Looking Awry* (1991); Adam Phillips, *Promises,
Promises* (2001); Jonathan Lear, *Love and Its Place in Nature* (1990); and Tim
Dean, *Beyond Sexuality* (2000). Richard Armstrong in *A Compulsion for Antiquity: Freud and the Ancient World* (2005) presents a deeply considered portrait of Freud's relation to classical literature and culture. Laura Quinney
draws usefully on Melanie Klein in *The Poetics of Disappointment* (1999). Finally, Mark Edmundson, "Freud and Shakespeare on Love," in *Raritan* 24:1
(Summer 2004), 51–74, makes a sophisticated protest against Freud's idea of
desire, and on behalf of Shakespeare's.

public sphere   The idea of the public sphere was first formulated by the German cultural theorist Jürgen Habermas in *The Structural Transformation of the Public Sphere* (1962). The public sphere is the realm in which private persons gather together and contribute to public opinion. In the eighteenth century, when it first became a substantial presence, the public sphere centered on coffeehouses where newspapers were read and discussed, literary societies, and intellectual clubs. The public sphere, Habermas wrote, presents a necessary challenge to the powers of the state. In other works Habermas drew a distinction between the "lifeworld" (*Lebenswelt* in German), which includes the public sphere, and the "system." The system consists of the forces of the market economy and the state, and it threatens to encroach on the lifeworld (the immediate social environment of individuals). The role of the public sphere is to defend the lifeworld against the system.

Later theorists of the public sphere include Niklas Luhmann and Hans Ulrich Gumbrecht. See also FRANKFURT SCHOOL, for a description of the tradition that stands behind Habermas's thought.

pure poetry   The term *pure poetry* (in French, *poésie pure*) is associated with the Abbé Henri Bremond, who delivered a lecture titled "Pure Poetry" in 1925 and published, the next year, *Prayer and Poetry*. The idea was then taken in a rather different, and more significant, direction by the great poet Paul Valéry in his essay "Pure Poetry" (1928). Poetry, Valéry suggested, aims to "give the impression of a complete system of *reciprocal* relations between our ideas and images on the one hand and our means of expression on the other—a system which would correspond particularly to the creation of an emotive state in the mind."

The "system of relations" that a poem builds, Valéry adds, should be "unconnected with the practical order." A pure poem would be a poem in which "the play of figures contained the reality of the subject," and in which "the transmutation of thoughts into each other appeared more important than any thought." Valéry immediately adds that such pure poetry is impossible and unattainable; but it remains a necessary ideal.

Valéry was influenced by the rather vague theories of Edgar Allan Poe that were inherited and adopted by French poets of the nineteenth century. Poe, in his essay "The Poetic Principle" (1850), argues that poems ought to be short rather than long, that they exist for the sake of beauty, and that they are damaged by any didactic content. (Before Poe, Samuel Taylor Coleridge had remarked, on the side of impure poetry, that "a poem of any length neither can be, nor ought to be, all poetry" [Coleridge, *Biographia Literaria* (1817), Ch. 14].) The familiar idea of poetry as a kind of literature that cannot be paraphrased, that depends on a faculty more intimate than reason, and that has a virtually mystical effect stems, in part, from Poe.

In the French tradition, a new impurity was consecrated by Guillaume Apollinaire in his *Zone* (1912). Apollinaire introduced peculiarities like the names of friends and favorite streets into his poems; his work particularly influenced the decidedly impure New York school poets (see NEW YORK SCHOOL).

Robert Penn Warren's important essay "Pure and Impure Poetry" (1943) argues effectively against Poe and his French inheritors. Poe's and Warren's essays can be read in Hazard Adams, ed., *Critical Theory Since Plato* (1971); for Valéry, see "Pure Poetry," in *The Art of Poetry* (1958), vol. 7 of *Collected Works of Paul Valéry*, ed. Jackson Mathews.

quatrain A stanza of four lines, one of the most popular forms in English poetry. It may be rhymed *abab, aabb, abba* (a scheme associated with Tennyson's *In Memoriam* [1850]), or in other ways—even *aaxa* (the form derived by the Victorian poet Edward Fitzgerald from the Persian *Rubaiyat* of Omar Khayyam). One of the best-known rhyme schemes for the quatrain is the "ballad stanza," which rhymes the second and fourth lines but not the first and third (as in this example by Herman Melville, "The Tuft of Kelp" [1888]):

All dripping in tangles green,
Cast up by a lone sea,
If purer for that, O Weed,
Bitterer, too, are ye?

See John Hollander, "The Quatrain," in Annie Finch and Kathrine Varnes, eds., *An Exaltation of Forms* (2002).

queer theory Queer theory, a critical approach that gained prominence in the 1990s, developed from the gay studies movement of the 1980s. Queer theory differs from gay studies, however, in several respects. Gay studies often focused on how the gay or lesbian identity of authors or literary characters had been covered up, and tried to bring these authors and characters "out of the closet." Queer theory, by contrast, is less interested in asserting a coming-out story, or realizing the fully fledged gay identity that is implicit in the literary work. Instead, queer theory is intent on studying how, in literature and culture, normative and nonnormative varieties of sexuality depend on, or interact with, one another: how the nonnormative helps to constitute the normative (and vice versa). (Thus the emphasis on the word *queer,* intended to connote not just homosexuality but anything odd, recalcitrant, or perverse in the realm of desire.) In general, queer theory sees both officially approved and "deviant" behaviors as the products of social construction, and discerns in social life the basis for an individual's desire. See Annamarie Jagose, *Queer Theory: An Introduction* (1996), and Robert Corber and Stephen Valocchi, eds., *Queer Studies: An Interdisciplinary Reader* (2003). See also GAY STUDIES; GENDER STUDIES.

quest romance The quest, or quest romance, is a prevalent literary form that over the centuries has generated bizarre, fascinating, and seemingly endless variations. Beginning in ancient literature (*Gilgamesh,* Homer's *Odyssey*), it refines itself in the epics of Ludovico Ariosto, Edmund Spenser, and William Blake, colonizes the novel from Henry Fielding to James Joyce, and expands into the sublime operas of Richard Wagner. Quest romance finds its current home in movies and television (*Star Wars, Star Trek*) and in video games (*Tomb Raider, Vice City*).

A quest is, before anything else, a hero's journey that involves various trials: usually, literal combat with fierce enemies, as well as the temptation to abandon the quest in favor of lower pleasures. The quest's classic form is that of the knightly search for the holy grail, or other chivalric reward. But the detective stories of Raymond Chandler (1888–1959), whose knight wears a cheap suit and carries a gun, are just as much quest romances as Browning's "Childe Roland to the Dark Tower Came" (1855) or Spenser's *The Faerie Queene* (1590–96).

A common theme of quest romance is the hero's movement away from his actual parents and his discovery of his true father, who might be a good king or an evil Darth Vader: Freud named this theme the family romance. The quest sometimes ends in the arrival at a place that feels both familiar and newly achieved. Such a true home, known well for the first time, hallows the whole enterprise of the journey, making it a discovery of self.

Some quests prove interminable: constant, perhaps eternal, attempts to find a truly adequate object of questing. In this sense the quest is "an allegory of purpose" (James Nohrnberg). Whether it is the garden idyll of Wagner's *Parsifal,* Augustine's *City of God,* the messianic paradise of Jewish mysticism, or the unimaginable alien civilizations of *Star Trek,* the end of the quest outshines easier satisfactions and redirects desire toward the unknown, the impending, the larger than life: "something evermore about to be" (Wordsworth).

The great critic of quest romance is indisputably Northrop Frye. See in particular Frye, *The Secular Scripture* (1976) and *Anatomy of Criticism* (1957). James Nohrnberg, *The Analogy of the Faerie Queene* (1976), Patricia Parker, *Inescapable Romance* (1979), and Jay MacPherson, *The Spirit of Solitude* (1982), are three brilliant treatments of romance by students of Frye. Harold Bloom, "The Internalization of Quest Romance," in Bloom, ed., *Romanticism and Consciousness* (1970), is an essential essay, departing from and advancing beyond Frye. Similarly important for the understanding of quest romance are the essays of Geoffrey Hartman in *Beyond Formalism* (1970). Ian Duncan in *Modern Romance* (1992) describes the importance of romance as a defining genre for British national consciousness in the nineteenth century. See also CHIVALRIC ROMANCE.

reader-response criticism In the 1970s, reader-response criticism was a well-known designation for a critical school occupied with understanding how readers actually experience texts. Pursuing a version of what the New Critics called the affective fallacy, such critics located the essence of a literary work in the reactions of the reader.

Reader-response criticism had two sources. First was I. A. Richards's study in *Practical Criticism* (1929) of individual readers' reactions, often fairly wild or misguided ones, when faced with a literary text. (Norman Holland's *Five Readers Reading* [1975] follows and develops Richards's work.) A second germ of reader-response criticism was Hans-Robert Jauss's statement in 1967 that literary criticism had largely ignored the reader's experience. Jauss emphasized the need to describe the expectations and reactions of a book's original audience. For Jauss, the reader was located in a particular time and place.

Reader-response criticism, though spurred by reception theory, was a distinct phenomenon in that it moved away from Jauss's interest in studying historically specific literary audiences. In much of Stanley Fish's criticism, for example, "the reader" could be anywhere in space or time, forever caught in the drama of a text's unfolding, tricky sentences. Fish's position is not consistent, though. Sometimes he identifies the reader's stance with perspectives common during the English Reformation (if Fish is reading Reformation literature, as he often does). Wolfgang Iser's theory of the implied reader suggested that readers have a more active and difficult role in the nineteenth-century novel than they did earlier, but the historical distinction was drawn broadly, in contrast to reception theory's emphasis on detailed description of the literary public at different points in history.

It is difficult to pin down what a reader's experience might have been in a vanished era; even contemporary readers may not be reporting their feelings and ideas very accurately or precisely. Reader-response criticism attempted to justify critical insights by grounding these insights in what an ordinary reader notices, and is able to describe. But that ordinary reader was, of course, a fiction developed by a critic: the critic's somewhat slower double or shadow.

Several important early essays on reception theory and reader response, by Jauss, Iser, Fish, Hayden White, and others, appeared in *New Literary History* 2:1 (Autumn 1970). See also Jane Tompkins, ed., *Reader-Response Criticism* (1980); Wolfgang Iser, *The Implied Reader* (1972) and *The Act of Reading* (1976). See also IMPLIED AUTHOR/IMPLIED READER; RECEPTION THEORY.

realism Near the beginning of Mark Twain's *Huckleberry Finn* (1885), Huck reports of Twain's earlier book *Tom Sawyer* (1876): "That book was made by Mr. Mark Twain. He told the truth mainly. There were things which he stretched, but mainly he told the truth." The claim of realism in literature is, mainly, to tell the truth, brushing away fantasies and wishful, idealized versions of the world. Realism, then, is allied to what Freud called the reality principle, the acceptance of the hard facts of life. But in nineteenth-century writers like Honoré de Balzac, Charles Dickens, and George Eliot, realism also involves a redemption of the world through wish fulfillment, with the aid of fabulous romance motifs: the triumph of the underdog, the happy marriage. (The grimmest exponents of the reality principle in fiction, the authors who exalt pessimism into a grand myth, are called naturalists rather than realists: authors like Theodore Dreiser, Émile Zola, and Frank Norris. See NATURALISM.)

Samuel Johnson, in his *Rambler* essay no. 4 (1750), writes, "The works of fiction, with which the present generation seems more particularly delighted, are such as exhibit life in its true state, diversified only by accidents that daily happen in the world, and influenced by passions and qualities which are really to be found in conversing with mankind." For Johnson, such realism proves itself by its contrast to the fables of romance, which involve such adventurous motifs as "a hermit and a wood, a battle and a shipwreck."

Realism in the eighteenth century was marked by a confluence, or confusion, between the novel and journalism, between fiction and the news. The subtitle of Balzac's *Père Goriot* (1835) is "all is true." Earlier, novelists like Daniel Defoe (1660–1731) had masqueraded as reporters of factual accounts. The novel in its early days presented itself at times as a quasi-legal deposition. At other times, novelists like Samuel Richardson in *Pamela* (1740) insured the realistic effect of their art by "writing to the moment": narrating events with a great impression of present-tense immediacy. Pamela is a young housemaid constantly grabbing ink and paper to recount the dangers that are threatening her—chiefly, a lecherous employer, whom she later marries. (The mode was effectively parodied by Henry Fielding in *Shamela* [1741].)

For the Hungarian Marxist critic Georg Lukács, writing in the 1930s, realism meant a total representation of society, including the interaction of its various classes. Such a panoramic social portrait proved that a novel had truly encountered history. See Lukács, *The Historical Novel* (written 1936–37), and *Realism in Our Time* (1958).

In its classic nineteenth-century form, realism requires the detailed recording of characters' sensory impressions, their styles of dress, and their visual or auditory perceptions, as well as the look of the houses and streets they inhabit. Such detail makes up what Henry James in "The Art of Fiction" (1884) calls "solidity of specification." In this respect, Joyce's *Ulysses* (1922), with its endlessly rich panoply of real-life details, fulfills the realist genre.

Erich Auerbach's *Mimesis* (1946) presents an innovative and influential theory of the birth of realism from the Christian gospels, as well as a survey of realistic fictional style through the centuries. (See STYLE.) Also useful are Richard Chase, *The American Novel and Its Tradition* (1957); George Levine, *The Realistic Imagination* (1981); Michael Davitt Bell, *The Problem of American Realism* (1993); Harry Levin, *The Gates of Horn* (1963); Eric Sundquist, ed., *American Realism: New Essays* (1982); J. P. Stern, *On Realism* (1973); and Nicholas Boyle and Martin Swales, ed., *Realism in European Literature* (1986). Robert Alter finds the origins of realism in the Hebrew Bible in *The Art of Biblical Narrative* (1981).

reception theory In 1967, the German scholar Hans-Robert Jauss, a recently appointed professor at the University of Constance, gave a lecture in which he called for a new aesthetics of reception (*Rezeptionsästhetik*). Jauss proposed a reorientation of literary history, in order to focus on the interaction of literary works and their readers in different times and places. In Jauss's summary description, readers have a "horizon of expectation": an awareness of genres and conventions which is then either confirmed or violated by a particular new piece of literature. In his description of the salutary disruption of readerly expectations Jauss was influenced by his teacher Hans-Georg Gadamer, and by the Russian formalist critics as well. (See CONVENTION; FORMALISM; HERMENEUTICS.)

The second important figure in reception theory is Wolfgang Iser, who also taught at the University of Constance. Iser was less interested than Jauss in the social and historical context of the reader; his work is closely related to reader-response criticism, a largely American school of interpretation (see IMPLIED AUTHOR/IMPLIED READER; READER-RESPONSE CRITICISM). See Hans-Robert Jauss, *Aesthetic Experience and Literary Hermeneutics* (1977; rev. ed., 1982); Wolfgang Iser, *The Act of Reading* (1976). A good introduction is Robert Holub, *Reception Theory* (1984).

recognition (In Greek, *anagnorisis.*) According to Aristotle in his *Poetics* (ca. 330 BCE), anagnorisis or recognition is, along with *peripeteia* or reversal, one of the two pivotal plot moments in tragedy. For Aristotle, the best kind of recognition is accompanied by a peripeteia, a reversal of situation (from happy to miserable, for example). Aristotle defines recognition as follows: "A change from ignorance to knowledge, producing love or hate between the persons destined by the poet for good or bad fortune."

Anagnorisis is the sudden realization, on the part of the protagonist and the audience, of a true state of affairs. In Aristotle's favorite example, Oedipus finally knows that he has killed his father and married his mother, and this recognition brings on the terrible conclusion of *Oedipus Rex.* In *Paradise Lost* (1667), Adam and Eve realize their fall, and this knowledge forms the somber, resolved culmination of Milton's epic. Like peripeteia, anagnorisis involves a change from a thing to its opposite. In the case of anagnorisis, the change is from innocence to hard knowledge.

Recognition occurs in comedy as well as tragedy. In Shakespearean comedy, the recognition scene is (as Terence Cave puts it) "the moment when strange tales are told and retold," and the characters suddenly understand where, and who, they are, as if through hearsay. At end of Shakespeare's *Twelfth Night,* for example, Viola touchingly proves her identity, along with her twin brother Sebastian's, by murmuring, "My father had a mole upon his brow." Shakespeare here furnishes an example of what Aristotle considers the lowest form of anagnorisis, recognition by tokens. The use of tokens is not just gimmickry, however, despite Aristotle's derogatory implication. Rather, it implies that small things demonstrate our identity: slight memories show us most truly.

Recognition does seem more fundamental to tragedy than to comedy. Comic characters are sometimes so blithely resilient that they can remain unaffected by a knowledge that would wound and destroy them in a tragedy. Don Quixote, one of the most memorable comic heroes, never experiences recognition: he never realizes he is laboring, and thriving, under a mere illusion (that he is a famous chivalric hero). See Terence Cave, *Recognitions* (1988). See also REVERSAL.

refrain Returning lines or words in a poem or song. John Hollander notes that refrain offers a restraint or brake on the movement of a lyric (the word *refrain* derives from the French *se retenir*, to bridle oneself).

Theodore Spencer writes that refrain can be used in at least three ways: for "rhythmical poignancy and contrast"; "to bind together and intensify the chief subject-matter of the poem"; and to "suppl[y] a background of natural description . . . and place the action in a definite environment." Spencer cites Edmund Spenser's "Epithalamion" (1595) as an example of this third type. Spenser's refrain goes

Sweete Themmes! runne softlie, till I end my song.

W. B. Yeats's Crazy Jane poems (1933), as Spencer mentions, offer a panoply of starkly inventive uses for refrain.

Another famous refrain is T. S. Eliot's in "The Love Song of J. Alfred Prufrock" (1915):

In the room the women come and go
Talking of Michelangelo.

Eliot's refrain, repeated only once, frames the solitary, anguished monody of the speaker in "Prufrock." It suggests a world of indifferent, polished chat just at the margins of the poem, unconcerned with its thematic center.

The category of the refrain blends with that of the chorus in popular song: the blues tradition, in particular, uses refrain to turn a song's verses into a kind of chorus. Often, in blues, the repeated lines of the verse give a direction, an anchor—insisting on, or driving, the argument. Consider the great Robert Johnson's lines from "Hellhound on My Trail" (sung in choked, frightened tones):

I got to keep moving, got to keep moving,
Blues falling down like hail.
Blues falling down like hail.

The speaker's fugitive song finds itself surrounded by a harsh weather: the blues itself. (The blues genre is also a state of the soul, one that descends—so it seems—inescapably, with no end in sight; refrains lock it in.)

Several important verse forms are based on refrain; see GHAZAL; SESTINA; VILLANELLE. See John Hollander, "Breaking Into Song: Some Notes on Refrain," in *Melodious Guile* (1988), and Theodore Spencer, "The Later Poetry of W. B. Yeats" (1933), in Morton Dauwen Zabel, ed., *Literary Opinion in America,* vol. 1 (3rd ed., 1962). See also BLUES; CHORUS.

Regency period The period between 1811 and 1820, so named because it was the reign of the Prince Regent during the madness of his father, George III. (The prince became King George IV in 1820.) Literature in England during the Regency was distinguished by the works of the Romantic poets and the novels of Jane Austen. The dandy Beau Brummel, who promoted high refinement in manners and dress, was a significant force in Regency society, which was devoted to fashionable balls, horse racing, and fastidious charm. The popular novels of society during this period are preoccupied by romantic plots, political gossip, wealthy dowagers, and social climbing. See Ellen Moers, *The Dandy* (1960).

reification Reification, in Marxist theory, occurs when a social phenomenon is made to appear permanent and natural: when it is solidified into the apparently substantial form of a thing (Latin *res*). The Hungarian Marxist critic Georg Lukács, in his book *History and Class Consciousness* (1923), writes that with reification a human connection "takes on the character of a thing and thus acquires a 'phantom objectivity,' an autonomy that seems so strictly rational and all-embracing as to conceal every trace of its fundamental nature: a relation between people."

The worker's labor is reified as, or into, the product of this labor. The product is a commodity that can be bought and sold (a car, a television set). But what is actually being bought and sold, according to Marx, is the worker's expending of his labor power for the employer. Therefore, the commodity becomes a mere objectified mask for the human relation between the worker and the owner of the means of production—a reified form.

The notion of reification has been important to Marxist theory in the mid- and late twentieth century, particularly in the work of Theodor Adorno and Fredric Jameson. For Jameson, reification is associated with "late capital-

ism," the reigning economic and social system, in which simulation, spectacle, and commodity fetishism have permanently altered our experience. See
COMMODITY; MARXIST LITERARY CRITICISM.

Renaissance literature In England, the great era of literature stretching from
the reign of Henry VIII, which began in 1509, through the execution of
Charles I (1649) and the ensuing Interregnum. (See also CAROLINE AGE;
ELIZABETHAN AGE; JACOBEAN AGE.) The English Renaissance was notably
belated: the Italian Renaissance of art, literature, and learning occurred in the
fourteenth and fifteenth centuries. The era was marked by an interest in the
revival of classical culture (hence the name *renaissance,* meaning "rebirth").
The Renaissance was also the age of exploration and discovery, the age of ab-
solutism, the age of the new science, and the age of humanism.

See HUMANISM and COURTLINESS for a more extensive portrait of Renaissance concerns (and for more bibliography). Walter Pater's *The Renaissance*
(1873) is the most important source for understanding the significance of the
Italian Renaissance to English Victorian and modern literature. On the Renaissance's inheritance of the classics, see R. R. Bolgar, *The Classical Heritage
and Its Beneficiaries* (1958), L. D. Reynolds and N. G. Wilson, *Scribes and
Scholars* (3rd ed., 1991), Anthony Grafton, *Commerce with the Classics* (1997),
and Thomas M. Greene, *The Light in Troy* (1982). Also Jacob Burckhardt,
The Civilization of the Renaissance in Italy (1860). For general views of the Re-
naissance, Thomas M. Greene, "The Flexibility of the Self in Renaissance
Literature," in *The Disciplines of Criticism,* ed. Peter Demetz, Thomas
Greene, and Lowry Nelson, Jr. (1968); A. Bartlett Giamatti, *Exile and Change
in Renaissance Literature* (1984); Harry Berger, *Second World and Green World*
(1988); Hiram Haydn, *The Counter-Renaissance* (1950); and Lisa Jardine,
Worldly Goods (1996). Marjorie Donker and George Muldrow's *Dictionary of
Literary-Rhetorical Conventions of the Renaissance* (1982) is a helpful resource,
as is Isabel Rivers, *Classical and Christian Ideas in English Renaissance Poetry*
(2nd ed., 1994).

repression Freud writes that "the essence of repression lies simply in turning
something away, and keeping it at a distance, from the conscious." The distinct character of repression as a trope or figure of knowledge lies in the fact
that one is not conscious of it (repression is unlike the deliberate suppression
of information): so the process of repression is itself repressed.

Paul Robinson remarks that Freud "inspires our belief that the mysteries of the present will become more transparent if we can trace them to their origins in the past, perhaps even in the very earliest past. . . . And, finally, he has created our heightened sensitivity to the erotic, above all to its presence in arenas . . . where previous generations had neglected to look for it."

In this comment Robinson defines the repressed by joining its two aspects: the repressed *origin* of a thing, and the repressed *character* of it. The repressed character of life, for Freud, is that it is infused with sexuality, though we are trained to ignore this. The erotic can be found where, in the past, people "had neglected to look for it," in cases of intense loyalty, furious rebellion, despairing self-involvement. The repressed origin of our feelings often seems to be a traumatic incident (or the fantasy of such an incident: the fantasized murder of the father, the imagination of the birth experience). Freud suggests at times that the origin that is repressed is not an event but a primal ambivalence (for example, the child's combined love and hatred of a parent).

For Freud, repression explains something. The ferocious strength of our beliefs or feelings has behind it a presence that the conscious ego denies: and the denial creates the strength.

In literary criticism, the concept of repression has been applied by Harold Bloom to the relation between the literary precursor, or ancestor, and his descendants. (See ANXIETY OF INFLUENCE.) See Sigmund Freud, "Repression" (1915); Paul Robinson, *Freud and His Critics* (1993).

Restoration literature Works written in the period from the coronation of Charles II in 1660, which restored the English monarchy following the Civil War, until about 1700. The two major poets of the era are John Milton and John Dryden; they are joined by the Earl of Rochester, Charles Cotton, Katherine Philips, Anne Finch, and others. In playwriting, William Congreve, Aphra Behn, and William Wycherly are significant presences. The age was marked by its devotion to satire and the comedy of manners: but also by the piety of John Bunyan's *Pilgrim's Progress,* the epic scope of Milton's *Paradise Lost,* and the scientific experiments of the Royal Society. See Earl Miner, *The Restoration Mode from Milton to Dryden* (1973); Martin Price, *To the Palace of Wisdom* (1964).

retirement The ideal of independent, pleasurable life in the countryside, away from the corruptions of the city: the moral stance of Horace (65–8

BCE), and widely echoed in the poetry of seventeenth- and eighteenth-century England. In the seventeenth century, the essays of Abraham Cowley, Ben Jonson's "To Sir Robert Wroth" (1616), and Andrew Marvell's "Upon Appleton House" (ca. 1650) are memorable evocations of retirement. Alexander Pope wrote significant poems of retirement, among them his Epistle to Burlington (1731) and his Imitations of Horace.

In addition to Horace, a famous chorus from *Thyestes,* by the first-century Roman philosopher and playwright Seneca the Younger, provides a touchstone for the retirement ideal, as do several of the poems of Martial (ca. 38–ca. 102 CE). Here Ben Jonson renders Martial's epigram "To Himself" (10.47):

> The Things that make the happier life, are these,
> Most pleasant Martiall; Substance got with ease,
> Not labour'd for, but left thee by thy Sire;
> A Soyle, not barren; a continewall fire;
> Never at Law; seldome in office gown'd;
> A quiet mind; free powers; a body sound;
> A wise simplicity; friends alike-stated;
> Thy table without art, and easy-rated;
> Thy night not drunken, but from cares layd wast;
> No sowre, or sullen bed-mate, yet a Chast;
> Sleep, that will make the darkest houres swift-pac't;
> Will to bee, what thou art; and nothing more:
> Nor feare thy latest day, nor wish therefore.

On Pope and retirement, see Maynard Mack's magisterial *The Garden and the City* (1969); for an excellent general treatment of the theme, Michael O'Loughlin, *The Garlands of Repose* (1978).

reversal According to Aristotle in his *Poetics* (ca. 330 BCE), *peripeteia* or reversal is, along with *anagnorisis* (recognition), one of the two crucial features of the plot of a tragedy. Reversal is a turn to an opposite situation: a surprising twist that is also probable or necessary. So, for example, Oedipus experiences a reversal from success and power at the beginning of Sophocles' *Oedipus Rex,* to tragic misery as the drama goes on. See also RECOGNITION.

rhetoric Cicero (106–43 BCE) tells the story of Zeno, the Greek philosopher, explaining the difference between logic and rhetoric. Zeno first displayed his clenched fist—the iron grasp of logic—and then, to illustrate rhetoric, opened his hand, showing a relaxed, spread palm. Following Zeno, we might say that rhetoric invites its audience, opens itself to them. Logic, by contrast, challenges or blocks their progress, showing up faulty reasoning. Through the centuries it is rhetoric's very openness that has led many to suspect it of lack of rigor, of merely currying favor with listeners and readers: wanting to please, and to win, at any cost.

Rhetoric is the technique of persuading an audience through the artful use of words. As such, it remains required equipment for the politician, the poet, and even the philosopher. For Aristotle (fourth century BCE), dialectic, associated with the methods of philosophy, bases itself on assumptions (*protaseis*) derived from universally held opinions. Rhetoric, by contrast, is craftily oriented toward the particular prejudices or opinions of the orator's audience. But Aristotle's distinction is, of course, questionable. From Socrates on, philosophers have often been accused of being mere sophists or rhetoricians, manipulators of argument rather than impartial seekers after truth. And the rhetor must be at least part philosopher, a student of the truth that includes probability (as Aristotle puts it, "what happens usually"). (See DIALECTIC.)

What is rhetorical success: winning over the mob, or gaining the approval of the discerning and judicious? This question haunts rhetoric, and clearly bears on its relation to political action. Is rhetoric a guide for politics, capable of refining it; or merely the politician's servant, his bag of manipulative tricks?

These matters go back to the ancient world. The sophists were a group of teachers who arrived in mid- and late-fifth-century Athens offering to instruct aspiring politicians in the ways of persuasion. Two of the most prominent sophists were Protagoras (ca. 490–ca. 420 BCE) and Gorgias (ca. 485–ca. 380 BCE), both of whom became the protagonists of Platonic dialogues. Protagoras was accused of making the worse case appear to be the better: a talent that became essential equipment for trial lawyers. For Gorgias, there was no objective or accessible criterion of truth, not in traditional standards of approved behavior and not in philosophical investigation. Like a modern-day advertising man or PR agent, Gorgias reveled in manipulating the audience. In his description, eloquence was like a drug or a magic spell. "Speech is a great prince," Gorgias remarked. "With a tiny body and unseen strength, he does marvelous works."

Lysias (early fourth century BCE) was an Athenian who contributed to the birth of forensic rhetoric, the kind of speechmaking designed to win a case before a jury. In addition to the forensic, oriented toward legal demonstration, the other two kinds of rhetoric are deliberative (trying to persuade an audience to do something, such as vote for someone or go to war) and epideictic (praising someone or something). Winston Churchill's addresses to the British nation during World War II are examples of deliberative rhetoric, encouraging his people to fight against Hitler. Pericles' Funeral Oration and Lincoln's Gettysburg Address, praising the dead, are epideictic speeches.

Rhetorical proofs or demonstrations can be divided into different categories. One might persuade a listener on the basis of ethos (the character of the speaker, or of the person who is the object of the rhetor's praise); by exploiting pathos (the audience's feelings or attitudes about the events that the rhetor describes, for example, its horror of murder or child molesting); or by relying on the strength of the logos, or argument, itself.

Rhetoric can also be understood on the basis of its intended effect. The Socratic *elenkhos* is a proof or demonstration that catches out, or shows up, Socrates' interlocutor, his conversational partner and victim—and (most frequently) reduces him to bafflement.

Isocrates (436–338 BCE) and Cicero developed the practice of arguing *in utramque partem* (a phrase that might be translated "on the other hand"). For centuries, students were asked to argue both sides of a case with equal effectiveness, showing that rhetoric in its professionalism aims to rise above too immediate an inclination to sincerity or truthfulness. Cicero's *controversia* are dialogues in which different formulations are placed in contrasting frames of reference, demonstrating rhetoric's flexible and pragmatic sense of the world.

Quintilian (ca. 35–ca. 95 CE) and Cicero both emphasized the civic responsibility of the orator, in an effort to counteract the dubious reputation of the sophist as rhetorician-for-hire. Quintilian's definition of rhetoric was "the power of judging and discoursing on civil matters": inspiring the citizens, defending the innocent, and protecting the truth.

Not all uses of language can usefully be called rhetorical. If this were the case, then rhetoric would lose its force as a concept. The dorm-room bull session, for example, though it (as the name implies) involves bullshitting, is less rhetorical, more sheerly wasteful and improvisatory, than the calculated use of bullshit to persuade or confuse an audience. (See Harry Frankfurt, *On Bullshit* [2005].)

The Renaissance writer Robert Burton in his *Anatomy of Melancholy* (1621) remarks, "Make the best of him, a good orator is a turn-coat, an evil

man, his tongue is set to sale, he is a mere voice . . . an hyperbolical liar, a flat-
terer, a parasite." A contemporary critic, Thomas Conley, in more balanced
fashion, remarks that rhetoric concerns the "tensions between privilege and
correctness, right and might, power and persuasion, and persuasion and ignorance."

See Thomas Conley, *Rhetoric in the European Tradition* (1994); Kenneth
Burke, *A Rhetoric of Motives* (1948); Brian Vickers, *In Defence of Rhetoric*
(1988); Wayne Rebhorn, *The Emperor of Men's Minds* (1995).

rhyme The repetition of the same, or a similar, vowel sound in the last
stressed syllable of two or more lines of verse. A feminine rhyme follows the
stressed syllable with others that also rhyme: *suitable/mutable* or *stranger/
danger* are examples. A masculine rhyme ends with the stressed syllable:
sound/pound. Slant rhyme or half rhyme, often seen in writers from Dickinson to the present, matches sounds that are similar but not identical: *moan/
swoon*.

Arthur Hallam, the Victorian writer and friend of Tennyson, defined
rhyme aptly as "the recurrence of termination." Rhyme stands for the summary effect, for finality: but for repeated, augmented, and even imposed, finality. It signifies the fact that a literary work presses on as it develops, but
also seals itself as complete.

Rhyme stirs and springs thought by means of regularity. Its opposite (so to
speak) is a device such as stream-of-consciousness, which flows organically
and unpredictably. Rhyme gives the verse foot its original shape, and is a
prime instance of what the linguist Roman Jakobson calls the "principle of
equivalence" in poetry. In rhyme, one word becomes not merely similar to
but compounded and symmetrical with another.

Rhyme has had its detractors. Milton protested the "bondage of rhyme" in
his preface to *Paradise Lost* (1667), a poem written in blank verse (unrhymed
iambic pentameter). Much later, Vladimir Nabokov speculated that rhyme
was perhaps the shoe or the bootspur of a line: mere ornament, rather than an
integral part of the final foot. See W. K. Wimsatt, "One Relation of Rhyme
to Reason" (1944), in *The Verbal Icon* (1954); Anthony Hecht, "On Rhyme,"
in *Melodies Unheard* (2003).

rhyme royal Sometimes called the "Troilus stanza" after its use in Geoffrey
Chaucer's *Troilus and Criseyde* (ca. 1385), rhyme royal consists of a stanza of

seven lines in iambic pentameter, rhyming *ababbcc.* For about a century after Chaucer, rhyme royal was pervasive in English poetry. In the Elizabethan era, Edmund Spenser relied on it in his *Fowre Hymns,* as did Shakespeare in *The Rape of Lucrece.* After the Renaissance, however, rhyme royal faded in importance and was rarely used by significant poets.

roman à clef (Pronounced RoMAN a CLAY.) In French, a novel with a key: featuring characters who are actual persons disguised by a change of name. The popular seventeenth-century novelist Madeleine de Scudéry was a founder of the genre. A contemporary example is *Primary Colors* by Anonymous (1996), based on the presidential campaign of Bill Clinton (named Jack Stanton in the novel). Thomas Love Peacock's *Nightmare Abbey* (1818) presents a lively roman à clef satirizing the Romantic poets: Shelley appears as the passionate Scythrop and Coleridge as Mr. Flosky, a lover of high obscurities. See also NONFICTION NOVEL.

romance. See CHIVALRIC ROMANCE; QUEST ROMANCE

Romanticism In the eighteenth century the word *romantic* was associated with the wild, eccentric, and bizarre, and mostly applied to natural scenery and landscape painting. In the early nineteenth century, German critics like Friedrich Schlegel and Heinrich Heine began using the term in something like its current meaning, to designate a kind of literature more vital and spontaneous than the opposing, "classical" kind. Then, as a result of Hippolyte Taine's *History of English Literature* (1863), "Romantic" became the name for the great English poets who wrote near the beginning of the nineteenth century: William Blake, Samuel Taylor Coleridge, William Wordsworth, Percy Bysshe Shelley, John Keats, and George Gordon, Lord Byron.

English Romanticism was influenced by continental authors, especially Jean-Jacques Rousseau and Johann Wolfgang von Goethe, along with the philosophers F. W. J. von Schelling and Immanuel Kant. Rousseau evoked the beauty of the soul's solitary conversations with itself (in *Reveries of a Solitary Walker* [1782]); Goethe, the desperate strength of youthful passion rebelling against social convention and intoxicated with its own freedom of thought (in *Wilhelm Meister's Apprenticeship* [1795–96] and his vastly popular *Sorrows of Young Werther* [1774]). English Romanticism was also substantially influenced by German lyrics of the 1770s, with their adaptation of popular traditions like the ballad and folk tale, and their passionate voicings of desire.

The beginning of literary Romanticism is sometimes given as 1798: the publication date in England of *Lyrical Ballads,* a collaboration between Wordsworth and Coleridge, and, in Germany, Schlegel's *Athenaeum* fragments. The restless simplicity of the *Lyrical Ballads* was an effort to evoke (in Wordsworth's phrase) "the real language of men." An alternative beginning for Romanticism is 1789, the year of the French Revolution: the 1790s saw significant work by Blake, Coleridge, Wordsworth, and William Godwin.

English Romanticism had two additional sources: the outpouring of liberating political energy during the French Revolution, and the native tradition of Protestant dissent, embodied especially in the writings of John Milton. Milton rebelled against official state religion in the name of the individual; Wordsworth's poetry, following Milton, "humanizes" religion. As Geoffrey Hartman notes, Wordsworth transfers the radical Protestant search for evidence of the soul's condition to the most ordinary realms of personal life, and makes it clear that this quest for blessing or sanctity within the everyday cannot be guided by any religious institution. Blake and the other Romantics sympathized with political revolution as an effort to free the exalted "whole man" of the imagination from bondage to what common opinion regards falsely as reality: the conventions, hierarchies, and social customs that surround us.

The rebel Prometheus was one of Romanticism's chief heroes. In Shelley's version, *Prometheus Unbound* (1819), Prometheus was ruthlessly punished by Zeus, but still remained intent on freeing the human soul from the secondhand beliefs that oppress it. In these respects Romanticism departed decisively from the eighteenth century's fear of creative imagination as a potential madness, and its adherence to norms of reason and hierarchy (in the works of Alexander Pope, Jonathan Swift, and Samuel Johnson, for example). To the Romantics, poets were, in Ralph Waldo Emerson's phrase, "liberating gods," not the slavish imitators of social reality. The prototype was expressed in William Collins's "Ode on the Poetical Character" (1746), which stars a "rich-haired youth of Morn": the inspired poet.

Even as it venerated the commonplace, Romanticism attended to the sublime voice from beyond familiar experience, in poems like Shelley's "Mont Blanc" (1816) and Keats's "On First Looking into Chapman's Homer" (1817). In their attention to both the merely human voice and the supernatural influence that informs or challenges the human, later writers like Emerson (1803–82), Emily Dickinson (1830–86), and Wallace Stevens (1879–1955) prove themselves definitive heirs of the English Romantics.

Romanticism had a powerful afterlife in the Victorian era. Alfred, Lord Tennyson (1809–92), Robert Browning (1812–89), George Eliot (1819–80), and John Ruskin (1819–1900) were among its inheritors. Though modernist writers frequently proclaimed their difference from the Romantics, more often than not they sustained Romantic arguments. The modernist difference was sometimes merely stylistic. The cold, hard poets of modernism rejected Georgian poetic diction, which was derived from the Romantic and Victorian lushness. (See GEORGIAN AGE.)

T. S. Eliot, a central modernist as well as the most influential critic of the mid-twentieth century, assailed the Romantic tradition as diffuse and weak-minded because it did not rely on an established, officially sanctioned system of ideas. With Eliot, the pendulum swung back to the eighteenth-century notion that the poet who does not conform to institutional norms might be mad, or at the very least eccentric and tiresome.

The commonplace denigration of Romanticism in the North American and British academy was reversed only in the 1960s and 1970s, chiefly through the works of the critics Harold Bloom and Geoffrey Hartman. Beyond the academy, Romanticism had a natural appeal for the liberationist element in the 1960s, who stormed the "gates of Eden" in their demand for a renewed innocence—though they often ignored the complex self-consciousness of the Romantic quest in favor of a willful, ignorant spontaneity.

A highly useful general treatment is Jacques Barzun, *Classic, Romantic, and Modern* (1961). On German Romanticism, see Marshall Brown, *The Shape of German Romanticism* (1979). On the French tradition, Henri Peyre's *What Is Romanticism?* (1942) is valuable; consult also Margery Sabin, *English Romanticism and French Tradition* (1976). Théophile Gautier's firsthand account *A History of Romanticism* (written 1849–74) is lively and instructive. On English Romanticism, consult M. H. Abrams, *The Mirror and the Lamp* (1953); Harold Bloom, *The Visionary Company* (1961, rev. ed. 1971); Geoffrey Hartman, *Wordsworth's Poetry, 1787–1814* (1971), and Harold Bloom, ed., *Romanticism and Consciousness* (1970). Anne Mellor, *Romanticism and Feminism* (1988), and Jerome McGann, *The Romantic Ideology* (1983), present later modifications of or arguments with Bloom and Hartman. On the Romanticism of the 1960s, see Morris Dickstein, *The Gates of Eden* (1977).

rondeau (French; plural, rondeaux.) The rondeau is a short verse form in which the first several words of the first line are repeated as a refrain at the end of the second stanza and the third (final) stanza. The rhyme scheme is (first stanza) *aabba;* (second stanza) *aab* + refrain; (third stanza) *aabba* + refrain. (There are several variations on this scheme.)

See the examples included in Thomas M. Disch, "Rondeaux and Roundels," *An Exaltation of Forms,* Annie Finch and Kathrine Varnes, eds. (2002).

saga A variety of heroic epic poem especially prominent in medieval Iceland from the twelfth through the fourteenth centuries, with all the central works of the genre stemming from the thirteenth century. Like the works of Homer, the sagas began in oral tradition and only later were written down (in Old Norse). Heavily alliterative in their prosody, the sagas are notably terse and realistic, even "hardboiled," in their style. They frequently state the necessity of submission to fate, along with a passionate attachment to honor and a marked interest in vengeance. The sagas' heroes are frequently outlaws, and their settings are agricultural and martial. *Njal's Saga* is probably the best known of the genre.

Some of the sagas are contained in the eddas, two collections of Icelandic literature from the thirteenth century. The *Elder Edda* narrates myths of the gods; Snorri Sturlison's prose *Younger Edda* offers an *ars poetica* (handbook of poetics). See Peter Hallberg, *The Icelandic Saga* (1962).

Sapphic stanza Named after Sappho, the sixth-century Greek poet from the island of Lesbos. English Sapphics are adapted from the classical Greek form. They are four-line stanzas, with a shorter final line (usually a dactyl plus a trochee, or a dactyl plus a spondee). Here is a Sapphic stanza by Fulke Greville (from his *Caelica* [1633]—an unusual example of a rhyming Sapphic):

> Reason is now grown a disease in reason,
> Thoughts knit upon thoughts free alone to wonder,
> Sense is a spy, made to do fancy treason,
>   Love I go under.

satire In the ancient world, satire began as a mixture of different, unevenly matched styles in verse (sometimes with prose added in): thus its etymology, from the Latin *satura* (a stew). Satire is in its origins a mishmash or jumble, and incongruity, the juxtaposition of high and low subjects, has always been centrally important to it. As the genre developed, the roving eye of the satirist became more pitiless, even ferocious. Often he depicted himself as an outcast, a vagabond; he was a furious decrier of corruption, or a mad dog barking raw words. The riotous irreverence of the satirist gave birth to another etymology, from *satyr,* the raucous and goatlike figure thought to populate the wild woods.

In ancient Rome, satire was a prime avenue for the venting of literary aggression. Menippean satire, usually written in a prose studded with mocking bits of verse, combines the jovial with the cynical and biting. The satires of Lucian (b. ca. 120 CE), written in Greek, are fantastic dialogues that look down laughingly on earthly folly. Lucian exposes our grand pretensions and fine, idealistic talk as petty, contentious, and peccadillo-driven.

The satirist is always in hot pursuit of his target: he has an intense drive toward condemnation. Satire depends, as comedy does not, on memorable, often grotesque images of humiliation, ridicule, and physical violence (as Ronald Paulson notes). The satirist is sometimes inclined to depict cannibalism, for example—not a normal comic subject. The classic satirical division is between the fool and the knave: the fool being the dupe or victim, and the knave the crass exploiter.

On one hand the satirist's ambition is mercilessly to expose human failings: to carve a window in the breast (an image that horrified Coleridge). On the other hand, though, satire can be gentle and forgiving of its victims, since we are all subject to folly. Thus the traditional division between the fierce indignation (in Latin, *saeva indignatio*) that characterizes Juvenalian satire, and the contrasting liberality of Horatian satire. Juvenal (second century CE) wrote nearly rabid denunciations of Rome's corruption; Horace [65–8 BCE], in an altogether more sociable fashion, poked fun at the habits of friends and enemies, and by implication included himself in the universal company of fools.

The satirist is often ambitious, almost prophetic in his height of voice. Milton writes, "For a Satyr as it was born out of a Tragedy, so ought to resemble his parentage, to strike high, and adventure dangerously at the most eminent vices among the greatest persons." (Milton refers to the satyr play that followed three tragedies in the Greek festival of Dionysus; see SATYR PLAY.)

W. H. Auden notes that "the commonest object of satire is a monomaniac," someone who has surrendered himself to one overriding desire (say, for money or fame). The target of satire feels no guilt or hesitation in his relent-less pursuit of satisfaction. Thus the grotesque or absurd character of satire originates in the satirist's subject matter, the person under attack.

Maynard Mack remarks, "As *naïf,* the satirist . . . is the child in the fairy story forever crying, 'But mamma, the king *is* naked.' As *vir bonus* [good man], on the other hand . . . he shows us he is stable, independent, urbane, wise. . . . And finally, as hero, he opens to us a world where the discernment of evil is always accompanied, as it is not always in the real world, by the courage to strike at it."

Mack's praise of satire impresses, but it also implies a balance and heroic virtue that is not always—or even, perhaps, usually—present in the genre. In prosecuting his case, the satirist often resorts (as James Wood notes) to cer-tain standard characterizations: he condemns hypocrisy, pompousness, fool-ishness, avarice, and so on. The rigidity of satire's code, its will to categorize, can make it a mean rather than a generous form of literary art, redeemed only by the satirist's inclusion of himself among the guilty mob he rails against.

The eighteenth century was the great age of satire in English literature, above all in the works of Alexander Pope (1688–1744) and Jonathan Swift (1667–1745). The Restoration had moved from a sense that literature ought to be heroic to an acceptance of satire as a basic mode: so the career of John Dryden (1631–1700) paved the way for Pope and Swift.

Some noteworthy and satisfying satires are Desiderius Erasmus's mock sermon *The Praise of Folly* (1511); Swift's *Tale of a Tub* (1704); Dryden's *The Hind and the Panther* (1687); Pope's *Dunciad* (1728–42); and, in the twenti-eth century, Nathanael West's short novel *Miss Lonelyhearts* (1933). Ronald Paulson's *The Fictions of Satire* (1967) and *Satire and the Novel in Eighteenth-Century England* (1967) are fundamental texts for an understanding of satire in the English tradition. See also John Sitter, *Literary Loneliness in Mid-Eigh-teenth-Century Britain* (1982); James Wood, *The Irresponsible Self* (2004); Michael Seidel, *Satiric Inheritance* (1979); Margaret Anne Doody, *The Dar-ing Muse* (1985); Claude Rawson, *Satire and Sentiment, 1660–1830* (1994); and the essays by W. H. Auden, "Satire," Northrop Frye, "The Mythos of Winter: Irony and Satire," and Maynard Mack, "The Muse of Satire," all collected in Ronald Paulson, ed., *Satire: Modern Essays in Criticism* (1971).

satyr play The satyr play was a burlesque presentation of Greek myth, often featuring satyrs (goat-gods) and the hairy, wild figure of Silenus. It was per-formed at the Greek tragic festivals as the fourth play, after three tragedies.

The satyr play apparently formed a kind of anti-masque, or parodic answer to the tragic competition. The only extant example of a satyr play is Euripides' *Cyclops* (ca. 410 BCE?).

scansion. See METER

science fiction Science fiction considers, in fictional form, the influence of scientific advances on human life. Frequently examining the possibility of existence on a higher plane, or in a future world, it instills fantastic literature with rational plausibility, and attends to the "technologically miraculous" (Northrop Frye). (See FANTASTIC.) The novelist and critic Brian Aldiss adds that science fiction conspicuously reaches back to the genre of the Gothic novel, with its frequent interest in the speculative and the monstrous (see GOTHIC).

Among the sources of science fiction are the fantastic Dialogues of the Greek writer Lucian (second century CE), as well as the tales of Edgar Allan Poe and two novels by Mary Shelley, *Frankenstein* (1818) and *The Last Man* (1826). Other notable influences are the tradition of utopian fiction, with its emphasis on social engineering, and the speculative "discussion novels" (as Aldiss calls them) of Thomas Love Peacock (1785–1866). Science fiction came into its own with H. G. Wells (1866–1946), whose novels are marvelous or nightmarish depictions of things to come, and, later, with the burgeoning world of American SF magazines from the late 1930s on, most prominent among them John W. Campbell's *Astounding Science Fiction*. Among the best-known American science fiction writers are Theodore Sturgeon, Isaac Asimov, Ray Bradbury, and Robert Heinlein, all of whom had their start in the "pulp" magazines. The Perelandra trilogy, by the literary critic C. S. Lewis, is also notable, as are three dystopian fictions of the future, Yevgeny Zamyatin's *We* (1924), George Orwell's *1984* (1949) and Aldous Huxley's *Brave New World* (1931). Among the science fiction writers taken most seriously by literary critics are Stanislaw Lem, J. G. Ballard, Philip K. Dick, Joanna Russ, and Ursula LeGuin. See Brian Aldiss, *Billion-Year Spree* (1973), and Marjorie Hope Nicolson, *Voyages to the Moon* (1949). Patrick Parrinder in *Science Fiction* (1980) identifies elements of fable and parable, as well as epic and romance genres, in SF.

semiotics Semiotics, or semiology, is the study of signs, with special emphasis on their conventional or systematic nature. In the 1870s, the American philosopher Charles Sanders Peirce (pronounced PERSE) inaugurated the modern investigation of the sign, distinguishing between signs that resemble their objects (iconic signs) and those that do not. The linguist Ferdinand de Saussure in his *Course in General Linguistics* (1916) defined a sign as consisting of an oral or written expression (the signifier) and an idea linked to this expression (the signified). The sign, Saussure noted, is part of a signifying system, and it depends for its meaning on the system, rather than on its referent (the object in the world to which it refers).

In the early twentieth century, he phenomenologist Edmund Husserl explored the role of the sign as a vehicle for human consciousness in his *Logical Investigations* (1900). Roman Jakobson in his linguistics investigated the link between sound and meaning in the sign. See PHENOMENOLOGY; SIGN, SIGNIFIER, SIGNIFIED; STRUCTURALISM. Later developments in the study of the sign, including the contributions of Roland Barthes and Jacques Derrida, are included under the entries DECONSTRUCTION; DIFFÉRANCE; POSTSTRUCTURALISM.

sensation novel A novel of breathless, suspenseful incident, popular in England in the 1860s. Among the major examples of the genre are Mary Elizabeth Braddon's *Lady Audley's Secret* (1861–62), Mrs. Henry Wood's *East Lynne* (1861), and the novels of Sheridan Le Fanu and Wilkie Collins. The most critically admired of these books are probably Collins's *The Moonstone* (1868) and *The Woman in White* (1860).

The thrills of the sensation novel were derived from those of Gothic, but with the Gothic's castles replaced by drawing rooms. Henry James wrote that Collins introduced into fiction "those most mysterious of mysteries, the mysteries which are at our own doors."

sensibility The Age of Sensibility (roughly, the later eighteenth century, especially the 1760s and 1770s) is marked by a valuing of refined emotion, by an acuteness of response and a quickness of perception and feeling. The plight of others is intimately felt: and the man of feeling congratulates himself on his thoughtfulness. This subtle emotional capacity is praised in works like Laurence Sterne's *A Sentimental Journey* (1768) and Henry Mackenzie's *The Man of Feeling* (1771). The novels of Jane Austen (*Emma* [1816], for example) reflect in complex ways on the cult of sensibility.

In Sterne's *Sentimental Journey*, there is a strange brew of pathos and comedy—as in this anecdote, about the poor maid Maria whose father has died, and whose "goat had been as faithless as her lover": "I look'd in Maria's eyes, and saw she was thinking more of her father than of her lover or her little goat; . . . the tears trickled down her cheeks. . . . I sat down close by her; and Maria let me wipe them away as they fell with my handkerchief.—I then steep'd it in my own—and then in hers—and then in mine—and then I wip'd hers again—and as I did it, I felt such indescribable emotions within me, as I am sure could not be accounted for from any combinations of matter and motion." Impressed by this incident, Sterne's narrator concludes, "I am positive I have a soul; nor can all the books with which materialists have pester'd the world ever convince me of the contrary."

Marshall Brown writes that, in the Age of Sensibility, "Intense feelings for nature and humanity were accompanied by . . . intense anxieties about the integrity of the self," even a fear of madness. Sentiment often steps in when the self is unsure of its reasons. "Even the lightest vibration of emotion will provoke a flood of tears or a torrent of rapture," Brown remarks. Dizzyingly, "feeling leads to more feeling," rather than to a gain in knowledge. Responsiveness, raised to an all-encompassing principle, makes all things, including the self, unstable. In this way, sensibility can become an instance of skepticism (see SKEPTICISM).

See Northrop Frye, "Towards Defining an Age of Sensibility," in *Fables of Identity* (1963); Marshall Brown, *Preromanticism* (1991); Louis Bredvold, *The Natural History of Sensibility* (1962); Frederic Bogel, *Literature and Insubstantiality in Later Eighteenth-Century England* (1984); Janet Todd, *Sensibility: An Introduction* (1986); and Jerome McGann, *The Poetics of Sensibility* (1996). See also SENTIMENT.

sentiment "We are astonished by thought, but sensation [i.e., sentiment] is just as marvelous," Voltaire wrote in his *Philosophical Dictionary* (1764). The role of sentiment in literature was especially an object of speculation in the eighteenth century, when, as Voltaire's statement indicates, feeling seems to become a rival for thinking. In its truest definition, though, sentiment means a union of feeling and thought, not a choice of one over the other. The implication is that the head needs the heart in order to know itself best, or most nobly. Lord Shaftesbury's *Characteristics* (1711) and Adam Smith's *Theory of the Moral Sentiments* (1759) were important contributions to the theory of sentiment.

In the eighteenth century, and at the beginning of the nineteenth, *sentimental* was a term of high praise ("everything clever and agreeable is comprehended in that word," one Lady Bradshaigh remarked in 1804). But in the 1820s and later, *sentimental* turns into a slur, the name for an unpardonable deviation from the dignity that ought to characterize great literature. It becomes associated with cheap and unworthy "tearjerkers," from Victorian penny dreadfuls to the daytime television of the present day.

Barbara Benedict in *Framing Feeling* (1994) notes that eighteenth-century epistolary novels by women, like those of Frances Brooke in the 1760s, stress the moralizing of feeling, along with the cultivation on the part of the reader of a proper blend of distance and sympathy. On the eighteenth-century "cult of feeling," consult R. F. Brissenden, *Virtue in Distress* (1974), and J. Paul Hunter, *Before Novels* (1990). See also Claude Rawson, *Satire and Sentiment, 1660–1839* (2000). See SENSIBILITY; also NAIVE AND SENTIMENTAL; SYMPATHY.

sestina A verse form of thirty-nine lines, divided into six stanzas of six lines each followed by a concluding triplet stanza (the envoi or send-off). The six end words of the first stanza (called teleutons) are repeated in a specific order at the ends of the later stanzas. In the envoi all six words are present, within and at the ends of the three lines. The form is said to have been invented by the twelfth-century Provençal troubadour poet Arnaut Daniel.

In the sestinas of the fourteenth-century lyric poet Petrarch, Robert Durling writes, "the recurrence of the six rhyme-words expresses the soul's obsession with its inability to transcend time." (See Durling's introduction to *Petrarch's Lyric Poems* [1976].) The best-known sestina in English is Philip Sidney's "Ye Goat-Herd Gods" (actually a double sestina), from his Elizabethan romance the *Arcadia* (1590–98). William Empson discusses Sidney's poem in *Seven Types of Ambiguity* (1930, rev. ed. 1947). Anthony Hecht reflects on the dolorous monotony that sestinas often aim to create in "Sidney and the Sestina," from *Unheard Melodies* (2003). W. H. Auden and Elizabeth Bishop, among other twentieth-century poets, wrote distinguished sestinas: see Bishop's "A Miracle for Breakfast" and Auden's "Paysage Moralisé," as well as Ezra Pound's "Sestina: Altaforte" and John Ashbery's "Farm Implements and Rutabagas in a Landscape."

short story A fictional form used early in European literature (in Giovanni Boccaccio's *Decameron* [1353], for example), and flourishing in the nineteenth and twentieth centuries. Among its major practitioners are Anton Chekhov, Henry James, Nathaniel Hawthorne, Guy de Maupassant, Edgar Allan Poe, E. T. A. Hoffmann, Isaac Babel, Flannery O'Connor, Franz Kafka, Ernest Hemingway, F. Scott Fitzgerald, Eudora Welty, Jorge Luis Borges, and Alice Munro. Often, the short story resembles the fable or the parable: it may turn on a surprise, or present a puzzle or a cryptic vignette.

Tzvetan Todorov writes that "the public prefers novels to tales, long books to short texts, not because length is taken as a criterion of value, but because there is no time, in reading a short work, to forget it is only 'literature' and not 'life.'" The short story, less expansive than a novel, generally does not permit the absorption in a narrative, and the identification of the tale with life itself, that the novel so often gives us. See Tzvetan Todorov, *The Poetics of Prose* (1971).

Frank O'Connor offers a critical approach to the short story in *The Lonely Voice* (1962). See FABLE; PARABLE; SKAZ.

sign, signifier, signified A trio of related terms proposed by the linguist Ferdinand de Saussure in his *Course in General Linguistics* (1916) and popular decades later in structuralist and poststructuralist theory. A word is a linguistic sign; it consists of two aspects, related to each other like the two sides of a sheet of paper: the *signifier* (the sound of the word) and the *signified* (the concept or idea implied by the sound). (A picture is also a sign; in this case the signifier is visual rather than sonic, but it is still paired with a concept.)

Saussure championed a system-centered view of language, based on the idea that meaning is generated by a network of differences. This is true on the level of the signifier (so that the sound "cat" is different from "cot" or "cut," and must be audibly distinct from both in order to mean what it does). More interesting, it is also true on the level of the signified. The concept "cat" has meaning only because it differs from the concept "lion," and differs as well from the concept "dog." These differences can often be understood as oppositions: in this case, a cat is "a domestic, rather than a wild, feline" (not a lion, tiger, etc.); or "the other main domestic animal, the one that does not bark or, generally, fetch" (not a dog). Signs are not individual units, picked out and matched to particular objects. Instead, they signify as members of a system—structurally.

According to Saussure, the things of the world are organized by signs, instead of being predetermined objects. The world, rather than being composed of extralinguistic referents (the things that signs refer to), incorporates, and is shaped by, a signifying system: language.

Theorists influenced by Saussure, including Roland Barthes and Jacques Derrida, sometimes use "signifier" to mean what Saussure means by "sign," and "signified" to mean "referent" (for Saussure, again, a signifier is simply the sonic aspect of a word, and a signified is the concept linked to this sound). For a presentation of Saussure that emphasizes his differences from later French theorists, see Raymond Tallis, *Not Saussure* (1995). See also STRUC-TURALISM.

Silver Fork novel Popular in the 1820s and 1830s, the Silver Fork novel described the elegant balls and fashionable society of the Regency period; it was the predecessor of the Regency romance. (See REGENCY PERIOD.)

The term *silver fork* was coined by William Hazlitt in 1827 in "The Dandy School," an attack on the trend. Later, William Makepeace Thackeray parodied the conventions of the silver fork novel in *Vanity Fair* (1847–48). Thackeray, like Hazlitt, was disturbed by the snobbery of the Silver Fork school, as well as the pretensions of the Silver Fork authors to knowledge of high society (most of them were middle class, and had no firsthand acquaintance with the luxurious and highly mannered scenes they described). Edward Bulwer-Lytton's *Pelham* (1828) was the prototypical Silver Fork novel; other authors included Catherine Gore and Theodore Hook. See Alison Adburgham, *Silver Fork Society* (1983); Ellen Moers, *The Dandy* (1960).

simile Usefully regarded as a subset of metaphor: a comparison of one thing to another that includes the words *like* or *as*. See EPIC SIMILE; METAPHOR.

sincerity Supplying some advice to struggling authors, the great Roman poet Horace wrote in *Ars Poetica* (Art of Poetry, ca. 20 BCE), "If you want me to cry, first be mournful yourself. . . . Then your misfortunes will hurt me." Horace's point does not concern the desirability of sincere feeling as such. Though he is not against inward passion, he is more interested in effective rhetoric: an author or orator ought to display the appropriate emotion, given the effect he wants to create. For ancient literary criticism, the inner reality, the question of whether the author is truly mournful or not, remains secondary.

Sincerity was once, from the Renaissance through (at least) the eighteenth century, an important ideal in literature and social life. Lionel Trilling in *Sin-*

cerity and Authenticity (1972) argues that sincerity was a fundamentally social virtue: being true to oneself in order, like Horatio in *Hamlet*, to be loyal and true to others. But in modern times, when sincerity comes to be seen as fundamentally self-concerned, and when we seem intent only on understanding our inner feelings without reference to the social use of such understanding, then sincerity begins to look shallow indeed. (Trilling links the decline in the status of sincerity with the rise of a new virtue, authenticity.) The final low verdict on sincerity has recently been passed by Harry Frankfurt, in the last sentence of his *On Bullshit* (2005): "Sincerity itself is bullshit." See also AU-THENTICITY.

skaz A Russian genre consisting of a fictional sketch written with colloquial verve, often imitating the manner of a cloddish, lowbrow, talkative narrator. Two of the masters of the form were Nikolai Leskov (1831–95) and Nikolai Gogol (1809–52). Influential discussions of the skaz are Boris Eikhenbaum's essay "How Gogol's Overcoat Is Made" (1919) and Walter Benjamin's "The Storyteller" (1936), reprinted in *Illuminations* (1968). See also Victor Erlich, "The Masks of Nikolai Gogol," in *The Disciplines of Criticism*, ed. Peter Demetz, Thomas Greene, and Lowry Nelson (1968).

skepticism John Wisdom defines the position of the philosophical skeptic: "The philosopher *laments* that we can never really know what is going on in someone else's mind, that we can never really know the causes of our sensations, that inductive conclusions are never really justified. He laments these things as if he can dream of another world where we can see our friends and our tables face to face, where scientists can justify their conclusions and terriers can catch hares."

Wisdom captures the sense of the skeptical impulse in philosophy familiar since René Descartes (1596–1650). The philosopher doubts that he can ever *really* know the meanings, causes, or true shape of the world. This kind of skepticism, begun by Descartes and continued by David Hume (1711–66), differs from ancient skepticism, a tradition of doubting inquiry that makes sure of things by testing their value and meaning. This older, practical skepticism, sometimes called Pyrrhonism, survives into the Renaissance in the works of Michel de Montaigne (1533–92). The skepticism of Descartes, unlike the ancient variety, is properly metaphysical, and liable to end anywhere, or nowhere.

Recently, Stanley Cavell has described the skeptical inclination in philoso-

phers like Ludwig Wittgenstein (1889–1951), but also in much modern literature from Shakespeare on, as a substituting of the question of knowledge for
the more properly intimate matter of our interaction with others. Our ac-
knowledgment or avoidance of other people is primary, but we are apt to
translate this involvement with them into a matter of knowing or proving, as
if we could assure our (and their) being through the possessing of information. So Othello, for example, in trying to demonstrate Desdemona's un-
chastity, shifts the ground of their relationship from love (which cannot, by
definition, be proved; and which needs no proof) to empirical knowledge.
Such skepticism, even in its destructive capacity, cannot be repudiated: it is
part of who we are.

See John Wisdom, "Philosophical Perplexity" (1936–37), reprinted in
Richard Rorty, ed., *The Linguistic Turn* (1967); and for a superb, original ac-
count of where the skeptical impulse may lead in literature and philosophy,
Stanley Cavell, *The Claim of Reason* (1979).

socialist realism Decreed at the Soviet Writers' Congress of August 1934, socialist realism mandated that both literature and literary criticism should reflect the revolutionary ideal of the "new man" and new society ostensibly being created in the Soviet Union. The "sincere writer" must give "a historically
concrete presentation of reality in its revolutionary development" (as a Soviet
government statement of 1932 put it).

Socialist realist fiction often centered on a "positive hero": for example, a
heroic worker who, through ardent love of the revolution, single-handedly
boosted quotas for production. (The real-life model for such fictional workers was the coal miner Alexei Stakhanov.)

Perhaps needless to say, much socialist realism comfortably occupies its
niche as propagandistic kitsch. But there are a few examples, like Mikhail
Sholokhov's *And Quiet Flows the Don* (1928–40), that are regarded as masterpieces. See Régine Robin, *Socialist Realism* (1988). *On Socialist Realism* (1959)
by Abram Tertz (Andrei Siniavskii), published in Paris, offers a searching critique of socialist realism by a Soviet dissident. William Empson discusses socialist realism in his essay "Proletarian Literature," the first chapter of *Some
Versions of Pastoral* (1935).

song In ancient Greece poetry was indistinguishable from song. Chanted to
the rhythm of the lyre, a stringed instrument, Greek lyric (like epic) poetry

was quantitative—similar to music, it was organized by the duration of sylla-bles rather than by their stress (see METER). Later European languages, in ad-miration of Greek and Roman poetry with their quantitative meters, have of-ten tried to replicate the musical character of ancient verse. Especially in the sixteenth century, but in other eras as well, poets have nostalgically hoped for a reunion of poetry and music. Renaissance English efforts to devise a quan-titative poetry came to nothing; but the works of Thomas Campion (1567–1620), with their exquisite melding of words and melody, take their place next to the matchless songs of Shakespeare's plays. In Campion and Shake-speare, verse and music meet.

Pastoral poetry relies on the fiction of what John Hollander calls an "out-door music, the blending of the human with the natural." In the April eclogue of Edmund Spenser's *Shepheardes Calender* (1579), the pastoral poet tunes his song "unto the water's fall." In Romanticism, Hollander suggests, the connection of the poet with the natural music of landscape becomes more troubled, as consciousness listens to itself, and knows its difference from nature: it hears its own music set against nature's.

The Aeolian harp, a stringed instrument placed in a window and acti-vated, or "played," by the errant breeze, was an important emblem of poetry for the Romantics, suggesting the spontaneity and openness of the soul to rapture, and to wayward feeling as well. The poet's escape from the officially literary into the freedom of the colloquial is often represented as a movement from mere rhetoric to song: Blake's *Songs of Innocence and Experience* (1789–94) and the *Lyrical Ballads* of Wordsworth and Coleridge (1798–1800) are ex-amples of this progress. Often in poetic theory, speech or even thought itself is represented as a kind of music, even an unheard melody (Keats). See John Hollander, "The Poem in the Ear," in *Vision and Resonance* (1975); James Winn, *Unsuspected Eloquence* (1984).

sonnet A short verse form of fourteen lines. It was invented in thirteenth-century Italy, probably at the court of Frederick II of Sicily. Among its major early practitioners were two great poets, Dante (1265–1321) and Petrarch (1304–74).

The Italian sonnet is divided into a first unit of eight lines, the octave (rhymed *abbaabba*), and a second unit of six lines, the sestet (variously rhymed, but often *cdecde*). Often, because of this bifurcation, the Italian son-net is suited to the asking, and then answering, of a lover's question. Sometimes, as Helen Vendler notes, an assertion is followed by a retraction, a description is faced by a moralizing summary, or a problem encounters a solution.

The Shakespearean sonnet, the other main form along with the Italian sonnet, consists of three quatrains (rhymed *abab cdcd efef*) followed by a couplet (*gg*). Frequently, the couplet summarizes, or draws the lesson of, the three preceding quatrains. English-language poets have written both Italian and Shakespearean sonnets in abundance.

During some periods in literary history, *sonnet* meant, more casually, a short lyrical poem, usually about love. John Donne's *Songs and Sonets* (1633) do not contain any poems that are actually sonnets, in terms of the technical definition given above.

In France, the sonnet was practiced by Pierre de Ronsard (1524–85), Joachim du Bellay (ca. 1522–60), and Louise Labé (1525–66); in Italian, by Gaspara Stampa (1523–54), like Labé an important woman poet of the Renaissance. Sonnets peppered the chief miscellanies (i.e., anthologies) of the Elizabethan Age, including *The Paradise of Dainty Devices* (1576), *A Gorgeous Gallery of Gallant Inventions* (1578), and the delightful *England's Helicon* (1600). There were a number of Elizabethan sonnet sequences, beginning with Philip Sidney's *Astrophel and Stella* (1591), which started a veritable sonnet craze in the 1590s. The lesser known but remarkable poems of Fulke Greville (1554–1628) followed in Sidney's wake. The other Elizabethan sequences that are still widely read are Edmund Spenser's *Amoretti* (1595), which are rhymed in linked fashion (*abab bcbc cdcd ee*) and, of course, Shakespeare's *Sonnets,* printed in 1609 but probably written in the 1590s. Shakespeare's sonnets, writes Helen Vendler, feature a speaker like none other in literature, "successively passionate, reproachful, abject, grieving, triumphant, coarse, deranged, and classical."

"Scorn not the sonnet," William Wordsworth pronounced: its narrow room can hold themes as ambitious and adroit as any larger verse form. In the seventeenth century, John Milton's sonnets are frequently political and satirical—modes not normally associated with the sonnet, which most often devotes itself to questions of love. In the eighteenth century, the sonnet was sometimes called the "lesser ode." Stuart Curran in *Poetic Form and British Romanticism* (1986) argues that the rebirth of the sonnet in the mid to late eighteenth century was linked to women's literary movements, centered on writers like Charlotte Smith (1749–1806). The Victorian Age produced at least two irreplaceable sonnet sequences, *Modern Love* (1862) by George Meredith (consisting of sixteen-line sonnets) and *The House of Life* (1870) by Dante Gabriel Rossetti. The sonnet, Rossetti memorably declared, is "a moment's monument."

Significant sonnets have also been written by American poets, from the underappreciated Frederick Tuckerman (1821–73) to Robert Frost (1874–1963). Frost's sonnets underline the tense air of privilege and the emblematic character sometimes carried by the sonnet form. Other American poets who have experimented with sonnet form are Mona van Duyn [1921–2004] and John Hollander, who in his *Powers of Thirteen* [1983] produces thirteen-line sonnets, each of whose lines have thirteen syllables.

Two still reliable accounts of the Renaissance sonnet are Lisle Cecil John, *The Elizabethan Sonnet Sequences* (1964), and J. W. Lever, *The Elizabethan Love Sonnet* (1956); F. T. Prince, *The Italian Element in Milton's Verse* (1954), has a fine discussion of the Italian sonnet tradition and its influence on Milton. On Shakespeare's sonnets consult Helen Vendler's introduction to William Shakespeare, *The Sonnets and Narrative Poems* (Everyman, 1992); also Vendler, *The Art of Shakespeare's Sonnets* (1997), and Stephen Booth, *An Essay on Shakespeare's Sonnets* (1969), along with Booth's edition of the sonnets with commentary (1977). Anthony Hecht's *Unheard Melodies* (2003) contains several stimulating essays on the sonnet form. Finally, Jennifer Wagner's *A Moment's Monument* (1996) brilliantly explores the sonnet tradition, with special attention to Romantic sonnets, Victorian "sonnetomania," and the modern sonnets of Frost.

sons of Ben A group of early-seventeenth-century poets associated with Ben Jonson (1572–1637) or devoted to his memory, including William Cartwright (1611–43), Richard Corbet (1582–1635), Thomas Randolph (1605–35), and Robert Herrick (1591–1674). Jonson and his poetic followers met in an upper room at the Devil Tavern in Fleet Street, London, known as the Apollo Room. Over its door was an inscribed poem ending with the exclamation, "O Rare Ben Jonson!" (later Jonson's epitaph).

Jonson's solid evocation of the pleasures of friendship and the frustrations of love, in round, honest verse, made him a significant image of the poet as committed man. Chief among the sons of Ben, the best poet and the one most dedicated to Jonson's memory, was Robert Herrick, who wrote in his *Hesperides* (1648):

When I a Verse shall make,
Know I have praied thee,
For old Religions sake,
Saint Ben to aide me.

Make the way smooth for me,
When I, thy Herrick,
Honouring thee, on my knee
Offer my Lyrick.
("His Prayer to Ben Johnson.")

sophists Wandering teachers of the art of persuasion who arrived in Athens
and other Greek cities in the fifth century BCE. The sophists were expert in
the techniques of argument, and ready to instruct others: anyone apt and energetic enough, they suggested, could master the art of persuasive speech.
They were men of method: masters of talking, rather than of wisdom; and
possessed of a professional attitude toward knowledge. The sophists manipu-
lated popular beliefs and plausible inferences for the practical purposes of argumentative success, in the law courts and elsewhere.

The main sophists were Gorgias, Protagoras, Prodicus, Hippias, and
Thrasymachus. Protagoras was famous for his ability to make the weaker argument the stronger. Socrates was charged with being a sophist by Aristophanes in the *Clouds* (423 BCE); it seems to have been a current accusation.
Despite the many differences between Socrates and the sophists, they both
bear witness to the importance of human reason and of persuasion in fifth-
century Greece. See Jacqueline de Romilly, *The Great Sophists in Periclean
Athens* (1992); Mario Untersteiner, *The Sophists* (1948); Leo Strauss, *Socrates
and Aristophanes* (1966). See also RHETORIC.

speech act The British philosopher J. L. Austin inaugurated the idea of the
speech act in *How to Do Things with Words,* a series of lectures given at Harvard in 1955 and published in 1962, after his death. Austin disagreed with the
usual idea that most statements describe a state of affairs or announce a fact:
that they are, to use his term, "constatives." To describe our words more fully,
Austin developed the notion of the "performative utterance." When I utter a
performative, I am not describing what I am doing; instead, my utterance is
itself the doing of an action (to say "I do" or "with this ring I thee wed" is to

marry someone; and to announce "I bet five dollars" is to place the bet). But the uttering of words is not the only thing needed for a successful performative. "Speaking generally," Austin comments, "it is always necessary that the *circumstances* in which the words are uttered should be in some way, or ways, *appropriate,* and it is very commonly necessary that either the speaker himself or other persons should *also* perform certain other actions, whether 'physical' or 'mental' actions or even acts of uttering further words. Thus . . . for (Christian) marrying, it is essential that I should not already be married with a wife living, sane and undivorced, and so on . . . and it is hardly a gift if I say 'I give it you' but never hand it over."

In Austin's witty and lucid account, the realm of the performative expands to include most of the statements that we make. For Austin, speech can no longer be separated from action: to speak is, in effect, to act. There are, Austin explained, at least two main kinds of performative utterances (though he experimented with many other categories): illocutionary (doing something *in* saying something) and perlocutionary (doing something *through,* or by means of, saying something). Some examples of illocutionary acts are warnings, assurances, and questions. Perlocutionary acts are far less tied to conventions and rules than illocutionary acts. Perlocutionary speech aims to produce an effect on the listener or reader: for example, to persuade, insinuate, shock, or surprise. The illocutionary, then, is rather more formula based than the perlocutionary: one can say "I warn you that . . ." or "I ask you that . . . ," but one cannot say "I surprise you that . . ." or "I persuade you that . . ."

John Searle develops and codifies speech-act theory in *Speech Acts* (1969). Shoshana Felman takes Austin in an altogether more playful way than Searle, in her book *The Literary Speech Act* (1980), which depicts the sly, straitlaced Austin as a seducer comparable to Don Juan. Charles Altieri interestingly draws on speech-act theory in *Act and Quality* (1981). Jacques Derrida's "Signature Event Context," in *Margins of Philosophy* (1972), accuses Austin of excluding the literary from his theory. (An exchange between Derrida and Searle ensued, partly reprinted in Derrida's *Limited INC* [1977].) In an important reading, Stanley Cavell criticizes Derrida for misunderstanding Austin in *A Pitch of Philosophy* (1994). See also PERFORMATIVITY.

Spenserian stanza A nine-line stanza invented by Edmund Spenser in his epic romance *The Faerie Queene* (1590–96). The Spenserian stanza consists of eight lines of iambic pentameter, with an Alexandrine (hexameter) line at the end. The rhyme scheme is *ababbcbcc*. The Spenserian stanza is in part Spenser's effort to outdo or "overgoe" the Italian poet Ludovico Ariosto, who in his *Orlando Furioso* (1516) used ottava rima, an eight-line stanza. William Empson describes the effect of Spenser's stanza form near the beginning of his *Seven Types of Ambiguity* (1930): "The size, the possible variety, and the fixity of this unit give something of the blankness that comes from fixing your eyes on a bright spot; you have to yield yourself to it very completely to take in the variety of its movement, and, at the same time, there is no need to concentrate the elements of the situation into a judgment as if for action." Spenser, Empson continues, "can pour into the even dreamwork of his fairyland Christian, classical, and chivalrous materials with an air, not of ignoring their differences, but of holding all their systems of values floating as if at a distance, so as not to interfere with one another, in the prolonged and diffused energies of his mind." See also ALEXANDRINE; OTTAVA RIMA.

stichomythia   From Greek *stikhos,* "row," and *muthos,* "speech." When characters trade alternating lines (or half-lines), a practice originating in ancient Greek drama, they are engaging in stichomythia. An example is the rapid, tense exchange between Oedipus and the herdsman in Sophocles' *Oedipus Rex.*

stream of consciousness   A technique originated by Edouard Dujardin in his novel *Les lauriers sont coupés* (We'll Go to the Woods No More, 1888). The phrase *stream of consciousness* was also used by William James in *The Principles of Psychology* (1890). As applied to literature, stream of consciousness describes a form of representation that stations itself inside the head of a character. The writer offers an unbroken, fleeting passage of thought and emotion, including jumbled or fragmented associations and states of half-awareness. (Stream of consciousness is sometimes associated with the related term interior monologue.) Some of the better-known examples of stream of consciousness are contained in novels by the modernist writers James Joyce and Virginia Woolf. See Melvin Friedman, *Stream of Consciousness* (1955); see also INTERIOR MONOLOGUE.

structuralism   Structuralism studies language, culture, or literary works by describing the governing system that determines their meaning. The foundations for structuralism were laid in part by Ferdinand de Saussure in his *Course in General Linguistics* (1916). Saussure distinguished between the diachronic dimension of language (the history of words over time) and its synchronic dimension. A language's synchronic aspect consists of the fact that its elements (its words or, in Saussure's terminology, signifiers) are all interrelated to form a perfect coherence. This coherence shows us that any language is a system retaining its basic form through time, no matter how individual words may change their meanings or fall into disuse. Saussure emphasizes the synchronic capacity of *langue* (language, the systematic competence that stands behind, or precedes, every utterance), and distinguishes this term from *parole* (the particular word or statement).

Structuralism, then, is the study of a language, or of a symbolic system modeled on language, as a synchronic entity: an organized set of signifiers. (For Saussure a linguistic sign always consists of two elements, the spoken or written *signifier* and the *signified*—the signified being the idea indicated by the signifier.)

The Russian-born linguist Roman Jakobson and the French anthropologist Claude Lévi-Strauss were later important figures in the development of structuralism. Jakobson insisted on the importance of the interlocking, total system of sounds that makes up a poem or other text. Lévi-Strauss, in his great intellectual autobiography, *Tristes Tropiques* (1955), and in *The Savage Mind* (1962), did the same thing with the myths of "primitive" cultures. But Lévi-Strauss worked on the level of theme rather than sheer sound: he demonstrated that these myths depend on a grid or diagram-like structure, and are governed by binary oppositions. For example, the stories told by a certain tribe might be oriented along different axes: life/death, autonomy/dependence, human/inhuman. Their myths would illustrate various combinations of these poles, or positions along them, culminating in a kind of equation. (Here is Lévi-Strauss's intricate reading of the Oedipus myth: "The overrating of blood relations is to the underrating of blood relations as the attempt to escape autochthony is to the impossibility of succeeding in [this escape].")

According to Lévi-Strauss, the polarity of nature and culture, the "raw" and the "cooked," is a chief orienting opposition in most mythic systems. Social relations, in Lévi-Strauss's work as in Roland Barthes's, act to confirm the ruling mythic dimension, with its vast metaphysical assertions. Every system of myths is culturally conservative, a hidebound ideology. So (for mainstream Americans at any rate) steak remains authentic, sushi merely fashionable; and homely, wholesome wood is always more honest than plastic.

Vladimir Propp's *Morphology of the Folktale* (1928) was another important influence on structuralism. Propp reduces stories to events of mediation (barter or exchange). In Fredric Jameson's crisp rendition of Propp's account, the hero of the folktale "meets the donor (a toad, a hag, a bearded old man, etc.) who after testing him for the appropriate reaction (for some courtesy, for instance) supplies him with a magical agent (ring, horse, cloak, lion) which enables him to pass victoriously through his ordeal." Thus the initial episode of the typical folktale, as Propp uncovers its basic structure.

Propp's work contributed to the related discipline of narratology. (See NARRATOLOGY.) An excellent summary and assessment of structuralism is contained in Geoffrey Hartman's essay "Structuralism: The Anglo-American Adventure," in *Beyond Formalism* (1970). See also Roman Jakobson and Claude Lévi-Strauss, "Les Chats," in Jacques Ehrmann, ed., *Structuralism* (1966); Frederic Jameson's account of structuralism, *The Prison-House of Language* (1972); Roland Barthes, *Mythologies* (1957); and Jonathan Culler, *Structuralist Poetics* (1975). See also POSTSTRUCTURALISM.

Sturm und Drang (German, "storm and stress.") A literary movement of German playwrights in the late eighteenth century. Their name is derived from a play by Friedrich Maximilian Klinger, *Sturm und Drang* (1777), a work full of agonized, yearning emotion. In *Sturm und Drang* the hero, Wild, wishes to be blasted into the air by a pistol, or stretched tight like a drumhead. Alan Leidner describes the characteristic emotion evoked by the Sturm und Drang writers as "the urge to be jarred into a life of greater decisiveness and expanse—to take on larger dimensions." Other important members of the movement were Heinrich Wagner (1747–79), Jakob Lenz (1751–92), and, most important, Friedrich Schiller, who wrote the best-known Sturm und Drang play, *The Robbers* (1782).

See Alan Leidner, ed., *Sturm und Drang* (1992). Barker Fairley in *A Study of Goethe* (1947) and Nicholas Boyle in *Goethe: The Poet and the Age* (1991) describe the impact of the movement on the greatest German writer, Johann Wolfgang von Goethe (1749–1832).

style From the Latin *stilus,* a stake, stem, or stalk; therefore also designating the pointed stylus used to make marks in waxed tablets (the ancient method of writing).

George Puttenham in *The Arte of English Poesie* (1589) writes that "*Stile* is a constant & continuall phrase or tenour of speaking and writing, extending to the whole tale or processe of the poem or historie." In this definition, Puttenham suggests that the style of a literary work pervades and characterizes it. Such an association between the style and the character of a piece of writing (often extending to the character of its author) is nearly universal.

Ancient literary critics sometimes divided style into the relaxed, or *eiromene* (pronounced ehROHmenay), which strings phrases loosely together, and the neatly compact, which relies on the repeated satisfaction of clauses and sentences that end with a resonant snap. Aristotle in his *Rhetoric* (fourth century BCE) writes, "Style will be made agreeable by . . . a good blending of ordinary and unusual words, by the rhythm, and by the persuasiveness that springs from appropriateness."

But such practicality as Aristotle's cannot account for the true scope of style. Style reveals character; it makes, in fact, an expression of character. The poet Paul Valéry remarks, "*Style* signifies the manner in which a man expresses himself, *regardless of what he expresses,* and it is held to reveal his nature, quite apart from his actual thought." Style is who we are: an intrinsic thing, Valéry adds, "something more than manner of being or doing."

For the discussions by Aristotle and Valéry see J. V. Cunningham, ed., *The Problem of Style* (1966); also D. A. Russell and M. Winterbottom, eds., *Ancient Literary Criticism* (1972). Margery Sabin, *The Dialect of the Tribe* (1987), offers a rewarding consideration of novelistic style. On poetic style, Donald Davie, *Purity of Diction in English Verse* (1952), is still eye-opening.

style indirect libre. See POINT OF VIEW

subaltern A term borrowed from the Italian Marxist Antonio Gramsci (1891–1937) and made popular by Gayatri Chakravorty Spivak in her essay "Can the Subaltern Speak?" (1985). Gramsci used the term to refer to social groups under the control of an elite that exercises hegemony, or rule over a society's values and ideas (see HEGEMONY). The subaltern is marginalized, subject to the power of others. Spivak applies *subaltern* to the position of natives in colonial society. Under colonialism, she writes, "the subaltern has no history, and cannot speak." Spivak further develops her theory of the subaltern in *A Critique of Postcolonial Reason* (1999). See POSTCOLONIAL STUDIES.

subject, subjectivity In recent criticism, the word *subject* is frequently used in place of *self*. *Self* is felt to connote an old-fashioned humanist ideal of authentic identity, whereas *subject* implies that identity is positioned or constructed by social and ideological pressures. *Subjectivity* names the realm of individual consciousness, feeling, and behavior that is affected and determined, at least in part, by social forces—and by wayward desires that cannot easily be explained. The use of these terms suggests that, as Freud remarked, the ego is not "master in its own house." Among others, Louis Althusser and Jacques Lacan have been instrumental in accomplishing the definition of subjectivity. See Althusser, *Lenin and Philosophy* (1969), and Lacan, *The Seminar of Jacques Lacan,* vol. 7 (1959–60). See POSTSTRUCTURALISM.

sublime The idea of the sublime goes back to Longinus (first century CE). Sublimity involves great thoughts, elevated diction, strong and lofty emotion—but also a violence inflicted on our sensibility. Noble emotion inspires our words with "a kind of madness and divine spirit," writes Longinus. He points to Sappho's remarkable lyric *Phainetai moi,* noting that Sappho is "cold and hot, mad and sane, frightened and near death, all by turns." The critic Thomas Weiskel comments that the reader "is scorched, pierced, inundated, blown down, and generally knocked about by the sublime, if Longinus is any guide."

Such interest in the violation of decorum and the violent disordering of words continued into the modern tradition of the sublime. Longinus was translated by Nicolas Boileau-Despréaux in 1674; Boileau's translation exerted much influence in European aesthetics. The two major treatments of the sublime in the eighteenth century, both heavily marked by the reading of Longinus, are Edmund Burke's *Philosophical Enquiry into the Origin of Our Ideas of the Sublime and Beautiful* (1757) and Immanuel Kant's *Critique of Judgment* (1790). In the eighteenth century, the sublime stands in contrast to two rival modes, the beautiful and the picturesque (see BEAUTIFUL; PICTURESQUE).

The sublime depends on the obscure, difficult, and threatening. Discourse breaks down; traumatic anxiety ensues. The terror of the storms in Homer, Satan's brilliant darkness and ruined grandeur in Milton's *Paradise Lost* (1667): Burke characteristically cites these for their sublime effect. Burke writes that the sublime is "a sort of delightful horror" that sets in "when without danger we are conversant with terrible objects," and feel ourselves shadowed by a superior power. (Here Burke picks up the discussion of the sublime in Joseph Addison's *Spectator* no. 418 [1712].)

For Kant, who followed and was influenced by Burke, the sublime involves a disequilibrium between the mind and its object. First the object overwhelms the mind, and then the mind recovers its balance. Being overwhelmed is reinterpreted as an indication of the mind's relation to transcendence. In Kant, then, the sublime moment turns out to be "reason's occasion for self-recognition" (Weiskel). Kant identifies a dynamic sublime (in which the mind is threatened by a power greater than itself) and a mathematical sublime (in which the mind feels dizzy, lost within a labyrinthine or seemingly endless space where it cannot locate itself).

Geoffrey Hartman defines the Wordsworthian sublime as "a dazzlement which draws the mind into a self-forgetful vortex": stranding the reader or spectator in an empty space, surrounded by his or her own struggling thoughts. Imagination finds itself baffled; a feeling of deprivation or desolation sets in. Then the burden is unexpectedly lifted. Imagination steps forward to provide an influx of power, as in this moment from Bk. 6 of Wordsworth's *Prelude* (1805):

> Imagination!—lifting up itself
> Before the eye and progress of my song
> Like an unfathered vapour, here that power,
> In all the might of its endowments, came
> Athwart me. I was lost as in a cloud,
> Halted without a struggle to break through,
> And now, recovering, to my soul I say
> "I recognize thy glory."

We see in Wordsworth's lines that the sublime has a humanizing effect. It marks a passage to a higher meaning, and makes this meaning ours. The sublime transcends, it gives an amazement or transport beyond ourselves, yet it exalts us as if we ourselves were the authors of it. As Longinus puts it, "Filled with joy and pride, we come to believe we have created what we have only heard." And Ralph Waldo Emerson adds in "Self-Reliance" (1841) that, when we experience literary greatness, our own thoughts come back to us "with a certain alienated majesty."

Wallace Stevens (1879–1955) is perhaps the twentieth century's chief American poet of the sublime. At times, Stevens detects imaginations independent of the mind that the mind cannot absorb: foreign sublimities. At other moments in Stevens, the mind, as dazzled author of its own sublime, produces imaginings that it does not know what to do with.

Finally, there are postmodern ideas of sublimity. The French thinker Jean-

François Lyotard describes the "postmodern sublime" as "that which . . . puts forward the unpresentable in presentation itself; that which denies itself the solace of good forms, the consensus of a taste which would make it possible to share collectively the nostalgia for the unattainable; that which searches for new presentations, not in order to enjoy them but in order to impart a stronger sense of the unpresentable."

See Samuel H. Monk, *The Sublime* (1935); Josephine Miles, "The Sublime Poem," in *Eras and Modes in English Poetry* (1964); Thomas Weiskel, *The Romantic Sublime* (1976); Neil Hertz, *The End of the Line* (1985); Jean-François Lyotard, *The Postmodern Condition* (1979); Kirk Pillow, *Sublime Understanding* (2000).

Surrealism An artistic movement extending from the late 1920s through the late 1940s, mostly centered in the visual arts but with repercussions in literature. Influenced by Futurism, Dadaism, and Freud's notion of the unconscious, the Surrealists explored bizarre, fantastic, hallucinatory juxtapositions of objects, intended to disconcert and enthrall the spectator (or reader). The movement's founder, André Breton, wrote in his *Surrealist Manifesto* (1924) that Surrealism is "based in the belief in the superior reality of certain previously neglected associations, in the omnipotence of dreams, in the disinterested play of thought."

In Surrealism the image is unmediated, as in dreams; we are directly exposed to associations and meanings, deprived of the distance required for measured or reflective interpretation. Yet along with the vulnerability that attends such exposure, there is often a wild, anarchic freedom implied by Surrealist practice.

Surrealist artists included Max Ernst, Salvador Dalí, René Magritte, Wilfredo Lam, and Joan Miró. In literature two of the main practitioners of Surrealism were the poet Robert Desnos and Breton himself, particularly in his novel *Nadja* (1928). The Surrealists were influential on the "deep image" poets of the American 1960s. See Mary Ann Caws, *The Surrealist Look* (1997), which explores affinities between the surreal and the baroque.

syllabics. See METER

symbol Samuel Taylor Coleridge, in his *Statesman's Manual* (1816), draws a distinction between allegory and symbol. "An Allegory is but a translation of abstract notions into a picture-language which is itself nothing but an abstraction from objects of the senses," he writes. A symbol, by contrast, "is characterized by a translucence of the Special in the individual or of the General in the Especial or of the Universal in the General." The symbol, adds Coleridge, "partakes of the Reality which it renders intelligible." For Coleridge, the symbol has an incarnational weight. Allegory, by contrast, is mere artifice. Coleridge's prizing of symbol over allegory is also present in the German Romantic writers Goethe and Schelling; A. W. Schlegel was another influential theorist of the symbolic in this period.

In the twentieth century, critics like Walter Benjamin in *The Origin of German Tragic Drama* (1928) and Paul de Man, who preferred allegory to symbol, were determined to combat the traditional inclination toward the symbolic. The New Critics, in the poems they studied, prized integrity and meaningful balance: the wholeness of the symbol. De Man argued instead that literary texts are allegories of their own workings; the symbol is a "mystified" or wishful entity, representing a unity that does not exist. See de Man, "The Rhetoric of Temporality" (1969), reprinted in his *Blindness and Insight* (rev. ed., 1983). In contrast to de Man, Susanne Langer in *Feeling and Form* (1953) makes an extensive and subtle effort to defend Coleridge's valuing of the symbol. On the symbol in German Romantic tradition, see Tzvetan Todorov, *Theories of the Symbol* (1977); on Coleridge's idea of the symbol, James McKusick, "Symbol," in Lucy Newlyn, ed., *The Cambridge Companion to Coleridge* (2002). Angus Fletcher's *Allegory: The Theory of a Symbolic Mode* (1964) innovatively considers allegory as a form of symbolic representation. See ALLEGORY.

Symbolism The Symbolist movement flourished in France between about 1885 and 1900; its main proponents were the poets Stephane Mallarmé and Paul Verlaine.

Anna Balakian characterizes Symbolism as proclaiming a "semantic transcendentalism," based on the near magical potency of the words that the poet has divorced from their everyday, utilitarian purposes. The Symbolists defended the obscure and the resonant in literary style and argued against didacticism and clear objective description. For them the verbal figure was an organizing principle, and one with consecrated power: suggestively incarnating the world but independent of the world. (In this they were inspired by Charles Baudelaire's poem "Correspondences" [1857].) The Symbolist tone was often one of composed beauty, airy moodiness, and abstraction: a sensuality refined and made musical. In Mallarmé, writes René Wellek, "Art reaches for the Idea, which is ultimately inexpressible, because so abstract and general as to be devoid of any concrete traits."

The essays on Mallarmé by the poet Paul Valéry are an excellent guide to understanding Symbolism (in Valéry, *Leonardo, Poe, Mallarmé,* vol. 8 of *Collected Works of Paul Valéry,* ed. Jackson Mathews [1956–75]). See also Marcel Raymond, *From Baudelaire to Surrealism* (1966), Arthur Symons, *The Symbolist Movement in Literature* (rev. ed., 1919), Bernard Weinberg, *The Limits of Symbolism* (1966), and René Wellek's essay on the Symbolists in *Discriminations* (1970). Richard Cándida Smith locates Symbolism within a larger historical and cultural setting in *Mallarmé's Children* (1999).

sympathy   A key word in eighteenth-century criticism, which was much concerned with the effects of literature on the reader's emotions. The Abbé du Bos, in *Critical Reflections on Poetry and Painting* (1719), argued that sympathy with others is the necessary foundation of society, and that artificial passions, presented in paintings or onstage, or in the reading of a novel, have civilizing effects. Even the horrors of tragedy are converted, in the viewer's mind, into touching sentiment, capable of bringing out our capacity for fellow-feeling. Artistic experience therefore confirms us in our humanness and our ethical purpose.

Eighteenth-century novels, from Samuel Richardson's *Pamela* (1740) to Denis Diderot's rather salacious adventure story *The Nun* (1760), excite extreme sympathy in the reader. Whether the excitement has moral motives, and whether it produces a moral result, were important questions during this era. Denis Diderot's "Éloge de Richardson" (1762) is a fervent evocation of the power of sympathy. See David Marshall, *The Surprising Effects of Sympathy* (1988). See also SENSIBILITY; SENTIMENT.

synecdoche   In rhetoric, the use of a part to stand for the whole ("fifty sails" = "fifty ships"). Closely related to METONYMY.

taste Etymologically, *taste* is related to *test:* savoring something is a way of proving it, checking its value.

The most common meaning of taste is social. Taste marks the difference between good and bad, with all the ethical implications that attend such a choice. Good taste requires a fine-tuned sense of decorum: it responds to the moment and the setting, and seeks an appropriate expression. (See DECO-RUM.) In Alexander Pope's Epistle to Burlington (1731), the poet disdains the elaborate, vulgar buildings of "Timon's" villa, the Trump Tower of its day. Instead, Pope advises, "Let Nature never be forgot." Budding architects should "consult the Genius of the Place in all."

In the eighteenth century, before Romanticism, taste normally meant such a sense of decorum as Pope expresses. When appreciating and evaluating an artistic work, the man of taste showed the ability to discern the sentiment he ought to display. The model of such propriety, it was often implied, was present in the work itself, and transmitted itself to the man. So David Hume, in "Of the Standard of Taste" (1757), discovers in certain classics the true measure of literary value, available across changes of time, place, and custom. Hume writes that "just expressions of passion and nature are sure, after a little time, to gain public applause, which they maintain forever. . . . Terence and Virgil maintain a universal, undisputed empire over the minds of men." Yet Hume also makes room for a more personal, even intimate standard of taste when he writes, "We choose our favorite author as we do our friend, from a conformity of humor and disposition. Mirth or passion, sentiment or reflection; whichever of these most predominates in our temper, it gives us a peculiar sympathy with the writer who resembles us." Immanuel Kant in his *Critique of Judgment* (1790) provides his own answer to Hume's ambivalent description of taste as both a public and a private matter. Kant argues that, even if taste could be publicly agreed on, as Hume desires, it would still be a fundamentally individual inclination.

In a Romantic critic like William Hazlitt, taste becomes, not the search for a common standard, but instead the varying exercise of sympathy between the author and the reader. (See David Bromwich, *Hazlitt* [1983].) For the great Victorian sage John Ruskin (1819–1900), the refining of the individual's taste was a moral imperative, deeply bound to Ruskin's prophetic vision of an improved society. (See JUDGMENT.)

In "Aesthetic Problems of Modern Philosophy" (1965), reprinted in *Must We Mean What We Say?* (1969), Stanley Cavell describes the idea of taste in terms of the responses that modernist art asks from us. The sociologist Pierre Bourdieu in *Distinction* (1979) offers a more skeptical view of taste as a mere desire for social prestige. E. E. Kellett, *The Whirligig of Taste* (1929), remains a useful study of the variations in literary taste. See also Denise Gigante's *Taste* (2005).

terza rima A verse form developed by Dante for his *Divine Comedy*, written at the beginning of the fourteenth century. Terza rima is composed of tercets that rhyme *aba bcb cdc ded* (and so on). It has been a rare form in English-language verse, though it was occasionally used in the Renaissance. The best-known English poem in terza rima is the sublime and devastating "The Triumph of Life" (1822), the final (unfinished) work by Percy Bysshe Shelley.

textual criticism The textual critic attempts to assess the authority of the surviving texts of a literary work, often to produce a scholarly edition of the work. As such, textual criticism should be a central part of literary study. Though we are often tempted to think of the work of editors and publishers as invisible, or as at most unwelcome interferences with the book we are trying to read, books rely for their very existence on editing, on the publishing process, and on authors who change their minds, often producing several different versions of a single work.

Textual editing depends on, and follows from, critical intelligence. As G. Thomas Tanselle points out, there is no sense in which textual scholarship precedes critical judgment; instead, it flows from critical judgment. Which has more authority: an author's first draft, his final revision—or the published edition that passed through the hands of an editor? Should we conflate successive versions with an eye to a composite text, or print them side by side? Should we reproduce without changes a particular published text of a work, or should we try to correct its errors (and how do we decide what is an error)? Textual criticism addresses these and similar questions in its work.

See Fredson Bowers, *Textual and Literary Criticism* (1959), Jerome Mc-

Gann, *A Critique of Modern Textual Criticism* (1983), and G. Thomas Tanselle, *Textual Criticism and Scholarly Editing* (1990).

theater. See DRAMA

theater of cruelty A concept developed by the French actor and writer Antonin Artaud, chiefly in *The Theater and Its Double* (1938). The theater, "like dreams, is bloody and inhuman," Artaud wrote, "a spasm in which life is continually lacerated" and in which order and hierarchy are disturbed.

The theater of cruelty, Artaud continued, "proposes to resort to a mass spectacle; to seek in the agitation of tremendous masses, convulsed and hurled against each other, a little of that poetry of festivals and crowds when, all too rarely nowadays, the people pour out into the streets." Artaud's "naked language" of theater urged "the transgression of the ordinary limits of art and speech." He advocated the liberation of theater from a focus on the text, instead seeking "a kind of unique language half-way between gesture and thought." Cosmic ideas of creation, chaos, and revolutionary upheaval played a central role. See also ABSURD.

topos In Greek, "place." A topos is a literary commonplace or (in Latin) *locus communis,* a recognizable spot. Topos implies literal location: we come upon certain familiar literary themes or subjects just as a traveler might discover a bend in the road or a broad meadow. (Over here is the Petrarchan beloved, yet again, with her ideal beauty and inaccessibility; over there, the ancient fable of green fields, the earthly paradise that returns us to a perfect childhood.)

Topos is comparable to the medieval English term *matere* (i.e., matter), which, as John Hollander remarks, implies a conjoined sense of "topic, question and realm." (The legends surrounding the court of King Arthur are the "matter of Britain," as opposed to the Carolingian "matter of France.") A literary topos is a place, but also an issue or argument, a point made clear in Northrop Frye's recasting of topoi (the plural of topos) as archetypes. In chivalric romance, for instance, the topos or archetypal motif of the heroic virgin asks a question, and makes a claim, about the integrity of the lonely self in a hostile social environment. See Northrop Frye, *The Secular Scripture* (1976). See also ARCHETYPE; INEXPRESSIBILITY TOPOS; MYTH.

tragedy Tragedy is the genre that comes after epic, in prestige as well as in historical sequence. Homer probably lived in the eighth century BCE; Aeschylus,

Sophocles and Euripides flourished three hundred years later, in the brilliance of fifth-century Athens. Tragedy began, possibly around 535 BCE, as the central part of the springtime festival of the god Dionysus. (The legendary first actor of tragedy was named Thespis, leading to our word *thespian*.) Usually, three tragic playwrights would compete against one another for the first prize, each of them taking a single day to present three tragedies followed by a satyr play (a brief, rather scurrilous comedy). (The festival also included sacrifices to Dionysus, the pouring of libations, and a procession of war orphans.)

How does tragedy differ from epic? The most obvious contrast between the two is that tragedy is staged, whereas Homeric epic was recited or sung by a single performer (called a *rhapsode*). But there are other differences as well. Kenneth Burke remarks that, "though the same magical patterns of fatality, magnification, and humility are present" in epic as in tragedy, "in tragedy these patterns are submerged beneath a more 'enlightened' scheme of causal relationships." Burke's point is borne out by the definitive examination of tragedy, Aristotle's *Poetics* (ca. 330 BCE), which lays a strict emphasis on reasonable causality. The hero's death (the most desirable result for a tragedy, according to Aristotle) is logically fated. This willing subjection to causality, to the inevitability of event, shows tragedy's seriousness, a major theme of Aristotle's discussion. Once the plot has been set in motion, no evasions are possible.

Tragedy's main contribution to human wisdom may be exactly this strange and frightening perspective: the idea that we might be subject to an irrefutable pattern of action, one that we could not possibly know in advance. In Greek mythology, Prometheus (hero of the tragedy *Prometheus Bound*) defied the gods by concealing from men the dates of their deaths. Tragedy assumes that our future is already determined, and that we mostly remain oblivious to this determination. Wagner's Siegfried, Milton's Eve, Sophocles' Oedipus: all three are equally unaware of their fates, until destiny descends on them.

According to Aristotle the tragic hero makes a mistake (in Greek, *hamartia,* a missing of the mark). A hero like Oedipus may be marked by the violent arrogance, or *hubris,* that often attends hamartia, but his tragic punishment is always vastly greater than he deserves.

In the eyes of the German Romantics, tragedy becomes a paradoxical sign that humans are autonomous and free, since the tragic hero freely takes on his suffering—accepts and knows it, even though it is cruelly imposed. The philosopher F. W. J. von Schelling in his *Philosophy of Art* (1802–3) describes the point of tragic heroism as follows: "To willingly endure punishment even for an *unavoidable* crime, so as to prove one's freedom precisely through the loss of this freedom."

Tragedy often relies on the principle of cosmic retribution. The hero has disturbed a balance, which must be corrected. This correction occurs impersonally. The author knows the hero will fall. Yet he refrains, as the melodramatist does not, from manipulating the plot. He refuses to save, or damn, his hero by artificial means.

Tragic drama invokes a rightness, or justice, originally drawn from ritual sources. The hero's death is a legitimate sacrifice, consumed by the audience, which participates as if at a religious ceremony. But the audience also recognizes a wrongness in the tragic destruction: a greater force (the gods, the author) has cruelly imposed the worst of catastrophes upon a hapless protagonist. While watching a tragedy unfold, we understand the causal logic of the hero's downfall, the ironclad plot that brings on the catastrophe. But a strange mystery inherent in the sacrificial character of the tragic still confronts us. Northrop Frye remarks that "the resolution of comedy comes, so to speak, from the audience's side of the stage; in a tragedy it comes from some mysterious world on the opposite side."

According to Friedrich Nietzsche in *The Birth of Tragedy* (1872), Euripides, the last of the great tragic playwrights, tries to dispel the mystery that clings to tragedy, attempting to make it a purely rational form. Socrates, the first anti-tragedian, exults in this decline of tragedy, this loss of its original power. So, in Nietzsche's version, philosophy wins out, for some centuries, over poetry—until the spirit of ancient, pre-Euripidean tragedy returns with the operas of Wagner.

For a fuller discussion of Aristotle's reading of tragedy, see ARISTOTELIAN CRITICISM. For an account of Greek tragic practices and their context, see Charles Segal, *Interpreting Greek Tragedy* (1986); John Winkler and Froma Zeitlin, eds., *Nothing to Do with Dionysus?* (1990); C. J. Herington, *Poetry into Drama* (1985); J.-P. Vernant and Pierre Vidal-Naquet, *Myth and Tragedy in Ancient Greece* (1986); and Martha Nussbaum, *The Fragility of Goodness* (1986). On tragedy as a genre, consult Northrop Frye, "Theory of Genres," in *An Anatomy of Criticism* (1957); Peter Szondi, *An Essay on the Tragic* (1961); Bernard Williams, *Shame and Necessity* (1993); and Stanley Cavell, "The Avoidance of Love," in *Must We Mean What We Say?* (1969, 2nd ed. 1976).

transcendentalism Transcendentalism began in the philosophy of Immanuel Kant (1724–1804). The term *transcendent* in Kant's sense asserts a necessary union between the mind's ways of understanding and the world outside the mind. Rejecting the idea of a "ready-made" objective world preceding the human consciousness that perceives and represents it, Kant argued that the foundations of knowledge and experience lie in our grasp of the world. Claims to validity cannot be referred to an objective reality independent of our understanding. Instead, validity inheres in our practices of judgment, feeling, and thought.

Kant's theories had a marked effect on literature. At the very end of the eighteenth century, the term *transcendental* was applied to poetry by Friedrich Schlegel; Kant and Schlegel in turn influenced the English Romantic Samuel Taylor Coleridge.

According to Louis Menand, American transcendentalism can be traced to the publication of James Marsh's edition of Coleridge's *Aids to Reflection* in 1829. Marsh protested against the empiricism of John Locke (1632–1704), which, as he saw it, reduced individuals to bland atomistic units, fully realized and capable of exercising the mature power of choice. Instead, Marsh wanted to emphasize the influence of community in shaping the individual. He also argued against Locke's separation between the evidence of the senses and matters of faith: a separation that reduced religious belief to merely inward, private sentiment. Marsh found in Coleridge a way of uniting the life of the senses with religious feeling.

The reading of Coleridge in Marsh's edition was a decisive stimulus for the group of Bostonians who, in the late 1830s, became known as the Transcendentalist Club. The most famous member of the club was Ralph Waldo Emerson (1803–82); other transcendentalists of the time, like Bronson Alcott and George Ripley, have largely faded from view (with the exception of Emerson's friend Henry David Thoreau). See Ernst Behler, *German Romantic Criticism* (1993), Andrew Bowie, *From Romanticism to Critical Theory* (1997), and Louis Menand, *The Metaphysical Club* (2001).

trochaic, trochee. See METER

trope The word *tropos* has a number of meanings in Greek: turning, way, manner, custom. In the *Odyssey*, Homer describes Odysseus as *polutropos*, a man of many ways. In literature, a trope is a turn of speech that also involves the turning, or inventive use of, the sense of a word: a turning away from proper or literal meaning. In Christian tradition, a trope was a brief addition, in the form of invented dramatic dialogue, to church liturgy (originally, Easter and Christmas services: at Easter, for example, the women at Jesus' tomb would announce that they were seeking the savior, and would be answered by angels). Trope, or *trop,* is also the method of chanting scriptural passages in a Jewish prayer service, whereby each word is given an inflected musical direction, bending it upward or downward.

In rhetoric, a trope is distinguished from a scheme, an arrangement of words that allows them to keep their usual meaning. Schemes can become tropes: a poem might, for example, reflect on the shape of its stanzas, or its rhyme scheme. (Jennifer Wagner comments that Robert Frost's sonnets "concern themselves with an unintelligibility whose source is each human being's limited perspective, his boundedness in a particular time and space that is troped by the conventional rigidity of sonnet boundaries"—a good example of how scheme is transformed into trope. See Jennifer Wagner, *A Moment's Monument* [1996].)

In his *Rhetoric* (ca. 350 BCE), Aristotle uses the term *metaphor* for what we call trope (later tradition has sometimes followed him). Among the tropes that Aristotle studies are analogy, use of genus for species (and the reverse), and comparison of kinds (see METONYMY).

Tropes can generate traditions. Here is one instance: the Hebrew prophet Isaiah proclaims that "all flesh is grass . . . the grass withereth, the flower fadeth" (Isaiah 40:6–7). In the mid-seventeenth century, Andrew Marvell carries further Isaiah's trope of flesh as grass in his "Damon the Mower." Marvell's poem is spoken by a pastoral character who mows first the grass and then, inadvertently, himself; distracted with love, he swings his sickle against his own flesh. Walt Whitman in *Leaves of Grass* (1855–92) carries the flesh-as-grass trope further, making the body of his book an incarnate person. He calls its pages leaves, and therefore parts of a "fleshy kosmos": the author Walt Whitman himself. And in the central poem of *Leaves of Grass,* "Song of Myself," Whitman answers a child's question, "What is the grass?" by murmuring, "I think that it is the beautiful uncut hair of graves." Here, instead of the flesh remaining cut down in death, it continues to grow, wild, to instill itself into Whitman's poetry.

troubadours A group of poets associated with the region of Provence, in southern France. They introduced the celebration of courtly love into European literature (see COURTLY LOVE and FIN AMORS for descriptions of the characteristic stance and style of the troubadours' lyrics). Among the best-known troubadours are Bernart de Ventadorn (fl. 1150–80), Bertran de Born (b. ca. 1140), Peire Vidal (fl. 1180–1205), and Arnaut Daniel (fl. 1180–1200).

An excellent introduction to troubadour poetry is Frederick Goldin's anthology with commentary, *Lyrics of the Troubadours and Trouvères* (1973). See also W. S. Merwin's *The Mays of Ventadorn* (2002), a moving evocation of the troubadours.

typology Christians have traditionally read the Hebrew Bible as an Old Testament that finds itself fulfilled in the Gospels, or New Testament. This kind of reading is called typology. In Romans 5:14 Paul speaks of Adam as a type (Greek *tupos*) of Christ. According to Paul, Christ is the antitype, the fulfillment or realization, of Adam. He is the new man who redeems our sins, instead of bringing sin: climbing the tree to be crucified, not to pluck dangerous fruit. (The prefix *anti-* in Greek means completion, not just opposition; both senses, but mostly the former one, are present in the word *antitype*.) The origins of typology lie in the works of early Christian writers: in addition to Paul, the second-century Justin Martyr and the late patristic writer John Cassian (who probably developed the system of fourfold exegesis; see FIGURA for a description).

Milton's *Paradise Lost* (1667; 12.310) uses the phrase "Joshua, whom the Gentiles Jesus call": Jesus is the real, or fulfilled, version of the Hebrew Bible's Joshua. In the last two books of *Paradise Lost* Milton's angel Michael is sent to inform the fallen Adam of future events, presented in the form of "shadowy types" (12.303). Michael presents to Adam a typological sketch of sacred history, from the murder of Abel to the apocalypse.

Northrop Frye writes that our modern ideas of historical process, our sense that events are heading somewhere and will come to a fitting conclusion, probably derive from biblical typology. Marxism is, or was, an especially typological brand of historical theorizing. For the Bolsheviks, Lenin fulfilled the prophecies of Marx and Engels.

Yet, despite this resemblance, there remains a difference between the modern sense of history and Christian typology. In his essay "Figura," Erich Auerbach describes typological (figural) reading (*figura* is the Latin equivalent of the Greek *tupos*). In typology, Auerbach writes, "History, with all its concrete force, remains forever a figure, cloaked and needful of interpretation. In this light the history of no epoch ever has the practical self-sufficiency which,

from the standpoint both of primitive man and of modern science, resides in
the accomplished fact; all history, rather, remains open and questionable,
points to something still concealed, and the tentativeness of events in the
figural interpretation is fundamentally different from the tentativeness of
events in the modern view of historical development. . . . In the figural system the interpretation is always sought from above; events are considered not
in their unbroken relation to one another, but torn apart, individually, each
in relation to something other that is promised and not yet present."

See Erich Auerbach, "Figura," in *Scenes from the Drama of European Liter-*
ature (1959); Northrop Frye, *The Great Code* (1982); Earl Miner, ed., *Literary*
Uses of Typology (1977); Paul Korshin, *Typologies in England, 1650–1820* (1981);
Sacvan Bercovitch, *Typology and Early American Literature* (1972); and John
Freccero, *Dante* (1986). See also ANAGOGIC; FIGURA.

ubi sunt (Latin, "Where are they?") A poetic topos lamenting the disappearance of beloved persons or things. The ubi sunt motif was familiar in medieval Latin poetry. (*Ubi sunt qui ante nos fuerunt?* was one version of the refrain: "Where are those who were before us?") It also appears in the Anglo-Saxon poem "The Wanderer" (eleventh century) and in a famous ballade by François Villon (ca. 1461). Villon asks, "Ou sont les neiges d'antan?" (Where are the snows of yesteryear?): recalling the Roman poet Horace's Ode 4.7, which is occupied with human transience.

unconscious Sigmund Freud explains in his essay "The Unconscious" (1915) that the psyche is filled with active ideas that are not present to the conscious mind. The unconscious, Freud's great discovery, leaves its mark in dreams, slips of the tongue, neurotic symptoms, and other elusive phenomena that seem to evade our self-awareness. Freud came to his conclusion that most of what occurs in mental life is unconscious, and that the core of the unconscious consists of wishful impulses attempting discharge or satisfaction, in a series of studies, including most importantly *The Interpretation of Dreams* (1900). According to Freud, the unconscious operates according to the laws of the primary process: a principle of mental functioning prior to the secondary-process considerations of plausibility, practicality, and sense-making associated with the conscious ego. Two main features of the primary process that rules the unconscious are timelessness, and the replacement of external reality by the psychic reality of wish and impulse.

Freud's understanding of the unconscious illuminates the themes, as well as the techniques, of many writers, including (among the modernists) James Joyce, Virginia Woolf, and Marcel Proust.

See "Unconscious," in J. Laplanche and J.-B. Pontalis, *The Language of Psycho-Analysis* (1967); see also REPRESSION.

unities. See NEOCLASSICISM

ut pictura poesis "As in painting, so in poetry": a famous motto from Horace's *Ars Poetica* (Art of Poetry, ca. 20 BCE). Horace was preceded by the Greek poet Simonides (ca. 556–468 BCE), who is said to have remarked that "painting is mute poetry, and poetry a picture with the gift of speech"; and by Plato, who compares literature to visual representation in his *Phaedrus* and in other dialogues.

Horace does not follow up on his remark very extensively; for him, it concerns the distance, and the angle of vision, that a spectator or reader may take with respect to the work of art or literature. But later writers make great use of the poetry-painting analogy. *Laocoön* (1766) by Gotthold Ephraim Lessing is a major statement in this tradition, revisionary because it claims a strong distinction, rather than a closeness, between verbal and visual art.

Lessing draws a clear distinction between painting and poetry. Speaking of Agamemnon's scepter as depicted in Homer's *Iliad,* Lessing writes that, unlike the painter who can supply only a single image of the object he decides to depict, Homer "gives us the history of the scepter: first we see it as worked by Vulcan; next it glitters in the hand of Jupiter; then it proclaims the dignity of Mercury; then it becomes the commander staff of the warrior Pelops; and then it is the pastoral staff of the peaceful Atreus."

In the eighteenth century, discussions concerning the analogy between poetry and painting were connected to the theatrical practice of *tableaux vivants,* and to the effort to determine the aim and nature of theatrical presentation. One important work in this vein is *Critical Reflections on Poetry and Painting* by the Abbé du Bos (1719). On "literary pictorialism," see Jean Hagstrum, *The Sister Arts* (1958). See also EKPHRASIS, EKPHRASTIC.

verse From Latin *versus,* the turning of a plow: implying that a line of verse is a kind of furrow. The farming metaphor suggests as well *boustrophedon,* "ox-turning": the way of writing common in the ancient world, with one line legible from right to left and the next from left to right.

The easiest definition of verse is that it is organized around line endings. In verse, unlike prose, lines of text are made to stop before the edge of the page, at the author's will. (The prose poem is a special exception; see PROSE POEM.) Such interest in determined form applies, as well, to the verbal choices shown in verse. Verse organizes and (often) makes regular or recurrent certain elements of language that are not as prominent in ordinary speech or in prose. Notably, verse will repeat similar sounds and rhythms to form verbal patterns.

Poetry is distinct from verse. Though most poems, except for prose poems, are written in verse, many works in verse are not poems. Doggerel is mere verse, rather than poetry (see DOGGEREL); so, for the most part, are limericks, rhymed riddles, nursery rhymes, and the like. A poem distinguishes itself from such genres by playing with, reflecting on, and understanding what verse is good for: what it can be made to say. Poetry, in other words, is a substantial use of form. (See POETRY.)

verse epistle A prominent form in early-eighteenth-century England (called the Augustan Age), modeled after the verse epistles of the Roman poet Horace (65–8 BCE). "When we speak of the Augustan verse epistle," William Dowling writes, "we are normally talking about a situation in which a male speaker, educated in classical values and seeking refuge, in the company of a few kindred souls, from a fallen social reality, addresses a male friend in a way meant to be exemplary for their society as a whole." In the Augustan Age, Dowling argues, the verse epistle takes over the place previously occupied by lyric poetry. The implication, perhaps, is that the epistolary form is able to supply a reassurance about literary communication that lyric cannot, due to the fact that a verse letter directs itself to a specific audience, the named addressee. (A dramatic monologue carries a similar quality; see DRAMATIC MONOLOGUE.) Among the memorable verse epistles of the Augustan Age are Alexander Pope's *Epistle to Dr. Arbuthnot* and *Eloisa to Abelard,* Mark Akenside's *Epistle to Curio,* and Charles Churchill's *Epistle to Hogarth.*

Verse epistles were also written by seventeenth-century poets like John Donne and Ben Jonson; by the Romantics, prominently Shelley and Byron; and by twentieth-century poets. Recent examples include W. H. Auden's *Letter to Lord Byron* (1936), Thom Gunn's imitation of Jonson, "An Invitation, from San Francisco to My Brother" (1992), and many poems by Frank O'Hara, which revise, and revive, the verse epistle genre. See William Dowling, *The Epistolary Moment* (1991).

Victorian Age Only in the 1870s did the adjective "Victorian" attain wide circulation as a literary term (for example, in Edmund Clarence Stedman's *Victorian Poets* [1875]). The period referred to is, of course, that of Queen Victoria's long reign, from 1837 to 1901.

Among the major themes of the Victorian era are the Higher Criticism of the Bible (the understanding of scripture as a historical document, spurred by Ernest Renan's *Life of Jesus* [1863]); the revival of Catholicism and quasi-Catholicism in the Oxford Movement of the 1830s and 1840s; the impact of science and the rise of religious doubt, particularly centered on the publication of Charles Darwin's *Origin of Species* (1859); movements for social reform, including the protest against the massive poverty associated with the Industrial Revolution and the agitation for women's rights; and the expansion of the British Empire, resulting in wars in the Crimea, North Africa, and elsewhere. The major Victorian writers include, in the novel, Charles Dickens, Emily Brontë, Charlotte Brontë, Anthony Trollope, George Eliot, Thomas Hardy, and William Makepeace Thackeray; in poetry, Alfred, Lord Tennyson, Robert Browning, and Gerard Manley Hopkins; and in nonfiction prose, Matthew Arnold, John Henry, Cardinal Newman, Walter Pater, John Ruskin, Thomas Carlyle, and Oscar Wilde.

The Victorian Age was preceded by a period of great loss for the English literary tradition: Keats died in 1821, Shelley in 1822, and Byron in 1824, all of them well before middle age and at the heights of their poetic careers. In part, the Victorian impulse was to continue the interrupted work of Romanticism. Later, modernist writers and critics (T. S. Eliot, Ezra Pound) sometimes voiced prejudices against their Victorian ancestors. F. R. Leavis, for example, criticized Victorian poetic style on account of its supposed preference for "nobility, sonority, and finish of phrasing" over intellectual content.

See Walter Houghton, *The Victorian Frame of Mind* (1957); Basil Willey, *Nineteenth-Century Studies* (1949); Steven Marcus, *The Other Victorians* (1966); Christopher Ricks's introduction to *The New Oxford Book of Victorian Verse* (1987); Peter Gay, *The Bourgeois Experience, Victoria to Freud* (1984–86). Lytton Strachey's *Eminent Victorians* (1918) is a mischievous and profoundly enjoyable account of some central Victorian figures.

villanelle One of the most acrobatic of English verse forms, derived originally from Renaissance Italy, and then France. The villanelle is divided into six stanzas: five tercets and a final quatrain. It has two alternating refrains and two rhymes. The two refrains first appear as the first and third lines of the opening tercet. The first refrain becomes the final line of the second and fourth tercet; the second refrain, the final line of the third and fifth tercet. The final two lines of the concluding quatrain consist of the first and the second refrain. Among the best-known modern villanelles are Elizabeth Bishop's "One Art" (1976), Dylan Thomas's "Do Not Go Gentle into That Good Night" (1952), and Edward Arlington Robinson's "The House on the Hill" (1921).

visual culture Seeking to define the relatively new field of visual culture studies, Nicholas Mirzoeff writes that "visual culture is concerned with visual events in which information, meaning or pleasure is sought by the consumer in an interface with visual technology"—whether the technology is that of an oil painting or a laptop computer. Concerned with architecture and landscape design as well as painting, sculpture, and the Internet, visual studies adopts from cultural studies its concerns with ideology and consumerism, in an effort to understand vision as an aspect of culture. See Nicholas Mirzoeff, ed., *The Visual Culture Reader* (1998).

Vorticism A pugnacious avant-garde movement initiated in London, in 1914, by Wyndham Lewis and Ezra Pound. Pound defined the vortex as the "point of maximum energy" that also "represents, in mechanics, the greatest effi-

ciency." Influenced by Italian Futurism (which they also criticized as "sensational and sentimental"), the Vorticists in their magazine *Blast* described England as an "industrial island machine." Unlike the Futurists, they rejected
images of chaos and fluid energy in favor of hard, disruptive clarity (though
Pound also suggested that Vorticism was, "roughly speaking, expressionism,
neo-cubism, and imagism gathered together"). The Vorticist manifesto declared a loyalty to the "timeless, fundamental Artist that exists in everybody.
The Man in the Street and the Gentleman are equally ignored."

The aesthetic of Vorticism was well represented by Lewis's paintings, with
their explosive, yet tightly controlled, angles and planes. Some of Lewis's
works from the 1910s and 1920s are collected in *The Complete Wild Body*
(1982); see also Michael Levenson, *A Genealogy of Modernism* (1984).

wit According to Aristotle (fourth century BCE), wit is the making of *asteia,* or elegances (*urbane dicta* in Latin). It therefore produces immediate understanding, in contrast to expressions whose force we admire but which we must struggle to understand. Wit's force depends on such instant facility.

Wit is, above all, efficient. Aristotle remarks that wit makes us see things as happening, rather than merely likely to happen. It is palpable rather than predictive: "How true, and I missed it!" should be the hearer's response to a witticism.

Wit had a somewhat different meaning in the Renaissance. Angus Fletcher describes Renaissance wit (similar to our term *imagination*) as marked by a considerable measure of anxiety and distraction, "the divided, wayward mind." In the 1580s and 1590s, the restless University Wits (Thomas Nashe, Robert Greene, and others) made their living as playwrights. Robert Burton's *Anatomy of Melancholy* (1621) presents an encyclopedia of wit's motions, its vast wandering and moody shapes.

"Wit," wrote Freud with a definitive snap, "permits us to make our enemy ridiculous": it allows us to voice the nastiness that we could not express in blunt, undisguised fashion. John Dryden in the preface to *Annus Mirabilis* (1667) defines wit more attractively as "some lively and apt description," and elsewhere as "a propriety of thoughts and words."

Wit can be the apt talent that Dryden and Aristotle describe, an ability to produce the cogent and fitting phrase—or else a mere knack, the insistent invention that overruns aptness, speeding off into foolish or manic hyperbole. Alexander Pope writes in his *Essay on Criticism* (1711),

> For wit and judgment often are at strife,
> Though meant each other's aid, like man and wife.

Before Pope, John Locke's *Essay Concerning Human Understanding* (1690; Bk. 2, Ch. 12) contrasted judgment's accuracy and sobriety with wit's giddy and pleasant "visions in the fancy." Despite Locke's disparagement, the late seventeenth and early eighteenth centuries were the age of wit par excellence. Joseph Addison (1672–1719), in his *Spectator* essays (nos. 58–63), distinguishes true from false wit: "True Wit consists in the resemblance of Ideas, and false Wit in the resemblance of Words."

Wit was a significant term for German Romantic writers. Friedrich Schlegel (1798) emphasizes wit's departure from decorum, its step into a new and unexpected dimension, when he writes that "wit is like someone who is supposed to behave in a manner representative of his station, but instead simply *does* something." (See also IRONY.)

See Angus Fletcher, "The Distractions of Wit in the English Renaissance," in *Colors of the Mind* (1991); F. R. Leavis, "The Line of Wit," in *Revaluation* (1936); also John Sitter, "About Wit: Locke, Addison, Prior, and the Order of Things," in J. Douglas Canfield and J. Paul Hunter, eds., *Rhetorics of Order/Ordering Rhetorics in English Neoclassical Literature* (1989).

witness Carolyn Forché's influential anthology *Against Forgetting* (1993) popularized the idea of the "poetry of witness." (Forché was inspired by the Polish poet Czeslaw Milosz, who wrote *The Witness of Poetry* [1983].) Forché grouped together poets from the twentieth century "for whom the social had been irrevocably invaded by the political in ways that were sanctioned neither by law nor by the fictions of the social contract." Their poems, she wrote, "call on us from the other side of a situation of extremity." Forché acknowledged the possibility that American poets may envy the suffering of foreign writers who have experienced the wars and deprivations that have largely spared the United States in the twentieth century. See also Edward Hirsch, "Poetry and History," in *How to Read a Poem* (1999).

zaum. See FUTURISM

zeugma From Greek *zeugnein,* to yoke or join. Zeugma is the pairing of two unlike items. "If I have broken your dish or your romance," remarks J. L. Austin in "A Plea for Excuses" (1956–57), then an excuse will prove more useful than a justification (the latter being, traditionally, the philosophers' preferred category). Here "dish" and "romance" are paired incongruously: two items that one might accidentally break. Austin's zeugma makes us reflect on the difference, but also the comic similarity, of the breaking in each instance. (Can I effectively say "oops" after I shatter your love affair?)

Probably the most famous zeugmas in English literature are contained in Alexander Pope's *Rape of the Lock* (1712–14):

> Or stain her Honour, or her new Brocade . . .
> Or lose her Heart, or Necklace, at a Ball . . .

See J. L. Austin, "A Plea for Excuses," in *Philosophical Papers* (1961).

INDEX

Page numbers in **boldface** type indicate the main entry for a term

Abish, Walter, 218

abject, abjection, **1**

Abrahams, Roger, 124

Abstract Expressionism, 241

absurd, **1–2**, 113

accommodation, **2**

Achilles, 5, 104, 159; shield of, 98–99, 105–6

act, **2–3**, 53

action, 113, 202

Adams, Henry, 41

Adams, Robert, 177

Addison, Joseph, 29, 58, 82, 109, 133, 202, 228, 290, 311; on imagination, 151

Adler, Stella, 94

Adorno, Theodor: aesthetics, 4; *The Dialectic of Enlightenment,* 77; Frankfurt School, 70, 84, 127; Marxist criticism, 66, 77, 175, 176, 177, 259; *Minima Moralia,* 21

AE (George Russell), 53

Aeneas, 99, 104

Aeolian harp, 281

Aeschylus, 5, 56, 63, 297–98; Dionysian, 22; *Oresteia,* 67, 84

Aesop, 37, 115

aestheticism, **3–4**, 20, 51; decadence, 79–80

aesthetics, **4;** beautiful, 37–38; Black Arts Movement, 41; cultural studies, 76; disinterestedness, 91; epistemology vs., 107; judgment, 164; Marxist criticism, 177

affectation. *See* decadence

affective fallacy, **4–5**, 254

African-American literature: ballad, 34; Bildungsroman, 40; Black Arts Movement, 41; blues, 43–44; call-and-response, 14; canonical, 49; flyting, 123; Harlem Renaissance, 140

Agamemnon, 5, 305

agitprop, **5**, 176

agon, **5**, 20

Akenside, Mark, 151, 215, 307

Albers, Josef, 41–42

Alberti, Leon Battista, 147

Alciati, Andrea, 101, 197

Alcott, Bronson, 300

aleatory, **6**, 31

Alexandrian, **6–7**, 28; concrete poetry, 68; epigram, 106; Neoplatonism, 202–3; pastoral, 6, 225

Alexandrine, **7**, 47, 285

Ali, Agha Shahid, 134–35

alienation, **7**, 66, 176

alienation effect, **7–8**, 106

allegory, **8–10,** 24, 192, 196; dream vision, 95; gnomic vs., 135; masque, 177; metaphor vs., 9, 181; parable, 222; quest romance, 252; symbol vs., 292–93. *See also* fable

alliteration, **10–11,** 270

allusion, **11–12;** echo, 96–97

Alpers, Paul, 198

Alter, Robert, 180, 189, 256

Althusser, Louis, 229–30, 290

Altieri, Charles, 91, 192, 285

ambiguity, **12,** 148, 223

American Renaissance, **12–13,** 207; transcendentalism, 300

Amis, Kingsley, 170, 171

amoebean song, **13–14,** 226

amor de longh, 123

amor fati, **14**

Amos, 101

Amygism, 128, 153

Anacreontic, **14**

anagnorisis. *See* recognition

anagogic, **14–15**

analogy. *See* conceit; metaphor; simile

analytic philosophy, **15–16,** 69, 70

anapest, 184, 185

anatomy, **16–17**

ancients and moderns (battle of the), **17–18,** 58–59

Anderson, Quentin, 13

Andre Capellanus, 75

Andrews, Bruce, 169

animal tales. *See* beast fable

animated films, 37, 45

Annales school, 205

anthropology, 77, 124, 195, 196, 242, 287

anti-essentialism (nominalism), 110

anti-masque, 177

anti-naturalist, 143, 144

antiphony, 224

antitheatrical, 3, 7–8, **18–19,** 188

antithetical, **19–20,** 22

antitype, 302

Antonioni, Michelangelo, 209

anxiety of influence, **20–21,** 31, 261; belatedness, 38–39; imitation, 153–54

Apelles, 31, 188

aphorism, **21**

apocalypse, apocalyptic, 14, **21–22**

apocrypha, apocryphal, 48

Apollinaire, Guillaume, 6, 129, 207, 250

Apollo, 22, 89

Apollonian, **22,** 88–89

Apollonius Rhodius, 6

aporia, **22–23**

apostrophe, **23**

Apuleius, Lucius, 212

Arcadia, **23–24,** 226

archaism, 24

archetype, **24–25,** 248, 297

Arendt, Hannah, 30, 31

Ariosto, Ludovico, 56, 132, 218, 252, 286

Aristophanes, 5, 63, 284

Aristotelian criticism, **25–27;** antitheatrical, 18, 19; antithetical, 19; catharsis, 52; character, 54; Chicago school, 55; comedy, 63; emotions, 5, 8; epic, 103–4; fiction, 120–21; form, 125; genre, 132; irony, 160; mimesis, 187, 188; poetic justice, 237; recognition and reversal, 199, 257, 262; rhetoric, 263; style, 289; tragedy, 25–27, 52, 60, 103, 237, 298, 299; trope, 301; unities, 60, 202; wit, 310

Aristotle, 16, 136; *Poetics,* 18, 25–26, 52, 54, 63, 103–4, 120–21, 124, 132, 188, 202, 236, 257, 262, 289, 298; *Politics,* 52; *Rhetoric,* 19, 26, 229, 230, 263, 301

Arnaut, Daniel, 276, 302

Arnold, Matthew, 111, 147, 307; grand style definition, 137. Works: *Culture and Anarchy,* 58–59; "Dover Beach," 224; "The Function of Criticism at the Present Time," 86, 91, 164–65; *On the Study of Celtic Literature,* 53

Arp, Hans (Jean), 78

ars poetica, **27**

Artaud, Antonin, 1, 94, 297

"art for art's sake," 3

asceticism, **27,** 131

Ascham, Roger, 100, 145, 189

Ashbery, John, 11, 98, 101, 207, 245, 276

Asimov, Isaac, 273

assonance, 10, **27–28**

Athanasius, 48

Athens, 28, 58

Attic, **28**

aubade, **28**

Aubrey, John, 41

Auden, W. H., 11, 21, 34, 183–84, 245; *The Dyer's Hand,* 222; "In Memory of W. B. Yeats," 100; *Letter to Lord Byron,* 170, 307; *Paid on Both Sides,* 193; "Paysage Moralisé," 276; "Satire," 271–72; "The Shield of Achilles," 99, 215

Auerbach, Erich, 82–83, 122, 189, 232–33, 256, 302–3

Augustan Age, **29,** 90, 237; verse epistle, 306–7

Augustine, Saint, 82, 146, 179, 252

Augustus, emperor of Rome, 29

d'Aulnoy, Marie-Catherine, 116

aureate, **29**

Austen, Jane, 49, 162, 259, 274; *Northanger Abbey,* 137, 211, 212, 224; *Pride and Prejudice,* 210; *Sense and Sensibility,* 212

Austin, J. L., 12, 15, 216, 229, 312; speech act, 69, 284–85

auteur theory, 122

authenticity, **29–30,** 230, 279

authorial intent. *See* intentional fallacy

authority, **30–31,** 231

autobiography, 41, 104; confessional poetry vs., 69

automatic writing, 31

avant-garde, **31–32,** 176; aleatory, 6; Dadaism, 78; difficulty, 88; Imagism, 150–53; nouveau roman, 209; Oulipo, 218–19; theater of cruelty, 1, 94, 297; Vorticism, 308–9

Ayer, A. J., 15

Babbitt, Irving, 147

Babel, Isaac, 277

Bacchylides, 56

Bacon, Francis, 17, 21, 71, 145, 147, 235; *Essays,* 109, 163; "Of Innovation," 217

Bakhtin, Mikhail, 50, 58, 84–86, 212–13

Balakian, Anna, 293

Ball, Hugo, 78

ballad, **33–35,** 66, 124, 170, 251, 267

ballade, **35,** 304

Ballard, J. G., 273

Balzac, Honoré de, 58, 104–5, 121, 210, 255

Baraka, Amiri (Leroi Jones), 41

Barber, C. L., 65, 94, 119, 205

bardic, **35–36**

Barish, Jonas, 18, 19

Barnfield, Richard, 227

baroque, **36.** *See also* mannerism

Barth, John, 180

Barthelme, Donald, 180

Barthes, Roland, 75, 196, 199, 242, 274, 278, 287

Barzun, Jacques, 59, 186, 268

Basho, 140

Bataille, Georges, 22, 87

Bate, W. Jackson, 38

bathos, **36–37**

Baudelaire, Charles, 3, 79, 86, 103, 139, 190,
    247; "Correspondences," 293; prose
    poem, 245

Baudrillard, Jean, 242

Baum, L. Frank, 9

Baumgarten, Alexander Gottlieb, 4

Bazin, André, 122

Beach Boys (music group), 29

Beardsley, Aubrey, 80

Beardsley, Monroe, 4, 5, 157–58

beast fable, **37**

Beatrice (Dante's beloved), 39–40

Beats, **37**

beautiful, 3, 4, **37–38,** 91, 234, 290

Beauvoir, Simone de, 118

Beccary, Madame, 107

Beckett, Samuel, 1, 3, 27, 180; *Endgame,* 62;
    Waiting for Godot, 2

Beerbohm, Max, 224, 225

Behn, Aphra, 261

belatedness, **38–39,** 104

Bell, Clive, 43

Bell, Quentin, 43

Bellay, Joachim du, 282

belletristic, **39**

Bellow, Saul, 40, 210

beloved, the, **39–40;** blazon, 42–43; cruel
    fair, 76; fame, 116; lyric, 173; ubi sunt,
    304

Benedict, Barbara, 276

Benedikt, Michael, 245

Benjamin, Walter, 10, 36, 76–77, 127, 176,
    177, 279, 293

Bennett, Arnold, 98, 191

Beowulf (Old English poem), 179, 183

Bercovitch, Sacvan, 164

Berger, Harry, 89, 227

Bergson, Henri, 63

Bernard of Chartres, 17

Bernart de Ventadorn, 302

Bernhard, Thomas, 27

Bernstein, Charles, 169

Berryman, John, 69

Bersani, Leo, 247

Bertran de Born, 302

Beuys, Joseph, 45

Bevington, David, 192

Bible: allegory, 9–10; allusion, 11; anagogic,
    14; antithetical, 19; apocalypse, 21; arche-
    type, 25; authority, 30–31; blues, 43;
    canons, 48; chapter and verse, 53; closure,
    61–62; decorum, 82–83; didactic, 86;
    emblem, 101; epic, 104; Erasmus' New
    Testament, 146, 232; exegesis, 112; figura,
    121–22, 164; higher criticism, 307; hortus
    conclusus, 144; iconography, 150; jere-
    miad, 163–64; Miltonian echo, 96;
    mimesis, 189; mystery play, 194–95;
    myth, 195, 196; panegyric, 220; parable,
    222; psalms, 43, 215, 220, 238; realism,
    256; typology, 164, 302

Bierce, Ambrose, 106

Bildungsroman, **40,** 167, 211

biography, **40–41,** 208

Birmingham School of cultural materialism,
    77

Bishop, Elizabeth, 45, 72, 276, 308

Black Arts Movement, **41**

Black Mountain, **41–42**

Blackmur, R. P., 204

Blair, Hugh, 137

Blake, William, 21–22, 35, 37, 102, 104, 195,
    252, 267, 281

Bland, Bobby ("Blue"), 43

blank verse, **42,** 73, 185, 265. *See also* iambic
    pentameter

blazon (or blason), **42–43**

Bloch, Ernst, 127, 176, 177

Bloom, Harold, 5, 31, 253, 261, 268; *The Anxiety of Influence,* 20–21, 38–39; *Blake's Apocalypse,* 22; Freudian theory, 247, 248, 261; gnosis, 136; kabbalah, 166–67; *Yeats,* 20, 191

Bloomsbury, **43**

blues, **43–44,** 49, 124, 135; refrain, 44, 258–59

Blue Stockings, **44**

Blume, Judy, 76

Blunden, Edmund, 133

Boccaccio, Giovanni, 80, 115, 145, 276

Boccioni, Umberto, 128, 129

body theory, **44**

Boethius, 179

Bogan, Louise, 184

Bogel, Frederic, 152, 275

Boileau-Despréaux, Nicolas, 202, 290

Bolshevism, 5, 302

bombast, **44–45**

Booth, Stephen, 12

Booth, Wayne, 55, 111, 155, 161, 200

Borges, Jorge Luis, 180, 277

Bos, Abbé du, 294, 305

Bosch, Hieronymus, 138–39

Boswell, James, 41

Boswell, John, 131

Bourdieu, Pierre, 76, 296

Bovarysme, **45**

Bowdler, Samuel, 45

bowdlerize, **45**

Bradbury, Ray, 273

Braddon, Mary Elizabeth, 274

Braque, Georges, 129

Braudel, Fernand, 205

Brecht, Bertolt, 94, 114; epic theater, 7–8, 106; Marxist criticism, 175, 176, 177

Bredvold, Louis, 275

Bremond, Abbé Henri, 249

Breton, André, 31, 176, 292

Breton lai. *See* lai

bricolage, **45**

Bridgewater, Earl of, 178

British Empire, 239–40, 307

broadside ballad, 34

Brodhead, Richard, 48

Bromwich, David, 164, 192, 243

Brontë, Charlotte and Emily, 307

Brooke, Frances, 276

Brooke, Rupert, 133

Brooks, Cleanth, 147–48, 162, 183, 203, 205, 223, 236; "The Heresy of Paraphrase," 223

Brooks, Mel, 46

Brooks, Peter, 44, 200, 236

Brothers Grimm. *See* Grimm brothers

Brower, Reuben, 61

Brown, Marshall, 275

Brown, Sterling, 34, 140

Browne, Thomas, 50, 163, 222

Browning, Robert, 61, 139, 252, 268, 307; "My Last Duchess," 94, 95

Brueghel, Pieter, 138–39

Brummel, Beau, 259

Bruni, Leonardo, 145

Bruno, Giordano, 143

Buber, Martin, 85, 144, 229

Büchner, Georg, 114

bucolics, **46,** 150, 225

Buffy the Vampire Slayer, 25, 137

Bullins, Ed, 41

bullshitting, 264, 279

Bulwer-Lytton, Edward, 278

Bunyan, John, 9, 261

Burckhardt, Jacob, 96, 147, 260

burden, **46**

Bürger, G. A., 34

Bürger, Peter, 32

Burke, Edmund, 37–38, 164, 234, 290

Burke, Kenneth, 26, 55, 65, 79, 129, 177, 204, 206, 247, 265, 298 burlesque, **46,** 272–73. *See also* satire

Burne-Jones, Edward, 244

Burroughs, William, 6, 37

Burrow, Colin, 105

Burt, Stephen, 100, 101

Burton, Robert, 16, 71, 163, 264–65, 310

Butler, Judith, 44, 131, 229, 230, 247–48

Butler, Samuel, 46, 92, 189

Butor, Michel, 209

Bynum, Caroline Walker, 44

Byron, Lord (George Gordon), 61, 168, 307; *Beppo,* 218; *Don Juan,* 160, 218; *The Vision of Judgment,* 170, 171, 218

cadence ending, 53

caesura, **47,** 184, 185

Cage, John, 6, 42

Cahiers du cinéma (journal), 122

call-and-response, 14

Callimachus, 6

Cameron, Sharon, 173

Campion, Thomas, 281

Camus, Albert, 1, 113

canon, canonical, **47–49,** 58–59, 76

canzone, **49,** 238

Cao Xueqin (Ts'ao Hsueh-ch'in), 211

capitalism, 7, 66, 127, 140, 211

Capote, Truman, 208

Caputo, John, 81, 82

Carew, Thomas, 72, 182

Carlyle, Thomas, 147, 307

Carnap, Rudolf, 15, 69

carnivalesque, **49–50;** dialogic, 85

Caroline Age, **50,** 260; Cavalier poets, 50, 52

carpe diem, **50–51,** 52

Carroll, Lewis, 95, 170, 227

Cartari, Vincenzo, 197

Cartwright, William, 283

Cash, Johnny, 34

Cassian, John, 112, 302

Castiglione, Baldassare, 74, 145, 146–47

castration anxiety, 246

catabasis. *See* katabasis

catalogue, **51–52**

catharsis, 26, **52**

Cather, Willa, 130, 167

Catholicism, 307

Catullus, 39, 67, 108, 238

causality, 298, 299

Cavalcanti, Guido, 92

Cavalier poets, 50, **52**

Cave, Terence, 257, 258

Cavell, Stanley, 8, 16, 62, 65, 119, 122, 138, 179–80, 217, 224, 229, 279–80, 285, 296

Céline, Louis-Ferdinand, 22

Celtic revival, **52–53**

cento, **53**

Cervantes, Miguel de: *Don Quixote,* 45, 56, 126, 210, 258; metafiction, 180

chance. *See* aleatory

Chandler, Raymond, 158, 252

Chapman, George, 163

chapter, **53**

character, **53–54,** 230; dramatic monologue, 94–95; ethics, 107; interior monologue, 158; point of view, 238–39; stock comedic, 63, 64; stream of consciousness, 286; style, 289

Charlemagne, 17, 56

Charles I, king of England, 50, 52, 177, 260

Charles II, king of England, 261

Charles d'Orléans, 35

Chase, Richard, 13, 201, 213

Chateaubriand, François René de, 190

Chatterton, Thomas, 34

Chaucer, Geoffrey, 24, 35, 115, 156, 179, 245; *The Book of the Duchess,* 95; *The Canterbury Tales,* 179; Franklin's Tale, 168; *The House of Fame,* 95; Knight's Tale, 75; *The Legend of Good Women,* 95; Merchant's

Tale, 144–45; Miller's Tale, 46, 115, 150; Nun's Priest Tale, 37; *The Parliament of Fowles*, 95; *Troilus and Criseyde*, 200, 265–66

Chekhov, Anton, 3, 58, 94, 277

Chester cycle, 194

Chesterton, G. K., 139

chiasmus, **55**

Chicago school, 26, **55**

chivalric romance, **55–56**, 178, 297; novel vs., 210; topos, 297. *See also* quest romance

chorus, **56–57**, 208, 258

Chrétien de Troyes, 56, 75

Christianity: allegory, 9–10; apocalypse, 21; apocryphal works, 48; archetype, 25; asceticism, 27, 131; canon, 48; cento, 53; courtly love, 75, 92; decorum, 82–83; figural scripture reading, 121–22; genealogy, 131; iconography, 149, 150; mythography, 196; trope, 301; typology, 302. *See also* Bible

Christine de Pisan, 35

chronicle, **57–58**

chronotope, **58**

Churchill, Charles, 307

Churchill, Winston, 264

Cicero, 17, 23, 146; *Orator*, 28, 82, 235; rhetoric, 262–63, 264

cinema. *See* film; film theory

Cixous, Hélène, 118

Clark, Kenneth, 137

classic, 17–18, **58–59**, 76, 295; humanism, 145–46, 260

classical, classicism, **59–60**, 82–83, 232, 238. *See also* neoclassicism

class struggle, 175, 176

Claude glass, 234

Cleveland, John, 60–61

Clevelandism, 28, **60–61**

Clinton, Bill, 266

close reading, **61**, 204, 205; explication de texte vs., 113–14; philology, 232

closet drama, **61**

closure, **61–62**; comic plot, 65

Clover, Carol, 119

Clurman, Harold, 94

Coleridge, Samuel Taylor, 41, 168, 266, 267, 271, 293; *Aids to Reflection*, 300; *Biographia Literaria*, 117, 152, 249–50; "The Eolian Harp," 71; "Frost at Midnight," 71; "In Xanadu did Kubla Khan," 55; *Lyrical Ballads*, 34, 267, 281; *Statesman's Manual*, 292–93

Colie, Rosalie, 90, 222

collage, 129

Collins, Wilkie, 212, 274

Collins, William, 35, 54, 152, 215, 267

comedy, 25, **62–66**, 132, 133, 161; recognition, 257–58; tragedy vs., 299

comedy of humors, 37, 64–65

comedy of manners, 64, 261

commedia del'arte, 63–64

commodity, **66**, 127; cultural capital, 76; fetishism, 66, 120, 176, 177, 259–60

common measure, **66**

complaint, **67**

Comus, 62–63

conceit, **67–68**; Clevelandism, 60–61

concordia discors. *See* discordia concors

concrete poetry, **68**

Condell, Henry, 124

confessional poetry, 30, 52, **69**, 230

Congreve, William, 64, 261

Conley, Thomas, 265

Conrad, Joseph, 98, 155–56, 208, 224

consciousness, 25, 231. *See also* unconscious

constative. *See* speech act

consumer culture. *See* commodity

continental philosophy, 15–16, **69–70**. *See also* existentialism contingency, 113

convention, **70–71.** *See also* decorum

conversation poem, **71**

Cooper, James Fenimore, 220

Coover, Robert, 180

copia, **71**

Corbet, Richard, 283

Corneille, Pierre, 59, 60, 201–2

cosmic retribution, 299

coterie poetry, **72**

Cottom, Daniel, 137

Cotton, Charles, 261

counterculture (1960s), 37, 149

country-house poem, **72**

couplet, **72–74;** blues stanza, 44; conclud-
     ing, 62, 73, 282; ghazal, 134

couplet envoi, 221

courtesy. *See* courtliness

courtier, 74, 226

courtliness, **74,** 260

courtly love, **74–75,** 178, 301–2; burlesque,
     46; cruel fair, 76; dolce stil nuovo, 92; fin
     amors, 123. *See also* chivalric romance

Cowley, Abraham, 182, 262

Craig, Hardin, 192

Crane, Hart, 101, 191, 223, 224; "Proem: To
     Brooklyn Bridge," 244

Crane, R. S., 55

Crashaw, Richard, 36, 101, 182

creole, creolizing, **75–76,** 124

Critchley, Simon, 70

Croce, Benedetto, 55

Cromwell, Oliver, 52, 220

cruel fair, **76,** 219

Cruikshank, George, 139

Cullen, Countee, 140

Culler, Jonathan, 23, 118

cultural capital, **76**

cultural studies, **76–77,** 148, 230, 308

culture, **77.** *See also* mass culture

culture industry, 127

Cunningham, J. V., 106

Cunningham, Merce, 42

Curtius, Ernst Robert, 138, 175, 221, 232–33

dactyl, 184; double, 92

Dadaism, 32, **78,** 129, 292

daemon, **79**

Dalí, Salvador, 292

dandy, 259

Daniel, Samuel, 218

Dante Alighieri, 75, 105, 122, 178, 228;
     beloved, 39–40; humanism, 145, 146;
     sonnet, 281. Works: *De Vulgari Eloquen-
     tia,* 49; *Divine Comedy,* 40, 92, 179, 296;
     Inferno, 153, 167; *Vita Nuova,* 40, 92

Darwin, Charles, 307

Dasein, 142, 148

Davenport, Guy, 41, 101, 136, 186

Davidson, Donald, 16, 180–81

Davies, Robertson, 61

dawn, salute to. *See* aubade

dead metaphor, 181

death: elegy, 99–100, 226; epitaph, 107–8;
     metaphor, 181; tragedy, 298, 299

death drive, 247, 248

"death of God," 2

débat, **79**

decadence, **79–80,** 123

de casibus, **80**

deconstruction, 10, **80–82;** ethics, 111; logo-
     centric, 171–72; semiotics, 274. *See also*
     différance; poststructuralism

decorum, **82–83,** 237, 295, 311

deep image poets, 292

defamiliarization, **83,** 125

Defoe, Daniel, 121, 210–11, 233, 239, 255

deism, 103

Dekker, Thomas, 144

De la Mare, Walter, 133

Deleuze, Gilles, 242

deliberative rhetoric, 221, 264

de Man, Paul, 10, 22–23, 81, 242, 293

Denham, John, 73, 74, 90

Dennett, Daniel, 16

Dennis, John, 202

De Quincey, Thomas, 109, 168

Derrida, Jacques, 70, 110, 148, 274, 278, 285;
    deconstruction, 81; "Différance," 86–88;
    feminist theory, 118; logocentric, 171–72;
    metaphor, 182; poststructuralism, 242

Descartes, René, 279

Descombes, Vincent, 70

Desnos, Robert, 292

detachment, 164

detective fiction, 236, 252

deus ex machina, **83–84**

Deuteronomy, 48, 104

Dewey, John, 243

dialectic, **84,** 176, 263

dialogic, **84–86,** 212–13. *See also* chronotope

dialogue, 141

diaspora, 124

DiBattista, Maria, 191

Dick, Philip K., 273

Dickens, Charles, 122, 179, 210, 212, 255, 307

Dickinson, Emily, 12, 48, 66, 102, 135, 265, 268

Dickstein, Morris, 268

diction, 133

didactic, **86,** 95

Diderot, Denis, 19, 102, 162, 294

différance, **86–88**

difficulty, **88,** 223; elliptical poetry, 100–101;
    language poetry, 168–69; in modernism,
    88, 169, 191. *See also* avant-garde

Dilthey, Wilhelm, 131, 141, 142

Diodore of Tarsus, 10

Dionysian, 22, **88–89,** 93

Dionysus, 56, 63, 89, 93, 298

Disch, Thomas M., 269

discordia concors (concordia discors), **89–90;** couplet, 73; paradox, 90

discourse, **90**

discursive, **90–91**

disinterestedness, **91**

dissociation of sensibility, **91–92,** 183

dithyramb, 56

doggerel, **92,** 306

dolce stil nuovo, **92**

domestic comedy, 63

Donaldson, E. Talbot, 168

Donne, John, 49, 91, 174, 222, 307; coterie
    poetry, 72; elegies, 47, 99; metaphysical
    poetry, 182, 183. Works: *Anniversaries,* 61;
    Songs and Sonnets, 282; "A Valediction
    Forbidding Mourning," 67

Doody, Margaret, 29

Doolittle, Hilda. *See* H.D.

Dostoevski, Fyodor, 85, 207–8, 238–39, 247

double dactyl, **92**

Douglas, Ann, 13, 118, 140

Dowling, William, 306–7

drab poets, 29

drama, **93–95;** absurd, 1–2; act, 2–3; agon,
    5; alienation effect, 7–8; antitheatrical,
    18–19; catharsis, 52; character, 54; chorus,
    56; chronicle, 57; classical, 60; deus ex
    machina, 84; Elizabethan, 2–3, 100; epic
    theater, 106; Jacobean, 91, 94, 163; melo-
    drama, 132, 179–80; morality play, 9,
    192; mummers' plays, 193; mystery play,
    194–95; neoclassical, 201–2; No, 208–9;
    plot, 235–36; poetic justice, 237; Restora-
    tion, 261; stichomythia, 286; Sturm und
    Drang, 288; unities, 60, 202. *See also*
    comedy; tragedy

dramatic monologue, **94–95,** 307

Drayton, Michael, 218

dream vision, **95**

Dreiser, Theodore, 200, 212, 255

Dryden, John, 59, 91, 170, 182, 188–89; heroic couplet, 73; Restoration literature, 261; wit definition, 310. Works: *An Essay of Dramatic Poesy,* 17, 202, 236–37; *Fables, Ancient and Modern,* 115, 156; *Georgics* translation, 133; *The Hind and the Panther,* 272; *MacFlecknoe,* 189–90; *Preface to Fables,* 154; "Song for Saint Cecilia Day," 215

DuBois, W. E. B., 140

Duchamp, Marcel, 78

Dujardin, Edouard, 286

dulce et utile, **95**

Dunbar, William, 29, 123

Duncan, Robert, 42

Duras, Marguerite, 209

Dylan, Bob, 34, 37

dystopian fiction, 273

early modern, **96.** *See also* Renaissance literature

Eberhardus Bethuniensis, 137–38

echo, **96–97**

eclogue, 14, 46, **97,** 99, 150, 225. *See also* pastoral

ecocriticism, **97–98**

edda, 270

Edgeworth, Maria, 107

editing, 296

Edmundson, Mark, 137, 229, 248

Edward VII, king of Great Britain, 98

Edwardian Age, **98;** modernism vs., 190–91

Eikhenbaum, Boris, 279

eiromene, 289

Eisenstein, Sergei, 122

ekphrasis, ekphrastic, **98–99**

Eleanor of Aquitaine, 75

elegiac mood, 100, 198

elegy, 60, **99–100,** 132, 226; epitaph vs., 107

Eliot, George, 40, 210, 255, 268, 307

Eliot, T. S., 49, 100, 163, 220, 238; classicism, 60; culture definition, 77; modernism, 190, 191, 241, 268; objective correlative, 214; Victorian Age, 308. Works: "Hamlet and His Problems," 214; "The Love Song of J. Alfred Prufrock," 258; "The Metaphysical Poets," 88, 91–92, 183; "Reflections on Vers Libre," 128; "The Three Voices of Poetry," 94–95; "Tradition and the Individual Talent," 154, 155; "Ulysses, Order, and Myth," 191; *The Waste Land,* 62, 94; "What Is a Classic?" 58

Elizabeth I, queen of England, 100, 163

Elizabethan Age, 2–3, 94, **100,** 227, 260; courtliness, 74; euphuism, 112; rhyme royal, 266; sonnet, 282

elliptical poetry, **100–101,** 207; language poetry vs., 101, 169. *See also* gnomic

Ellison, Ralph, 40, 44, 49

Elyot, Thomas, 89, 100

emanations, theory of, 203

emblem, 68, 90, **101–2**

Emerson, Ralph Waldo, 12, 13, 41, 48, 49, 267, 268; character, 54; essay, 109; genius (daemon), 79; gnosis, 136; transcendentalism, 300. Works: "The American Scholar," 40, 159; "The Poet," 51; "Self-Reliance," 216, 291

emotions: affective fallacy, 4–5; alienation effect vs., 8; catharsis, 52; impersonality vs., 154; objective correlative vs., 214; objectivity, 224; pathos, 229; sensibility, 274–75; sentiment, 275–76; sympathy, 294

empiricism, 243, 300

Empson, William, 12, 55, 177, 198–99, 204, 224, 227, 248; *Seven Types of Ambiguity,* 276, 286

ending. *See* closure

Engels, Friedrich, 175, 302

English Renaissance, 29, 100, 144, 145, 260. *See also* Elizabethan Age

English Romantics. *See* Romanticism

enjambment, 184–85

Enlightenment, **102–3,** 142

ennui, **103.** *See also* decadence

environmentalism, 98

envoi, 221, 276

epic, **103–5,** 211, 216, 238; catalogues, 51; chivalric romance vs., 55; didactic, 86; epithet, 108–9; as genre, 132, 297; georgic vs., 134; heroic couplet translation, 73; invocation, 159–60; katabasis, 167; meter, 99; mimesis, 188, 189; mock, 46, 189–90; muses, 193, 194; ottava rima, 218; saga, 178, 270; tragedy vs., 298

epic simile, **105–6**

epic theater, 7–8, **106**

epideictic, 221, 264

epigram, 21, **106–7,** 238

epistemology, **107**

epistolary novel, **107,** 121, 211, 276

epitaph, 29, **107–8;** epigram, 106

epithalamion (or epithalamium), 42–43, **108,** 133, 221

epithet, **108–9,** 216

epoché (reduction), 231

equivalence, principle of, 265

Erasmus, Desiderius, 71, 146, 154, 232, 272

Ernst, Max, 292

Erskine-Hill, Howard, 29

esoteric wisdom, 48–49

essay, **109–10**

essentialism, **110–11,** 119

Estienne, Henri, 101

estrangement. *See* defamiliarization

eternal return, **111**

ethics, 107, **111**

ethnicity, 76

ethos, 264

Euphemerism, **111**

euphuism, **112**

Euripides, 5, 56, 63, 273, 298, 299

evasion, 136

everyday. *See* ordinary

Everyman (morality play), 9, 192

evil, 166

exchange value, 66

exegesis, **112**

existentialism, 70, **112–13,** 148; absurd, 1–2; authenticity, 30; phenomenology, 231

Exodus, 48, 104, 150

exoteric teaching, 48–49

explication de texte, **113–14**

expressionism, **114,** 309

expurgation. *See* bowdlerize

Ezra, 48

fable, 9, 37, **115,** 212, 277. *See also* parable

fabliau, **115–16,** 167

Fairport Convention (music group), 34

fairy tale and folk tale, **116,** 199, 266. *See also* folklore

fame, **116**

fancy, **117**

Fanon, Frantz, 240

fantastic, **117,** 136, 203, 273

Farber, Manny, 122

Father Time, 196–97

Faulkner, William, 137, 200

Felman, Shoshana, 285

female Bildungsroman, 40

feminine rhyme, 265

feminist theory, **117–19,** 122, 131, 247; essentialism, 110, 111, 119

Fenellosa, Ernest, 209

Fergusson, Francis, 93

festive, **119,** 205; anthems, 221; carnivalesque, 49; comedy, 62; folklore, 124; green world, 138 fetishism, 66, **120,** 176, 177

Fetterly, Judith, 118

Ficino, Marsilio, 203

fiction, **120–21;** character, 54; interior monologue, 158; metafiction, 180; narrator, 200; plot, 235–36; poetic justice, 237; point of view, 238–39; realism, 121, 255–56; science fiction, 273; short story, 276–77; socialist realism, 280; stream of consciousness, 286. *See also* fable; novel

Fielding, Henry, 252; *Shamela,* 121, 211, 224, 256; *Tom Thumb,* 185

figura, 14, 112, **121–22,** 164, 302–3

figures of speech: Attic style vs., 28; euphuism, 112; metaphor, 180–82

film: beast fable, 37; bombast, 45; comedy of humors, 64–65; dream vision, 95; Gothic, 137; green world, 138; horror, 1, 19; mass culture, 77; melodrama, 179; nouveau roman, 209; poetic justice, 237; point of view, 238; quest romance, 252; travesty, 46

film theory, **122;** feminist theory, 119

fin amors, 75, **123,** 301–2

Finch, Anne, 261

fin de siècle, **123**

Fish, Stanley, 254, 255

Fitzgerald, Edward, 251; style indirect libre, 239

Fitzgerald, F. Scott, 277

Flaubert, Gustave, 3, 239; "Art as Ascetic Religion," 27; *Dictionary of Received Ideas,* 226–27; *Madame Bovary,* 45, 210; *Salammbo,* 80

Fletcher, Angus, 10, 136, 181, 310

Fletcher, Dana, 98

Florin, John, 44

flyting, **123**

focalization, **123,** 239

folio, **123–24**

folklore, 116, **124,** 193, 232. *See also* fairy tale and folk tale

fool, the, 139

foot, 184, 185

Forché, Carolyn, 311

Ford, Ford Madox, 98, 155

Ford, John, 163

forensic rhetoric, 221, 263–64

formalism, 83, **124–27,** 236, 256. *See also* structuralism

Forster, E. M., 54

Foster, Hal, 241

Foucault, Michel, 31, 77, 110, 148, 230, 242; *Discipline and Punish,* 206; "The Discourse on Language," 90; *The History of Sexuality,* 130, 131; "Nietzsche, Genealogy, History," 131–32

fourfold exegesis, 112, 302

Fowler, Alastair, 68, 72, 133

Frank, Joseph, 85, 86

Frankfurt, Harry, 264, 279

Frankfurt School, **127,** 249; continental philosophy, 70; dialectic, 84; Marxist criticism, 176; mass culture, 76–77, 127

"Frankie and Johnnie" (ballad), 34

free association, 31, 159

free indirect style, 239

free rhyme, 49

free verse (vers libre), **127–28,** 170, 183, 184; Imagism, 153; line length, 186

Frege, Gottlob, 15, 69

French Revolution, 267

French Symbolists, 153

Freud, Sigmund, 6, 41, 43, 81, 87, 231, 290; essentialism, 110; feminist theory, 110, 118, 247; fetishism, 120; free association, 31, 159; psychoanalytic criticism, 246–47, 248; quest romance, 252; reality principle, 255; repression, 260, 261; wit, 310. Works: "Creative Writers and Daydreaming," 246; *The Interpretation of Dreams,* 246, 304; "The Theme of the Three Caskets," 246; "The Uncanny," 117, 246; "The Unconscious," 242, 292, 304

Friedman, Michael, 16

Frost, Robert, 88, 243, 245, 283, 301

Frow, John, 76

Fry, Roger, 4

Frye, Northrop, 210, 299; *Anatomy of Criticism,* 14–15, 16–17, 24, 102, 133, 161; archetypes, 24, 25, 297; comedy, 64, 65, 299; genres theory, 133; *The Great Code,* 122, 302, 303; lyric, 173, 174; myth, 195, 196, 248; *A Natural Perspective, 138;* quest romance, 252–53

Fulgentius, 196

Fuller, Buckminster, 42

Fuller, Margaret, 13

Fuss, Diana, 111

Fussell, Paul, 29

Futurism, **128–29,** 292, 309

Gadamer, Hans-Georg, 38, 70, 84, 155, 256; *Truth and Method,* 141–42, 143

Gallagher, Catherine, 205–6

Gallop, Jane, 247

Galsworthy, John, 98, 191

gangsta rap, 34

Garber, Marjorie, 131

garden of Adonis, 145

Gascoigne, George, 29

Gass, William, 180

Gates, Henry Louis, 12

Gautier, Théophile, 3

gay studies, 119, **130,** 131; queer theory vs., 251

gaze, 19, 119, 122

Geertz, Clifford, 124

Geisteswissenschaft, **130–31**

gender studies, **131;** essentialism, 110; feminist theory, 117–19; gay studies, 130; performativity, 229; phallologocentrism, 172; queer theory, 251–52

genealogy, **131–32**

Genesis, 48, 104, 121–22, 217

genetic fallacy, 4

Genette, Gérard, 123, 199–200

genius, 79

genre, **132–33.** *See also* comedy; elegy; epic; lyric poetry; melodrama; romance; satire; tragedy

Geoffrey of Monmouth, 57

George III, king of Great Britain, 259

George IV, king of Great Britain, 259

George V, king of Great Britain, 133

Georgian Age, **133,** 152, 191, 268

georgic, **133–34**

German Romanticism. *See* Romanticism

ghazal, **134–35,** 259

ghost story, 117, 136

Giacometti, Alberto, 190

Gilbert, Sandra, 118

Gilgamesh (epic), 25, 252

Gilpin, William, 233–34

Ginsberg, Allen, 37

Giovanni, Nikki, 41

Globe (London theater), 100

gnomic, **135–36,** 167

gnosis, Gnosticism, **136,** 166, 203

goat-song. *See* eclogue

God, 103, 138, 217; "death of," 2; Great Chain of Being, 138; kabbalah, 166

Godard, Jean-Luc, 209

Godwin, William, 267

Goethe, Johann Wolfgang von, 10, 41, 288, 293; "Erlkönig," 34; *Faust,* 61; *Roman Elegies,* 99; *Sorrows of Young Werther,* 266; *Westöstlicher Divan,* 134; *Wilhelm Meiser's Apprenticeship,* 40, 211, 266

Goffman, Erving, 16, 93, 124

Gogol, Nikolai, 279

Goldberg, S. L., 192

Golden Age, 226

Golden House of Nero, 139

golden poets, 29

Gomringer, Eugen, 68

Góngora, Luis de, 36

Googe, Barnabe, 29

Gore, Catherine, 278

Gorgias, 28, 263, 284

goslars, 216

Gothic, **136–37**, 211, 212, 273, 274; chronotope, 58; parody of, 137, 224; picturesque,
235

Gower, John, 24, 29, 35

Graff, Gerald, 233

Graham, Jorie, 42

Gramsci, Antonio, 141, 289

grand style, **137–38**

Graves, Robert, 24, 133

Gray, Thomas, 35, 100

Great Chain of Being, **138**

"great man theory," 144

Greek Bible. *See* Septuagint

Greek chorus, 56–57

Greenberg, Clement, 4

Greenblatt, Stephen, 205, 207

Greene, Robert, 310

Greene, Thomas, 105

green world, **138;** locus amoenus, 171

Gregory, Lady Augusta, 52–53

Greimas, A. J., 199

Greville, Fulke, 270, 282

Grierson, Herbert, 182–83

Griffith, D. W., 179

Grimm brothers, 116, 232

Grooms, Red, 45

Grosz, George, 114

grotesque, 50, 60, 71, **138–39;** satire, 271,
272

grotto style, 139

Group Theater, 94

Gubar, Susan, 118

Guillaume de Lorris, 95, 179

Guillory, John, 76

Guinizelli, Guido, 92

Gumbrecht, Hans Ulrich, 249

Gunn, Thom, 307

Habermas, Jürgen, 127, 241, 249

Hafiz, 134

haiku, **140,** 184

half rhyme (slant rhyme), 265

Hall, Stuart, 77

Hallam, Arthur, 265

Halpern, Nick, 216

hamartia, 298

Hammer, Langdon, 192, 223

Hansen, Miriam, 176, 180

Hardy, Thomas, 98, 307

Harington, John, 218

Harlem Renaissance, 44, **140**

harmonious discord. *See* discordia concors

Harpham, Geoffrey, 139

Hartman, Geoffrey, 253, 267, 268, 288, 290

Harvard University, 61, 243

Hassan, Ihab, 241

Hawks, Howard, 64

Hawthorne, Nathaniel, 12, 220, 277

Haywood, Eliza, 107

Hazlitt, William, 109, 111, 164, 189, 278, 296

H.D. (Hilda Doolittle), 153

Hebrew Bible. *See* Bible

Hecht, Anthony, 92, 93, 224, 244, 245, 265,
276

Hegel, G. W. F., 70, 161, 230; dialectic, 84

hegemony, **141,** 289

Heidegger, Martin, 16, 69, 87, 112; *Being and Time,* 142; *Destruktion,* 81; "Letter on Humanism," 110, 148; phenomenology, 70, 231

Heine, Heinrich, 34, 162, 266

Heinlein, Robert, 273

Hellenistic. *See* Alexandrian

Heller, Erich, 191, 245–46

Heminges, John, 124

Hemingway, Ernest, 64, 277

Hendin, Josephine, 241

Henry VIII, king of England, 260

Heraclitus, 135

Herbert, George, 50, 101–2, 182, 222; "The Altar," 68, 102; "Heaven," 97; *The Temple,* 101–2

hermaphrodite, 90

hermeneutics, 70, **141–43,** 155

Hermes Trismegistus, 143, 203

hermetic, **143,** 203

Herodotus, 40, 120

heroic couplet. *See* couplet

Herrick, Robert, 14, 29, 52; "Gather ye rosebuds, while ye may," 50; *Hesperides,* 283–84; self-epitaph, 107–8; "A Ternary of Littles, Upon a Pipkin of Jelly Sent to a Lady," 192–93

Herskovits, Melville, 124

hexameter, 99

Hickey, Dave, 17

hip-hop, 92, 123

Hippias, 284

Hirsch, Edward, 311

historical novel, 211

historicism, **143–44,** 158. *See also* new historicism

history: chronicle, 57; fiction, 120; figura, 122; genealogy, 131–32; historicism, 143–44; humanism, 146; new historicism,

205–7; nonfiction novel, 208; typology, 302

Hitchcock, Alfred, 64, 119, 137

Höch, Hannah, 129

Hoffmann, E. T. A., 139, 246, 277

Holiday, Billie, 43

Holinshed, Raphael, 57

Holland, Norman, 254

Hollander, John, 54, 68, 93, 97, 98, 99, 120, 217, 221, 258, 259, 281, 283, 297

Holmes, Oliver Wendell, 109

Holquist, Michael, 58

Holy Roman Empire, 17

Homans, Margaret, 118

Homer, 115, 146, 189, 198, 220, 228, 290; authority, 30–31; catalogue, 51; cento, 53; didactic, 86; ekphrases, 98–99; epic, 104, 132, 188, 238, 297, 298; epic division, 53; epic simile, 105–6; epithet, 108–9; heroic couplet, 73; *Iliad,* 5, 31, 51, 86, 98–99, 104, 105–6, 108–9, 132, 138, 159, 305; inspiration, 156; invocation, 159; *Odyssey,* 86, 104, 108, 132, 153, 156, 167, 171, 252, 300; oral literature, 216

homoioteleuton, 28

homosexuality. *See* gay studies; queer theory

Hook, Thomas, 278

Hope, A. D., 91

Hopkins, Gerard Manley, 307

Horace, 198, 238; antitheatrical, 18, 19; *Ars Poetica,* 3, 18, 27, 82, 95, 104, 139, 278, 305; Augustan Age, 29; carpe diem, 50, 51; decorum, 82; dulce et utile, 95; imitation, 153, 154; *Odes,* 50, 116, 153, 173, 214, 215, 304; retirement, 261–62; *Satires,* 194, 271; verse epistle, 306

Horkheimer, Max, 70, 77, 127, 177

horror, 1, 18, 19, 137

hortus conclusus, **144–45**

Hoskins, John, 67

Houghton, Walter, 308

Housman, A. E., 57, 67, 159

Howard, Richard, 94

Howe, Irving, 86, 191, 201, 212, 239, 241

hubris, 298

Huggins, Nathan, 140

Hughes, Langston, 44, 140

Hugo, Victor, 7, 224

Huizinga, J., 179

Hulme, T. E., 60, 153

humanism, **145–48;** courtliness, 74; Elizabethan Age, 100; essentialism, 110; Renaissance, 260

Hume, David, 102, 164, 279, 295

humor: blazon parody, 43; double dactyl, 92. *See also* comedy

humors, 37, 64–65

Hunt, William Holman, 243

Hunter, G. K., 29

Hurd, Richard, 137

Hurston, Zora Neale, 40, 49, 140

Husserl, Edmund, 70, 81, 113, 230–32, 274

Hussey, Christopher, 235

Huxley, Aldous, 273

Huysmans, Joris-Karl, 3, 80

Huyssen, Andreas, 241

hymn, 66, 178, 215

hyperbole, 180

iamb, iambic, 184, 185, 244

iambic pentameter, 7, 127; blank verse, 42, 185, 265; heroic couplet, 73; ottava rima, 218; rhyme royal, 266; Spenserian stanza, 285

Ibsen, Henrik, 3, 94, 114

Icelandic saga, 178, 270

iconography, **149–50**

idealism, 84

Idel, Moshe, 167

idyll, **150,** 225

illocutionary act, 285

imagination, **150–52,** 246, 267, 310; beauty, 4; fancy vs., 117; muses, 193–94; poetry, 238

Imagism, 128, 140, **152–53,** 192, 309

imitation, 20, **153–54,** 159. *See also* mimesis

impersonality, 42, **154–55,** 207, 209, 214

implied author/implied reader, **155,** 200, 254, 257

impresa. *See* emblem

impressionism, **155–56**

improvisation, 124

inconsistency, comedic, 65

inexpressibility topos, **156**

influence, **156;** anxiety of influence, 20–21, 31, 261; belatedness, 38–39; imitation, 20, 154, 159

inspiration, 79, **156–57;** invocation, 159–60

instrumental reason, 176

intentional fallacy, 4, **157–58**

interior monologue, **158,** 286

interlude, **158**

internal focalization, 120

International Style, 241

interpellation, 229–30

interpretation, 70, 114; exegesis, 112; figura, 121–22; hermeneutics, 141–43; implied author/implied reader, 155; intentional fallacy, 157–58

Interregnum (Britain), 260

invention, **158–59;** conceit, 67. *See also* imitation

inversion, 55

invocation, **159–60,** 244

Ionesco, Eugene, 1–2

Irigaray, Luce, 118

Irish literary renaissance. *See* Celtic revival

Irish National Theater, 53

irony, 133, 148, **160–62,** 204, 223, 311

Isaac, binding of, 121–22

Isaiah, 19, 46, 121, 301

Iser, Wolfgang, 155, 254, 255, 257

Isocrates, 28, 264

Italian Futurists, 128–29

Italian Renaissance, 260; humanism, 145. *See also* Renaissance literature

Italian sonnet, 281–82

Jacobean Age, **163,** 260; drama, 91, 94, 163; masque, 163, 177–78

Jakobson, Roman, 126–27, 129, 181–82, 187, 265, 274, 287

James, C. L. R., 240

James, Henry, 48, 66, 98, 130, 212, 220, 237, 243, 274; "The Art of Fiction," 256; canon, 48; character, 54; estrangement, 125–26; irony, 162; parody of, 224, 225; point of view, 239; short story, 277; *The Turn of the Screw,* 117, 200

James, Jesse, 33

James, William, 203, 243, 286

James I, king of England, 163, 177

Jameson, Fredric, 66, 83, 127, 177, 241, 288; reification, 259–60

Jardine, Alice, 118, 247

Jarry, Alfred, 128

Jason, 5, 6

Jaspers, Karl, 112

Jauss, Hans-Robert, 254, 255, 256, 257

jazz, 49

Jean de Meun, 95, 179

Jefferson, Thomas, 134

Jeffrey, Francis, 168

jeremiad, **163–64**

Jeremiah, 163

Jerome, Saint, 53, 146

Jesus, 25, 121–22, 161, 302

John, Gospel of, 2

"John Henry" (ballad), 34

John of Salisbury, 17

Johnson, Barbara, 81–82

Johnson, James Weldon, 40, 140

Johnson, Robert, 43, 258–59

Johnson, Samuel, 227, 267; ballad parody, 33; decorum, 82; on difficulty, 88; discordia concors, 89; on metaphor, 181; on metaphysical poetry, 182, 183; on mimesis, 188–89; on realism, 255. Works: *Dictionary of the English Language,* 215; *Life of Cowley,* 182; *Lives of the English Poets,* 40–41; *Preface to Shakespeare,* 235–36; *Rambler* no. 4, 210

Jones, Chuck, 45

Jones, Ernest, 246

Jones, Inigo, 163, 178

Jonson, Ben, 41, 235, 238, 307; comedy of humors, 64; Elizabethan Age, 100; emblem, 101; epigram, 106; imitation, 20; masque, 163, 178; sons of Ben, 163, 283–84; wit, 183. Works: Cory-Morison Ode, 56; "On the Famous Voyage," 189; *Pleasure Reconciled to Virtue,* 62–63, 178; "To Himself," 262; "To Penshurst," 72

Joshua, 302

journalism: essay, 109; novel, 121, 210–11, 255

Joyce, James, 41, 212, 239, 252, 304; allusion, 11; interior monologue, 158, 286; modernism, 190, 191, 192, 240. Works: "The Dead," 55; *Finnegans Wake,* 195; *Portrait of the Artist as a Young Man,* 40, 167; *Ulysses,* 51–52, 105, 125, 158, 190, 191, 212, 236, 256

Judaism: canon, 48; kabbalah, 166–67; trope, 301. *See also* Bible

judgment, **164–65;** wit vs., 311

Jung, C. G., 24, 195, 248

Jünger, Ernst, 22

Juno, 104

Justice, Donald, 23–24

Justin Martyr, 302
Juvenalian satire, 271

kabbalah, **166–67**
Kafka, Franz, 1–2, 190, 212, 222, 277
Kalstone, David, 72
Kant, Immanuel, 102, 266; aesthetics, 4, 38, 164; *Critique of Judgment,* 4, 38, 91, 164, 238, 295; sublime, 290–91; taste, 295; transcendentalism, 300
katabasis, **167**
Keats, John, 39, 60, 100, 307; agon, 5; inspiration, 157; metaphor, 181; on negative capability, 201. Works: "La belle dame sans merci," 34; *The Fall of Hyperion,* 95; *Hyperion,* 95; "Ode on a Grecian Urn," 99; Odes, 92, 215; "Ode to Psyche," 157; "On First Looking into Chapman's Homer," 267
Kennedy, Adrienne, 41
Kennedy, Walter, 123
Kenner, Hugh, 66, 139, 153, 191
kenning, 167
Kermode, Frank, 58, 59, 62, 115, 196, 226; *English Pastoral Poetry,* 227
Kerouac, Jack, 37
Kerrigan, John, 67
Kerrigan, William, 247, 248
Ketuvim, 48
Keynes, John Maynard, 43
Khlebnikov, Velimir, 129
Kierkegaard, Søren, 22, 112, 161
Kilmer, Joyce, 92
King, Edward, 60
King Arthur and his Round Table, 56, 75, 297
King James Bible, 19, 43, 163
Kingsley, Charles, 228
Kinzie, Mary, 186
Kipling, Rudyard, 98

Kirsch, Adam, 69
Klein, Melanie, 248
Klinger, Friedrich Maximilian, 288
Knight, G. Wilson, 25
Knight, Richard Payne, 234
knighthood, 55–56, 74–75, 168, 252
knowledge: epistemology, 107; Gnosticism, 136; phenomenology, 231; repression, 260
Koch, Kenneth, 207, 215
Kokoschka, Oskar, 114
Kollwitz, Käthe, 114
Kracauer, Siegfried, 127
Kripke, Saul, 16
Kristeva, Julia, 1, 242
Kruchenykh, Alexei, 129
Kunstlerroman, **167**. *See also* Bildungsroman

Labé, Louise, 282
labor: alienation, 7, 66; reification, 259
Lacan, Jacques, 110, 118, 242, 247, 248, 290
Laclos, Pierre Choderlos de, 107, 211
La Fayette, Madame de, 211
La Fontaine, Jean de, 17, 115
Laforgue, Jules, 67, 128
lai, **168**
Lake Poets, **168**
Lam, Wilfredo, 292
Lamb, Charles, 64, 109
landscape: ecocriticism, 97–98; locus amoenus, 171; pastoral, 225–26; picturesque, 233–35; Romanticism, 266, 281
Langer, Susanne, 4, 293
language poetry, **168–69;** elliptical poetry vs., 101, 169
Lanyer, Emilia, 72
Larkin, Philip, 185
La Rochefoucauld, François de, 21
Larson, Nella, 140
late capitalism, 66, 127

Latin Bible. *See* Vulgate
Latin poetry, 178
Laura (Petrarch's beloved), 40
Laverdant, Gabriel-Désiré, 31
Lawrence, D. H., 40, 133, 167
Lazarillo de Tormes (anonymous), 233
Leacock, Stephen, 56
Lear, Edward, 170
Lear, Jonathan, 246
learning play, 8
Leavis, F. R., 191, 308
Leconte de Lisle, Charles-Marie, 224
lectio difficilior, **169**
Le Fanu, Sheridan, 137, 274
LeGuin, Ursula, 273
Lehman, David, 140, 221–22, 245
Leishman, J. B., 183
Lem, Stanislaw, 273
Lenin, V. I., 302
Lennox, Charlotte, 107
Lentricchia, Frank, 61
Lenz, Jakob, 288
Leonardo da Vinci, 147
Leskov, Nikolai, 279
Lessing, Gotthold Ephraim, 102, 305
letter writing. *See* epistolary novel; verse
    epistle
Levenson, Michael, 128, 153, 191, 309
Lévinas, Emmanuel, 87, 111, 231
Lévi-Strauss, Claude, 45, 195, 241–42, 287
Leviticus, 48, 104
Lewis, C. S., 29, 75, 105, 273
Lewis, David Levering, 140
Lewis, Matthew, 137, 211–12
Lewis, R. W. B., 13
Lewis, Wyndham, 129, 308, 309
Lichtenberg, Georg Christoph, 21
life vs. art, 29–30
light verse, **169–71**
Lincoln's Gettysburg Address, 264

literary influences. *See* influence
Living Theatre, 89
Livy, 146
Locke, John, 300, 311
locus amoenus, 138, **171**
Lodge, David, 121, 187
logic, 15, 69, 89; rhetoric vs., 262–63
logical positivism, 15
logocentric, **171–72**
Lomax, John and Alan, 124
London theaters, 100
long eighteenth century, **172**; neoclassicism,
    202; realism, 255–56; satire, 272; sensibil-
    ity, 274–75; taste, 295
Longenbach, James, 72, 192, 238
Longfellow, Henry Wadsworth, 225
Longinus, 27, 36, 290, 291
Lord, Albert, 216
Lorraine, Claude, 233, 234
Louis VII, king of France, 75
Lovecraft, H. P., 1
Lovejoy, Arthur O., 138
Lovelace, Richard, 52
love poetry: beloved, 39–40; blazon, 42–43;
    canzone, 49, 238; chivalric romance, 55–
    56; dolce stil nuovo, 92; elegies, 99; fin
    amors, 123; lai, 168; medieval, 178. *See
    also* courtly love; troubadours
Lowell, Amy, 128, 153
Lowell, Robert, 69, 72, 215
Lowenthal, Leo, 127
Lowth, Robert, 215
Lubbock, Percy, 239
Lucan, 29
Lucian, 271, 273
Lucretius, 104, 105, 238
Luhmann, Niklas, 249
Lukács, Georg, 127; commodity, 66; dialec-
    tic, 84; Marxist criticism, 176, 177.
    Works: *The Historical Novel*, 212, 256;

History and Class Consciousness, 259; *Realism in Our Time,* 158, 201, 256

Luria, Isaac, 166

Lydgate, John, 29

Lyly, John, 111

Lynch, David, 95, 138–39

Lyotard, Jean-François, 241, 242, 292

lyric poetry, 132, **172–74,** 238, 307; beloved, 39–40; canzone, 49; carpe diem, 50; elegy, 99–100; elliptical, 100–101; emblem, 102; irony, 162; ode, 214–26; song, 280–81; sonnet, 282

Lysias, 263–64

McGann, Jerome, 268, 275

Machiavelli, Niccolô, 17, 145

machinelike. *See* mechanical

Mack, Maynard, 262, 272

McKay, Claude, 140

Mackenzie, Henry, 211, 274

McKeon, Richard, 55

MacLeish, Archibald, 27

MacPherson, Jay, 253

Macrobius, 97

magic. *See* fantastic

Magnetic Fields (music group), 67

Magritte, René, 292

Mailer, Norman, 208

Malay poetry, 221

male authority, 118, 172

male friendship, 131

male gaze, 119, 122

Malevich, Kasimir, 129

Mallarmé, Stephane, 103, 293, 294

Malory, Thomas, 56, 75

Mankind (morality play), 192

Manley, Lawrence, 71

Mann, Paul, 32

Mann, Thomas: essay, 110; interior monologue, 158; modernism, 190, 240. Works: *Buddenbrooks,* 212; *Confessions of Felix Krull,* 233; *Death in Venice,* 80; *The Magic Mountain,* 103, 212; *Tonio Kröger,* 167

mannerism, 36, **175**

Mansfield, Katherine, 98

Marcus, Greil, 44

Marcus, Steven, 308

Marcuse, Herbert, 7, 127, 176

Marie de France, 56, 75, 168

Marinetti, Filippo Tommaso, 128, 129

Marino, Giambattista, 36

Mark, Gospel of, 161

Marlowe, Christopher, 73, 100, 226

Marotti, Arthur, 72

Marquis, Don, 170

marriage: archetype, 25; comedy, 25, 65; emblem, 90; epithalamion (epithalamium), 42–43, 108, 133, 221; novel, 210

Marsh, Edward, 133

Marsh, James, 300

Marston, John, 144

Martial, 106, 238, 262

Marvell, Andrew: as metaphysical poet, 182; multum in parvo, 192; paradox, 222, 223; pastoral, 226. Works: "Damon the Mower," 301; "The Definition of Love," 223; Horatian Ode, 220; "To His Coy Mistress," 50–51; "Upon Appleton House," 61, 72, 262

Marx, Karl, 302; alienation, 7, 176; *Capital,* 66, 120, 199; *The Holy Family,* 175

Marxist literary criticism, 120, **175–77,** 176, 177; commodity, 66, 176, 177, 269; dialectic, 84, 176; formalism, 125; Frankfurt School, 127, 176; mass culture, 77; New Criticism vs., 204; reification, 259–60

masculine rhyme, 265

masculinity, 131

Masefield, John, 133

mask, 208, 230

masque, 62–63, 119, 163, **177–78**

mass culture, 76–77, 127; capitalist hege-
    mony, 140; folklore, 124; quest romance,
    252

Masters, Edgar Lee, 128

matere (matter), 297

mathematics, 15

Matthiessen, F. O., 12–13

Maupassant, Guy de, 277

Mayakovsky, Vladimir, 129

mechanical, 63, 128, 309

Medea, 5

medieval literature, 7, 9, **178–79**; aureate
    poets, 29; ballad, 35; canzone, 49; chival-
    ric romance, 55–56; courtly love, 74–75;
    débat, 79; dolce stil nuovo, 92; dream
    vision, 95; ennui, 103; fabliau, 115; fin
    amors, 123; Gothic, 137; Great Chain of
    Being, 138; humanism vs., 146; mum-
    mers' plays, 193; mythography, 196; pan-
    egyric, 221; saga, 178; topos, 297; trouba-
    dours, 74–75, 92, 123, 178; ubi sunt, 304

Meisel, Perry, 191, 247–48

melancholy, 16, 42, 103

melodrama, 132, **179–80**, 201

Melville, Herman, 12, 13, 48, 49; *Billy Budd,*
    81; *Moby-Dick,* 244; "The Tuft of Kelp,"
    251

memoir, 41

Menand, Louis, 243, 300

menander, 63

Mendelssohn, Moses, 102

Menippean satire, 271

Meredith, George, 283

Merleau-Ponty, Maurice, 70, 231

Merrill, James, 61, 104

Merritt, Stephin, 67

metafiction, **180**

metaphor, 24, 143, **180–82;** allegory vs., 9,

181; anagogic, 14–15; conceit, 67–68;
    metonymy vs., 181–82, 187; simile, 278;
    trope, 301

metaphysical poets, 91, 163, **182–83,** 222

meter, **183–86;** Alexandrine, 7; ballad, 33;
    blank verse, 42; common measure, 66;
    couplet, 73; doggerel, 92; double dactyl,
    92; elegiac, 99; epithet, 109; free verse,
    127, 128; light verse, 170; prose, 244;
    song, 281

method acting, 94

metonymy, **186–87,** 301; metaphor vs., 181–
    82, 187; synecdoche, 294

Michaels, Walter Benn, 206

Michelangelo, 149–50, 175, 203

Middle Ages. *See* medieval literature

Middle Comedy, 63

Middle English, 24

Middleton, Thomas, 163

Mikics, David, 206, 241

Mill, J. S., 173

Millais, John Everett, 243

millennium, 14

Miller, D. A., 206

Miller, J. Hillis, 111

Miller, Perry, 163–64

Millett, Kate, 118

Milosz, Czeslaw, 79, 311

Milton, John, 24, 41, 170, 267; blank verse,
    42, 73, 265; canzone, 49; Caroline Age,
    50; dissociation of sensibility, 91, 92;
    enjambed lines, 184; epic simile, 105;
    Freudian theory, 247; humanism, 145; in-
    spiration, 156–57; invocation, 159–60;
    masque, 178; Restoration, 261; on satire,
    271; sonnet, 282. Works: "At a Vacation
    Exercise," 156–57; *Comus,* 178; "Lyci-
    das," 47, 49, 60, 88, 99, 226; Nativity
    Ode, 7, 196; *Paradise Lost,* 2, 5, 11, 42, 51,
    55, 73, 92, 96, 104, 134, 159–60, 181, 189,

Milton, John (*continued*)
190, 192, 194, 217, 257, 261, 265, 290, 298, 302; *Samson Agonistes,* 61
mimesis, **187–89,** 190, 198, 202; comedy, 65; ut pictura poesis, 305
Miró, Joan, 292
Mirollo, James, 175
Mirzoeff, Nicolas, 308
Mitchell, Juliet, 118, 247
Mitchell, Lee Clark, 201
mixed genres, 132
mock epic, 46, **189–90**
modernism, 6, **190–92;** authenticity, 30; Bloomsbury, 43; classicism, 60; comedy, 66; coterie poetry, 72; difficulty, 88, 169, 191; Dionysian, 89; Edwardian Age vs., 98; free verse, 128; Georgian diction vs., 133, 268; Imagism, 150–53, 192; impersonality, 42, 154, 155, 207, 214; impressionism, 155; naturalism, 201; nouveau roman, 209; novel, 212; postmodernism, 240, 241; prose poem, 245; Romanticism, 268; unconscious, 304; Victorian Age, 308
modernity, 247; classic vs., 17–18, 58, 59; early modern, 96; Frankfurt School, 127; Futurism, 128–29
Modleski, Tania, 119
Moi, Toril, 111, 119
Molière, 64
monologue. *See* dramatic monologue
Monro, Harold, 133
Monroe, Harriet, 214, 223
Monroe, William, 7, 111
montage, 122
Montague, Lady Mary Wortley, 44
Montaigne, Michel de, 44, 109, 145, 162, 230, 279
Monte, Steven, 245
Moore, G. E., 15, 43

Moore, Marianne, 72, 183
morality play, 9, **192**
moralizing, 3, 276; beast fable, 37; didactic, 86; Edwardian Age, 98; ethics vs., 111; mythography, 196
More, Paul Elmer, 147
More, Thomas, 145
Moretti, Franco, 40
Morris, Edmund, 208
Morris, William, 3–4, 7, 244
Morrison, Toni, 40
Moses, 9, 48, 96, 104, 150, 196
Moses de Leon, 166
mourning. *See* elegy
movies. *See* film; film theory
Mücke, Dorothea von, 117
Mulholland Drive (film), 95
multum in parvo, **192–93**
Mulvey, Laura, 119, 122
mummers' plays, **193**
Munch, Edvard, 114
Munro, Alice, 277
Murasaki, Lady, 211
Murdoch, Iris, 113
Murray, Albert, 44
Muse, 156, 159–60
muses, **193–94,** 224
music: African-American canon, 49; ballad, 34; blues, 43–44; chorus, 57; common measure, 66; conceit, 67; doggerel, 92; folk, 124; masque, 177–78; modernism, 190; song, 280–81
Muslim canon, 48
Musset, Alfred de, 224
mystery play, **194–95**
mysticism, 143, 166–67, 203, 252
myth, **195–96;** archetype, 24–25, 248; Celtic, 52; iconography, 149, 150; masque, 177; modernism, 191; muses, 193–94; psychoanalytic criticism, 246;

satyr play, 272–73; structuralism, 195, 287; tragedy, 298

mythography, 149, **196–97**

Nabokov, Vladimir, 162, 247, 265

Nachträglichkeit (deferred action), 87

Nagel, Thomas, 16

Nagy, Gregory, 188, 189

naive and sentimental, 18, **198–99**, 227

narrative, 143; plot, 235–36; poetic justice, 237

narrative poem, lyric vs., 172–73

narratology, **199–200**, 287, 288; focalization, 123, 239

narrator, **200**; point of view, 238–39

Nashe, Thomas, 233, 310

Nasruddin, 222

national identity, 75

naturalism, 143, 144, **200–201**, 212, 231; historicism, 143–44; realism vs., 200, 201, 255

nature, 133, 134, 138; ecocriticism, 97; idyll, 150; locus amoenus, 171; pastoral, 226. *See also* landscape

Neal, Larry, 41

negative capability, **201**

Nelson, Victoria, 139

Nemerov, Howard, 88

neo-baroque, 36

neoclassicism, 26, 60, **201–2**

Neoplatonism, 149, 166, **202–3**

Neruda, Pablo, 215

Nerval, Gerard de, 79

Neviim, 48

New Comedy, 63

New Criticism, **203–5**; affective fallacy, 254; ambiguity, 12; Chicago school, 55; close reading, 61, 204, 205; dissociation of sensibility, 92; humanism, 147–48; irony, 162, 204, 223; metaphysical poetry, 183; paradox, 223; symbol, 293

new historicism, 119, 148, **205–7**, 230

new humanism, 147

Newman, Cardinal John Henry, 307

New Masses (periodical), 176

new novel. *See* nouveau roman

New Testament. *See* Bible

New York Dadaism, 78

New York school, **207**, 250

Nicholas of Guilford, 79

Niedecker, Lorine, 214

Nietzsche, Friedrich, 16, 65, 81, 87, 118; Apollonian and Dionysian, 22, 88–89; "death of God," 2; eternal return, 111; existentialism, 112; nihilism, 207. Works: *The Birth of Tragedy,* 22, 88–89, 299; *Daybreak,* 122, 232; *The Gay Science,* 14, 21, 111, 138; *Genealogy of Morals,* 27; "On the Use and Disadvantage of History for Life," 144; *Toward a Genealogy of Morals,* 27, 131–32; *Twilight of the Idols,* 89

nihilism, 78, **207–8**

Nohrnberg, James, 104, 105, 109, 252, 253

Nolde, Emil, 114

nominalism, 110

nonfiction novel, **208**, 266

nonsense verse, 170

nonsensical, 31

No play, 308–9

Norris, Frank, 200, 255

nouveau roman, **209**, 212

Novalis, 54

novel, **209–13**; Bildungsroman, 40, 211; Bovarysme, 45; character, 54; dialogic, 85, 212–13; epistolary, 107, 121, 211, 276; fiction, 121; Gothic, 136–37, 211, 212; Kunstlerroman, 167; metafiction, 180; metonymy, 187; mimesis, 187; modernism, 190–91; naturalism, 200–201, 212; nonfiction novel, 208; nouveau roman, 209, 212; plot, 236; point of view,

novel (*continued*)
238–39; quest romance, 252–53; realism, 210, 212, 255–56; Regency period, 259; roman à clef, 208, 266; science fiction, 273; sensation, 274; short story vs., 277; Silver Fork, 278; story vs. plot, 126; sympathy, 294; Victorian era, 307

novella, 209

Numbers, 48, 104

nursery rhymes, 170

Nussbaum, Martha, 86, 111, 148, 229

objective correlative, **214**

objectivism, **214**

objectivity, 164, 224

obscurity, 31, 32, 169, 223

occult. *See* fantastic

O'Connor, Flannery, 277

O'Conor, Charles, 35

octavo, 124, 281

ode, **214–16**, 220, 238

Odysseus, 104

Oedipus myth, 26, 160–61, 246, 257, 262, 287, 298

O'Hara, Daniel, 20

O'Hara, Frank, 207, 307

Old Comedy, 63

Old English, 167, 178, 183

Old Norse, 167, 270

Olds, Sharon, 69

Old Testament. *See* Bible

Olson, Charles, 42

Olson, Elder, 55

O'Neill, Eugene, 94

ontology, epistemology vs., 107

Oppen, George, 214

oral literature, **216**; ballad, 33–35; epithet, 108–9, 216; fairy tale and folk tale, 116; saga, 270. *See also* epic; folklore

oratory. *See* rhetoric

ordinary, 15, **216–17**

originality, **217–18**

Orwell, George, 110, 273

Ossian, 35–36

ostranenie. *See* defamiliarization

Other, the, 77, 231

ottava rima, **218,** 286

Oulipo, 6, **218–19**

Ovid, 30, 75, 115, 153; *Amores,* 73, 116; *Art of Love,* 126, 194; *Elegies,* 99; *Metamorphoses,* 51, 97, 104, 196; *Tristia,* 29

Ovide Moralisé (commentary), 196

Oxford Movement, 307

oxymoron, **219**

paleface and redskin, **220**

palinode, **220**

Panchatantra (Sanskrit text), 222

panegyric, **220**

Panofsky, Erwin, 23, 24, 36, 149, 150, 196–97, 203

pantoum, **221–22**

Pappas, Nickolas, 25, 26

parable, 9, 101, 212, **222**, 277

Paracelsus, 45

paradox, 90, 148, 161, **222–23;** couplet, 73; deconstruction, 81; oxymoron, 219

parallel syntax, 19

paraphrase, **223–24**

Parker, Dorothy, 169–70

Parker, Patricia, 253

Parnassians, **224**

parody, **224–25;** of ballad, 33; of blazon, 43; cento, 53; of chivalric romance, 56; of conceit, 67; of epistolary novel, 121, 211, 256; of Gothic, 137; of katabasis, 167; of Silver Fork novel, 278

Parry, Milman, 109, 216

parts of speech, 53

Pascal, Paul, 92–93

pastoral, 6, **225–28;** amoebean song, 13–14; Arcadia, 23, 226; bucolics, 46; catalogue of trees, 51; echo, 97; eclogue, 97; ecocriticism, 97; elegy, 99, 226; georgic vs., 134; idyll, 150; naive and sentimental, 198–99; song, 281

Pater, Walter, 27, 80, 153, 164, 307; *The Renaissance,* 3, 51, 260; "Style," 154–55

pathetic fallacy, **228**

pathos, 36, 173, **229,** 264

patriarchal bias, 118

pattern poetry, 68, 102

Paul, Saint, 10, 11, 27, 121, 302

Paulson, Ronald, 233, 272

Peacock, Thomas Love, 221, 266, 273

Pearl (dream vision), 95

Pease, Donald, 13

Peirce, Charles Sanders, 243, 274

Peire Vidal, 302

pentameter, 99. *See also* iambic pentameter

Percy, Thomas, 34

Perec, Georges, 218

perfectionism, **229**

performativity, **229–30**

Pericles' Funeral Oration, 264

peripeteia. *See* reversal

perlocutionary act, 285

Perrault, Charles, 17, 116

persona, **230**

Petrarch, 75, 123, 178; beloved, 40; blazon, 42; canzone, 49; humanism, 145, 146; *Rime Sparse,* 40, 42; sestina, 276; sonnet, 281

Peyre, Henri, 268

Phaedrus, 115

phallologocentric, 172

phenomenology, 70, 84, 113, **230–32;** hermeneutics, 143; semiotics, 274

Philips, Katherine, 261

Phillips, Adam, 41, 103, 246

Phillips, Dana, 98

philology, 147, 158, **232–33**

philosophical definition, 24

phonemes, 126

phonetic poetry, 78

phonocentric, 172

Picabia, Francis, 78

picaresque, 58, **233**

Picasso, Pablo, 129, 190

Pico della Mirandola, 147, 203

picturesque, **233–35,** 290

Piers Plowman (dream vision), 95

Pindar, 56, 153, 173, 214–15, 220, 238

Pinsky, Robert, 90–91

place, 58, 60, 199, 202

plain style, 28, **235**

Plath, Sylvia, 69, 230

Plato, 16, 26, 40, 81, 136, 231; antitheatrical, 3, 18, 19; Apollonian, 22, 89; canonical and noncanonical texts, 48–49; classic, 58; dialectic, 84; dialogues, 171–72, 263; mimesis, 188; perfectionism, 229. Works: *Apology,* 79; *Ion,* 86, 188; *Phaedrus,* 84, 157, 171, 220, 305; *Republic,* 19, 25, 77, 86, 188, 229; *Symposium,* 139, 203; *Timeus,* 196. *See also* Neoplatonism; Socrates

Plautus, 63

playing the dozens, 123

plot, 54, **235–36;** comic, 65; deus ex machina, 83–84; narratology, 199; poetic justice, 237; story vs., 126, 236; tragic causal logic, 298, 299; unities, 202

Plotinus, 202–3

Plumptre, James, 234

Plutarch, 40

Poe, Edgar Allan, 12, 49, 273, 277; Gothic, 137; grotesque, 139; metaphor, 181; "The Poetic Principle," 249, 250; "The Raven," 126

Poem of the Cid (medieval poem), 179

poetic justice, **236–37**

poetry, **237–38;** ars poetica, 27; blank verse, 42; canzone, 49, 238; concrete, 68; coterie, 72; elliptical, 100–101; free verse, 127–28; Georgian, 133; haiku, 140; Imagism, 150–53; invention, 159; Lake Poets, 168; language, 168–69; light verse, 169–71; medieval, 178–79; metaphysical, 91, 163, 182–83; meter, 183–86; modernism, 191, 192; naive and sentimental, 198–99; New York school, 207; objectivism, 214; ode, 214–16, 238; painting analogy, 305; palinode, 220; pastoral, 225–28; proem, 244; prose poem, 245; psalms, 43, 215, 220, 238; pure, 249–50; quatrain, 251; refrain, 258–59; sonnet, 281–83; verse vs., 306; Victorian Age, 307; of witness, 311. *See also* epic; lyric poetry; song; troubadours

Poetry (magazine), 214

point of view, **238–39;** focalization, 123

Poirier, Richard, 61, 66, 191

polarity, 287

politics: authority, 30; fable, 115; rhetoric, 263; satire, 63

polyphonic novel, 85, 213

Pope, Alexander, 71, 237, 267, 307; Augustan Age, 29; bathos, 36, 37; classicism, 59, 60; decorum, 82; heroic couplet, 73; mock epic, 46, 188–89; retirement, 262; satire, 272. Works: *Dunciad,* 46, 190, 272; Epistle to Burlington, 295; *Essay on Criticism,* 73, 202, 310; *Peri Bathous, or the Art of Sinking in Poetry,* 36; *The Rape of the Lock,* 46, 167, 189–90, 312; *Windsor Forest,* 90

Popper, Karl, 110; historicism, 143–44

popular culture. *See* mass culture

pornography, 19

Porter, Cole, 51

Porter, James, 89

postcolonial studies, 76, **239–40**

postmodernism, **240–41;** sublime, 291–92

poststructuralism, 118, **241–42,** 277

Potter, Robert, 215

Pound, Ezra, 24, 42, 60; avant-garde, 31; coterie poetry, 72; difficulty, 191; epic, 104; free verse, 127, 128; Imagist credo, 152–53; modernism, 133, 191, 241; No play, 209; objectivists, 214; Victorian Age, 308; Vorticism, 129, 308–9. Works: *Cantos,* 62, 104; "In a Station of the Metro," 153; "Sestina: Altaforte," 276

Poussin, Nicolas, 23–24, 233

Powys, John Cowper, 49

Praed, W. M., 170

pragmatism, 203, **243**

prejudice, 19, 142, 164

Pre-Raphaelites, 4, 153, **243–44**

Price, Martin, 37, 190, 235

Price, Uvedale, 234

primal scene, 87

Primary Colors (anonymous), 208, 266

Prodicus, 284

proem, **244**

proletarian literature, 175–76

Prometheus, 267, 298

propaganda, 5, 175–76, 280

Propertius, 39, 194

Propp, Vladimir, 199, 287–88

prose, **244–45;** essay, 109–10; verse vs., 306; Victorian Age, 307

prose poem, **245,** 306

Protagoras, 22, 263, 284

Protestantism, 19, 124–25, 247, 267

Proust, Marcel, 41, 54, 76, 190, 240, 304; *In Search of Lost Time,* 62, 212

proverb, 21, **245**

Prudentius, 9

Psalms, 43, 215, 220, 238

psychoanalytic criticism, 118, 122, 242, **245–48**

psychologism, 231

public sphere, **249**

pun, 87

Punch and Judy shows, 64

pure poetry, **249–50**

puritanism, 19, 163–64

Puttenham, George, 12, 14, 67, 106, 108, 288–89

Pynchon, Thomas, 22, 105, 212

pyrrhic foot, 184

Pyrrhonism, 279

Pythagoras, 203

quantitative meter, 183

Quarles, Francis, 101

quarto, 123–24

quatrain, 72, 92, **251,** 282, 308

queer theory, 119, 130, **251–52**

Queneau, Raymond, 218

querelle des anciens et des modernes, la. See ancients and moderns

quest romance, 56, 133, **252–53**

Quine, W. V. O., 16

Quint, David, 105, 134

Quintilian, 264

Quixotism, 45

Quran, 48

Rabelais, François, 71, 85, 145

race, 76

Racine, Jean, 59

Radcliffe, Ann, 137, 211

Rahv, Philip, 220

Rakosi, Carl, 214

Rambach, J. J., 155

Randolph, Thomas, 283

randomness. *See* aleatory

Ransom, John Crowe, 88, 203

Raphael, 175, 244

rap music, 92

Rasmussen, Mark, 67

Rauschenberg, Robert, 45

reader-response criticism, **254–55,** 257

reading: close, 61, 204, 205; closet drama, 61; closure, 62; ethics, 111; feminist theory, 117–19; hermeneutics, 141–43; implied author/implied reader, 155, 254; invention, 158–59; perfectionism, 229; reception theory, 256; sympathy, 294

ready-mades, 78

Reagan, Ronald, 208

realism, 83, 86, 110, 121, **255–56;** metonymy, 187; mimesis, 187; naturalism vs., 200, 201, 255; novel, 210, 212, 255–56. *See also* socialist realism

reality principle, 255

reason, 22, 89; Enlightenment, 102–3

Rebhorn, Wayne, 74, 265

reception theory, 254, 255, **256–57**

recognition, 26, 125, 199, **257–58,** 262

redskin. *See* paleface and redskin

reduction, 231

reductiveness, 246

Reformation, 19, 124–25, 247

refrain, **258–59;** blues, 44, 258–59; burden, 46; chorus, 57; rondeau, 269; villanelle, 308

Regency period, **259,** 278

reification, 66, **259–60**

relativism. *See* anti-naturalist

Renaissance literature, 17, **260;** act, 2, 3; anatomy, 16; baroque, 36; commedia del'arte, 63–64; complaint, 67; conceit, 67–68; copia, 71; coterie poetry, 72; courtliness, 74, 260; cruel fair, 75, 219; daemon, 79; discordia concors, 89–90; dulce et utile, 95; early modern, 96; elegies, 99; Elizabethan Age, 100; emblem,

Renaissance literature (*continued*)
101; epigram, 106; essay, 109; fabliau,
115–16; festive, 119; genre, 132; Great
Chain of Being, 138; humanism, 145–47,
148; humors, 64; imitation, 20, 153, 154;
mannerism, 175; masque, 177–78;
melancholia, 103; meter, 183; mimesis,
187; mummers' plays, 193; mythography,
196, 197; Neoplatonism, 203; new historicism, 206; ottava rima, 218; paradox,
222; pastoral, 226, 227; philology, 232;
plain style, 235; sonnet, 281–82, 283; wit,
310. *See also* American Renaissance;
Celtic Revival; English Renaissance
Renan, Ernest, 53, 307
renga, 140
repression, **260–61**
rest. *See* closure
Restoration literature, 172, 202, 237, **261;**
satire, 272
retirement, 215, **261–62;** country-house
poem, 72
retrospective fantasy, 87–88
Revelation, 9–10, 14, 21, 48
revelry. *See* festive
reversal, 26, 125, 199, 257, **262**
revolution, 176
Reynolds, David, 13, 206
Reynolds, Henry, 226
Reznikoff, Charles, 214
rhetoric, 19, **262–65;** Aristotelian criticism,
26; copia, 71; dialectic, 84; panegyric,
221; pathos, 229, 264; persona, 230; plain
style, 235; poetry vs., 238; sophists, 284;
synecdoche, 294; trope, 301
rhetorical criticism, 26
rhyme, **265;** ballad, 33; ballade, 35; blues, 44;
canzone, 49; common measure, 66; cou-
plet, 72–74; doggerel, 92; double dactyl,
92; free verse, 127–28; ottava rima, 218;

quatrain, 251; rondeau, 269; sestina, 276;
sonnet, 281, 282; Spenserian stanza, 286;
terza rima, 296; villanelle, 308
rhyme royal, 218, **265–66**
rhythm, 47, 306; doggerel, 92; meter, 183,
184
Richards, I. A., 4–5, 117, 152, 162, 204;
reader-response criticism, 254
Richardson, Dorothy, 49
Richardson, Samuel, 107, 121, 210, 211, 224,
255–56, 294
Ricks, Christopher, 11, 12, 137, 160, 308
Ricoeur, Paul, 70, 142–43, 236
riddles, 173, 178
Rilke, Rainer Maria, 99, 100, 103
Rimbaud, Arthur, 37
Ripa, Cesare, 101, 197
Ripley, George, 300
Ritchie, Jean, 34
ritual, 93, 94, 119, 188, 189, 299
road movies, 58
Robbe-Grillet, Alain, 209, 212
Robin Hood, 33
Robinson, Edward Arlington, 308
Robinson, Paul, 261
Rochester, Earl of, 261
roman à clef, 208, **266**
romance, 132, 201; chivalric, 55–56; medieval, 178; novel vs., 209–10, 211; quest,
133, 252–53, 256
Romance of the Rose (dream vision), 95, 179
Romanticism, 10, 18, 23, 103, 169, **266–69;**
ballad, 34; classicism vs., 59, 60; convention vs., 71; conversation poem, 71; coterie poetry, 72; dream vision, 95; essay,
109–10; gnosis, 136; irony, 160, 161–62;
judgment, 164; Lake Poets, 168; light
verse, 170; in long eighteenth century,
172; lyric, 173; ode, 214, 238; Parnassians
vs., 224; pathetic fallacy, 228; picturesque,

235; Regency period, 259; song, 281; symbol, 293; taste, 296; tragedy, 298–99; transcendentalism, 300; verse epistle, 307; Victorian Age, 308; wit, 311
rondeau, **269**
Ronsard, Pierre de, 67, 282
Rorty, Richard, 16, 217, 243
Rosa, Salvator, 233
Rose, Jacqueline, 247
Rosen, Stanley, 18, 208
Rosenmeyer, Thomas, 23, 24
Rosenthal, M. L., 69
Rossetti, Dante Gabriel, 4, 243, 283
Rothenberg, Jerome, 2
Rothman, William, 119, 122
Roubaud, Jacques, 218
Roundheads, 52
Rousseau, Jean-Jacques, 81, 102, 266; *Confessions,* 41; *Letter to d'Alembert,* 19
Rowley, William, 163
Rueckert, William, 97
Ruskin, John, 3, 307; humanism, 147; judgment, 164; "Of the Turnerian Picturesque," 234; pathetic fallacy, 228; preRaphaelites, 244; taste, 296; *The Stones of Venice,* 7, 136
Russ, Joanna, 273
Russell, Bertrand, 15, 43
Russell, George. *See* AE
Russian formalists, 83, 125–26, 236, 256
Russian Futurists, 129
Ruthven, K. K., 67, 195
Ryle, Gilbert, 15
Rymer, Thomas, 202, 237

Sackville, Thomas, 80
Sa'di, 134
saga, 178, **270**
Said, Edward, 240
Sainte-Beuve, Charles-Augustin, 58

Saint George's Day, 193
Saint-Simon, Henri de, 31
Sakya Pandita, 222
Sanchez, Sonia, 41
Sapphic stanza, **270**
Sappho, 108, 194, 238, 270, 290
sarcasm, irony vs., 160
Sarraute, Nathalie, 209
Sarris, Andrew, 122
Sartre, Jean-Paul, 1, 70, 112–13, 148, 231
Saslow, James, 131
Sassoon, Siegfried, 133
Satan, 217
satire, 63, 132, 198, 233, 238, **270–72;** comedy, 63; light verse vs., 171; poetic justice, 237; Restoration, 261
Saturn, 197
satyr play, 271, **272–73,** 298
Saussure, Ferdinand de, 81, 87, 187, 242, 274, 277–78; structuralism, 286–88
Scaliger, J. C., 106
scansion, 184
Scarry, Elaine, 44
Schelling, F. W. J. von, 266, 293, 299
scheme, 68, 301
Schiller, Friedrich, 198, 199, 288
Schlegel, A. W., 18, 59, 293
Schlegel, Friedrich, 21, 266, 267, 300, 311; irony, 160, 161–62
Schleiermacher, Friedrich, 131, 141, 142
Schlick, Moritz, 15
Schnackenberg, Gjertrud, 160
Schoenberg, Arnold, 190
Scholem, Gershom, 167
Schopenhauer, Arthur, 21
Schuller, Gunther, 44
Schuyler, George, 140
Schuyler, James, 207
science, 147, 230, 231, 261, 307
science fiction, 1, **273**

Scott, Walter, 34, 56, 168

Scottish literature: ballads, 33–34; bardic, 35–36; flyting, 123

screwball comedies, 65, 138

scripture. *See* Bible

Scudéry, Madeleine de, 211, 266

Searle, John, 285

secular immortality. *See* fame

Sedgwick, Eve Kosofsky, 131

seduction, 50

sefirot, 166

Segal, Erich, 65

self. *See* subject, subjectivity

self-epitaph, 107–8

semiotics, **273–74**

Seneca the Younger, 2–3, 109, 153–54, 262

sensation novel, 212, **274**

sensibility, 211, 212, **274–75;** dissociation of, 91–92, 183

sentiment, 13, 18, 118, **275–76;** epistolary novel, 107, 276; novel, 211–12; taste, 295. *See also* naive and sentimental

Septuagint, 48

serialization, 212

sermons, 49

sestet, 281

sestina, 259, **276**

setting. *See* place

Severini, Gino, 128–29

Sexton, Anne, 69

sexual fetishism, 120

sexuality, 130, 251, 261

Shaftesbury, Lord, 275

Shakespeare, William, 2, 14, 29, 35, 41, 92, 122, 193, 201; archetypes, 25; bowdlerizing of, 45; canon, 49; character, 54; chorus, 56; chronicle plays, 57; comedy, 65–66; courtliness, 74; Elizabethan Age, 100; euphuism, 112; festive rituals, 119, 205; First Folio, 124; Freudian theory, 246, 247, 248; historicist critics, 144; imagination, 151; meter, 185, 186; quarto, 124; recognition, 257; skepticism, 280; song, 281. Works: *Antony and Cleopatra*, 92; *As You Like It*, 16, 42, 226; *Coriolanus*, 9; *Hamlet*, 103, 132, 161, 235, 247, 279; *Henry IV, Part 1*, 112; *Henry IV, Part 2*, 44–45; *Henry V*, 56; *Henry VI, Parts 1–3*, 57; *Julius Caesar*, 160; *King Lear*, 158, 163, 246; *Love's Labour's Lost*, 169; *Macbeth*, 163; *Measure for Measure*, 12; *A Midsummer Night's Dream*, 10–11, 138, 151, 185; *Much Ado About Nothing*, 65; "The Phoenix and the Turtle," 222; *The Rape of Lucrece*, 266; *Romeo and Juliet*, 28; *Sonnets*, 40, 62, 72, 116, 186, 282, 283; *The Taming of the Shrew*, 64; *The Tempest*, 46, 185; *Troilus and Cressida*, 138; *Twelfth Night*, 43, 76, 257; *The Winter's Tale*, 56

Shankman, Steven, 58

Shaw, George Bernard, 98

Shearman, John, 175

Shelley, Mary, 273

Shelley, Percy Bysshe, 23, 49, 170, 266, 307; *Adonis*, 100; *The Cenci*, 61; "Mont Blanc," 267; *Prometheus Unbound*, 267; *The Triumph of Life*, 95, 296

shepherd and shepherdess. *See* echo; pastoral

Shetley, Vernon, 88

Shines, Johnny, 43

Shklovskii, Viktor, 83, 126

Sholokhov, Mikhail, 280

short story, **276–77**

Showalter, Elaine, 117

Sidney, Philip, 29, 74, 95, 97, 99–100; *Apology for Poetry*, 120, 187, 238; *Arcadia*, 23, 276; *Astrophel and Stella*, 100, 282; "Ye Goat-Herd Gods," 276

sign, signifier, signified, 274, **277–78,** 287

Silenus, 272

Silver Fork novel, **278**

simile, **278;** epic, 105–6

Simon, Claude, 209

Simonides, 305

Simpsons, The, 64

sincerity, **278–79**

Sirk, Douglas, 179

"Sir Patrick Spens" (ballad), 33–34

skaz, **279**

Skelton, John, 92

skepticism, 155, 275, **279–80**

slant rhyme (half rhyme), 265

Smith, Adam, 275

Smith, Bessie, 43

Smith, Charlotte, 282

snobbery, 76

Snodgrass, W. D., 69

Snorri Sturlison, 270

Snow, Edward, 188

Social Darwinism, 200–201

socialist realism, 176, 227, **280**

Socrates, 40, 81, 86, 139, 188, 196, 264, 299; as Apollonian, 22, 89; daemon, 79; irony, 161; logocentric, 171–72; *Protagoras,* 22; sophists, 284

Sokel, Walter, 114

song, **280–81;** amoebean, 13–14; blues, 43–44; chorus, 57; lyric, 173; refrain, 258–59

Song of Deborah, 220

Song of Roland (Old French poem), 179

Song of Songs, 43, 48, 144, 145

sonnet, **281–83**

sons of Ben, 163, **283–84**

sophists, 28, 79, 263, 264, **284**

Sophocles, 56, 58, 63; *Oedipus Rex,* 26, 160–61, 246, 257, 262, 286, 298

Southey, Robert, 168

Spacks, Patricia Meyer, 100

spectacular, 19

speech act, 69, 229, **284–85**

speechmaking. *See* rhetoric

Spencer, Theodore, 258, 259

Spengler, Oswald, 80, 191

Spenser, Edmund: chivalric romance, 56; complaint, 67; courtliness, 74; elegy, 99–100; emblem, 101; fabliau, 115–16; influence, 156; locus amoenus, 171. Works: *Amoretti,* 282; "Astrophel," 99–100, 252; *Epithalamion,* 42–43, 108, 258; *The Faerie Queene,* 7, 9, 24, 51, 56, 100, 101, 105, 116, 132, 145, 171, 197, 218, 219, 226, 252, 285–86; *Fowler Hymns,* 265; Mutabilitie Cantos, 196; *Shepheardes Calendar,* 13–14, 100, 281

Spenserian stanza, 7, 218, **285–86**

Spiegelman, Willard, 42, 61, 86

spiritual autobiography, 41

spirituals, 49

Spitzer, Leo, 232–33

Spivak, Gayatri Chakravorty, 289

spondee, 184, 185

sprezzatura, 74

Staël, Madame de, 59

"Staggerlee" (ballad), 34

Stakhanov, Alexei, 280

Stalin, Joseph, 125

Stalinism, 175–76

Stampa, Gaspara, 282

Stanislavski, Konstantin, 98

stanza: ballad, 33, 66, 251; blues, 44; chorus, 57; couplet, 72–74; ottava rima, 218, 286; pantoum, 221; quatrain, 251; rhyme royal, 265–66; rondeau, 269; Sapphic, 270; sestina, 276; Spenserian, 7, 218, 285–86; villanelle, 308

Star Trek, 25, 252

Statius, 29

Stedman, Edmund Clarence, 307

Steele, Danielle, 76

Steele, Richard, 109

Stein, Gertrude, 62, 101, 191, 212, 243, 245

Steiner, George, 88

Stendhal, 58, 187

Stern, Daniel, 180

Sterne, Laurence, 180; *A Sentimental Journey,* 211, 274–75; *Tristram Shandy,* 126, 200, 212, 236

Stesichorus, 220

Stevens, Wallace, 97, 268; belatedness, 39; elliptical poetry, 101; gnomic, 135; inspiration, 157; modernism, 190, 240; on pathetic fallacy, 228; pragmatism, 243; sublime, 291. Works: *Adagia,* 21; "Anecdote of the Jar," 99; "Imagination as Value," 152; "Notes Toward a Supreme Fiction," 27; "Sunday Morning," 181; "Tea at the Palaz of Hoon," 157; "Thirteen Ways of Looking at a Blackbird," 135

Stevick, Philip, 53

Stewart, Stanley, 145

stichomythia, **286**

Stock, Lorraine, 179

Stoker, Bram, 107, 137

story vs. plot, 126, 236

storytelling, 199

Strachey, James and Alix, 43

Strachey, Lytton, 43, 308

Strasberg, Lee, 94

Strauss, Leo, 18, 144

Stravinsky, Igor, 190

stream of consciousness, 158, **286**

stressed syllable, 265

Strindberg, August, 94, 114

Strong, George, 225

structuralism, 83, 181–82, 277, **286–88**; myth, 195; narratology, 199, 287; post-structuralism, 118, 241–42; semiotics, 274

Sturgeon, Theodore, 273

Sturm und Drang, **288**

style, **288–89**

style indirect libre, 239

subaltern, **289**

subject, subjectivity, **289–90**

sublime, 27, 36, 136, 137, 173, 234, 267, **290–92**; beautiful vs., 37–38, 290; ode, 215; psychoanalytic criticism, 247

Suckling, Sir John, 52

Sue, Eugène, 175, 179

Sukenick, Ronald, 180

Sükind, Patrick, 139

supernatural, 117, 137

superstition, 137

Surrealism, 2, 31, 32, 129, 176, **292**

Surrey, Henry Howard, Earl of, 29, 42

Swales, Martin, 40

Swenson, May, 68

Swift, Jonathan, 29, 83, 237, 267; bathos, 37; *Battle of the Books,* 18; *Gulliver's Travels,* 83; *Tale of a Tub,* 272

Swinburne, Algernon Charles, 35, 80, 185, 225; "August," 27–28

syllabics. *See* meter

symbol, 10, 142–43, **292–93**; iconography, 149–50; mythography, 196

Symbolism, 153, **293–94**

symmetry, 265

Symons, Arthur, 80

sympathy, **294**

synchronic entity, 287

syncretism, 196, 203

synecdoche, 187, **294**

Synge, J. M., 53, 98

systematic artifices, 218

tableaux vivants, 305

Taine, Hippolyte, 266

Tallis, Raymond, 82, 278

tanka, 140

Tasso, Torquato, 218, 226

taste, 91, **295–96**

Tate, Allen, 203

Tatlin, Vladimir, 129

Taylor, Archer, 245

Taylor, John (the Water Poet), 170

Taylor, Mark, 81

teleuton, 276

Tennyson, Alfred, Lord, 57, 60, 153, 268, 307; *Idylls of the King*, 150; *In Memorium*, 100, 244, 251; "Ulysses," 94

Terence, 63, 295

Teresa, Saint, 36

terror, 136

Tertullian, 17

terza rima, **296**

textual criticism, **296–97**; close reading, 61; philology, 232–33

Thackeray, William Makepeace, 278, 307

theater. *See* drama

theater of cruelty, 1, 94, **297**

theater of the absurd, 1

Theatre (London), 100

Theocritus, 6, 23, 46, 99, 150, 225

Theognis, 116

Theophrastus, 54

Thespis, 298

39 Steps, The (film), 64

Thomas, Dylan, 308

Thomas Aquinas, Saint, 179

Thompson, Stith, 124

Thomson, James (eighteenth century), 134

Thomson, James B. V. (nineteenth century), 244

Thoreau, Henry David, 12, 48, 300

Thrasymachus, 284

Thucydides, 40, 120, 208

Tibullus, 194

tikkun, 166

Tillyard, E. M. W., 138

time, 143; chronotope, 58; unities, 60, 202

Titanic sinking, 33

Todd, Janet, 275

Todorov, Tzvetan, 10, 117, 148, 199, 277, 293

To Have and Have Not (film), 64–65

Tolstoy, Leon, 187

Tompkins, Jane, 118

topos, **297**; inexpressibility, 156; locus amoenus, 171; ubi sunt, 304

Torah, 48, 86, 104

Tourneur, Cyril, 163

tragedy, 122, **297–99**; antitheatrical, 18–19; Aristotelian criticism, 25–27, 52, 60, 103, 237; catharsis, 52; chorus, 56–57; comedy vs., 62, 65; Dionysian, 22, 89, 93; epic vs., 103–4; formal features of, 125; as genre, 132, 133; mimesis, 188; philology, 232; poetic justice, 237; recognition and reversal, 26, 125, 199, 257–58, 262; satyr play, 272–73, 298; unities, 60, 202

transcendentalism, **300**

Transcendentalist Club, 300

transience, 304

transvestism, 131

travesty, 46

tree catalogue, 51

Trilling, Lionel, 30, 86, 98, 111, 162, 191, 230, 247; *Sincerity and Authenticity*, 278–79

trochaic, trochee, 184, 185

Trollope, Anthony, 212, 307

trope, 68, 153, **300–301**; irony, 160–62

Trotsky, Leon, 5, 175, 176

troubadours, 74–75, 92, 123, 178, 276, **301–2**

Trumpener, Katie, 75–76

Tuberville, George, 29

Tuckerman, Frederick, 283

Turgenev, Ivan, 207

Twain, Mark, 58–59, 220, 255

typology, 164, **302–3**; exegesis, 112

Tzara, Tristan, 78

ubi sunt, **304**

uncanny, 117

unconscious, 31, 190, 242, 247, 292, **304;** repression, 260–61

underworld, 167

unities, 60, 202

University of Chicago. *See* Chicago school

University Wits, 310

unpredictability, 113

unreliable narrator, 200

Unsworth, John, 241

Untermeyer, Louis, 88

Urania, 194

use value, 66

utopian fiction, 273

ut pictura poesis, **305**

Valéry, Paul, 21, 59, 215, 249, 289, 294

value, 66

Van Doren, Mark, 105

van Duyn, Mona, 283

Vasari, Giorgio, 136, 139

Vaughan, Henry, 182

Vendler, Helen, 61, 173, 223–24, 282

Verfremdungseffekt. See alienation effect

Verlaine, Paul, 293

vernacular poetry, 178

verse, **306;** doggerel, 92, 306; light verse, 169–71; rhyme, 265; rondeau (roundel), 269; sestina, 276

verse epistle, 71, **306–7**

verse riddle, 170

vers libre. *See* free verse

Vickers, Brian, 265

Victoria, queen of Great Britain, 98, 307

Victorian Age, **307–8;** femininity stereotypes, 118; humanism, 147; idyll, 150; novel, 212; Romanticism, 268; sonnet, 282–83

video games, 256

Vienna Circle, 15

villanelle, 259, **308**

Villon, François, 35, 37, 304

violence: nihilism, 207; theatrical, 18–19

Virgil, 23, 153, 189, 295; Augustan Age, 29; cento, 53; classic, 58, 146; ekphrasis, 99; epic, 104, 132, 238; epic simile, 105, 106; epithet, 108; heroic couplet, 73; invocation, 159. Works: *Aeneid,* 31, 42, 58, 99, 104, 108, 132, 156, 159, 167; *Eclogues,* 14, 46, 97, 99, 100, 225; *Georgics,* 133, 134

Virgin Mary, cult of, 92

visual arts: bricolage, 45; emblem, 101–2; ephrastic text, 98; expressionism, 114; Futurists, 129; grotesque, 138–39; iconography, 149–50; mannerism, 175; masque, 177–78; mimesis, 188; modernism, 190; New York school, 207; picturesque, 233, 234; poetry analogy, 305; postmodernism, 241; pre-Raphaelites, 243–44; Romanticism, 266; Surrealism, 292

visual culture, **308**

Vitruvius, 139

voice, dialogic, 84–86

Voltaire, 102, 275

Vorticism, 129, **308–9**

vowel sounds, 55

Vulgate, 53, 146

Wagner, Heinrich, 288

Wagner, Richard, 196, 252, 298, 299; *Parsifal,* 80, 252

walking, 159, 234

Walpole, Horace, 136–37, 211

Warburg, Aby, 149

Warren, Robert Penn, 100, 147–48, 183, 203; "Pure and Impure Poetry," 250; *Understanding Poetry,* 205, 223

Warton, Joseph, 215

Wasserman, Earl, 90, 203

Waters, Muddy, 43

Watts, Isaac, 66

Waugh, Patricia, 180

Webster, John, 163

Wedekind, Frank, 114

Weinberg, Bernard, 95

Weiskel, Thomas, 290

Wellek, René, 36, 91, 187, 294

Wells, H. G., 98, 191, 273

Welty, Eudora, 277

West, Nathanael, 272

Western Marxism, 176–77

West Indies, 76

Whedon, Joss, 137

White, Bukka, 43

White, Hayden, 57, 58, 255

Whitman, Walt, 12, 37, 39, 42, 98, 220, 230; catalogues, 52; free verse, 128, 186. Works: "Crossing Brooklyn Ferry," 186; *Leaves of Grass,* 51–52, 301; "When Lilacs Last in the Door-yard Bloom'd," 100

Whitney, Geoffrey, 101

Wilamowitz-Moellendorff, Ulrich von, 232

Wilde, Alan, 241

Wilde, Oscar, 3, 20, 21, 80, 307

Willey, Basil, 308

Williams, Bernard, 16

Williams, Linda, 119, 122

Williams, Raymond, 77, 120, 177

Williams, William Carlos, 42, 94, 104, 153, 214, 245

Wilson, Brian, 29

Wilson, Edmund, 175, 177

Wilson, Robert, 98

Wimsatt, W. K., 4, 5, 55, 157–58, 203, 205, 265

Winckelmann, Johann, 22

Winkler, John, 131, 200

Winnicott, D. W., 248

Winters, Yvor, 29, 223, 224

Wisdom, John, 279

wit, 21, 102, 183, **310–11;** light verse, 170

witness, **311**

Wittgenstein, Ludwig, 15, 69, 216, 280

Wittmann, Anna, 137

Wizard of Oz, The (film), 9, 95

Wölfflin, Heinrich, 36

women: beloved, 39–40; Bildungsroman, 40; Blue Stockings, 44; canonical writers, 49; courtly love, 74–75; cruel fair, 76; epistolary novel, 107, 211, 276; essentialism, 110; fairy tale authors, 116; fin amors, 123; Hollywood melodramas, 179; as readers, 117–18. *See also* feminist theory; gender studies

Wood, Mrs. Henry, 274

Wood, James, 8, 213

Woolf, Leonard, 43

Woolf, Virginia, 43, 98, 212, 304; essay, 110; impressionism, 155; interior monologue, 158, 286; modernism, 190–92. Works: "Modern Fiction," 190–91; "Poetry, Fiction, and the Future," 190–91; *A Room of One's Own,* 117

Wordsworth, William, 25, 41, 71, 170, 252; canon, 49; discursive, 91; inspiration, 156; invention, 159; invocation, 160; as Lake Poet, 168; ordinary, 216; picturesque, 235; Romanticism, 59, 228, 267; on sonnet, 282. Works: "Character of the Happy Warrior," 54; "Imitations of Immortality," 215; *Lyrical Ballads,* 34, 159, 227, 244–45, 267, 271; "Ode to Duty," 215; *The Prelude,* 69, 71, 104, 160, 244, 291; "Tintern Abbey," 71

World War I, 98

World War II, 22, 105, 264

wrenched accent, 186

Wright, Charles, 42

Wright, Richard, 200

writer's block, 79

Wycherly, William, 261

Yates, Frances, 143

Yeats, William Butler, 4, 98, 238; antithetical, 19–20; Celtic revival, 52–53; coterie poetry, 72; modernism, 240, 241; mythic system, 195; No plays, 209. Works: "Among School Children," 218; *The Celtic Twilight*, 52; "The Circus Animals' Desertion," 218; Crazy Jane poems, 258; *Dramatis Personae*, 20; "In Memory of Major Robert Gregory," 100; *The Trembling of the Veil*, 19–20; *The Wanderings of Oisin*, 52

Yosemite Sam, 45

Young, Edward, 137, 217

Yugoslavian bards, 216

Zamyatin, Yevgeny, 273

zaum, 129

Zeno, 262–63

zero focalization, 123

zeugma, **312**

Zeuxis, 188

Zirmunskij, Viktor, 187

Zizek, Slavoj, 242, 247

Zohar, 166

Zola, Émile, 200, 212, 255

Zukofsky, Louis, 214

Zurich Dadaism, 78

Mikics's *Handbook* is ideal for classroom use at all levels, from freshman to graduate. Instructors can assign individual entries, many of which are well-shaped essays in their own right. Useful bibliographical suggestions are given at the end of most entries. The *Handbook*'s enjoyable style and thoughtful perspective will encourage students to browse and learn more. Every reader of literature will want to own this compact, delightfully written guide.

David Mikics is professor of English at the University of Houston. He is the author of several books, including *The Romance of Individualism in Emerson and Nietzsche* and *Who Was Jacques Derrida?* (forthcoming from Yale University Press).